Frederick the Great

Frederick the Great

Theodor Schieder

edited and translated by
Sabina Berkeley and H.M. Scott

Longman
London and New York

Pearson Education Limited
Edinburgh Gate,
Harlow, Essex CM20 2JE, United Kingdom
and Associated Companies throughout the world.

Published in the United States of America by Pearson Education, New York.

First published 2000

ISBN 0–582–01768–8 CSD
ISBN 0–582–01769–6 PPR

Visit our world wide web site at http://www.awl-he.com

British Library Cataloguing in Publication Data

A catalogue entry for this title is available from the British Library

Library of Congress Cataloging-in-Publication Data

Schieder, Theodor.
    [Friedrich der Grosse. English]
    Frederick the Great/by Theodor Schieder; edited and translated
by Sabina Berkeley and H.M. Scott.
        p.   cm.
    Includes bibliographical references and index.
    ISBN 0–582–01769–6 (PPR). — ISBN 0–582–01768–8 (CSD)
    1. Frederick II, King of Prussia, 1712–1786. 2. Prussia—Kings
and rulers Biography. 3. Prussia (Germany)—History—Frederick II,
1740–1786. I. Berkeley, Sabina. II. Scott, H.M. (Hamish M.),
1946– . III. Title.
DD404.S2813   1999
943′.053′092
[B]—DC21   99–20828
                                                                   CIP

Set by 35 in 10/12pt Graphic Bembo
Produced by Addison Wesley Longman Singapore (Pte) Ltd.,
Printed in Singapore

Contents

List of maps

Preface to the English edition

We have produced this abridged translation of Theodor Schieder's study of Frederick the Great with the demands of English-language teachers and students in mind. We have therefore excluded sections which were part of the original study but which are primarily of interest to German readers and to specialists: the section on the King and German literature, the accounts of Frederick's rather tangential contacts with some of his contemporaries (though by far the most important of such relationships, that with Voltaire, is included in the English version) and the rather rambling chapter which closes the volume on the subject of historical greatness, have all been cut. We have also removed the footnotes, believing that specialists will consult the original German edition, and have substituted a guide to further reading in English, together with a chronology of the major events. In translating Schieder's Baroque German, we have removed some of the many repetitions found in his text, together with a few passages of purely German interest, but have tried to retain something of the distinctive style of the original. Not infrequently the German text has seemed ambiguous to us, and we are of course entirely responsible for any errors in the English version which may have resulted.

Sabina Berkeley
H.M. Scott

Introduction to the English edition

When it first appeared in German in 1983, Theodor Schieder's study of Frederick the Great was immediately recognised as a major contribution to the study both of Prussia's most important King and of Europe's eighteenth century. Until then Frederician historiography had been dominated by Reinhold Koser's panoramic life-and-times, completed just before the First World War and consolidating the previous half-century's scholarship on the King.[1] Though the next generation saw numerous publications on Frederick and his reign, together with the inevitable distortions introduced by the Third Reich, no book emerged to rival Koser's political biography in scope and scholarly authority. After 1945, earlier epochs in German history and especially Prussia's eighteenth century were neglected in favour of an understandable preoccupation with Germany's traumatic recent past.

During the later 1970s and early 1980s a noted revival of popular and, to a lesser extent, academic interest in Prussia's earlier history, the so-called 'Prussian Wave' (*Preussenwelle*), was apparent, stimulated in part by the large-scale 1981 Berlin exhibition, and this has gathered pace during the past fifteen years.[2] It was further encouraged by the two-hundredth anniversary of Frederick's death, which was celebrated in 1986. Though standing rather apart from the 'Prussian Wave', Theodor Schieder's book was one of the earliest contributions to the King's anniversary and also the most substantial. It was immediately recognised in Germany as a distinguished study, the most important single contribution to the field since Koser. The product of a lifetime's study of and reflection upon the whole course of modern German and European history, Schieder's book was characterised by sharp and penetrating

1. *Geschichte Friedrichs des Grossen* 3 vols. (6th–7th edns.; Berlin, 1925), but essentially completed before 1914.
2. See the catalogue, and the four volumes of scholarly essays which accompanied it: *Preussen: Versuch einer Bilanz* 5 vols. (Hamburg, 1981). For Frederick the Great's reign, the publications of the distinguished East German scholar Ingrid Mittenzwei stand alongside Schieder as the most enduring legacy of the 'Prussian Wave': see her *Preussen nach dem Siebenjährigen Krieg* ([East] Berlin, 1979), and her short biography, *Friedrich II. von Preussen* ([East] Berlin, 1980).

insights and was a landmark in the historiography of Prussia's eighteenth century. Yet it received surprisingly little attention in the Anglo-Saxon world, where it has only been known and admired by specialists. The year after its publication it was the subject of a notable review by T.C.W. Blanning, but with this single exception it does not seem to have been reviewed in a major British or North American historical journal.[3] It here appears in an abridged English version, which requires a few words of introduction for an Anglophone readership who may find its format and approach rather distinctive and even unusual.

Schieder's purpose, as he makes clear in his 'Afterword',[4] was not to produce a biography in the conventional sense of the term: that is, a chronological life, a study which follows its chosen subject from the cradle to the grave. His intention was rather to write – and thereby demonstrate the value of – what he termed a 'structural biography'. Since the 1950s, when the term came into widespread use, 'structural history' (*Strukturgeschichte*) has been the Holy Grail for a generation of German scholars who have focused primarily upon the social dimension of the past. Schieder's own interests by contrast were more exclusively political, though in his studies of parties and political change he was a forerunner of the 'social history of politics' associated with the Bielefeld school. His belief that 'structure' was 'the social and historical matrix that shaped and constrained the actions of individuals' underpinned his biographical study of Frederick and determined its contours.[5] This study is episodic in the sense that it focuses upon certain key phases or dimensions of the King's life which Schieder believes were crucial in his development and that of his state. Frederick slowly emerges out of his own times and out of the Prussian and European context, as a picture of his remarkable personality is built up piece by piece. In the 'Afterword' the author, in order to describe his book's distinctive format, employs the metaphor of a photographer who continually changes his viewpoint in order to provide the most lifelike pictures of the subject, which presented a contrasting series of faces.[6] Schieder believed that frequent changes of perspective were essential if all the dimensions of the King's multifaceted personality and impact upon his age were to be fully comprehended.

A series of overlapping essays is therefore devoted to central themes in Frederick's life and times: the contest with Austria for the possession of Silesia

---

3. See the *Bulletin of the German Historical Institute London* no. 16 (1984), pp. 10–13. Schieder's book was subsequently mentioned by Professor Blanning in the course of a major and notably lively review article on 'The death and transfiguration of Prussia', *Historical Journal* 29 (1986), 433–59, which provides an excellent introduction to the 'Prussian Wave'. It does not seem to have been reviewed in the *English Historical Review, History*, the *American Historical Review* or the *Journal of Modern History*.
4. Below, p. 268.
5. James Van Horn Melton, 'Introduction: continuities in German historical scholarship, 1933–1960', in Hartmut Lehmann and James Van Horn Melton (eds), *Paths of Continuity: Central European Historiography from the 1930s to the 1950s* (Washington, D.C., and Cambridge, 1994), pp. 1–18, at p. 15.
6. Below, p. 269.

which dominated the first half of the reign; Frederick's troubled relations with Russia; his changing attitude towards the Holy Roman Empire; his role in government; his position as a 'soldier-king'. Though this inevitably leads to a degree of repetition across the individual chapters, unity is provided by Frederick's own personality and attitudes which emerge as the central core of the entire book. Successive essays slowly build up an overall picture of the King and a unified interpretation of his reign. With this aim in view, Schieder therefore provides an account in the first chapter of the dramatic episodes which shaped the life of Frederick before he became King and did so much to form his character and to determine his distinctive psychology: his education, the attempted flight from Prussia in 1730 and subsequent trial, and the reconciliation with his father, Frederick William I (1713–40), which followed. His education and upbringing are seen as having created a distinctive personality with an indestructible core, in this way exerting an influence upon Prussian and European history during the half century after 1740.

One legacy of his formative years was the dichotomy between the French-educated Crown Prince who signed himself 'Frederick the philosopher' and the heir-apparent to the spartan, militaristic Prussian state, a ruler in waiting whose education and training aimed only to prepare him for the role of King within a highly personalised monarchy. The distinctive Prussian social and administrative system is examined at length in the second chapter, which provides an essential context for the remainder of the study. This dichotomy, which was strengthened by Frederick's upbringing, is viewed by Schieder as one of the several unresolved tensions within the King's personality, which were apparent in his actions and his statecraft. The German version was given the sub-title *Ein Königtum der Widersprüche*. This is very difficult to render into idiomatic English, but has the sense of 'A King full of contradictions' or the 'Janus King'. It accurately expresses the central dialectic within Schieder's portrait of Frederick the Great: the extent to which the King was a transitional figure who both looked back to earlier dispensations in Prussian and European history, and forward to the political structures of a later age, a tension which once again is only fully articulated in his 'Afterword'.

Such an interpretation came naturally for Theodor Schieder, who turned to the study of the Prussian eighteenth century towards the end of a very distinguished career, a career which had been devoted primarily to writing about the problems of history and historiography during the nineteenth and twentieth centuries, both in Germany and more widely in Europe.[7] His study of Frederick the Great was his last important work. The King's life and reign are frequently illuminated by means of comparisons and perspectives informed by its distinguished author's wide-ranging knowledge of later German and

7. Biographical information can be found in the extended obituary and tribute by Lothar Gall, 'Theodor Schieder, 1908–84', *Historische Zeitschrift* 241 (1985), 1–26. A difficult but rewarding introduction to Schieder's historical thought is provided by Jörn Rüsen, 'Continuity, innovation, and self-reflection in late historicism: Theodor Schieder (1908–1984)', with a comment by Charles S. Maier, in Lehmann and Melton (eds), *Paths of Continuity*, pp. 353–96.

European history. One dimension of Schieder's wider historical and methodological interests may puzzle an Anglophone readership: the appearance in
the text of several quotations from the writings of the nineteenth-century
cultural historian Jacob Burckhardt. During the second half of his own career
Schieder – like Friedrich Meinecke before him – was increasingly drawn to
Burckhardt's writings and attracted to his concept of cultural continuity as the
mainspring of human history. This appeared a way of resolving the fundamental problem with which all post-war West German historians wrestled:
that of dealing with the discontinuity of the Third Reich, which at times
almost seemed to invalidate history itself, or at least the established historicist
paradigm.

Schieder had himself lived through Germany's time of troubles and experienced at first hand the many vicissitudes of its twentieth-century history.
Born in Bavaria in 1908, he was a central figure in the West German historical
profession during the generation after the Second World War. For many years
a professor at the University of Cologne, he was also editor of the *Historische
Zeitschrift*, at that time the leading German-language historical periodical, and
President of the Bavarian Academy of Sciences. His influence as a scholar,
teacher and organiser was enormous. More importantly, he played a central
role in – and was himself undoubtedly influenced by – the agonised reappraisal
of the nature and value of history in West Germany after 1945. During the
generation which followed the Second World War Schieder stood at the very
heart of the West German historical establishment and contributed significantly to its evolution. He himself wrote extensively about the history of nation-
state formation, the history of political parties and the problem of revolution
during the nineteenth and twentieth centuries, and participated in the intense
methodological debates which characterised these decades.

In other respects, however, the study of Frederick the Great arose naturally
out of certain of Schieder's enduring concerns as a historian. He had written
his dissertation on nineteenth-century Bavarian party politics and his publications as a mature scholar were largely to be on the period after the French
Revolution. But he had briefly been at the University of Königsberg (in what
had been the eighteenth-century Hohenzollern province of East Prussia) and
had in fact written his all-important *Habilitationsschrift* (that is to say: his
second-level thesis which secured entry into an academic career) on the political culture of Royal (after 1772 West) Prussia over the period from the Union
of Lublin until the second Partition of Poland.[8]

---

8. It was published as *Deutscher Geist und Ständische Freiheit im Weichsellande: Politische Ideen und
politisches Schrifttum in Westpreussen von der Lubliner Union bis zu den polnischen Teilungen (1569–
1772/93)* (Königsberg, 1940); its conclusions are summarised in 'Landständische Verfassung,
Volkstumpolitik und Volksbewusstein: Eine Studie zur Verfassungsgeschichte ostdeutscher
Volksgruppen', in H. Aubin, O. Brunner et al (eds), *Deutsche Ostforschung: Ergebnisse und Aufgaben
seit dem Ersten Weltkrieg* vol. ii (Leipzig, 1943), pp. 257–88. At this period in his life Schieder was
involved with the *Ostforschung* school of German historians who emphasised their nation's decisive contribution to the development of 'Slavic' areas in Eastern Europe, and he subsequently
sponsored editions of documents on this theme: Michael Burleigh, *Germany Turns Eastwards: a*

His study of Frederick was also a logical culmination of Schieder's long-standing interest in the role of personality in history.[9] Albeit not a biography in the conventional sense of the term, his study of the Hohenzollern King was primarily a study of the impact of a towering personality upon the Prussia and Europe of his own day. That personality, however, was animated by distinctive ideas, rather than simply pragmatic responses to the situations he faced and the context within which he operated, far less any belief in historical materialism. Here the distinctive intellectual approach associated with German idealistic philosophy and particularly with Hegel clearly left its imprint upon Schieder. Throughout his career, the author believed that individuals were primarily driven not by economic forces but by the power of ideas, which were of fundamental importance throughout human history. As he notes in the German edition of his study, it was based almost entirely on printed material and especially the King's own writings.[10]

Schieder presents a complex and persuasive analysis of Frederick's intellectual development, across the half-century from the 1730s to the final years of his reign, and this stands at the heart of his interpretation. Time and again quotations from Frederick's own voluminous writings, both works of philosophical speculation and practical statecraft, are used to illuminate an argument or buttress a conclusion. More characteristically, Schieder sees Frederick's actions and policies as the working out in practice of a distinctive philosophical system. Once again he identifies tensions within Frederick's intellectual world-view: primarily between his idealism, seen at its clearest in the *Anti-Machiavel* (which is discussed at length, particularly in Chapter 3), and the exigencies of power-politics and Prussia's distinctive geostrategic position.

In other respects, however, Schieder's portrait of Frederick is firmly within an established German – and German nationalist – tradition. This goes back to the second half of the nineteenth century, when historical writing in Germany underwent a scientific revolution associated above all with the career and influence of Leopold von Ranke, who himself contributed significantly to the study of Frederick the Great and whom Schieder cites on several occasions, always with approval. Scholarly study of Prussia's leading eighteenth-century King began during the period which saw first the Unification of Germany during the wars of 1864–71 and then the consolidation of a Prussian-dominated German Empire. This imparted a nationalist tone to studies of Frederick the Great which has endured. Since Germany had been 'unified' by means of the expulsion of Austria, and since this process had begun in the 1740s, when

---

Study of Ostforschung *in the Third Reich* (Cambridge, 1988) provides the essential German perspective. There is a real problem establishing Schieder's intellectual development during the Weimar and Nazi periods: after a careful survey of the evidence, Jörn Rüsen concluded that, although Schieder was involved in some politically driven projects during the early phases of his career, he was more influenced by 'folk' history than by the ideological programme of Nazism: 'Continuity, innovation and self-reflection', p. 367.

9. Gall, 'Theodor Schieder', p. 20.
10. *Friedrich der Grosse* (Frankfurt/M.-Berlin-Vienna, 1983), p. 495.

the King had seized the Habsburg province of Silesia, Frederick became a kind of patron saint for a united Germany. A nationalist historiography of the King developed, which rested upon the publication of great documentary series devoted largely or even entirely to Frederick's reign.[11]

There are echoes of such an approach in Schieder's study, though they are far less dominant than in earlier studies and particularly in the last book on the King by a major German scholar to be published in an English translation, Walther Hubatsch's Prussophile study of Frederician government and administration.[12] Anglophone readers will value the insights as well as the underlying ambiguity of Theodor Schieder's portrayal of the dominant Prussian as well as a central European personality of the eighteenth century, with its picture of a King as a transitional figure who was wedded to the old order, which his own actions would do so much to undermine.

H.M. Scott

---

11. Above all the *Acta Borussica* which began publication in 1892 and produced volumes of documents in several series bearing on the internal development of eighteenth-century Prussia, and the *Politische Correspondenz Friedrichs des Grossen*, ed. J.G. Droysen et al (46 vols.; Berlin, 1879–1939), which is the major source for the King's foreign policy.
12. *Frederick the Great: Absolutism and Administration* (trans. P.F. Doran; London, 1975).

CHAPTER 1

Frederick's youth: the international situation and personal destiny

The ruler known to history as Frederick II of Prussia was born on 24 January 1712. He was the son of the Prussian Crown Prince, Frederick William, and his wife, Sophia Dorothea of Hanover. The couple's fourth child, Frederick followed two brothers who had died in infancy and a sister, Wilhelmina, who was three years older than him. Destiny had determined him to be the heir to the Prussian throne in accordance with the law of succession through male primogeniture.

These simple facts record an event which was to have an extraordinary effect upon the history of Germany and Europe during the eighteenth century. It was unusual for men of real distinction to ascend Europe's monarchical thrones, whether by traditional right or as a result of veiled usurpation. The offspring of marriage alliances formed within the narrow confines of ruling families were unlikely to have inherited any extraordinary qualities. They were influenced rather by an upbringing in a world which, despite placing them in positions of authority, expected a certain, but often limited, talent for the tasks of political and military leadership. A prince was, from the very beginning, put on a pedestal. In public it was never questioned whether he merited this elevated position as a man, statesman and military leader. The world of the ruler was a traditional one, and it did not encourage or expect great achievements from the favoured individual, since power and splendour were bestowed upon him as a matter of course. The situation was quite different from that in revolutionary societies, in which the ascent to power involved exceptional risks and possessed none of the safeguards, provided by inherited right, which could prevent a fall into the abyss. Most legitimate rulers, in any case, contented themselves with upholding the status quo. Those who attempted to do more than this were compelled to extract herculean efforts from the state apparatus which they had inherited and attempt a revolution from above.

The eighteenth century offers several examples of such men: Charles XII of Sweden appeared to many, including Frederick himself, to represent the epitomy of failure; Peter the Great of Russia provided the model for creating a powerful empire through internal and external reorganisation. Since the time of the Elector Frederick William (the Great Elector, 1640–88) in the seventeenth century, Prussia had been a second-rate state, showing little, if any, signs of ever playing the role of a great power. In order for it to become a great power, decisive dynastic leadership was needed, and this was provided first by the Great Elector and then by King Frederick William I (1713–40). The leader who wished to transform Prussia into a great power had to rely on and make use of the existing administration and army. The option of proceeding, as Napoleon and Lenin would do, after a destruction of the existing political and military order, did not exist. In order to achieve the goal of territorial aggrandisement and political expansion, such a leader was not obliged continually to destroy his enemies, but needed only to summon the 'courage of his soul' (J. Burckhardt) to deter external foes. Frederick overthrew Europe's existing political order, not Prussia's social order, which he was always concerned to uphold.

This overthrow depended for its success upon Frederick's possession of three qualities rarely found in the same person: political decisiveness, an aptitude for military leadership and practical administrative talent. It is pointless to ask why and from whom the King had inherited these traits of character. His ancestors included such outstanding personalities as the leader of the Dutch Revolt, William the Silent, and the French Huguenot, Admiral de Coligny, both of whom possessed such qualities, but these names can also be found in the genealogies of other rulers. The enigma of great ability cannot be solved through recourse to ancestral lineage, nor simply through an analysis of the historical context. More important is the process whereby circumstances and trends combine with individual potential and allow it to develop. To chart this interaction is the specific responsibility of historical scholarship. Frederick, marked by his fateful youth, sought and found the great opportunity in the history of his time.

He was born during the final stages of the War of the Spanish Succession. In the month before his birth, diplomats assembled at the Peace Congress of Utrecht and this led, a year later in April 1713, to the conclusion of the Peace of Utrecht. Resistance to France's hegemony and her claim to the Spanish inheritance (the possession of which would have made her unassailable) led to the introduction of a new principle of political order, the balance of power. Its proponent was England, the island state which was preparing to rule the oceans, dominate maritime trade, and build an Empire beyond the seas. Since the Glorious Revolution of 1688/89, it had begun to develop a new type of constitutional structure in which power was shared by Crown and Parliament, at a period when absolute monarchy was the order of the day in most other European states. From that time onwards, the struggle for supremacy on the world stage revolved around the Anglo-French conflict, on which

King Frederick II's calculations depended so vitally when he embarked on his first, decisive action, an action which was to have a determining influence on his whole life – the conquest of Silesia. Once the great western conflict of the Spanish Succession was on the wane, the simultaneous struggle in northern and eastern Europe continued unabated. Peter the Great's wide-ranging internal reconstruction and the increased influence which European technology and ideas now had within Russia had prepared the way for her formidable advance westwards. She drove Sweden from the Baltic coast, destroyed the Swedish great power position and made her own presence felt throughout the Baltic region. Poland-Lithuania, too, became totally caught up in the maelstrom of Russian politics. The Empire of the Tsars had carved its way into the whole European states system. Europe's politics could no longer be conducted without paying due regard to the rising power on its eastern rim.

As a result of her extended geographical position, straggling across the territory between the rivers Rhine and Memel, Prussia was located directly between the two spheres of conflict in East and West. Various treaties tied her to the Grand Alliance against Louis XIV, and compelled her to provide troops to serve in the Southern Netherlands, Italy and the Rhineland. This did little to advance Prussia's own interests, except perhaps in the Lower Rhine region. Only after the Peace of Utrecht did the main focus of her own military activity shift to the neighbouring territory of Pomerania, which lay to the north of Brandenburg. In October, 1713, Russia allowed Frederick William I, who had become King on 25 February of that year, to occupy the important port of Stettin and the territory up to the river Peene until the peace settlement should be concluded. This important acquisition was not formally approved until 1720, when Frederick was just eight years old.

During the years when the eighteenth-century power constellation was taking shape, a new generation of monarchs and even new ruling families ascended Europe's thrones. These changes were particularly significant at a period when political power, in continental Europe at least, was personified by absolute monarchy. In 1711 Emperor Joseph I had died after only a brief reign. The resulting accession of his brother, Charles VI, made it inevitable that the Spanish inheritance would be separated from the Austrian Habsburgs, and thus laid the seeds for the destruction of the great alliance between the two branches of the Habsburg family. The year 1714 saw the accession to the British thrones of the Hanoverian dynasty in the person of George I, brother of the Queen of Prussia. This, too, was an event with considerable repercussions for German politics. On 1 September 1715, Louis XIV died. He had been responsible for the most glorious epoch in France's history, but at the same time it had become clear that the power of the French monarchy had reached its zenith at home and abroad. The concept of a French 'universal monarchy', the foundation of which would have been the union of France and Spain, had clearly failed. No European alignment could henceforth come about without the approval of Great Britain. For some time, however, it was impossible to prevent the hegemony of the French language, French thought and

French culture, a process which did not reach its climax until the age of the Enlightenment, even though the English contribution to that movement was to be significant.

The death of Louis XIV signalled a transition which was already under way: Europe lost its monarchical focal point from which the other continental rulers had all taken their lead. The move away from the image of kingship personified by this sovereign can nowhere be more clearly observed than with the accession in 1713 of Frederick William I, the son of the first King in Prussia. The change of personnel in the five years between 1710 and 1715 did not produce a European crisis, unlike the momentous and almost simultaneous changes in 1740 in Prussia, Russia and Austria, with the deaths of Frederick William I, the Russian Empress Anna and the Emperor Charles VI. The earlier changes, however, certainly did not have a stabilising effect, since the exhausted French monarchy henceforth faced severe domestic problems which proved enduring, while the dynastic change in Britain as well as the question of the succession in Austria brought with them difficulties which would loom large during the ensuing decades.

Following the establishment of the French Bourbon dynasty in Spain in 1700 and the resulting gain by a French company of the monopoly for the black slave trade to Spanish America, Britain secured a share in this odious human commerce, gaining the right to send an annual ship under the Asiento agreement (March 1713), an addition to the Anglo-Spanish peace settlement. Spain had declined economically as well as politically; while the Dutch Republic had lost its dominant position both in the Baltic grain trade and in commerce with the East Indies, and had been decisively eclipsed by Great Britain. Sweden's *dominium maris baltici*, her military and political dominance of the Baltic, which was also based upon economic control of its ports, had slowly been eroded since its peak around 1660; now, with the loss of Stettin, a further important component of its position was removed. The French monarchy never recovered from the strains caused by the wars of Louis XIV and by France's simultaneous emergence as a maritime as well as a continental power. Nevertheless, in the eighteenth century she entered once more into a worldwide conflict with England, in North America and India. Frederick II's seven-year struggle with Austria (the Seven Years War of 1756–63) was merely a sideshow in this crucial global struggle which was being fought to secure the riches of the New World.

In the years following the conclusion of the War of the Spanish Succession, Europe entered a new age in other respects too. Paul Hazard, describing the period 1680–1715, spoke of a 'crisis of the European conscience' and highlighted two distinctly opposing cultures: 'Hierarchy, discipline, an order secured by authority, dogmas which regulated life with a firm hand – that's what the people of the seventeenth century craved; force, authority, dogmas are what the people of the eighteenth century, their immediate successors, cordially detested . . . The majority of Frenchmen used to think like Bossuet, and yet suddenly the French think like Voltaire; it is a revolution . . .'. Pierre

Bayle referred to the two forms of thought as that of the 'believers' and that of the 'rationalists', whose struggle for adherents was watched with interest by all Europe's intellectuals. A few decades later this struggle was played out afresh within the Prussian King's own family, in the conflict between Frederick William I and his son, Crown Prince Frederick, the friend of Voltaire.

What role did Prussia play in the world in which Frederick grew up? It was still not a unified state, as the name might imply, and took its designation from the most eastern of the Hohenzollern territories. East Prussia was that land which was 'of no importance to anyone but God and its own subjects' and which had been elevated to the status of a kingdom by the Elector Frederick III (1688–1713), after 1701 'King in Prussia' as Frederick I. Since Kings, unlike Electors, could create titled nobility, the Hohenzollerns were obliged to locate their royal dignity outside the Empire, within which that right was a powerful and profitable Habsburg monopoly which Vienna was determined to uphold. Apart from the other ruling titles and possessions held by the Prussian monarchy, the Hohenzollerns significantly held sway over the Electorate of Brandenburg. From this core the authority of the ruling family extended to all the outlying territories. At the time of the accession of Frederick William I, however, the process of territorial integration was only in its infancy. What Voltaire would later refer to mockingly as a 'kingdom of mere border strips' was an 'aggregate of territories' which stretched from the Rhine to the Memel, but did not amount to a solid, unified geographical area except in its central province, the Electorate of Brandenburg.

Apart from the functions exercised by the court and the absolute ruler himself, along with his councillors and close advisors, the only institution which covered all the Hohenzollern territories was the Prussian army, which was to be considerably strengthened under Frederick William I. Under the previous ruler, Frederick III/I, it had been the enormously lavish court with its array of honorific offices which had represented the rudimentary elements of a unified state, though it conveyed the impression rather than the reality of power and also devoured the monarchy's budget. The international position of the Prusso-Brandenburg state was that of an auxiliary whose army could decisively tip the military balance and which was therefore courted by all sides, as – for example – were other second-rank states such as Savoy-Piedmont or Bavaria. Prussia still lacked most of the essential attributes of a real great power. The adolescent Hohenzollern monarchy simply displayed the intention to become one, particularly since becoming a kingdom. It did not possess decisive political clout, despite the efforts of the Great Elector. The principal reason for the weakness of this political entity was its territorial fragmentation; this was much more acute than that of other dynastic creations within the Empire. In contemporary eyes, its size in 1713 of 2,043.67 square miles and population of 1.65 million qualified it, at most, as a second-rate power.[1]

---

1. The author here and elsewhere gives the size in the much larger German miles. One 'German mile' = 4.6 English miles.

The capital was as incomplete as the state itself. Berlin had only existed as a unified town since 1709 and the amalgamation of the city with the outlying districts of Cölln, Dorotheenstadt, Friedrichsstadt and Friedrichswerder. With around 56,000 inhabitants, the capital was more than double the size of the 'Royal residence and principal town of East Prussia', Königsberg, which had barely 25,000 inhabitants. By the end of Frederick the Great's reign, the disparity was even more striking: Berlin's population numbered 147,000 in 1786, while Königsberg at much the same time had only 48,692 inhabitants. Berlin grew along with the Hohenzollern monarchy: the city was politically and socially a creation of the state and its court. It had a military garrison, factories, palaces and a distinct social structure. Around 1720, the proportion of Huguenot refugees amounted to some 9 per cent of the total population. This percentage was considerably higher than the national average and was indicative of the fact that the state had not yet mustered the strength to build up its capital by itself.

Unlike the cities of Karlsruhe, Ludwigsburg or Rastadt, which were also the seats of ruling families and the locations of their princely courts, Berlin was not an artificial creation, but grew from humble beginnings as a small provincial town to become the capital city of an expanding territorial state. In its expansion, the years around 1700 were of particular importance architecturally, when the ambitious first King in Prussia and his Queen, Sophia Charlotte, provided artistic momentum to the Hohenzollern state. The focal point of this building programme was Berlin's late-sixteenth-century Renaissance town palace, which may well be described historically as a 'memorial in stone to the Hohenzollern dynasty'. Significant alterations were made in Frederick I's time, when Andreas Schlüter, entrusted with the rebuilding, transformed it by converting three wings of the inner courtyard and refurbishing the façade into a Baroque construction of such colossal splendour that it conveyed the impression of a powerful Prusso-Brandenburg state, even if the reality was a little different. It resembled the palace in Stockholm with its massive block shape, which gave the impression of a fortress, and blended the particular North German Baroque style with an Italian influence. The further rebuilding, following Schlüter's downfall, was supervised by the Swedish architect Johann Friedrich Eosander, Freiherr von Göthe, who wished to give expression to the confidence of the new kingdom by adding a high dome, which was not, however, completed until the nineteenth century. Eosander von Göthe worked in Berlin from 1707 to 1715. During that time, his endeavours created the palace as it was known to the young Crown Prince Frederick. Many of Eosander's great plans, however, remained uncompleted.

In the years around 1700 the Hohenzollerns followed the example of their own high nobility who, through the building of castles, had erected princely memorials for themselves, and it was only this which transformed Berlin into a city which was fit to be a royal capital. Between 1695 and 1699, Lietzenburg palace was built near the village of Lietzow for the Electress, later Queen, Sophia Charlotte. After her death in 1705, it was renamed Charlottenburg.

The garden palace of Monbijou, built by Eosander between 1703 and 1710, was a present from Frederick I to the Queen, who gave concerts and balls there. It was to remain the private residence of subsequent Prussian Queens. This architectural programme, which also included ecclesiastical buildings such as the church of Sophia, built in 1712, formed the basic core of the new royal capital, before the focal point of the monarchy moved to Potsdam. The plans for the rebuilding of Berlin's cathedral, a task for which the Dutchman Jean de Bodt was signed up, were never completed. Likewise the colossal plan adopted by Frederick I in 1704 to allow the architect Johann Bernhard Fischer von Erlach to create a Prussian Versailles never came to fruition, though Fischer von Erlach did submit plans. The scheme's purpose had been to put the young kingdom on an equal footing with the established powers – a bold concept, though one which was somewhat premature.

The world of the court stretched beyond the capital into the Mark Brandenburg, and here two locations are of particular interest: Königswusterhausen and Rheinsberg. Königswusterhausen, or 'Wendisch-Wusterhausen' as it was originally known, belonged as early as 1683 to the Crown Prince, later King, Frederick, who passed it on to his ten-year-old son, Frederick William, in 1698. Throughout his life, Frederick William had a special affection for this palace, which he rebuilt and refurbished. There, he created a model of an idealised state, and spent at least two months a year during the hunting season. It was already clear that this was a favoured retreat when, after his own accession as King, it was used in the autumn of 1713 for festivities dominated by hunting. The gloomy palace of Königswusterhausen had notably cramped living conditions. According to her memoirs, Princess Wilhelmina was forced to share two small attic rooms with one of her sisters. Königswusterhausen was a hateful place for her and for her brother, Fritz, the location where the conflict between father and son was to reach intolerable heights in 1728.

Königswusterhausen is always associated historically with Frederick William I. Rheinsberg, on the other hand, is remembered as the place where, between 1736 and 1740, Crown Prince Frederick spent his happiest years. In the previous century, it had been bestowed by the Great Elector on General Du Hamel, who promptly sold it. Frederick William I acquired Rheinsberg in 1734 and bestowed it upon his son, who employed the noted architect Georg Wenzeslaus von Knobelsdorff to rebuild it between 1737 and 1739. The result was distinctly reminiscent of the Trianon at Versailles, since Frederick envisaged transplanting 'a piece of France . . . into the sandy Mark' (P. Gaxotte). The transition from Schlüter to Knobelsdorff also reflected a decisive change in architectural style.

FATHER AND SON

Frederick was barely one year old when the death of the first King on 25 February 1713 brought his father to the Prussian throne. Frederick William I's accession was far more than a simple change of ruler. It brought about a fundamental transformation in the whole lifestyle, political world and established hierarchies of the Prussian monarchy. Frederick I, like many other seventeenth- and eighteenth-century German princes, had been a representative of a form of absolutism which had taken as its model the France of Louis XIV. What distinguished his own position from that of his fellow German rulers was the honour of the royal title which lent greater dignity to the sovereign territory which lay beyond the boundaries of the Empire. Two other Electors, those of Hanover and Saxony, did of course rise to royal rank by becoming Kings of Great Britain and Poland-Lithuania, while other German dynasties concluded marriage alliances with foreign crowned heads. For the Kings of Great Britain, however, Hanover sank to the status of a secondary possession, while the association of the Saxon Elector Augustus the Strong and his son with the Polish throne can hardly be viewed as having represented a real increase in power and income for their homeland of Saxony; at most it was a considerable gain in prestige. Only for the Elector of Brandenburg did the royal dignity act as an integrating factor for all his widely scattered lands. Admittedly this process had scarcely begun by the time of the first Prussian King. Frederick III/I announced a claim through the display of royal ceremonial, which thus had a different function than in the established kingdom of France. The coronation of 1701 was an act of usurpation, the launching of a programme which challenged the established monarchies.

Prussia's new King did not yet have at his disposal a state which was a closed territorial unit internally or externally, but he possessed a court of substantial size: with a *Schlosshauptmann* (literally 'head of the palace', that is to say majordomo), *Hofmarschall* ('marshal of the court'), *Oberschenk* ('principal cup-bearer'), sixteen *Kämmerer* (chamberlains), thirty-two *Kammerjunker* (gentlemen of the bedchamber), seven *Hofjunker* (gentlemen of the court), twenty-four pages, and a great number of chamber and household servants. Below these were the liveried servants (*Heiducker*), valets and royal stablehands, the court's chief cook, five royal cooks, eight master chefs, three bakers, seven pastry cooks, five butchers, two fish-keepers, one poultryman. In its upper echelons, there thus existed a network of holders of largely honorific posts, exactly the situation at the courts of many minor German rulers.

In contrast to the French court, its Prussian counterpart did not hold an irresistible attraction for noblemen, who based themselves in the provinces; for a time it remained an artificial creation, lacking any function. Norbert Elias's celebrated explanation of the French court and of court society in general, namely that it served to deprive the aristocracy of its independence and strengthen its reliance upon the King, the court thus performing the double function of providing for and at the same time taming the high nobility, did not yet apply in the case of Brandenburg-Prussia. The Prussian court, understandably, could not hope to match the dimensions of the French where the King's own household employed a staff of 4,000. The inherent weakness of the rapidly established court system of Frederick I explains the ease with which his successor was able to destroy it.

As Crown Prince, Frederick William had already come to appreciate the inherent fragility of his father's regime, particularly the large state debt and the dependence upon foreign powers and their subsidies. Soon after taking over the reins of government, therefore, the new King overthrew in a matter of weeks the prevailing absolutism which had reached its climax in the court and its institutions. Most of the court posts were abolished, while the number of appointments and salaries was drastically reduced and all forms of luxury suppressed. In place of the court society with its extravagant tastes and hierarchy of posts, the holders of which seemed solely concerned with the prestige which accrued, a military system of ranks and offices was established. The 'Table of Ranks' of 21 April 1713 confirmed the dominant position of the army: whereas until then the *Oberkämmerer* (Lord High Chamberlain) had represented the peak of the pyramid, the field-marshal now took his place. The *Grandmaître* of the court was demoted from fourth to seventh position and was now responsible to the lieutenant-general, the *Schloßhauptmann* to the major-generals. The chamberlains were ranked below colonels, who were moved upwards from forty-third to nineteenth position. The *Kammerjunker* were placed under the captains, who were thus promoted by no less than fifty-five places in the hierarchical ladder.

In the new King's state, stripped of its Baroque embellishments, the existing social hierarchy remained, but it was now governed by military ranks. Aristocratic principles were still important, but the new social order was clothed in military uniform. This was evident in a sharp rise in the size of the army, whose numbers rose, first from 40,000 in 1713 to 60,000 and, finally, to 80,000 by 1740. Its composition was also changing: although the proportion of foreign mercenaries was still considerable, that of native soldiers from rural areas was rising. Individual regiments were each allocated particular recruiting districts known as cantons. The officer corps was recruited exclusively from the ranks of the nobility and this process was at times enforced through draconian measures. Brandenburg – Prussia was an almost entirely agrarian state, and the whole economy was geared towards the army, while the royal domain lands were enlarged and their yield increased by rational farm management. The army, instead of the court, was now the largest consumer, often devouring more than two-thirds of the state revenues, while the court only secured one per cent. Prussian mercantilism was a state-directed economic programme to support the army. Any surplus income was stored up in the *Tresor*, the state treasury, which, by the end of Frederick William's reign, contained 8,000,000 thaler. The mercantilist theory of an increase in the monetary pool as the goal of trade and other economic activity, in this case, had a distinct purpose. In this way a material base was established which provided his successor, Frederick, with political freedom of action.

After 1725, Frederick William I constantly wore a uniform, a fashion which caught on amongst the European aristocracy, even if the Prussian system it represented was not adopted. Militarism was inherent in the Prussian state created by Frederick William. It was its *raison d'être*, born out of the enormously overstretched resources of a poor country, which did not possess the means to support a great power role, but which, through its attempt to play such a role, was constantly exposed to foreign threats. Standing armies had been created in all the larger German territorial states after the end of the seventeenth century, but these forces played a politically neutral role. In Prussia by contrast the army took over the whole state apparatus and was assimilated by it. The aristocratic duty of the officer was the basis of a military state machine. Militarism was not an end in itself, but an instrument of the state's quest for power and this led to the modernisation of the administration and the army. The relatively passive foreign policy pursued by Frederick William I, however, largely confined the Prussian regiments to the barrack square. There were minor exceptions but, in the main, the military system had time to become established within Prussia itself.

Those contemporaries who were affected by the King and his policies did not regard Frederick William as the instigator of deeply considered reforms, but as a hostile destroyer of culture, governed by unpredictable moods. Indeed, his personality, full of contradictions and lacking in social grace and conviviality, made it difficult to see him as an inspired creator. Throughout his life, he failed to curb his dangerous tendency to displays of violent temper, brutality and contempt for his fellow man, which conveyed the impression that he was the archetypal inhuman despot. Excessive in anger, he was also excessive in repentance and remorse. He was torn by violently conflicting emotions which seemed quite irreconcilable with the calculated and rational policies which he pursued. Nevertheless, both aspects of his personality were evident in these policies as well as in the upbringing of the Crown Prince. Bearing in mind his father's Baroque display of splendour, Frederick William's puritan austerity and harshness, which as in his treatment of his own son could reach the level of mental cruelty, were particularly noticeable. Although externally he gave the impression of a puritan, his basic principles were governed more by the influences of Pietism, to which he had been introduced by General Dubislav von Natzmer. His association with August Hermann Francke, the founding father of German Pietism, allowed him to experience the proven Christian value of practical action, but this need for practical action was not directed at man, but at the state, in which context human happiness was irrelevant. Power was to be found on the battlefield, where one must seek 'one's temporal welfare' as he put it. It is possible to perceive a curious combination of Lutheran and Calvinist principles; the concept of predestinarianism had such an unsettling effect on the Calvinistically raised King that he rejected it and did all he could to preserve his son from contamination by it. This in no way meant that he shrank from the responsibilities which his royal house and his own state demanded of him; quite the reverse, in fact. Like a person possessed, he did everything to prove to himself that his contribution to the rise of Prussia merited his being one of God's elect.

Frederick's childhood and early youth coincided with the first decade and a half of Frederick William's reign, a critical test period for the newly established

General Directory which transformed the state apparatus and the administrative order. This synchronisation of personal evolution and state development can be confirmed by specific dates: in the early part of 1722, the King drew up his Political Testament, intended to guide his successor in statecraft. At the end of the same year, the great 'Instruction' was issued, bringing into being the new governmental institution, the General Directory. The nervousness with which the King viewed any deviation on the part of the Crown Prince from the principles of statecraft laid down by Frederick William, may be explained by his awareness that these were still in their vulnerable infancy and that any divergence from the prescribed path could not be endured.

The conflict which began to brew between father and son, and later escalated into a full-scale crisis, can be attributed to several factors which must not be viewed separately, but whose combination and interaction served to fuel the struggle. First of all, there was clearly a generation gap, one that coincided with and was sharpened by the general abandonment of seventeenth-century values in favour of those of the 'century of Enlightenment', a development of which the participants were not necessarily aware. In addition, it was also a contest between contrasting political objectives, which was particularly highlighted by the question of marriages for Frederick and his older sister, Wilhelmina. Ultimately, it was, of course, a father–son conflict, which was exacerbated by their totally opposing natures. Freudian analysis based upon the notion of an 'Oedipus complex' is futile, since in Frederick's case the basic prerequisite of a strong maternal bond was lacking. Frederick William's character was divided by an untamed choleric temperament which combined in him a violent temper, brutality, unpredictability and lack of tact on the one hand, with calculated rationality, immense diligence, an attention to detail in his daily business but also pedantry and stubbornness. Side by side with a puritan work ethic, the King derived what appeared to be a barbaric pleasure from the company of coarse men. Similarly contradictory is the deep, religious feeling of remorse which often followed outbursts of unbridled temper. Frederick William was the archetypal autocrat in whom an incredibly assertive will was united with a mastery of the smallest details which allowed him to be competent in nearly all the areas of political life. He had at his disposal a state which although in every sense incomplete, was sufficiently malleable to allow him to make his mark.

Frederick William's basic concepts of statecraft were simple. Emphasis is often given to their pragmatic origins, but their intrinsic unity and interdependence must not be overlooked: state power was totally at his disposal and at best it only served its people indirectly, life and the well-being of the individual were of no consequence. This systematic disregard corresponded with the King's own nature, since the possibility of self-determination for his subjects did not occur to him – only a religiously determining influence was acceptable: 'One must look to God for eternal salvation, but to me for everything else.'

Frederick William subjected his state and his subjects to a harsh learning process, imposed from above and carried out by governmental institutions, but not based on the conscious cooperation of those it affected. The sons of Junkers, for example, were forced to become cadets in military academies set up to provide a steady stream of officers for the army. At this point, similarities can clearly be detected between the rigorous educative policies imposed upon the state and the upbringing of the Crown Prince. Frederick William determined that the latter be conducted according to a plan which his father had laid down for his own education in 1695 and which also incorporated some of Leibniz's ideas. He was untroubled by the fact that, in the past, he himself had demonstrated that these intractable instructions could not be implemented. As soon as the Crown Prince reached the age of six in 1718, responsibility for his education was placed in the hands of two senior officers, Lieutenant-General Graf von Finckenstein and Colonel von Kalckstein, who had been instructed by the King to employ the programme of 1695, which had shaped his own childhood, embellished by Frederick William's own pietistic additions, as the basis for their teaching. Thus, fear of God was to be given the utmost importance since 'great princes who recognise no humanly imposed punishment or reward' cannot, unlike other mortals, be encouraged to do good or, conversely, prevented from doing evil by rewards or punishments imposed by the highest of legal authorities. It was, therefore, the religious ties which served to remind the absolute monarch of the only limitation upon his power. It was in keeping with the spirit of Pietism that the individual should display personal piousness with the 'ultimate aim of attaining God's eternal salvation'; as a result, the King expected that 'operas, comedies and other such worldly vanities' would be foregone. In addition, the preservation of orthodoxy was an important component of religious education – this meant guarding against 'all sects and aberrations intent on malicious destruction, such as the Atheist–Arian–Socinian society, and also . . . against the Catholic religion'. Moreover, the King prohibited what he regarded as the deeply disturbing teaching of predestinarianism, the 'particularist' doctrine which limited God's grace to only a chosen few. It had been a recurring nightmare of Frederick William's own youth that he did not belong to the elect. He had, unknowingly at first, awakened the same fear in the young Crown Prince, who saw the sense in a preordained fate for man. The subject remained a constant topic of discussion right up to the great crisis of 1730.

In the educational plan, it is possible to detect basic Pietist ideas: for example, the breaking of a natural self-will pitted against God as the final goal of the educative scheme and the assimilation of 'Christian teaching' which dictated that such wisdom should then affect the actions of those who had acquired it. However, the Crown Prince was to become not only a pious Christian, but also a 'good host' and to be prepared 'to play the part of an officer and a general'. It clearly did not seem difficult for the King to reconcile the idea of a chivalrous lifestyle with his own religious ideals: next to the fear of God, he believed, there is nothing which stimulates the princely mind to do good and discourages it from doing evil more than 'the true splendour of and yearning for glory, honour and bravery'. This peculiar synthesis of ethical guiding forces was to be one source of Frederick's almost vocational search for glory. It is this which clearly provided the impetus for his invasion of Silesia. Glory was virtually a royal status symbol, as honour was for the nobility. In all aspects of the educational plan, strong emphasis was placed upon questions of morality. This applied both to the 'moderate exercise' that had been planned for the Prince, as well as to times of 'honorable recreation' engaging in 'certain decent games, but not cards or games of chance'. The purely pedagogic element played something of a secondary role, whereas in other educational plans it occupied a dominant position as, for example, in that of Frederick's younger contemporary, the future Joseph II.

Although it is impossible merely to limit one's analysis of Frederick's education to broad generalisations, certain trends are discernible. It seems almost as if this severely practical education was an anticipation of things to come; Latin and Ancient History were scrapped and the main emphasis placed upon Mathematics, Artillery, Economy, Geography, Modern History, and a knowledge of the affairs of state. History served to convey an understanding of practical action. Accordingly, the King ordered the study of the 'History of the House of Hohenzollern' and insisted that the histories of those states particularly associated with Prussia – England, Brunswick and Hesse – also be given especial emphasis. The absence of any mention of the history of Austria, as well as that of the Empire, reflected a certain political naiveté. Regular teaching in 'Natural Law and in the Law of Nations' was not, however, overlooked. This was an area in which Joseph II, too, was to be given detailed instruction by legal scholars. In a complementary clause of 1721 to the Educational Instruction, the King laid down that the present condition of European states, 'the strengths and weaknesses, size, urban wealth or poverty of all the European powers' be taught, possibly along the lines of Pufendorf or even just using the *Theatrum Europeum.*

All of this bore the King's somewhat unsystematic, arbitrary stamp, which can also be detected in many other areas. The Instruction of 1718, although very much in the tradition of other princely political testaments and writings on education, had purely pragmatic goals. Its theoretical content was peppered with contradictions and its educational value is questionable, not least because it lacked any understanding of an adolescent's psyche. Much more influential than the educational programme, however, was the personal relationship between Frederick William and his son. This was shaped by a series of factors which silently interacted. Like any father, Frederick William undoubtedly hoped to mould his son in his own image, or even the idealised image of himself which he had striven for but failed to attain. Behind this lay the dreadful fear that Frederick could re-establish the odious, ruinous system of government of Prussia's first King: the semblance of power, the trumpery of a dazzling culture without the solid basis of a healthy economy, the claim to royal sovereignty at the cost of dependence upon a power-hungry nobility. This trauma of a return to obstacles which had already been surmounted weighed heavily upon the King's mind. Added to this, especially with the passing years, was probably a certain jealousy of his son, of 'the rising sun', while experiencing his own physical decline. All this made it difficult, even impossible, for the King to remain objective with regard to Frederick and to exercise moderation in his dealings with him. Nevertheless, in spite of the fact that eventually he could not bear him as a person, he was obliged to raise the heir to the throne in the fashion laid down by *raison d'état*.

When one speaks of the educational programme for the Crown Prince, one is referring not only to the regulating of discipline and the subject-matter of learning, but the total regimentation of daily life. Frederick's day was organised down to the last minute – much like the quotidian routine of the members of the General Directory after the Great Instruction of December 1722. The need to carry out his prescribed daily tasks proved to be an overwhelming strain on the Crown Prince, whose constitution was stretched to its limits by this regime. The King perceived this regimentation to be the pivotal point of his son's education, an education which did not allow for normal adolescent development, but only aimed at coercing Frederick into a system. 'He truly believed that a mind can be trained like a regiment, and that a soul can be cultivated like a royal demesne' (Carl Hinrichs). Flexibility or a regard for the psychological needs of the individual played no part in this educational system. Everything had to be done as laid down by the programme. The Crown Prince constantly heard the same, seemingly inflexible formulae: he was to prepare to become 'God's bureaucrat', a 'good host' and a 'soldier and general'. He was perhaps most touched by the example of the 'honnête homme', the high social ideal which stemmed from France and to which the rest of the European aristocracy aspired. In the mind of Frederick William, who used the term constantly, the idea acquired overtones of German uprightness and respectability, and it became for him simply a description of an honourable man, who, while not repudiating the still largely aristocratic moral code, turned more for guidance towards the truths of the Christian faith. Though Frederick William was steeped in the continuing tradition of Western chivalry, this had little direct impact on his utterances. One thing cannot be overlooked: all these models served a single purpose, that of turning the Crown Prince into an autocrat; not an autocrat wallowing in luxury and majesty, but one dedicated to work and subject to the 'majesty of God'.

It is difficult to establish precisely how the young Prince was affected by these exacting educational demands. There is very little documentation from contemporary observers and next to nothing written (at that time, at least) by Frederick himself. The only option left for the historian is therefore to examine later material, and in particular the chapter entitled 'The Education of the Crown Prince' in Frederick's own first Political Testament, finalised in 1752. Here Frederick refers to many incidents and experiences from his own upbringing, and it is possible to unearth a great deal of hidden criticism of his father's educational methods. For example, there is the ironic remark about the parents of a Prince striving to turn him into a model of perfection and completeness (*modèle parfait*), one free of enervating passions, and one who, at the age of fifteen, was to have reached the level of intellectual maturity that a Frenchman would only achieve at forty. On religious matters, which were allocated such an important place within Frederick William's educational plan, Frederick remained silent. He dismissed the practice of early marriage, since in his opinion this could only turn out badly. His own experience of an adolescence filled with conflict seems to lie behind his recommendation that a young Prince should be allowed the freedom to do as he chooses. His governor should refrain from following him everywhere, but should scold or punish him for any pranks. Thus, the Prince will learn to discipline himself, and fear of retribution will make him wise in his own way. A love of hunting, music, dancing and games should be encouraged to such an extent that he himself will learn to tire of them.

Despite the veiled critique of his own upbringing, however, one of Frederick William's basic educational principles, against which Frederick had reacted during his own youth, was now fully accepted and recommended: this was the encouragement of a love of militarism, since both father and son were fully aware that the army was the very foundation on which the Prussian state was built. Frederick only stipulated that this should be taught in the guise of an enjoyable game, rather than be turned into an oppressive chore. There are further echoes of the Crown Prince's own youth when Frederick recommended that a Prince who has completed his training in the lower ranks of the army, should be given a regiment for which he would be responsible in the same way as a regular officer. Frederick William's educational system continued to exercise this dual influence over Frederick, at times encouraging, at others deterring him, even when the original wounds it had inflicted had long since healed. It is indicative of the strength of Frederick's own character, with its blend of enthusiasm and scepticism, that it was not broken by this exacting upbringing. Not until the first Political Testament, however, did he find words of thanks and gratitude, indeed admiration, for his father. With the passing of time, shared work brought them closer, but their personalities remained incompatible and the gulf between them could never be bridged. Their opposing positions became more entrenched in the years of increasing conflict and one has to look to Frederick's childhood and adolescence to find the origins of their attitudes.

Quite unlike his father's physical robustness, the Crown Prince as a child had a delicate, frail constitution. The latter's appearance was reminiscent of his Guelph ancestors, while his father's fuller figure recalled that of the Great Elector as portrayed by Andreas Schlüter in the famous equestrian statue. Frederick William's predisposition to convulsive attacks was not inherited by his son; indeed, in his first few years, it appeared that Frederick positively lacked liveliness. In her memoirs, which are a questionable source, his sister, Wilhelmina, claimed that he was slow to learn; others, however, dispute this and cite discontentment as its cause. Frederick certainly was not a precocious child prodigy (*Wunderkind*), in spite of the fact that traces of intellectual ability did reveal themselves at an early age. His inner turmoil found expression in

the melancholy air in which he enveloped himself, and the habitually disdainful, apparently haughty, attitude he adopted. In a painting by Antoine Pesne
of 1718, a curious, pensive streak can be perceived in him: his eyes already
have that piercing look which does not betray anything of his innermost self.
There is little doubt that from the very beginning he reacted against the harsh
reality of his existence. This later manifested itself in his predisposition towards mockery and arrogance – the result of a slow and gradual process of
development, which owed much to the influence of the personalities who
surrounded him. In the first few years of his life, women played a decisive
part, in particular the French *émigrée*, Madame de Rocoulle, who had already
brought up Frederick's own father. From 1716 onwards, the Crown Prince
was placed in the care of Jacques Egide Duhan de Jandun, a French refugee
and a highly educated dilettante whom Frederick William had met in the
trenches during the siege of Stralsund. It is interesting to note that Huguenot
émigrés clearly made a valuable contribution to the rising Prussian monarchy,
while simultaneously being in the forefront of opposition to the growth of
French absolutism.

In 1718 two high-ranking officers of East Prussian extraction were made
responsible for the Prince's military education, and these men were to remain
his tutors until 1729. Neither General Graf von Finckenstein nor Colonel von
Kalckstein were strictly army-oriented or stiff military personnel; instead both
men were imbued with distinct humanitarian principles. It was they who
were also entrusted with the implementation of the Educational Instruction of
1718. There was never a formal breach of the kind that had occurred between
Frederick William and his own tutors (indeed, later in life Frederick continued
to express his gratitude to Duhan), but he did not bare his soul to anyone save
his older sister, Wilhelmina, the future Margravine of Bayreuth.

Frederick's affection for his elder sister stemmed less from a sense of sib-
ling allegiance and more from a desire to break free from family bonds. The
family over which his father held sway clearly inhibited natural development.
To an extent, Frederick was later to thank his father for not allowing him or
his brothers and sisters to become royal showpieces at the mercy of court
ceremony, but for bringing them up like ordinary children with common
family mealtimes. There was, however, a limit to how far this could go. The
total isolation of a private enclave within the court and court society contravened all social laws and was only just becoming an acceptable characteristic
of bourgeois society. Despite the radical transformation of the role of the
court in 1713/14, when it lost its Baroque status of being the centre of the
social universe and the King was stripped of his aura of majestic inaccessibility
and aloofness, the position of the royal family at court was preserved.

Continuity in personnel and appearance masked a decisive change in the
roles assumed and played by the members of the court; henceforth, military
rank determined status. 'When one speaks of the Berlin court,' ran a contemporary report, 'one is referring only to the military personnel, of which the
court is almost entirely composed.' The nobility no longer held the monopoly

of power, since under Frederick William there were marginally more middle-class than noble councillors. The noble officers resided with their regiments which were based, for the most part, in small garrisons or in Potsdam. The court, although controlled by political factions, became a sober governmental headquarters, much curtailed in its extravagance and displaying 'little splendour or riches'. Only the visit of a foreign Prince could restore its former glory, and then only temporarily. The claustrophobic environment and the lack of refined social and cultural intercourse, as well as the material restrictions imposed upon court society, made it, in many respects, the perfect breeding ground for intrigue and widespread corruption. This, of course, contrasted sharply with the King's puritanical austerity. Most notable in this respect was the role played by the monarch's personal confidant and former comrade-in-arms, Graf Friedrich Heinrich von Seckendorff, the Imperial envoy. He formed a close association with the most powerful man at court, Friedrich Wilhelm von Grumbkow, which, in time, was cemented by financial bribes.

The Prussian royal family, lacking the strong hierarchical order which existed in Vienna, threatened to fragment into opposing groups and factions, each courted and encouraged by the diplomatic envoys of foreign powers. The latters' attempts to gain influence were considerably facilitated by the fact that a deep rift divided the royal household. This division was common knowledge, since Queen Sophia Dorothea made no attempt to conceal her abhorrence of her husband's distasteful, brutish habits and his periodic mental crises. The political manoeuvring surrounding the projected marriages of Frederick and Wilhelmina to the offspring of the Guelphian King of Britain served to accentuate the gulf between the King and Queen to the point where it became explosive enough to destroy family unity completely.

Frederick's close relationship with Wilhelmina already contained the germ of his rebellion against the enforced system of his father. It was part of an attempt to build his own world, one which was quite separate from the other, increasingly despised one. Outwardly, the Crown Prince fulfilled all the tasks which were required of him, so that it is impossible to judge how far he allowed his inner self to become involved and how far it was an act of dissimulation – an art which he was easily able to master from an early age, since court life demanded the constant suppression of one's emotions. When the Crown Prince was six years old, the King established for him a company of cadets comprising 131 boys, which Frederick, in due course, was to command himself. This 'playing at soldiers', which clearly contained a tendency to treat children as small adults, was taken quite seriously by its inventor and was designed to be an effective educational device. It should not be ruled out, therefore, that Frederick's later devotion to the military lifestyle may have owed more to such adolescent army games than has generally been appreciated.

In these early years, the Crown Prince did not make use of the little free time left to him for more serious preoccupations; in keeping with his youth, he preferred to engage in casual daydreaming. It was Wilhelmina, his older and more energetic sister, who encouraged him to pursue higher things. The nine-year-old, therefore, began to read novels. Fénelon's *Télémaque* made the strongest impression upon him, perhaps less because of its moral emphasis and more because of its colourful content; at any event, the book had a lasting impact and constituted his first experience of political education. One has to beware, however, of detecting premature intellectual development. The earliest traces of intellect in Frederick seemed to have been sparked by religious topics, which held his interest well into his eighth year. Despite the King's dismissal of the court chaplain Andreä in 1725, after the latter had acquainted Frederick with the theological question of predestinarianism, it was this particular religious problem which excited him for the longest time. Nevertheless, by the age of thirteen, his religious statements were no longer clear cut; they contained undercurrents of political criticism which flowed into his metaphysical speculation. Two years later, his tutors were forced to confess that, for some months their religious instruction had no effect, which prompted a characteristic reaction from the King: the amount of religious teaching which the Crown Prince was to receive was doubled. By the time of Frederick's confirmation in April 1727, this unsatisfactory state of affairs, as it was perceived by Frederick William, persisted. The Crown Prince had, without doubt, already taken the decision to sever all his religious ties. A little later, he signed his name for the first time as 'Frédéric le philosophe' and thus declared his belief in the 'religion' of reason as advocated by the Enlightenment, a movement of thought with which he had become acquainted principally through the Abbé Fénelon and Pierre Bayle.

The intellectual road along which the young Crown Prince chose to travel was that of the philosophical intelligentsia of his century. In Frederick this intellectual strata of society won an ally who was to become politically powerful and of whom it could be expected that he would transform the newly acquired theories into political fact. This expectation became one of the great hopes of the eighteenth century, but unfortunately it was never to be fulfilled.

It is tempting to associate Frederick's emancipation from religion with the various stages of increasing tension between himself and his father. Indeed, it is possible to find links between the two processes. Among the earliest evidence confirming the growing alienation between the Crown Prince and the King is a statement by Frederick William, dated March 1724, in which he complained that he was unable to fathom 'what went on in that little head; I know that he does not think as I do, and that there are people who teach him different views and encourage him to question everything; they are scoundrels . . .'. In short, the King is here expressing his distaste for his son's opposition, his alternative religion and his obsession with criticism. In 1726, at a time when Frederick's religious indifference had already become established, the Crown Prince became involved in a major clash with his father. By October, 1728, with memories of the irritating visit to the Saxon court still fresh in his mind, the dispute had escalated to a point where the tension seemed almost unbearable.

The King reacted by ordering a new companion for his son. Lieutenant-Colonel von Rochow was issued with strict instructions which required him to make clear to Frederick that 'all effeminate, lascivious, feminine pursuits were highly unsuitable for a man'. But even Rochow failed to bring about a change in the Crown Prince. The hostility between father and son increased. More and more, the King displayed the violent side of his nature and took to ridiculing his son mercilessly in front of the servants and the officers of his regiment. After one of his beatings, he shouted at the Crown Prince that had his father treated him thus, he would have shot himself. Frederick, however, continued to endure everything. What was happening here was no longer an educational tactic; these were outbreaks of unbridled hatred designed morally to destroy the Crown Prince. But even this failed. Frederick's sense of self-preservation was strong enough to withstand this extreme form of harassment, if at the price of inner hardening and an increasing talent for dissimulation. His innate character traits were intensified to the point where they marked his whole personality and engendered the prerequisite impenetrability and inscrutability of a person wishing to play the power game successfully. It could be argued that these early experiences were possibly of greater importance in the development of his character than any subsequent influences.

The King's bitter letter to Rochow concerning his wayward son still contained the instruction that the Crown Prince should continue to pray and read the Bible regularly. But, in this matter too, the point of no return had been reached. By now Frederick had created his own secret world of music, poetry and philosophy which he shared with his sister. The tangible evidence of this was a library, secretly acquired with Duhan's help, which contained all the great names of the Enlightenment: over 3,000 books (including Descartes, Bayle, Locke and Voltaire) which Frederick catalogued himself. It was located in a building near the royal residence, but it proved impossible for the Crown Prince to find the time or the opportunity to instigate any kind of systematic reading programme. The library, nevertheless, represented a symbol of his rejection of the traditional world of religious values, of Christendom; it was the partially open door to a new phase in his internal development.

The father–son conflict, meanwhile, had acquired a new dimension: it became entangled with a highly sensitive political question, the explosive nature of which both the King and Frederick were, at first, unaware. It concerned the projected double marriage of the Crown Prince to the British Princess Amalia and Frederick's sister, Wilhelmina, to the Prince of Wales. This would be a third-generation inter-Guelph union and, as such, more of a question of traditional family politics than a matter of state. But already in the opening round of negotiations in 1725, when the alliance between Prussia, Britain and France was concluded at Herrenhausen, difficulties arose which, for King George I at least, were clearly of a political nature. George II's accession to the throne in 1727 occasioned further moves by Frederick William to bring about the double marriage. Prussia's King necessarily continued to view this as a family matter, since he had no wish to jeopardise his *rapprochement* with Austria through apparent political ties with Britain. British foreign policy, however, took exactly the opposite stance, preferring instead to use the marriage to advance the political objective of securing Prussia for the alliance of the Western powers.

The decisive factor in this affair proved to be the emergence at the court in Berlin of a highly active group striving to prevent renewed family links with London. It was centred around the Imperial representative, General Graf von Seckendorff, and the Prussian minister, General Friedrich Wilhelm von Grumbkow, with whom Seckendorff had cultivated close links, in part through bribery, and who was described by Ernst Lavisse as 'one of the most devious cabinet ministers in Europe'. It was this Imperial faction, prepared to do anything to attain its goal, with which the Queen had to contend in her vigorous efforts to advance the English marriage plan. She hoped that its realisation would go some way towards compensating her for the neglect, sacrifice and humiliation she had been subjected to in what she considered to be the relative backwater of Berlin. Sophia Dorothea counted on the support of her relatives in London, as well as that of her two eldest children, who were, after all, to be the ultimate beneficiaries of this project. In time, Anglo-Austrian diplomacy ensured that the marriage plan was catapulted into the mainstream of European great power politics. The Berlin court, with its intrigue, bribery, espionage and competing factions always on the alert, became the 'battlefield of diplomacy' (E. Lavisse). This was clearly not an issue of such proportions as the dynastic problems which had threatened the European equilibrium during the Spanish Succession conflict or the crisis surrounding the Habsburg Pragmatic Sanction. Nevertheless, it was still a matter which threatened to draw in the great powers who would inevitably be forced to take one side or another.

The marriage negotiations took many dramatic turns. Significantly, their effect at Berlin was to polarise the existing tensions within the Prussian royal family. The King, who had originally been quite prepared to entertain the concept of a double marriage, eventually only supported the plan for that of his daughter, and rejected all idea of a proposed English bride for his son, not least because he was unwilling to incur the political risks which were involved. The Queen, at the mercy of her unbridled ambition, threw all caution to the wind in the hope of a great future for her children; she championed Guelph, not Prussian, policy and thus entered the dangerous waters of intrigue and conspiracy with her English relatives, without ever being able to persuade them to abandon their sober calculations and caution.

The Crown Prince and his sister were dragged into her game and actively furthered its course. Frederick established new links and cultivated old contacts, while making promises to the English which would keep them interested. Although his ultimate goals were unclear, he already displayed remarkable skill in his political dealings. The marriage question was the masterpiece which he completed in this courtly diplomatic game, without being in any way personally affected by it. Princess Amalia, the prospective bride, remained unknown to him, while his inclination towards the Western powers was not rooted in political sympathy, but was more of an expression of emotional inclination and, above all, a protest against the policy pursued by the King's party. In the manoeuvring for position with Grumbkow and Seckendorff, in making risky revelations to the French and English diplomats – Count Rothenbourg, Sir Charles Hotham, the *chargé d'affaires*, Guy Dickens – in all this, his tactical abilities and his talent for dissimulation grew to the point where he did not even shy away from a reckless disregard for the interests of the state.

When the game was lost, he seized upon thoughts of escape, having toyed with the idea when visiting the notoriously licentious Saxon court and the nearby encampment of Mühlberg-Zeithain. One should beware, however, of viewing the escape as a direct reaction to the failure of the marriage project, but rather see it as a way of eluding the unbearable constraints, the insults and humiliation to which the Crown Prince would now be subjected even more brutally by the King. Frederick prepared for the flight with a paradoxical mixture of far-reaching calculation and careless rashness, an idiosyncratic combination which was also to become a hallmark of some of his later actions. The first attempt, at the time of August the Strong's[2] visit to the Mühlberg encampment, was precipitated by an overwhelming desire to rebel against his father's mistreatment, and failed miserably. Already at this early stage, his closest ally and helper was Lieutenant Hans Hermann von Katte of the *Gens d'Armes* regiment. During the weeks of preparation, Frederick succeeded in making careful diplomatic arrangements for his flight, but failed to apply similar diligence to the necessary practical preparations for such an undertaking. Indeed, he treated this aspect of the preparations with almost reckless disregard. At Mühlberg he had already revealed his plans to the English diplomatic *attaché*, Guy Dickens, and asked for English support in Paris, where he hoped to gain temporary political asylum. On returning from a trip to England, however, Guy Dickens informed him that the Crown Prince would not be welcome in London and that the British government advised against any attempt to escape. The French *chargé d'affaires*, Sauveterre, on the other hand, assured him that he could count on a warm reception in France. It seemed much more difficult to find trustworthy helpers and suitable opportunities, travel routes and intermediate stops.

When it became clear that the King wanted to take the Crown Prince on a journey to Southern Germany, the final decision for flight was taken in spite of new obstacles, such as the inability of his fellow conspirators to take part. Lieutenant Peter Christoph Carl von Keith had been transferred to Wesel by the King, as a direct consequence of the influence which he had exerted upon Frederick, and Katte had failed to gain permission to go on a recruiting trip for his regiment. The Crown Prince was, nevertheless, resolved to make the attempt, and he was so sure of success that he ignored advice to be cautious

---

2. King Augustus II (the Strong) of Saxony-Poland (King of Poland, 1697–1733 and Elector of Saxony, 1694–1733).

since not one of his steps went unobserved. He was almost intoxicated by the idea of escape, while at the same time displaying the obstinacy with which he pursued any goal once determined upon, even if this meant abandoning all reason. This was surely a character trait which pointed towards things to come. The purpose of the red coat, which he had specially made for the journey, remains a mystery. Was it supposed to symbolise the freedom he hoped for, or was it simply a means of disguise? Did he not once again risk his safety for an irrational obsession with being noticed, at a time when it would presumably have been better for him to have remained as inconspicuous as possible? When, on the night of 4–5 August 1730, he attempted to slip away from the royal camp near the village of Steinfurt, it became apparent that his movements had been carefully monitored and he was quickly surrounded. He did not find the way to the freedom that he had imagined, but fell into the hands of a father trembling with rage.

The consequences had Frederick's plan succeeded do not bear thinking about. The British government was in no doubt, and had indeed intimated to the Crown Prince that, in the present political situation, his flight would fan the flames of international tension. The heir apparent to the Prussian throne receiving political asylum from Great Britain – such an occurrence could have provoked Frederick William to initiate a reprisal action against neighbouring Hanover or drive the King to some other unpredictable deed. The only person who was seemingly unconcerned about this was Frederick himself. To him, this was purely an adventurous bid for freedom, the consequences of which were obviously as unclear to him as the goals he hoped to attain. In the event, it led to the first great personal crisis of his life. This was as decisive a factor in the shaping of his character as the seizure of Silesia ten years later was for the development of his statecraft. Whether the Crown Prince met this crisis with a character already formed or whether it precipitated a total change in his nature remains to be seen and will be examined later.

THE COURT MARTIAL OF THE CROWN PRINCE AND
FREDERICK'S EVENTUAL REHABILITATION

It would be misleading to attribute the Crown Prince's attempted flight to any political motives. To him this was not an act of political rebellion; his search for foreign allies was aimed at securing personal independence, rather than a means of blackmailing, far less ousting, his father, as the latter in his anger had at first suspected. Even the proposed marriage with Princess Amalia did not constitute the actual reason for his desire to break free. He thirsted for freedom, since this seemed the only way of escaping the humiliations and obligations to which his father subjected him at the Prussian court. It appeared that King and Crown Prince were complete opposites: opposites in character, in lifestyle, in interests. Each failed to understand the other. Frederick William not only displayed the typical behaviour of a father who wished to impose his way of life upon his son, and gradually became aware of his inability to do so, but also that of a ruler who had built a state and now feared that it would be destroyed by his successor. It was not the traditional, historical *mise-en-scène* where the Crown Prince represented new political ideals, but a conflict of minds which was fuelled by the King's overwhelming fear that his life's work, the inheritance he would hand on to his son, would be gambled away. In the King's eyes Frederick seemed not to have any feeling for what constituted the cornerstone of the Prussian state, namely its military foundations, to which everything else, the whole of administrative and financial policy, was subordinated. Even subtle personal details highlighted this fact. The Crown Prince, for example, described his military uniform as his death shroud. Although he carried out his duties as an officer, he did so without displaying any particular leaning for or personal involvement with the tasks he discharged. Frederick William, therefore, could not help but be haunted by the ghost of his own father, whose only concern seemed to have been the appearance of power, not its reality.

A closer comparison reveals that the father's insecurity may not have been entirely unfounded. His son entertained ideas, centred on the higher planes of human knowledge such as fine art and philosophy, which, although they merely represented a personal world of freedom for the Crown Prince, were quite incompatible with contemporary political reality. The King's raw, barbaric manner contrasted sharply with his son's precocious intellectualism. The latter's undoubtedly greater popularity, as demonstrated by the crisis of 1730, does not, however, furnish proof that he possessed the more attractive personality. Most contemporary accounts, largely culled from diplomatic dispatches, describe the Crown Prince as being arrogant, given to mockery and, especially, to dissimulation. This final character trait was Frederick's way of asserting himself against what he perceived to be the unbearable world constructed by his father and it corresponded perfectly with the laws of behaviour in court society. It would be wrong to assume that it was the court martial which followed his flight that caused this particular aspect of his nature to come to the fore, although the trial was, of course, a matter of life and death and not merely the covering up of a somewhat playful private adventure. The ability, which Frederick developed to the point of virtuosity, to clothe untruths in the mask of truth, presupposed intelligence of the highest degree as well as a total absence of feeling. Often it was impossible to tell whether the Crown Prince was hiding his feelings or simply lacked them completely. He was, thus, a true child of his times, when the ascendancy of feelings over reason had not yet begun and where strict social convention dictated that any flicker of individuality be relegated to the very depths of one's being.

The details of the attempted flight and its goals can be reconstructed fairly precisely from the statements of the Crown Prince and his friends, Katte and Keith. Of course, much appears shrouded in mystery and contradictions abound, but, on the whole, the subsequent investigation yielded an accurate account of events. It is certain that the Crown Prince aimed to escape at first to France where he had hoped to obtain temporary sanctuary before proceeding to his relatives at the English court. The fact that he ignored London's warnings and refusals of help, as conveyed by the British *attaché*, Guy Dickens, shows Frederick's lack of understanding of the international repercussions which would inevitably result from the presence of a Prussian Crown Prince at a foreign court. A private adventure could suddenly be transformed into an affair of state, and the English marriage project jeopardised if Frederick had turned up as an asylum-seeking *émigré* who had thrown away his rights to the Prussian throne.

During the inquiry into the affair, Frederick at least had sufficient sense to perceive the extremely precarious situation in which he found himself, and he did everything in his power to obscure the link with England. On 15 August, when asked, during one of the final interrogations, whether he had not intended to seek refuge in England rather than France since the former seemed a more natural choice because of his relatives there, he answered: 'while laying plans for the flight, his thoughts had touched on England as a possible *retraite*, but, upon reflection, he concluded that this would only lead His Majesty [i.e. the King] to think that he had determined to undertake the planned marriage and, as he had no wish to further complicate matters in this affair, he had resolved to seek political asylum in France'. This was certainly only part of the truth. At other times, he attempted to hide behind the general excuse that he had only intended to stay away for a short time and to return 'when the King was willing to treat him differently'.

Frederick William, and those officers and officials employed by him, were certainly anxious to uncover the English plans together with the extent to which the Queen and Princess Wilhelmina had been involved, or, at least had acquiesced, in the plot. While this element of family complicity remains a grey area, however, extensive details of the negotiations with the English, particularly with Guy Dickens and the ambassador, Hotham, were provided by Lieutenant von Katte. It seems that these discussions were already well under way by the time of the visit to the Saxon encampment at Mühlberg-Zeithain, and information supplied by Katte included the embarrassing and incriminating revelation concerning the Crown Prince's request to have his debts (the figure for which was vastly inflated) paid by the English. Nevertheless, even after the final interrogation on 16 September, led by Auditor-General Christian Otto Mylius, many questions pertaining to the ultimate objectives of the Crown Prince remained unanswered.

The final report, detailing all the evidence of the case, is the most important document of the trial, which, far from following the usual legal process, had been conducted along the lines of an inquisition. It is worth noting that Mylius, the person responsible for drawing up the final document and, indeed, who had conducted the entire proceedings, was a disciple of August Hermann Francke, that is, he was a Pietist. On several occasions, he had obviously endeavoured to intervene on the accused person's behalf, calling for moderation in the way the trial was being handled. This led to gossip at court, a point which the Imperial envoy, Graf von Seckendorff, raised in a dispatch to Vienna.

Mylius had, initially, avoided describing the Crown Prince's action as desertion, and only after the King had crossed out the word '*retraite*' which had originally been used, did he replace it with the term 'desertion'. Even more serious was Mylius's attempted protest against the final article, which the King himself had formulated and which clearly aimed at extracting an admission of guilt from the accused. The article contained the following questions, initially concerning general points of morality but which then merged with more pertinent political matters:

179. What did he consider to be a fit punishment for his action?
180. What does a person who brings dishonour upon himself and plots desertion deserve?
181. Had he not seen enough examples [of such a crime] in his own regiment?
182. Did he believe that he still deserved to consort with honest people?
183. Did he consider that he still merited becoming King?
184. Did he wish his life to be spared or not?
185. Since in saving his life, he would *ipso facto* lose his honour, and, in effect, be unable to succeed [as King of Prussia], would he thus stand down in order to save his life, and renounce his right to the throne so that this [action] could be confirmed by the entire [Holy] Roman Empire?

These questions far exceeded the boundaries of normal investigation, a fact which Mylius recognised, remarking that 'he could not have drawn up such questions in the light of the evidence available to him'. The King, however, insisted on these articles, and merely conceded that 'I myself will be responsible for them being put to the Crown Prince.' As a result, the records contain a special preamble in which those leading the examination distanced themselves from having formulated the above: 'Here at His Royal Highness's command follow the questions, formulated by His Majesty himself, which were put to the Crown Prince.'

Frederick's answers to these inflammatory questions, which appeared to highlight the most extreme consequences of the conflict, have always been regarded as proof of his quick-wittedness and political acumen. This becomes clear especially when one considers where Frederick William was ultimately leading and what his intentions were. It is quite probable that at times the execution of his son became a distinct possibility to him, and the acceptance of such an idea would be entirely compatible with his character, temperament and the depth of anguish he was experiencing. Frederick responded to the pertinent question with only an assurance of his submission to the King's will and mercy. We may assume that at this moment Frederick William's thoughts focused, if not on a death sentence, then at least on the loss of Frederick's right to succeed to the throne; and the Crown Prince seems to have sensed this. The question of 'whether he would renounce his right of succession' was not precisely formulated, but indicated that renunciation of the throne presented the possibility of escaping the death sentence. Frederick's answer was evasive: 'His life was not that dear to him, but His Royal Highness would surely not be so harsh in his treatment of him.' Such an evasive answer failed to conceal the fear for his own life which he was indeed experiencing, while making no mention of abjuring his rights of succession. His slick, quickly formulated exclamations did not obscure the fact that he was seized by violent emotions, to the point of being scared to death. Although initially this pretence was a means of self-preservation and self-assertion, it was to produce severe emotional tensions. In the course of the proceedings, his remorse grew, as is evident in the closing statement of the report dated 16 September, and even more in the additional interrogation of 11 October which the Crown Prince had requested. Here is documented his increasing fear, not so much of death or the loss of the throne, but of lengthy or life-long imprisonment which seemed an unbearable prospect, until it was pointed out to him that in this respect 'nothing had been proposed'.

From the very start, Frederick William built the case around the charge of desertion, and refused to allow any other description, such as retreat (*retraite*), withdrawal (*retirade*), escape or flight, to be used in the formal record of the trial. This corresponded with the Prussian military state system to whose laws each member of the army was subject. Another reason was that the crime of desertion – a frequent occurrence in the armies of absolutist states where the rank-and-file had often been press-ganged into service, which was subjected to increasingly draconian penalties to counteract this phenomenon – was best suited to being tried according to the *Kriegsgerichtsordnung* (or regulations governing courts martial) of 1712, since all other civil procedures entailed legal and practical problems when a member of the royal family, especially the Crown Prince, was being subjected to trial. Thus, after a certain amount of hesitation, the King initiated proceedings according to the prescribed code, against 'Prince Frederick, resident at Küstrin' and his accomplices, the 'Lieutenants von Ingersleben und Spaen, the former Lieutenant von Katte, and the deserter, Lieutenant Keith'.

In view of the exalted rank of the principal defendant, the court was composed of three major generals, three colonels, three lieutenant colonels, three majors and three captains under the chairmanship of Lieutenant General Graf Achaz von der Schulenburg, who, like Mylius, was of Pietist sympathies. The members of each military rank collectively had one vote, and the chairman a sixth. They were made to swear a special oath, and proceeded to perform the unusual task required of them with a remarkable degree of objectivity and fairness. The only serious divergence of opinion occurred during the sentencing of Katte, whose crime the majors, colonels and lieutenant-colonels felt warranted the death sentence, while the captains and major-generals favoured life imprisonment. The casting vote of chairman von der Schulenburg decided the issue – life imprisonment was to be the punishment, since actual desertion had not yet taken place.

The principal charge against the Crown Prince, however, confronted the court with an insoluble problem. How could the monarchy's strict rules of hierarchy and precedence be reconciled with the concept of officers or vassals sitting in judgement upon a member of the royal family? The major-generals perceived this as 'pushing the loyalty they owed the Prussian state to its very limits', and the colonels declared that neither a court martial nor any other earthly judge had the right to comment upon the King's disciplining of his son motivated as it was by fatherly concern and religious faith. Lieutenant General von der Schulenburg reported to Frederick William that the special court had determined not to pass a verdict on the Crown Prince, but 'to entrust this family matter and affair of state to the great mercy of Your Royal Highness'. As officers, vassals and subjects, they were not at liberty to intervene in this matter, 'especially since Your Majesty is better placed to punish Your son, both as father and as King'. The King failed to acknowledge this declaration of the court's position, even though it seems certain that he had already reserved for himself the final judgement on the Crown Prince.

Frederick William's anger, combined with his embittered craving for revenge against those who had supported 'the rising sun', focused upon Lieutenant von Katte. Despite the King's objection to the sentence of life imprisonment imposed upon Katte, the court stood by its decision with notable tenacity and courage. Frederick William, however, was prepared to go to extremes, overturned the verdict and replaced it with the death sentence. To his blinkered way of thinking, coloured by the requirements of the military state, an officer's breach of duty (especially when committed by one attached to the Royal *Garde Gens d'Armes*) amounted to a crime of *lèse-majesté*. In the King's opinion, this demanded the most brutal form of execution, that is the tearing of limbs by red-hot irons, followed by hanging. Beheading was, therefore, deemed to have been a considerable moderation in the method of execution, and was certainly implemented only out of consideration for Katte's family. It is indicative of the King's mentality that he was seriously convinced that an example had to be made of someone in order to discourage the thought in others that Katte had received too lenient a sentence. His chief target was in any case the Crown Prince. Katte's execution was to be a horrifying means of punishing Frederick. The events support this theory: the Crown Prince, placed under the strictest detention at Küstrin and hermetically sealed off from the outside world, was sentenced to watch his friend's beheading from the window of his prison. This severe means of punishment, which reduced its unhappy victim to the status of merely being a means to an end, was thought to have been unusually harsh even by contemporaries accustomed to barbaric penal practices. Frederick William's reply to the 'irksome discourse' which Katte's execution occasioned in England, was filled with utterances of the utmost severity: 'If there were 100,000 Kattes, I would have them all placed on the rack.' Such a reaction was clearly more an indication of extreme vulnerability than firm resolve.

The execution of Lieutenant von Katte marked the peak of the disciplinary excesses set in motion to punish Frederick. The Crown Prince, however, remained convinced that this was merely a preliminary to his own execution.

The King, meanwhile, was undergoing a change of heart, although it is difficult to establish when this began or what influences led Frederick William to
this decision. It seems improbable that the Emperor Charles VI's handwritten
note, a plea on Frederick's behalf, played any part, since the chronology of
events rules this out. A more feasible explanation appears to lie in the theory
that only now had the King become fully aware of the difficulties associated
with breaking the established royal succession, and that, in any case, Katte's
death had assuaged his fiercest anger. What followed was the Crown Prince's
gradual, painfully slow pardoning (*Pardonierung*), involving Frederick's social
rehabilitation and the renewed assumption of his duties and privileges. The
whole process was undertaken in the spirit of Pietism, and has been termed
'an attempt at pietistic conversion which reached terrible heights' (C. Hinrichs).

It began with religious instruction administered by the army chaplain, Johann
Ernst Müller of the Regiment *Gens d'Armes*, who, a few days prior to Katte's
execution, had been charged by the King with the task of 'reasoning with him
[the Crown Prince] and convincing him that those who turn away from God
and forsake His blessing, will be condemned to do only wicked, never good,
deeds'. Frederick William, according to the teachings of Pietism, had a deeply
felt awareness of the sins committed by his son, whom he described as 'a sly
piece of work'. He felt obliged to guide him towards 'true remorse' and a
'repentant heart', while never failing to impress upon the preacher the importance of also conveying to Frederick an understanding of the perniciousness
of Predestinarianism, the corrupting influence exercised by the notion of the
elect. Army chaplain Müller had to be present when Frederick was forced to
observe his friend's execution and witnessed the Crown Prince's resulting
collapse. In the days immediately after Katte's execution he stood by the
shattered Crown Prince, as the latter awaited his own death in mortal agony.
Was this, as has been argued, the moment at which there took place in Frederick
a radical change of character, a 'transformation'? What supposedly emerged,
the theory continues, was a kind of 'artificial man', who had assumed a personality imposed upon him, but who had little, if anything, in common with
Frederick's true nature.

Proponents of this psychoanalytical hypothethis, however, have failed to
consider two things: firstly, there is the deep-rooted sense of tradition associated with the royal house of Hohenzollern and the Prussian state which was
clearly inherent in the Crown Prince, and although Frederick's early lifestyle
appears to be at variance with this, his sense of tradition was only obscured,
never replaced, by his protests. Secondly, there has to be the realisation that
humiliation and mental and physical torment not merely failed to break
Frederick, but actually awakened in him a special zeal to disprove in deed and
achievement his father's contempt for and low opinion of him. The Crown
Prince's wealth of talent, which was also, of course, the prerequisite for the
contradictions in his character, allowed him the strength not to give up on
himself and to develop in the face of adversity. His 'transformation' did not
lead to a total eclipse of his original character, but merely to inner shifts of

emphasis. The 'discipline of terror' (L. von Ranke) did not result in 'a completely altered way of thinking'; at most, it led to a change in the hitherto one-sided direction he pursued. New initiative and impetus were awakened in Frederick, something which had been lacking in him or, at least, had earlier been overshadowed. Here then lies the explanation for Frederick's mysterious dual nature: the often fluid coexistence of political Machiavellianism and military lifestyle with moral/philosophical speculation and playful, yet, at times, serious involvement in the arts. All these combined to form different facets of the same man. Admittedly, this conglomerate ruled out the possibility of complete emotional stability. Not until he had surmounted the most exacting of tests did Frederick eventually achieve a type of inner equilibrium in the form of stoicism. There was to be only one further occasion when he physically and mentally collapsed: after the defeat at Kunersdorf in 1759.

Such results reflect all the various aspects of the educational programme instituted by the King, except the conversion which Frederick William had hoped to bring about. The Crown Prince would never be a good Christian, but if he was to follow his father's principles and become a good officer and a 'good host', he now possessed the willingness to do so. The King continued to employ similar educational methods to those followed earlier, except that they now assumed a slightly different guise. He kept the Crown Prince, who was absent from court and cut off from the royal family, informed of administrative details and fiscal and economic developments, and eventually drafted him into the army.

It is due to the peculiar extent to which Prussian and Imperial politics were interwoven, that the first draft of the 'Generalplan' (that is, the 'project' of 'what was further to be done' in the handling of the pardoned Crown Prince) was submitted by the Imperial envoy, Graf von Seckendorff. In its final form, however, one can detect a large measure of the King's ideas and influence. The instructions issued to the Crown Prince's new governor at Küstrin, Privy Councillor von Wolden, bear the unmistakable hallmarks of Frederick William's style of thought. His pre-empting of his son's decisions and the regimentation of Frederick's daily life differ only slightly from the educational plan of 1730 in that they now contained a greater degree of rational thinking. Seckendorff had the further idea of making Frederick swear another oath, a curious assurance of good behaviour under threat of 'forfeiture, completely and forever, of the royal and electoral succession'. Frederick duly took this vow. The draconian restrictions on his personal freedom were gradually lifted, and the Crown Prince was allowed to move to the town and was appointed, for the time being without the right to vote, as 'Auskultator' at Küstrin's *Kriegs-und Domänenkammer* (that is to say, the 'War and Domains Chamber', the provincial administrative authority directly subordinate to the General Directory). This was to be an exercise in practical administration, strictly confined to concrete detail without ever touching upon wider political matters. Frederick was allowed to discuss – and, incidentally, in no language other than German – only the following subjects: 'the word of God, the economy, the condition of the territory, the manufacturing industries, matters of minor local policy, ordering [supplies] for the local community, the reduction of debts, the details of leases of Crown lands, the order of court cases and the ways in which the "Rendanten" (or local accountants) should assign moneys and keep the accounts'.

Such restrictions upon what Frederick might discuss were, of course, difficult to enforce. They were somewhat easier for the Crown Prince to bear when his conversational companions at Küstrin were affable and educated men such as the President of the War and Domains Chamber, Christian Ernst von Münchow or, more especially, the Director of the local collegial chamber, Christoph Werner Hille, with whom he could speak about 'economy' and literature as well as theological matters such as predestination. Nevertheless, both men were subject to constant controls by the permanently distrustful Frederick William, and would not have been able to maintain their benevolent disposition towards the Crown Prince without the support of Grumbkow, who, in spite of having had a hand in the catastrophic events that had passed, was now actively encouraging a reconciliation between King and Crown Prince. Of the two young *Kammerjunker* (gentlemen of the bedchamber) assigned to him, Dubislaw von Natzmer became a close confidant; it was in a letter to him that Frederick made his first substantial pronouncement on a point of high politics.

Frederick William's educational plan failed to make allowance for any deviations of the kind that would be regarded as perfectly usual when a number of men were living within the confines of a small town. The King knew only hard work, 'respectable things' and not 'irresponsible pursuits', and in order to please him the Crown Prince 'played the economist'. He produced proposals, the authorship of which, however, the King disputed, and he appears to have shown an interest in improving the economy of the surrounding domain lands. But all this was certainly only one side of his nature. Had he not successfully led a double life for some time now? He continued to discuss questions of philosophy and composed poetry which Hille considered quite good for a Crown Prince, but not particularly so for an ordinary person. In Frederick the balance of interests had only shifted slightly: the interest in economics and government was not feigned, even if it failed to fulfil him.

Neglect and humiliations continued to be heaped on the Crown Prince by his father; he was once more exposed to both at the official reconciliation during Frederick William's first visit to Küstrin on 15 August 1731. Nonetheless, all that was now left for him to do in order to buy his freedom from the 'prison galley' of Küstrin was a final act of submission to the King, by agreeing to marry Princess Elizabeth Christina of Brunswick-Bevern, a cousin of the Empress. In Vienna, the powerful Prince Eugene of Savoy viewed this union as the only way to bind the heir to the Prussian throne to the Habsburgs. The great statesman did not, however, prove himself a good judge of character; his plan was doomed to failure. Crown Prince Frederick at first did everything to avoid marriage to a woman he did not love, who was clearly his intellectual inferior and whose physical appearance aroused little attraction.

However, could he afford to pit himself against his father's express wishes, when abiding by them was the only means of securing the freedom he longed for? He did not dare contravene his father's will and resigned himself to his fate, with a significant proviso: one could be sure, he wrote in a letter to Grumbkow, dated 26 January 1732, that the Princess of Bevern, 'if I am forced into marriage with her, will be rejected (*"elle sera repudiée"*) as soon as I am King'. This was no empty threat, as events were soon to show: immediately she assumed the rank of Queen of Prussia at the end of May 1740, Christina became the 'poor woman', whose fate Frederick had already decreed in 1732. To the Crown Prince, this marriage was merely a 'purchase price', as he wrote to Grumbkow, who had become the recipient of numerous frank letters. It was, in effect, the price of his own freedom.

In the time between the formal engagement and the eventual wedding in June 1733, the Crown Prince enjoyed a temporary reprieve during which time, rehabilitated as an officer, he was obliged to do garrison duty in Nauen and Ruppin: 'I have just come from military drill, I am engaged in military drill, I shall be engaged in military drill.' These are words which, quite distinct from their original meaning, proved prescient for the future. No contemporary ruler would match the courage and endurance Frederick was to display in times of war; nor could they hope to equal his stature as a philosopher, poet and musician. The genius of a nature racked by contradictions was doubtless something which was inborn, but it was also, to an extent, the result of a process of education and development. Frederick William I's rigid educational plan was in itself less influential than in the general environment it created – a youth marked by regimentation and fateful episodes is bound to play a part in the shaping of a character. When one attempts to take stock of the effect which Frederick William's pedagogical experiment had on the Crown Prince, one emerges with the impression that it served to awaken positive strengths as well as an ability to withstand negative forces. The years in Küstrin, for example, led Frederick to the realisation that a flourishing economy was the source of political power. Furthermore, in Nauen and Ruppin, while enduring the monotony of garrison life, he came to acknowledge that being a professional soldier was not totally alien to his nature. In this way, positive forces were indeed released from the subconscious.

Even more effective, however, were the restrictions imposed upon the Crown Prince against which he reacted with such sustained vigour as to awaken and nurture a strong sense of self-confidence, an enormous resilience and a powerful will. The psychological scars inflicted upon him in his youth never healed, and his character remained marked by them. His cynicism, contempt for mankind and arrogant haughtiness all reflected his attitude towards life and go some way towards explaining his almost limitless, and often uncalculated, willingness to take risks in the early years of his youth and reign. His remarkable intellect had not yet encountered an equal among his peers, nor had it been allowed to find adequate expression; that would only come with the years at Rheinsberg, and subsequent to his meeting with Voltaire. In any case, the contrasting impact of his earlier years must never be underestimated: the religious instruction which he was compelled to endure did not transform him into a 'good Christian', on the contrary, it totally alienated him from Christian belief; while the attempt to force him into conservative, German/Protestant court and family life drove him into the arms of the French Enlightenment. Frederick's character developed fully as a result of family, social and political influences. How differently, in another environment, this character – in conjunction with such considerable abilities as intelligence of the highest degree, artistic talent and enormous willpower – would have unfolded can only be the subject of conjecture.

The Crown Prince only reached full maturity during the four years he spent at Rheinsberg, from the autumn of 1736 until his assumption of the reins of government on 31 May 1740. It was not the idyll Frederick would later idealistically contrive it to have been, but after the first dramatic episodes of his life, Rheinsberg represented a calmer phase of self-discovery and improvement, prior to the further unfolding of his life's drama.

CHAPTER 2

The King and his Prussia

The court, within an absolute monarchy, constituted the focal point of state and society. Its very composition, its functions and authority bore witness to the fact that in the presence of the absolute ruler, established social privileges and rights meant nothing, and only proximity to the King himself determined rank and reputation. The French court under Louis XIV is frequently cited as the prototype of absolutist court life, but as far as etiquette and lifestyle are concerned, Spain's court during her Golden Age preceded it chronologically and probably exercised a much greater influence over the rest of Europe. Philip the Fair in the early sixteenth century had transferred his experiences of Burgundian courtly refinement to Castile, from whence Ferdinand I, raised at the Spanish court, introduced it to Vienna. As a result, Spanish etiquette still held sway over the Viennese court of Maria Theresa, having been at its height during the reign of her father, Charles VI.

Prussia, by comparison, was a young monarchy without ancient traditions or long-established monarchical roots. Frederick I's elevation to royal rank in 1701 had only been possible through an appeal to foreign precedents, and for some time the new Hohenzollern monarchy continued to appear as artificial and inorganic as the attempt to call upon the fabled Borussian kingdom for historical legitimation. Only the splendour of Baroque court life could detract from the reality that this was no more than a chimera, a glittering façade obscuring the inherent weakness, or more precisely, impotence, of the new creation. The accession of Frederick William I heralded the systematic dismantling of the recently established court system, and despite its thoroughgoing nature, this was less damaging to the foundations of the young monarchy than the subsequent conscription of the peasantry and nobility into the army. A monarchy centred upon a courtly world of honorific posts, festivities and luxury was swept aside, and the military state was born.

As Crown Prince, Frederick grew up in a world where lifestyle was dictated by a combination of middle-class values and military discipline. Courtly ceremony, which had evolved over the centuries from early Byzantine beginnings via Burgundy, Spain and France, was limited to the barest essentials, and was only retained at all because of Prussia's bilateral links with other European courts. A comparison with her German neighbours at this time clearly demonstrates that Prussia was following her own distinctive path. The contrast between her and the sumptuous court culture of neighbouring Saxony, where German Rococo had found its fullest expression, is particularly striking. Indeed, the Crown Prince had already encountered its attraction and allure during the monarchical visits of 1728 and 1730 to the court of Augustus the Strong. Frederick's own court, however, deliberately set itself apart from this world; instead, it came to represent a distinctive fusion of military discipline and intellectual pleasure. His fateful adolescence, and the draconian educational regime to which he was subjected after his attempted flight, had brought him into contact with only the bureaucratic and military elements of the state. Even after his rehabilitation and garrison life in Nauen and Ruppin, this continued to be the case. It was not until his move to Schloß Rheinsberg in 1736 that he acquired, though without real financial independence, the freedom to fashion his own life as he wished. The Crown Prince's court in this rural setting far from the royal residence, represented his first and only attempt to create a court which corresponded to Frederick's own mind and spirit.

The Rheinsberg years made a distinctive contribution to Frederick's emergence as one of the geniuses of his age. At the court of Rheinsberg, neither courtly etiquette nor military discipline prevailed, and instead free social intercourse, the exchange of enlightened ideas and the cult of friendship were encouraged in true Rococo spirit. Noble birth was no guarantee of inclusion in this courtly society, to which even the musicians of the court orchestra could claim to belong. The two individuals closest to Frederick were the native of Courland, Dietrich von Keyserlingk, nicknamed 'Caesar', whom the Crown Prince promoted to colonel and adjutant-general, and Karl Stephen Jordan, a descendant of Huguenot refugees from Normandy, who was later employed as a Privy Councillor at the Berlin Academy. Apart from the aesthetes, Christoph Ludwig von Stille and Heinrich August de la Motte-Fouqué, with whom Frederick struck up a friendship, officers at court, some from the Crown Prince's own regiment of Ruppin, played an insubstantial role. The official Chancellor at Rheinsberg, von Wolden, was also of secondary importance, and only the household of Frederick's wife, Elizabeth Christina was maintained along traditional lines. Ladies, as in all Rococo society, played a part in the court's social life, although it should be noted that there were no official favourites or mistresses. Rheinsberg did not represent a court in the usual sense of the word. In accordance with the Crown Prince's wishes, it was to be a forum for all the arts, where guests, whether celebrated or not, could gather from around the world. One such example was the Italian writer Algarotti who, at Frederick's instigation, took up permanent residence in Berlin in 1740.

The Crown Prince, partly due to conventions of etiquette and partly because of his own intellectual ability, formed the centre of the court's social life, discussions and recreations. Nonetheless, he always remained the ascetic hard worker who read and studied at night and so acquired an extensive education, encompassing a wide-ranging knowledge of many diverse fields. He contrasted visibly in this respect with his contemporary monarchs, for whom he would later show such disdain. However, despite study, conviviality, theatre, music and the inexhaustible possibilities that presented themselves to this youthful company, Rheinsberg – in some ways reminiscent of the Weimar of the young Carl Augustus – remained the court of a future King. Frederick eagerly followed events in Berlin and throughout Europe, while foreign envoys vied with each other for his favour. Here, however, diplomatic intrigue wore the mask of social diversion, a game at which the French envoy and occasional guest at Rheinsberg, the Marquis de La Chetardie, excelled. Frederick received warnings about every foreign minister: 'however devoted and charming he may appear, he will always be willing to sacrifice all for the small profit of conveying items of news to his employer'. Such caveats were hardly necessary for a Crown Prince who in his younger years had skilfully weathered much stormier diplomatic waters at the court of Berlin. Rheinsberg, in any case, lacked the impressive backdrop of a politically sensitive royal court, with all its factional intrigues and opposing viewpoints. Nevertheless, the period did represent a prelude, and amidst the convivial distractions and intellectual discussions, Frederick prepared for his future role as King. There exists no other contemporary example of such self-disciplined drive, hidden as it was behind the glittering façade of Rococo society. Self-education and the possession of a work ethic were no longer purely an expression of the aristocratic lifestyle, but began to be influenced by emergent middle-class principles.

At Rheinsberg, the Crown Prince, according to contemporary practice, founded an order which combined elements of freemasonry and secret societies with traditional knightly virtues. The reasons behind this order, which was based on the French Order of Bayard, 'Les Chevaliers sans peur et sans reproche', are disputed. A certain amount of playful seriousness was undoubtedly involved. It is questionable, however, whether one could regard it as 'morally restrained warlike idealism' (A. Berney) or even as a 'group of people of certain rank focusing on the science of war, the theoretical preparation for the art of war' (W. Elze). The order did not exercise a visible influence over life at court. Like King Arthur's round table, it had twelve members, among them the brothers of the Crown Prince, Augustus William and Henry, two Brunswick princes as well as Frederick's closest friends headed by the order's Grand Master Heinrich August de la Motte-Fouqué. Enduring ties were certainly not formed through membership of the order, even though it continued in existence for many years after Rheinsberg. The whole exercise was marked by a spirit of non-committal vagueness, and it was as much an attempt to adhere to old ways in changed times as was exemplified by the use of archaic French in written communications. To Frederick it probably signified a momentary divergence from his increasingly radical rationalism, in which a sense of duty and service to the state mattered more than romantic, noble ideals.

Rheinsberg already displayed some of the traits which were to characterise the later court of Frederick the Great. Above all, the dichotomy between a military and an intellectual aristocracy was evident, although at that time the artistic, intellectual component was clearly numerically dominant. At Rheinsberg, prestige was based on intellect, whereas in future it would depend upon one's place within the military hierarchy staffed by those of feudal-aristocratic descent. In those early days, the latter group was physically separated from Rheinsberg society, in the garrison of Frederick's regiment at Ruppin.

Soon after the Crown Prince's accession to the throne, it became clear that the members of the Rheinsberg circle were to have little influence over the future shape of Frederick II's Prussia. It was not long until 'les Rheinbergois' awoke from the dream that a great political future awaited them. Keyserlingk, the 'Caesar' of Rheinsberg society, was particularly disappointed and had to content himself with the position of adjutant-general, a post virtually devoid of functions. Soon there was talk of a Day of Dupes. The young King's decision in favour of strictly personal monarchy was both a reaction against possible dependence on personal friends and an emphatic rejection of the playful elements of the Rheinsberg days. Even more surprising was Frederick's reinstatement at his accession of the royal household which his father had almost completely abolished. Here his motives are not clear. It seems reasonable to suppose that the restoration of a framework of representative monarchy was to be a means of impressing foreign courts, a way of projecting an image of Prussian might, which, unlike the era of the first King, was underpinned by that most important instrument of power, an increasingly strong army. Although the majority of German rulers used courtly splendour as a means of masking military weakness, Prussia was to follow a different path. The new King did not, however, assign undue importance to courtly appearance. Of the nine positions of 'Oberhofcharge' (the highest positions at court) which he instituted, five still remained unfilled by the time of his death. None of the incumbents of posts such as *Oberkammerherr* (chief gentleman of the bedchamber), *Oberstallmeister* (head of the royal stables) or *grandmaître de la guarderobe et de la maison royale* had much influence. As a Frenchman ironically remarked, referring to the Privy Councillor, Michael Gabriel Fredersdorff: 'the King has a chancellor who never speaks, a chief huntsman who does not dare to kill a quail, a chief steward who does not order anything, a master of wines who does not know if there is any wine in the cellar, an equerry who is not empowered to saddle a horse, a chief gentleman of the bedchamber who has never handed him a shirt, a *grandmaître de la guarderobe* who is unacquainted with the court tailor . . .'. Such sarcasm failed to take into account, however, that this was a general phenomenon: by the mid-eighteenth century, formal titles everywhere had lost the functions for which they had originally been designated. It is noteworthy that these posts were largely filled not by members of the Prussian nobility but by representatives of aristocratic families from neighbouring German territories. The King considered his own nobility too good to occupy meaningless honorific posts. Two members of the royal household, however, neither of them from the Prussian high nobility, held special and undoubtedly influential appointments. One of them was Michael Gabriel Fredersdorff, whom Frederick appointed chamberlain and minister of finance, and subsequently ennobled. Voltaire described him as 'Frederick's great factotum'. As a result of his exceptional height, he had once fallen into the hands of Prussian recruiting officers, and the Crown Prince had already made his acquaintance at Küstrin. The court post which he held was in his case only a veneer which masked a significant personal contribution, the exact nature of which is difficult to gauge. Much the same applied to Pierre Louis Moreau de Maupertuis, who, as President of the Berlin Academy after 1747, was numbered among the *Oberhofchargen*, thus signifying the elevated position of importance accorded to intelligence within the social system of the Frederician era.

The role in Prussia of Frederick the Great's court cannot be equated with that of Louis XIV's in France as described by Hippolyte Taine or Norbert Elias. These classic analyses of courtly society, as well as a series of more recent specialist studies, largely ignore the Prussian court because of its atypical structure. Voltaire's description was short and to the point. In his memoirs he wrote: 'Frederick lives without advisers, without a court and without the external trappings of monarchy.' Many elements contributed to the fact that courtly life lacked social appeal, hope of advancement and respect. The King's own character dictated that an individual was judged either along intellectual/aesthetic or military lines and emphatically *not* according to the established contemporary courtly 'virtues'. The effective exclusion of Elizabeth Christina from the royal court and her banishment to Schönhausen meant that the Prussian court was a court without a Queen, although it should be said that it was also one free of mistresses and favourites. Finally, of course, Frederick's years of absence during the Silesian Wars in the first half of his reign paralysed the embryonic court life. After the wars of 1740–63, the King's reclusive lifestyle and growing isolation at Sans Souci, the small palace at Potsdam which became his personal refuge, was indicative of a 'philosophically inspired renunciation of the great role of monarchical representation' (J. Kunisch). This corresponded with the way in which Frederick conducted policy, which limited the monarch's contacts with his ministers almost entirely to exchanges of letters.

The King had totally divorced himself from the style of an artificial imitation of Baroque, of the kind that his grandfather had initiated, but without ushering in a return to his father's harsh German puritanism. His enlightened intellectualism fuelled an increasing lack of interest in, and eventual disdain for, court ceremony. He sensed that it contained elements akin to ritualistic and ecclesiastical rites. Addressing this point in the Political Testament of

1752, Frederick lays down that the abandonment of etiquette should extend to contact with foreign emissaries, whom he would in any case avoid meeting as far as possible: 'Prussia does not have hierarchical ranks, etiquette or ambassadors. Thus we are preserved from all quarrels arising from questions of precedence and above all, from the pride of Kings, which at other courts commands serious attention and consumes time which is better spent working for the public good.' In reality, quite such a radical abandonment of traditional court practices was impossible. Contemporary observers confirm, however, that a particular style emerged, one free of 'tiresome, that is to say ceremonial, dealings', combining 'a spirit of militarism' with the 'finest manners, intellect, wit and philosophy'. This also applied to relations with foreign envoys, 'who would wish with all their might to be treated according to traditional court ceremony'.

The King was perfectly aware, moreover, that 'because of the weakness and sensuousness of humankind', a ruler could not entirely abandon representative functions and the ceremonies associated with his position. Each year he therefore dedicated a part of the winter in Berlin to such duties, when the period of Carnival occasioned great festivities at court, designed, above all, to entertain the rural nobility in the capital. At such times, he knew to appear 'with all the splendour of a great Prince' and 'precisely observed etiquette, unforced and with personal dignity'. It is questionable whether the word 'unforced' truly reflected the King's mood, since he himself disliked such official functions. Although his appearance commanded respect for his position as King, it did not generate sympathy for his person, and coolness and distance would be more descriptive of the reaction he aroused. A contemporary account, the diary of Count Ernst Ahasverus Heinrich von Lehndorff, tells of an encounter with the King: 'The forty persons who were in the best of spirits in the antechamber, turned, as soon as the King entered, into forty statues. Why does power occasion more fear than love?'

The yearly reviews and parades, where strict military etiquette prevailed, were quite another matter. Here, as commander-in-chief of his regiments, the King appeared not as a stranger among strangers but as the head of a homogeneous hierarchy. It was in this sphere, rather than in service at court, that personal advancement was possible; in the Prussian army, achievement was generously rewarded by the King, but, at the same time, failure could result in the imposition of harsh penalties. In the Political Testament of 1752, Frederick gives detailed descriptions of the basic process of selection which took place at the yearly reviews in the provinces. These were conducted, according to precisely laid-down guidelines, between the end of May and the end of September, not under combat conditions but while undertaking the parade-ground drill which was the basis of the Prussian army's superiority. 'At the reviews, invalid officers are to be discharged, and those whose conduct was not in keeping with their position or who did not behave honourably are thrown out. Those dismissed are to be replaced from among the regiment's ensigns. Those who appear brightest, conduct themselves correctly and have received the best reports from the staff officers are to be selected.' The criteria for dismissal were thus clearly laid down: invalidity, inability to carry out duties efficiently, and dishonourable conduct. Occasionally a whole company could be disciplined or even lose seniority because its performance at a review was unsatisfactory. Advancement, on the other hand, was given to those displaying intelligence, qualities of leadership, and other particular military attributes.

The whole system, a conscious state policy designed to maintain the established social hierarchy, was in keeping with the trends of the times and the contemporary art of war. In Prussia, however, it reached a much higher degree of efficiency than elsewhere and took its lead from a distinctive monarch; its end was deemed to coincide with the death of this remarkable King. Political and military autocracy did not produce a climate in which solid traditions could become established, however much their importance was emphasized. The myth of the Great Frederick undoubtedly formed and nurtured the Prussian concept of statehood, but set unattainable standards for succeeding monarchs. Herein lies the dichotomy to which the uniqueness of Frederick gave rise. The resulting strains placed upon Prussia's social and political fabric meant that an eventual breaking point was more or less inevitable.

The 'Princes of the Blood' occupied a curious position at court. Frederick, in the Political Testament of 1752, describes them as a kind of hermaphrodite (*'une espèce d'être amphibie'*) who are neither potentates nor private citizens and increasingly difficult to govern. 'Their high birth [the King continued] imbues them with a certain arrogance which they term aristocratic. It makes obedience unbearable to them and any kind of subjection hateful . . . In Prussia they have less power than anywhere else.' The best means of dealing with them was to 'put emphatically in his place the first person to raise the flag of independence, to treat them all with the respect their high birth demanded, overwhelm them with honours, but keep them away from affairs of state and only entrust them with a military command if one is quite certain of them, that is, they must possess talent and a dependable character'. These words, written before the King's subsequent problems with his brothers, Augustus William and Henry, display only a reluctant acceptance of dynastic and family ties, which are viewed with cool detachment. As a matter of necessity, such ties were of secondary importance to the exigencies of *raison d'état*. Frederick, nonetheless, made full use of the opportunity to heap 'superficial honours' upon his brothers, Ferdinand, Augustus William and Henry, the latter being the most important of the three. The King also bestowed on them appanages large enough to maintain opulent courts: Augustus William, who had been named heir to the throne in 1744, at Castle Oranienburg, Henry at Rheinsberg. For the time being, the brothers were kept well away from affairs of state. Two of them, Augustus William and Henry, were then given high military posts and the latter was subsequently entrusted with important political responsibilities. Augustus William threw away his prospects as a result of mistakes made during the disastrous retreat from Bohemia in the autumn of

1757, was dismissed in disgrace and died still in disfavour with the King. During the Seven Years War, Henry rose to second in command, and despite quarrelling with the commander-in-chief on a number of occasions, made a valuable contribution to Prussia's survival. He was never able to escape the conflict between a relationship with the King which bordered on love–hate and the demands of *raison d'état*, but his career underlined the extent to which the royal family was integrated into the state, a role determined for it by Frederick.

The royal family, or more precisely the King's siblings, were never closely identified with the Prussian court and state since they all led separate existences. His brothers had their own courts and his sisters, with the exception of Amalia, for whom the King procured a sinecure as Abbess of Quedlingburg after a particularly sensational escapade, all lived outside Prussia as a result of their marriages with minor German princes and Louise Ulrike's with Sweden's King Adolf Frederick, who ruled from 1751 to 1771. Frederick was never inclined to promote any such identification, although he continued to be conscious of a sense of family which, in spite of actions which appeared to negate this (such as the humiliating treatment of his brother, Augustus William), he never lost sight of and which may be supposed to have provided a strong emotional driving force. A sense of dynasty and family had formed the basis of the state-building policy pursued by European powers during the previous century. The fact that this was not fully apparent in Frederick was a consequence both of the traumatic experiences of his own youth and a gradual, universal shift in attitude whereby the state was increasingly viewed as an abstract concept and one which took precedence over dynastic considerations. This can clearly be demonstrated with reference to the resolution of the succession question through the application of the law of male primogeniture. The consequent triumph over the principle of partible inheritance had facilitated the initial state-building activities of the larger German territories. The Golden Bull, governing rights of succession, had already determined that the law of primogeniture was to be applied in the Electorates, although this provision was not universally implemented. The Hohenzollern *Dispositio Achillea* of 1473 clearly took it into account when it specified that the Brandenburg Mark was not to be partitioned, but, paradoxically, cleared the way for the fragmentation of the Franconian principalities. Although the principle of primogeniture was not fully enforced in neighbouring Hanover until an Imperial confirmation in 1683, it remained unassailable within the Hohenzollern family. This was to cause considerable problems during the reign of Frederick II.

The King must have recognised quite early on, perhaps at around the age of twenty-nine, that he would remain without an heir of his own body. Authoritative sources to ascertain the reasons for this cannot be found and officially they are shrouded in mystery. Nor are there any medical records documenting sterility. This gave rise to malicious rumours, to which Voltaire contributed by insinuating that suspicions of homosexuality were not unfounded. The most convincing explanation seems to be that provided by

Frederick's physician, Johann Georg Ritter von Zimmermann. He claimed that the Crown Prince, before his marriage, had contracted venereal disease and underwent surgery, which supposedly caused 'impotence and self-imposed chastity'. Frederick does indeed appear to have been sterile and, as far as the succession to the throne was concerned, this was a source of great anxiety to him. As early as the eve of the battle of Mollwitz, on 8 April 1741, he wrote to his brother, Augustus William: 'You are my only heir.' In a directive dated 30 June 1744, written before he embarked on the second Silesian War, Frederick decreed that Augustus William was to be known as 'Prince of Prussia', 'without the addition of Christian or any other names', which amounted to an official declaration that he was the heir apparent. Following Augustus William's death in 1758, the succession passed without complications or opposition to his son, Frederick William. The King, in his personal will and testament of 8 January 1769, refers to him throughout as the heir designate and as the person to whom he would bequeath all his territories.

Such events masked grave personal and political problems. Chief among these was the fact that Frederick regarded his legitimate heir, Frederick William, as incapable of living up to the demands of his position. In his final years he even became anxious that Prussia's neighbours posed a threat to her future security which his successor would be unable to withstand. He never considered changing the succession, however, since the law of male primogeniture represented a central element in *raison d'état*. Thus, even at the most critical point of the Seven Years War in the summer of 1758, Prince Henry, as second in line of succession to the throne, was merely designated as guardian of the underage Frederick William. In case of the King's death, the imposition of oaths upon officers was to be performed by the latter. Unlike Russia's Peter the Great, Frederick did not stretch autocracy to the point of personally naming his successor. Instead he submitted totally to the binding laws of male primogeniture.

Once King, Frederick could not and did not exist within the narrow confines of a conventional court. The man who called himself a philosopher had been inspired by the Enlightenment to seek alternative forms of intellectual sociability and conviviality which, for the most part, replaced traditional courtly life. Accordingly, the dinner parties which the King gave right up to his final days became the forum where Frederick's personally chosen guests would mingle. In the summer months these were held in the Marble Hall at Sans Souci and in the winter, in Potsdam's town palace. Admittance to this privileged circle, whose origins went back to the Rheinsberg days, was not determined by rank or influence, but by intellect and merit. Its composition changed with the years and by the later phase of the Frederician era had lost much of its glamour and appeal. Nevertheless, despite all the changes, and the premature exclusion of some of the King's close friends, it remained an enlightened enclave, the nucleus of a court society. Frenchmen predominated in its make-up and provided its most brilliant members: chief amongst them were Voltaire during his brief sojourn at Potsdam, his rival and eventual successor, Pierre

Louis Moreau de Maupertuis, and Jean Baptiste de Boyer, Marquis d'Argens. The last two were distinguished scholars whom the King valued for their encyclopaedic knowledge while not perhaps being quite able to take full advantage of it. The Italians were represented by such men as Francesco Algarotti, already a participant in earlier Rheinsberg gatherings, who, in spite of being ennobled by Frederick on his accession eventually moved to the Saxon court of Augustus III, and Giovanni Battista Bastiani, who acted as a go-between with the Papacy. Politically and militarily active men such as the Scots brothers, George and Jacob Keith, were also welcome. Exiled from Great Britain for their Jacobite sympathies, they found employment in the service of Prussia. George was eventually elevated to the post of Prussian envoy – first in Paris, then in Madrid – while Jacob, as field marshal, was killed in action at Hochkirch in 1758. The circle's German contingent was limited to a few literary-minded officers such as Christoph Ludwig von Stille, whom the King employed as a tutor for his brothers, Henry and Ferdinand, and Count Frederick Rudolf von Rothenburg, a Brandenburg nobleman who carried out important diplomatic negotiations for Prussia in Paris. It is remarkable how few of these individuals held official posts, most serving only in a semi-official capacity.

The composition of this round table changed constantly over the decades, but never to the extent where it became a focus of favourites or flattering courtiers. Instead it remained a free élite, based on personal contacts and Frederick's own intellectual inclinations. It exercised little, if any, influence over political matters. Its effect on policy was, at most, indirect. Members of the royal *Kabinett*, such as its secretary, August Friedrich Eichel, were not admitted to this private society. Karl Stephan Jordan, a member of the French colony in Berlin who had already enjoyed the Crown Prince's friendship during the Rheinsberg years, distinguished himself during the Silesian Wars by becoming the King's principal correspondent. This role was later taken up by the Marquis d'Argens during the Seven Years War. Frederick's letters directed towards them and other members of the King's inner circle, document his thoughts and moods at times of war.

In addition to the round table, the role played by the Berlin Academy must not be overlooked. Although certain of its members, principally its President, Maupertuis, and the Marquis d'Argens were also part of the King's inner social circle, the Academy possessed a life of its own. It failed, however, to fulfil the King's expectations of excellence or to achieve the international standing he hoped it would attain. The dispute between Voltaire and Maupertuis, although undoubtedly the former's fault, seriously damaged its reputation. It comes as no surprise, then, that the King's invitation to the leading encyclopaedist, Jean Baptiste le Rond d'Alembert, to succeed Maupertuis as its President met with an almost brusque refusal following the Frenchman's two-month sojourn at Berlin in 1763. In Prussia, pronounced d'Alembert, intellectual life was neither good nor bad, it was simply non-existent. The earlier attempts to recruit the Swiss Albrecht von Haller and Christian Wolff, the philosopher whom Frederick William I had expelled, also ended in failure.

The Academy was clearly an intrinsic component of enlightened monarchical display, as Catherine II was to demonstrate in Russia. Nevertheless, Frederick's enthusiasm for and involvement with the Berlin Academy eventually waned, probably because the King was basically less interested in academics with specialised fields of learning. He failed to attend any of its meetings, and others read out his instructions for the Academy's future transactions. Not until the years following the Wars of the Bavarian Succession did he begin to invite individual members of the Academy to become part of his round table.

The Berlin Academy and the gatherings at Sans Souci were in any case integral parts of Frederician court society, the other important element being provided by the military élite with its own distinctive ritualism. The dichotomy which ran through the entire Frederician system was clearly highlighted by these heterogeneous components.

ARMY AND OFFICER CORPS

Mirabeau is deemed to have coined the *bon mot* that 'Prussia was not a state, but simply the territory on which the Prussian army subsisted.' If this were a truism, it should follow that in Frederician Prussia the army was the dominant force in society; all other social groups depended upon it and their individual roles within the state machinery were dictated by it. This certainly seems to have been the case, except that Frederick II's army was no longer simply an end in itself, as it had been during the reign of Frederick William I. Under Frederick, it clearly became a means to an end, that is to say, it acted as the most important instrument of Prussian state-building. As long as *raison d'état* governed state and society, the needs of this army, with its claims upon Prussia's population and particularly its need for recruits, undoubtedly took precedence over those of the economy. Contrary to popular opinion, however, the result was something of a flawed system. Paradoxical overlaps arose, for example, concerning the interests of the army itself: while the nobility and peasantry provided the majority of recruits for the officer corps and the rank and file, town-dwellers were exempt from military service because the dictates of the mercantilist state demanded that they increase their manufacturing productivity in order to satisfy the army's economic needs. Those exempt also included the comparatively small number of intellectuals living in towns, who, in spite of limited contacts with the mainly foreign *literati* at court, facilitated the growing influence of the Enlightenment and as such constituted a somewhat heterogeneous element within the military state. The successful integration of these opposing elements eluded the Frederician state. It was a problem which was not to be seriously addressed until the catastrophic failure of the *ancien régime* ushered in an era of reform.

The nobility's traditional role – that of a warrior caste – survived in most early modern European states as a relic from a more violent age. In Prussia, however, the reigns of Frederick William I and Frederick II were characterised by a determined transformation of this role into a new type of military aristocracy responsible to and disciplined by the state. Although politically emasculated, the nobility under Frederick William I continued to enjoy the manorial rights guaranteed by the Great Elector while, at the same time, gradually assuming a new function within the structure of the state, through service in its army and, to a lesser extent, its bureaucracy. It goes without saying that the nobility, with its tenacious spirit of independence, did not readily assume its new function and had to be coerced into doing so. One inducement to conform presented itself to the lower nobility in the form of opportunities for their younger sons who now had the possibility of politic- ally rewarding careers as officers, rather than having to rely on ecclesiastical patronage, a system which in Protestant Prussia was, in any case, dying out. Yet the stage where the noble landowner was fully compensated for his milit- ary service was never quite reached. The economic losses incurred through years of absence from his estates were only partially counterbalanced by the prestige attached to advancement within the military hierarchy. The wars of Frederick II made such preferment much more possible than had been the case during the comparatively peaceful reign of Frederick William I. It is here, and not in an acceptance by the nobility of an ideology of military service, that the essential difference between Frederick William I and Frederick II lies. Aristo- cratic military service was not termed a '*métier d'honneur*' ('profession of hon- our') until the test of war had brought with it the realisation that monarchical aggrandisement as well as the army's continued existence, its *raison d'être*, depended on its victories.

Frederick William had established the principle that the nobility alone would exercise command in the army, but never fully realised this aim in practice. Under Frederick the Great, it became the norm. Frederick justified this prac- tice on several occasions, citing various different reasons. The *Allgemeine Landrecht* (the Prussian General Law Code of 1794), not promulgated until after his death but very much bearing his stamp, represented the legal codifica- tion of the social order in the final phase of the *ancien régime*, the Society of Orders ('*Ständische Gesellschaft*'). It described the nobility straightforwardly and unequivocally as 'the first Order in the state'. 'Its position' obliged it 'to undertake to defend the state, to protect and uphold both its external dignity and the fabric of its internal structure'. This pronouncement was referring not to an artificial, political creation, but a natural partnership between Crown and nobility. Frederick frequently declared his allegiance to and support for this partnership, and this has given rise to speculation that he understood noble privilege to be a birthright and the natural product of the Society of Orders. This would surely be highly uncharacteristic of a man steeped in the ideas of the Enlightenment who sought and preferred the company of middle-class intellectuals to stimulate his mind. His assertion that the nobility should form the backbone of the army's officer corps stemmed from his determination to impose discipline rather than from any social prejudice. Noble *corps d'ésprit* was essential to guarantee the strength of the army, whose rank-and-file was held together by no other means than a rudimentary sense of patriotism.

Frederick, however, rigorously enforced almost complete social segregation, a strict division between nobleman and commoner. Accordingly it was forbidden for members of the nobility to open offices in trading towns because 'they would then be distracted from following their *métier d'honneur* and some would perhaps serve the interests of commerce more than the military duties which they owed [to the state]'. Indicative of this mode of thought is the 'Instruction for Infantry Officers' of 11 May 1763 – that is, at the end of the Seven Years War, during the course of which it had not always been possible to maintain a noble monopoly in the officer corps. It states: 'Officers are forbidden to keep the company of low-born people or townsfolk, and must limit their associations to those with higher officers and their comrades, thus conducting themselves in a seemly manner and nurturing ambition.' These sentences are not related in any way to the establishment of prescribed social privileges; much more, they form the guidelines for the maintenance of a strong service ethic. Strict rules governing consent to marriage were also rigorously applied, especially where a nobleman was considering marrying a member of the middle classes. This led to a large proportion of the younger officers remaining unmarried and a corresponding neglect of sexual morality.

The caste ethic imposed by the King on his nobility represented a code of conduct that did not necessarily come naturally to the élite, but along with their military duties had to be instilled into them. At the centre of the nobility's code of conduct lay the notion of ambition. This concept had an iridescent aura about it. Although sometimes used in the negative sense, it was fundamentally understood to be a concept with strongly positive connotations, encompassing different elements: fame, ambition, the will to lead, a quest for honour and glory and an acknowledgement of one's achievements. It formed a new social norm for the officer, replacing, for example, the aristocratic code of virtue. The number of citations in the King's decrees and instructions referring to the concept of ambition point to the fact that it was elevated to a prominent position in the noble officer's scale of values, one which it had not held under Frederick William I. Earlier military writers such as the Frenchman, de Guinard, can lay claim to having initiated such a development: a military career, he says, is the only one where ambition is deemed to be a virtue, although it can often be a burden. Frederick reiterated this maxim throughout his reign. As early as 1740, in an instruction dated 30 June to Lieutenant Colonel von Oelsnitz, the commander of the cadet corps, he asserts that he considers it to be of 'the first and foremost importance' that 'cadets should be taught a reasonable degree of ambition'. A cabinet order from the final chapter of his life, dated 28 August 1785, ran along identical lines. Addressed to Major General von Götzen, it stated that the principal aim should be 'to instil better discipline into officers, and that efforts should be made to teach them a sense of honour and ambition'.

Honour and ambition were here deemed to go hand in hand, and they do belong together. Both require the framework of an *esprit de corps* which in its turn dictates that the honour and ambition of the officers as a group be channelled towards serving the regiment, the army and, by extension, the state. In the wake of the state's nationalisation of the army, the individual concept of honour and pride and the practice of satisfying injured personal honour through duelling was increasingly questioned. Since the seventeenth century, rulers had sought – in the face of fierce noble opposition – to eradicate this troublesome practice. In Brandenburg-Prussia, the Great Elector had outlawed duelling as early as 1652 and this had been followed in 1688 by a further edict issued by the Elector Frederick III. Frederick William I somewhat modified its requirements in 1713, by imposing imprisonment rather than a death sentence on the participants of a duel in which blood was not spilled. Frederick the Great confirmed this last decree, but he, like his predecessors, was unable to bring about significant change. Not until the late nineteenth century could the aristocratic code of honour be subjugated in any way to state discipline. Frederick's reaction to the ineffectiveness of these measures is worth noting: in 1749, after reading Montesquieu's *Spirit of the Laws*, he published a discourse entitled *Dissertation sur les raisons d'établir ou d'abroger les lois* (Treatise upon the Reasons for Establishing or Abolishing the Rule of Law). In it, he often admits that the laws against duelling were ineffectual: 'a misguided but widely felt sense of honour serves to defy the power of the ruler who can only uphold the law through recourse to draconian measures'. Frederick is clearly aware of the difficulty of preserving the honour of the private individual while at the same time upholding the rule of law. The King obviously sympathised with the noble code of honour; it was *raison d'état*, however, that determined that he consider how 'a misguided sense of honour in Europe has lost so many honourable lives which could instead have been employed in great service to their state' and how this destructive practice could be eradicated. This led to his utopian thought that all Europe's rulers should assemble at a congress and agree 'to heap shame upon those who, in spite of the ban on duelling, continue to attempt to kill themselves, to withhold all sanctuary for this type of murderer, and to punish heavily anyone who seeks to insult another verbally, either through the written word or by deed. Unless this can be agreed upon, duelling will not cease.' Frederick's proposal is particularly interesting because the *raison d'état* of the individual state is surrendered in favour of a general agreement based on common ground within feudal-aristocratic Europe; however, habit and European tradition governed relationships, not understanding and agreement.

Military service for the nobility was an age-old tradition, but in whose pay or in which country this was to be carried out was not always certain. At least since the seventeenth century, the period of the Thirty Years War and the French and Turkish wars, there existed a European pool of professional soldiers from which even the positions of command were filled and among whom celebrated military leaders such as Prince Eugene of Savoy were numbered. Even in the age of Frederick the Great, the French marshal, Maurice de Saxe, the Livonian Gideon Ernst von Laudon, who served in the Austrian army, eventually rising to become field marshal and who was to be one of the most important of Frederick the Great's opponents, and the Prussian field marshal Jacob Keith, who was of Scottish noble descent, are all examples of this military cosmopolitanism – all three had served in the armies of different powers. Keith was, however, something of an exception in the Prussian army, the recruitment for which tended to be limited to members of neighbouring minor princely dynasties, such as the Princes of Anhalt. In any case, by the middle of the eighteenth century such mercenary soldiering which ignored dynastic or nationalistic considerations had become less usual. Since the reign of Frederick William I, noble emigration was actively discouraged in Prussia through the application of moral as well as material pressure and entry into the service of foreign states was forbidden. Noblemen were only to serve the King of Prussia. If a noble failed to comply, he was considered to be a deserter and treated as such: as, indeed, was the case in the trial of the Crown Prince after his attempted flight. The army was yoked to King and country and the newly established cadet schools became training grounds for young noblemen. The itinerant element, which had predominated among the officer corps of the early absolutist period and made possible the development of a standing army, disappeared and was replaced by a new dynastically and territorially orientated aristocratic stratum.

This, however, applied only to the officer corps and not to the army's rank-and-file, which will be discussed later. The steady increase in the army's size during Frederick William I's reign meant a corresponding increase in the pressure on the Prussian nobility. In 1740 it required the services of at least 3,116 officers, while by the end of Frederick the Great's reign that total had risen to 5,511. Of that number, 90 per cent were of noble descent in the year of Frederick's death. At the end of the Frederician era, the proportion of commoner to nobleman in the positions of command ranging from major to general was 22 to 689, that is, the balance had moved even further in favour of the nobility. It was easiest for commoners to become officers in the Hussars, a regiment whose origins lay in the light cavalry, and in the artillery, of whose revolutionary impact upon the conduct of warfare, clearly evident under the pressure of the Seven Years War, the King had written in his Second Political Testament, finalised in 1768. Nevertheless, this limited penetration by bourgeois elements had little impact upon the overall social composition of the army. The King did not, or simply refused to, acknowledge that the artillery represented a potential starting point for the infiltration of bourgeois intelligence into the army. By 1806, out of 7,000–8,000 officers, including the lower grades, only 695 were not noblemen; of those, 131 were in the infantry, 289 in the artillery, 84 in the cavalry and 37 in the other corps. The number of non-noble staff officers was just over 30. These figures demonstrate that the system had run its course: the increased importance now attached to the bourgeois element in society was in no way reflected in the development of the officer corps. This, as well as the backward-looking ethos of the corps, was surely one of the numerous causes of the Prussian army's collapse in 1806. The theory that the considerable losses suffered by the nobility during the

Austrian Succession War and the Seven Years War only made themselves felt in the two decades between Frederick's death and the downfall of the old Prussia should not be dismissed either. In the three Silesian wars, a total of 1,550 officers, among them 60 generals, lost their lives. The impact upon individual noble families could be severe: the Kleists lost 23 of their number, the Münchows fourteen, the Seydlitz, Frankenbergs and Schenkendorffs each lost eight, and the Winterfeldts, Korsigks, Arnims, Bredows, Schulenburgs, Sydows and Puttkamers seven. So considerable were the losses that not only were young boy cadets drafted as officers, but also a not inconsiderable number of commoners were commissioned. The King, however, quickly shut off this temporary opening at the conclusion of the Seven Years War. This is why the year 1763 saw the most rigidly favourable Instructions for the nobility.

The Seven Years War had brought the education of the officer corps to a virtual standstill, with the result that young officers frequently left cadet school without even a basic knowledge of reading and writing. Frederick thus placed particular emphasis on the education of the new generation of officers after the war. Erudite and scholarly officers such as Christoph Ludwig von Stille, whom the King had already known in his youth and who became tutor to Frederick's brothers Henry and Ferdinand, clearly existed, but they were not typical of the general level of education prevailing among members of the Prussian officer corps. In his obituary for Stille, the King bemoaned the fact that 'among men of standing, it was rare to find any with such an enlightened mind' as his. On the other hand, the lack of education within the army was not as widespread as general opinion would have it. This also applies to the era of Frederick William I, during which Prince Leopold von Anhalt-Dessau exercised considerable influence. He was the archetypal military professional, whose knowledge of warfare was extensive, but whose acquaintance with intellectual life was limited. Certain common principles can be detected in the educational system implemented for the new generation of officers and for the Crown Prince himself. The cadet corps, based in Berlin since 1717, saw 1,612 cadets passing through it from the time of its inception to Frederick William's death; these were instructed largely in the practical aspects of warfare and soldiering, though the teaching also had pietistic overtones. The basic educational principles of the Noble Academy at Kolberg, the most important of those established (1653) by the Great Elector, were upheld and instruction encompassing the 'realism' of mathematics and the natural sciences retained, but theoretical studies were limited.

Frederick paid little heed to the intellectual formation of his officers during the first half of his reign. His own theoretical writings on warfare and the extensive chapters concerning the army in his Political Testaments, even in that of 1768, contain practically nothing on this matter. The young King's first instruction to the commander of his cadet corps on 30 June 1740, betrayed little of the former's acquaintance with the pedagogical optimism associated with the Enlightenment. Although it prescribed a certain reduction in the severity of punishments, when compared to the era of Frederick William I, the King was less concerned with humanitarian considerations than with in-stilling in the commander a sense of respect for the cadets, who were not after all 'to become professional musketeers' but officers. Study of Brandenburg's history or Feuquières's writings on warfare was made compulsory so that 'the cadet would read before he could receive his food'. The cadets heard nothing of philosophical ideas, except that they were to be instructed in 'logical thought, which they should be taught as soon as they can read and write, so that from youth onwards they become accustomed to sensible and ordered thought and judgement'. This educational programme clearly proved unsuccessful. Not only did the lenient punishment regulations lead to a decline in discipline, but the instruction in logic totally failed to take into account the young cadets' limited ability to comprehend such matters. It was thus completely wasted on them.

The King only displayed an increased interest in the education and intellec-tual formation of his young officers after the conclusion of the Seven Years War. This was undoubtedly occasioned by the catastrophic educational stand-ard of most young officers, some having been forced into active service at a very early age, as well as by the calculation that the successful efforts at reform in the Austrian army could give it an advantage over its Prussian counterpart. In any case, Frederick was now prepared to break down the barriers that had strictly separated his enlightened thought, which until now had been limited to philosophical enquiry, and the military world. He at-tempted to overcome the dichotomy which he found in himself, and to effect a synthesis between the two different worlds in which he lived. These efforts were ultimately doomed to failure. Frederick endeavoured to improve the education of officers both through his writings on the formation of officers and through the establishment of institutions of learning. The most significant element in this was the *Académie des Nobles* or *Académie Militaire*, opened on 1 March 1765, which was to be a noble academy on a higher, intellectual plane. The idea seems to have originated with the King himself, as did the '*Instruction pour la Direction de l'Académie des Nobles*'. This was especially note-worthy for the strong and, indeed, exaggerated emphasis upon the theoret-ical study of philosophy, encompassing a history of the fine arts as well as metaphysical instruction which was to conclude with Locke, on whom the teacher should spend most time. In addition, history, geography, mathematics and a limited amount of law were to be taught, along with 'the so-called law of nations' which he considered nothing more than an 'empty phantom'.

The philosophical system, if such it may be termed, was to form the basis of lectures at the Academy and is in itself a clear indication of the changes in Frederick's beliefs which his experiences during the war had occasioned: self-esteem (*l'amour propre*) and utilitarianism form the basis of his moral teach-ings, and he believed that this should be conveyed in a convincing way to the pupils at the Academy. To this end he wrote the 'Dialogue de moral à l'usage de la jeune noblesse' five years later. He sought to establish self-respect and self-interest as the basis of morality, without conflicting with traditional religiously based ethical principles and, above all, the social-ethical precepts of the nobility, whose youth it was destined to educate. Central to this were three guiding forces: ambition, honour and fame. It is interesting to note that in this document the King places less emphasis upon the otherwise much vaunted ideal of ambition and in its stead holds up '*émulation*' (competitive zeal) as a virtue, while discrediting ambition as often being excessive and almost an encumbrance. Competitiveness encourages one to surpass one's rivals without envy 'by discharging one's duties better than them'. A sense of honour ('*point d'honneur*') can be maintained through the avoidance of everything that makes a person distasteful, and pursuing one's duty to use all honest means to defend and advance one's good name ('*réputation*'). Not only the social virtues of 'a man of standing' ('*un homme de condition*') are said to lead to honour, but Frederick introduces a whole catalogue of virtues which, in the true spirit of the Enlightenment, were of relevance to everyone and encompassed noble as well as bourgeois values: respectability, well-mannered behaviour, knowledge, diligence, vigilance, bravery, noble deeds ('*les belles actions civiles et militaires*'), 'in a word, all that places the human being above human weakness'. Service of the citizen for the fatherland and the individual striving of the private person towards lasting fame are also raised as an objective: the fatherland can demand the sacrifice of life, but would it not be better to attain fame willingly through this death and 'to immortalise one's name until the end of time' ('*perpétuer mon nom jusqu'à la fin des siècles*')?

The pedagogic guidelines for the *Académie des Nobles* contained significant concessions to the enlightened spirit of the age and seemed to spell an end to social rigidity. The paradox, however, lies in the fact that the course was only open to members of the nobility and thus much of its educational value was lost. The overwhelmingly noble officer corps, in spite of a few notable personalities, was not prepared to participate in Frederick's attempted reconciliation between the traditional noble military values and the ideas inherited from the Enlightenment. The army of 1806 contained several generals who had been students at the *Académie des Nobles*; none, however, were imbued with a reforming spirit which might have provided the basis for a successful confrontation with the armies of the French Revolution. Of Frederick's contemporaries, Count Wilhelm von Schaumburg-Lippe, who was to instruct the future Prussian general and military reformer, Gerhard von Scharnhorst, exercised a much greater degree of influence.

The noble officer corps was a strictly closed body, something that was emphasised by the fact that from ensign to colonel, all external manifestations of rank were dispensed with. Even the King himself wore only a simple officer's coat. The social equality of officers of differing ranks distinguished the Prussian army from all other European armies. Subordination was only of relevance in cases of royal service since, observed one contemporary, 'in the normal course of affairs, the youngest of ensigns could find himself in the company of a general or even at court'. The officer corps was also hermetically sealed off from the rank-and-file of the army. At the inception of the standing army, officers and men both had held the status of mercenaries who were only distinguished from one another through the type of payment they received. While in seventeenth- and early eighteenth-century Prussia the officers grew together into a corps based on common feudal, aristocratic principles with a special relationship to its ruler, the ordinary soldier remained a mercenary, recruited, frequently from outside the Hohenzollern lands, for specific military service. He was subject to a draconian system of punishment which was the product of a fear of mass desertion. Frederick William I reverted to ideas of a generalised obligation to serve, prohibited the press-ganging of native Prussians through edicts of 1714 and 1721, and issued circular orders to all regiment commanders on 10 May and 15 September 1733, which introduced arrangements known as the 'Canton System'. It entailed the dividing up of Prussia into individual recruiting districts for the different regiments, the so-called cantons, from which the regiments could augment the number of their men. Those with farms, only sons of such landowning farmers, urban merchants, those with a considerable fortune and those with middle class, town-based occupations were all exempt from compulsory cantonal service. In the course of time, these exemptions were extended even further. At first the Canton System conscripted mainly sons of farmers and skilled tradesmen, who were obliged to render only three months' service annually with their regiment, while being free to pursue their civilian occupations throughout the rest of the year. The pay for those on leave was received by the company commander and used to finance the recruitment of mercenaries.

This system, which could not yet be viewed as one of universal conscription, reinforced the underlying inequalities inherent in the social order. In times of peace, it met the requirements of the agrarian economy, but placed undue strain upon a peasantry already overburdened by their duties to the manorial lord.

Symptomatic of the division between officers and men is the fact that after 1713 each group was treated differently by the Articles of War: after that date non-commissioned officers and common soldiers had to swear the same oath on the Articles as all mercenaries had been obliged to give since the sixteenth century. Officers, on the other hand, had to swear to uphold 'all the rules and customs of war which the military service regulations and royal edicts encompassed'. Thus the soldiers' oath and the oath of obedience and service of the officers were neatly separated, the first continuing to sanction the fact that the ordinary soldier stood under constant threat of punishment, while the second was bound up with the aristocratic *esprit de corps* and its code of honour. When Frederick William I changed the punishment imposed on Lieutenant von Katte to a death sentence during the Crown Prince's court martial, he justified the necessity of his action by claiming that otherwise the King could rely on neither officer nor servant bound to him 'in oath and duty'. This comment was a reminder to the noble officer corps of its special relationship with the King.

Prussian Kings displayed conflicting attitudes to the soldiers from the cantons. On the one hand they favoured their use because of the beneficial influence they exercised on the general maintenance of discipline within companies. In his 1768 Political Testament, Frederick, with the lessons of the Seven Years War still fresh in his mind, stipulated that each company should contain sixty youths from the localities: 'these sixty youths are from one and the same area; many are acquainted with or related to each other. Mixed with the foreigners, they make up excellent regiments. The cantons encourage competitive vigour and bravery . . . and friends or relations who fight together do not easily desert each other . . .' On the other hand, however, in order not to jeopardise agricultural production, the Kings of Prussia also sought wherever possible to limit the number of native cantonists. Two-thirds of the army of Frederick William I still consisted of indigenous recruits but Frederick the Great intended to reduce that proportion by half although he only briefly succeeded in achieving this. Losses suffered during the Seven Years War had to be made up by soldiers from the cantons and by the end of the conflict the army consisted almost entirely of Prussian subjects. It has yet to be researched in detail whether this led to a reduction in the number of desertions. After the war, the proportion of foreign soldiers rose once again, to the point where by 1768, the number of native soldiers from the cantons had sunk to below half. In 1776, a numerical balance between Prussian and foreign soldiers was established. Foreign mercenaries were usually enlisted from neighbouring German territories such as Hanover or Mecklenburg, and highly questionable recruiting tactics on occasion led to serious friction and conflict with them.

The Prussian army under Frederick the Great was thus rarely, or more precisely only in the years of grave national crisis, composed of a majority of native Prussians. At such times patriotic loyalty to the King was surely a more significant factor in motivating it towards its achievements than would have been the case in the Austrian army which, in spite of an officer corps undoubtedly imperial and monarchical in its affiliations, suffered from its heterogeneous composition. More important than this vague, embryonic patriotism was Frederick's charisma as a military leader, which, when coupled with strict discipline (enforced by inhuman punishment) spurred the Prussian troops on to incredible feats of bravery and endurance. The success of Frederick's charismatic influence lay in his breaking down all the established barriers between officers and men and personally participating – along with his generals and officers – in all the dangers and privations of war. In no other army were the losses of generals so enormous or the personal, sometimes foolhardy, exposure to danger of the Soldier-King (*Roi-Connétable*) so great as in that of Prussia. In this respect, Frederick took Charles XII of Sweden as his example; but what Charles with his more primitive nature achieved through the exertion of puritan strength, Frederick attained through arduous, stoic, philosophical self-discipline. When the relationship between Enlightenment and absolutism is examined, this dimension of it must not be overlooked. The fundamental evil of absolutist armies, the treatment of its rank-and-file as mere pawns or objects, was thus only eradicated at the moment when a military community encompassing King right down to the last grenadier was established.

This fundamental evil, of course, existed in the armies of all absolutist states. Karl Mannheim described the Prussian type of absolutist army as the first great institution 'which invented rational methods not only to enforce military discipline to produce artificially homogeneous mass behaviour, but also to employ these methods to educate a great mass of people (mostly from the lowest classes) to act and, if possible, think in a prescribed way'. Clearly, then, the lines along which the Prussian army was organised met with quicker success and better results than any other form of mass organisation; since, however, overly centralised and disciplinarian techniques leave little room for the individual to be assimilated successfully 'they are unable to accommodate problems arising from social expansion'. Whether it is here that one should seek the origins of the Frederician state's premature destruction is difficult to say. The catastrophe which befell its army, unforeseen under Frederick, arose in the final analysis out of a confrontation with a military force governed by a different social discipline. This army offered far greater scope for the assimilation of the individual, if less in the sense of humanitarian individualism than in the spirit of collective participation in a revolutionary experience.

SOCIETY OF ORDERS: *GUTSHERRSCHAFT*[1] AND PEASANT SUBORDINATION

While England witnessed the dawn of its industrial revolution, Germany in the mid-eighteenth century remained largely an agrarian country. The old Imperial cities were for the most part economically moribund. A few towns benefited from international trade and, like Frankfurt, prospered as a result. But these were in the minority. Only a handful of the towns in the various German territories succeeded in generating the kind of economic upsurge enjoyed by Leipzig in Electoral Saxony. None of the towns located in the Hohenzollern lands, including Berlin (with 90,000 inhabitants in 1740), Halle and Königsberg, could possibly compete, since the major trade routes either passed Prussia by or were blocked following the Prussian annexation of Silesia. Its most economically developed areas lay in the Rhineland territories in the west and in newly acquired Silesia. Prussia's economy was based upon agriculture. Although fiscal considerations were not unimportant, rigid social conditions which governed the distribution of estates and their legal organisation exerted greater influence upon the agrarian economy. It is important to note here that a disproportionate amount of land was shared between the state and the nobility. Around 1740, almost a quarter of the country's surface area was directly owned by the Crown, the most extensive holdings being in Prussia and Prussian Lithuania, where over 3,200 villages were under direct royal control (*Grundherrschaft*), while the nobility owned not quite 900. In the central Hohenzollern provinces the proportions of land held were reversed. In the second half of the eighteenth century, 652 villages in the Electoral Mark were in royal, and 1,262 in noble, possession; the proportions in Pomerania

1. Demesne farming with serf labour.

were similar, with 652 royal and 1,276 noble villages. Under Frederick William I, the purchase of noble *Grundherrschaften* for the royal domain had been actively undertaken – a trend which in the neighbouring territory of Anhalt had led to the virtual selling off of noble land. Under Frederick II, however, there was an important change where the ownership of land was concerned. The Political Testament of 1752 had already laid down as a matter of policy that the King of Prussia should preserve the nobility and, as a corollary, prevent 'middle-class acquisition of noble estates'. This warning was principally aimed at the acquisition of noble estates by purchase from the treasury which the King strictly forbade civil servants to sanction. Frederick's reasons for such a policy centred solely around the military role which the territorial nobility was obliged to play. The nobleman's sons 'defend the land and improve the race to such an extent that they must be rewarded and conserved in every way'.

Frederick was determined that landownership should continue to provide the material base of the Prussian nobility. Such a policy, however, required that noblemen be based upon, or rather tied to their estates, managing and farming them personally while, at the same time, providing new generations of personnel to officer the army and staff the administration. Inevitably, this was not possible everywhere, since noble estates were mostly of moderate size and often heavily encumbered by debt. The explanation for this lies principally in the way in which the nobility's corporate status and its landed possessions were legally defined. In 1717, in return for a minimal tax, Frederick William I had relinquished his rights as feudal overlord over most of his territories (with the exception of East Prussia, to which it was extended in 1732), and thus relieved the nobility of feudal services, and especially military obligations, in respect of those fiefs, which now became allodial land. In 1723, the *Lehensverfassung* allowed each family to determine the nature which the feudal bond between Crown and nobility was to take in the future. As a result, a plethora of family contracts was drawn up and numerous disputes arose. Fiefs became independent property which, at the death of each owner, could be freely disposed of and sold. Added to this were the encumbrances occasioned by the practice of partible inheritance, which gave equal shares to all male heirs, as well as the compensation paid to widows or daughters, all of which led to enormous debts. The division and fragmentation of noble estates were clearly real dangers. The King sought to reverse such developments by promoting the establishment of entails, by which a single male descendant inherited all landed property, while the remaining sons received minimal financial compensation from the family's moveable assets. A cabinet order of 3 April 1754 recommended that 'under the circumstances' the nobility should establish 'a system of primogeniture within their families' since this was beneficial to the preservation of noble lineages. A decade later the economic situation of the nobility had declined even further, as a consequence of the Seven Years War. Frederick's response was to send a forceful circular in 1765 to the provincial administrations of Brandenburg, Pomerania, Magdeburg and Halberstadt repeating his earlier recommendation. It had come to his notice, he wrote, that the noble families of his territories were allowing themselves to decline as a result of the repeated division of their estates; he had considered the problem and would like to see a system of primogeniture established in all the provinces and would strongly commend such a course of action to the nobility. The nobility took little notice of the King's suggestion, however, probably because, had they followed his advice, the legal rights and financial interests of younger sons would have been severely damaged.

It was this group, the younger sons of noble houses, who placed the greatest strain on the finances of their families. Since the division of noble estates was discouraged, their economic situation forced them to seek employment in state service, either in the army or, to a lesser extent, in the administration. In addition, of course, the social glamour attached to an officer's career exercised a considerable degree of attraction: not only for younger sons but for many eldest sons as well. The incorporation of the landed nobility into the state machinery and its almost complete transformation into a military aristocracy was completed under Frederick II. It has been calculated that in the Electoral Mark, only 27 per cent of noblemen were resident and dependent on their estates, while the rest earned their living through army service or in the civil administration. This situation was broadly similar in other provinces, or at least in the eastern core territories of Brandenburg, Pomerania and East Prussia. It has to be remembered, of course, that the nobility could not maintain itself by the ownership of land alone, since the 20,000 noble families far exceeded the number of noble estates available: there were three times as many families as estates. The resulting surplus of noblemen could not be fully accommodated in either the bureaucracy or the army and, as involvement in 'bourgeois' occupations such as trade was forbidden to them, widespread impoverishment of many élite families ensued. This was evident in the increasing numbers of young, poverty-stricken, landless noblemen entering the cadet schools.

With such a narrow economic base, Frederick's attempt to prevent a further deterioration in the material position of the nobility in Prussia was understandable, though success was necessarily incomplete. The complicated inheritance system which established the so-called *Agnatenconsens*, whereby encumbrances were subject to the agreement of the numerous agnates (relatives on the male side of the family) brought into question the King's much-vaunted notion of noble solidarity and led instead to litigation and feuding within the nobility. Such developments coincided with the aftermath of the Seven Years War which had significantly increased noble indebtedness. The option of disposing of heavily mortgaged lands to wealthy middle-class buyers naturally became an attractive proposition, but legislation restricting the sale of noble land made this means of escaping financial ruin increasingly difficult, to the point where it became quite impossible.

Under such circumstances, Düring's plan for a 'General Credit Bank for Estates and [Noble] Houses' fell on fruitful ground. A Berlin merchant, he proposed that the noble estates be valued and put up as collateral to finance mortgages for two-thirds of their worth. Individual provincial banks were to provide financing for the enterprise, and the money was to be used by noble landowners to pay off creditors. In January 1767, the Great Chancellor of the State Council of Justice was requested to establish the amount of property owned by the nobility in Pomerania and the New Mark and to determine the extent of their indebtedness. Concrete action, however, was first taken in Silesia, so severely crippled by the war. There, the nobility concluded an agreement in the summer of 1770, the potential success of which was considerably aided by a substantial monetary contribution from the King: within the newly founded Silesian *Landschaft* (Rural Credit Institute, membership of which was limited to noble estate owners) the nobility now acted as a cooperative, pledging its entire fortune to those estates propped up by mortgages. A similar decision was taken in 1777 by the nobility in the Electoral and New Mark, where the *Kreditsocietät* (Credit Society) had a membership consisting entirely of the owners of mortgaged estates. Here, too, the state provided financial assistance in the form of a pool of 200,000 thaler. In Pomerania, such a credit bank was established in 1780. Finally, on 20 December 1783, a *Hypothekenordnung* (edict for mortgages) was issued for the whole state. The basic concept at the heart of all these new credit institutions was, of course, that of the landowning élite's joint surety for noble debt. Such an idea naturally ran counter to the individualism and sense of independence which characterised particular noble families, and ultimately threatened to destroy the very thing it aimed to preserve: the landed estates which were the power base of the nobility. The idea was, therefore, doomed to failure since it failed to gain sufficiently widespread support to allow for a fundamental rehabilitation of the élite.

The King's concerns with the nobility's declining material wealth were clearly well founded. His efforts to reverse the trend certainly met with some success, but his wars, which demanded participation by the nobility at great personal cost, played a major part in inflicting a damaging blow to the noble agrarian economy. This would explain why royal material aid was confined largely to the period after the Seven Years War. At a time when continued easing of the social restrictions within the army would have been appropriate, however, Frederick firmly re-established aristocratic predominance within the officer corps. His reasons for doing so are open to debate. The King was too closely in touch with the Enlightenment and enlightened thinkers for the contemporary debate about the problems of noble power and privilege to have escaped his attention. Indeed, on occasion he even sympathised with enlightened objections to inherited privilege; in his essay *Über die Erziehung* (On Education) dating from 1769 he wrote:

> The glory attached to a career in the judiciary, the diplomatic corps, the army or in finance is undoubtedly attractive to a nobleman. However, all would be lost if the state placed birth above ability. The pursuit of such a

principle is as wrong as it is ludicrous, and the government which seeks to adopt it, would soon experience disastrous consequences.

The inherent contradiction between sentences such as these and later Frederician state policy is so stark that one is forced to question whether the established dichotomy between the King's thinking and his actions provides a sufficiently satisfactory explanation. It is possible that the defence of noble privilege stemmed from the desperate position in which the élite found itself. The King probably wanted to ensure the survival of the nobility, an increasingly difficult task, by reserving prestigious positions for them within the state machinery, especially in the army. Aristocratic participation in profitable middle-class occupations continued to be disregarded as a possibility, an attitude which survived, if in a slightly modified form, in the *Allgemeine Landrecht*: 'Noblemen should on the whole refrain from engaging in any kind of bourgeois profession or trade' (Vol. II, Section 9, paragraph 76). Yet this provision is weakened by the provision that, 'Where the business is not bound to a guild, a nobleman may engage in such a trade', which clearly refers only to cases where he is the sole entrepreneur. In Silesia, for example, noblemen had for some time played a leading role in the metal mining and smelting industry. By the end of the eighteenth century, Count Colonna operated the largest ironworks in Upper Silesia, taking advantage of less restrictive Bohemian work practices and combining them with heavy noble investment.

Throughout most of Europe, eighteenth-century agrarian society was composed of legally and socially segregated strata, whose interrelationship was usually dictated by the dependence of the underprivileged on the privileged. This relationship could merely entail an obligation for the dependant to pay certain taxes, but at the other extreme, it could also signify the kind of subordination which transformed human beings into mere objects which lacked any human qualities. Prussia, apart from its possessions in Western Germany, tended towards the latter, although the gradations of servile status varied considerably. There were tenant farmers of widely varying legal and social status. Personally and economically independent free peasants, on the other hand, could only be found in the east, in the provinces of Prussia and Prussian Lithuania; these so-called *Kölmer* (the free peasantry of the Kingdom of East Prussia) were relics of the colonisation programme in the east and still enjoyed the favourable rights which had been accorded to new settlers there. Around the middle of the eighteenth century, their numbers were comparatively small – only 10,355 compared to 41,188 tenant farmers who were bondsmen of their lords. All other peasants on the domain as well as those on noble *Grundherrschaften* (manorial estates) can be classed as serfs, subject to the jurisdiction, discipline and church patronage determined by the overlord. Serfdom bound peasants to the soil in hereditary subjugation (*glebae adscriptus*). Serfs were not allowed to marry without the lord's consent and they required his permission to leave the estate. Their most important function within the agrarian economy was their obligation to pay taxes and to perform labour services which could amount to as much as six days a week. The inclusion of the peasant labour force in the economic system of manorial estates eventually transformed eastern German *Grundherrschaften* (that is to say, demesne farming where, although the peasant was dependent fiscally and juridically, he had relative freedom to cultivate) into a general system of *Gutsherrschaft*, in which peasants on noble land were unfree, bound in perpetuity to the soil, could not marry or move without the lord's permission, and were compelled to perform labour services which were often heavy.

Within the generalised condition of serfdom, different gradations of rights and ownership existed. The most favourable of the bonded peasants were the *Erbzinsbäuer* who leased their land from the lord's estate, enjoyed some security of tenure and were in a position to sell the land provided the lord gave his permission. They were subject to the lord's authority only in respect of the land leased from him and, if they sold, their servile status ended. *Erbzinsbäuer* predominated in the Old Mark, Magdeburg and Lower Silesia. Settlers in the numerous areas of colonisation around the Oder and Warthe rivers, in the Priegnitz and in Eastern and Western Pomerania, were accorded similar rights and enjoyed additional privileges such as exemption from military conscription and from the obligation to perform compulsory labour services on domain estates, while only minimal services were required of them on noble estates. The *Laßbauer* was another type of lease-holding peasant whose tenancy could be inherited by one of his children, although the landlord possessed the right to choose the inheritor. The *Unerbliche Laßbauer*, however, only held his lease for the duration of his own lifetime, or sometimes only for a period determined by the seigneur, and was frequently also liable to render labour services. The latter's position was very similar to that of a tied serf, and differed legally only in respect of the *Laßbauer's* ability to own personal items of property and the fact that he could not be sold unless the manorial lord were selling his entire estate.

The lines of division between subservient and servile status soon became blurred, however, and a tendency to view serfdom in its widest possible sense and sphere of application could clearly be detected among the landowning aristocracy. Not only the extent of manorial lordship, but also the areas where serfdom prevailed, were expanded through the use of monetary payments. Evidence exists, for example, to suggest that even in the eastern provinces, serfs were openly bought and sold. An advertisement in a local newspaper, the *Königsberger Wöchentliche Nachrichten oder Intelligenzblatt*, dated 2 May 1744, announced that 'the following serfs are being offered for sale'. This is of particular historical interest since it occasioned a documented reaction from Frederick, who noted its appearance 'with considerable displeasure' and instructed his royal *Fiskal* to submit 'a detailed report on the matter'. The dispute over the difference between subservience and serfdom was, in any case, an academic and meaningless one. This is clearly demonstrated by the reply of the Estates of Eastern Pomerania and Kamin to the King's instruction in 1763 to abolish serfdom. They agreed that they would forthwith moderate the term 'serfdom' to that of 'subservience', but the change was, of course, in name only. Since the 'Peasants, Shepherds and Domestic Servants Decree' of 1616, the Pomeranian peasants had been serfs, and so they remained.

Here the critical point of the feudal agrarian system can be seen to have been reached. It was a system based on the limitless exploitation of the peasant workforce and one which transformed tenant farmers into wholly dependent agricultural labourers. Eighteenth-century enlightened writers and liberal, or at least realistic, landowners both put up objections to the system. These can be broadly divided into two main kinds. One argument was based on purely humanitarian grounds and followed Immanuel Kant's proposition that all human beings had the right to be free and should not be treated like objects or be at the mercy of others. The other, less idealistic and more pragmatic argument asserted that only personal interest provided the motive for diligent labour, and when this was lacking 'one can only expect a morose workforce, producing poor quality work'. This view was advanced by the cameralist, Johann Heinrich Gottlob von Justi, in his 1767 treatise on *The Principal Obstacles to Agricultural Production*. When one examines Frederick's opinions on the structure of agrarian society throughout most of Prussia and his conduct in this sphere, it becomes apparent that his enlightened conscience was concerned with two things: the abolition of the odious term 'serfdom' and the reduction of the number of days on which labour services were to be performed. This seems a very limited approach given the fundamentally enlightened opinions which he expressed in his writings. An answer may lie in his 1777 essay on *The Forms of Government and the Duties of a Ruler*, in which he admits the impossibility of reconciling humanitarian considerations with the existing social order. 'In most European states,' he writes,

> he [the sovereign] will find provinces in which the peasants are tied to the soil as serfs of noblemen. Of all human conditions, this is the most unfortunate, and the one which most deeply offends the human spirit. No man is born to be another's slave. It is only right to abhor this barbaric custom and to think that all one requires to abolish it, is the will to do so. Unfortunately, this is not so; it is based on ancient contracts between landlord and settler. Agriculture is dependent upon the labour services provided by the peasantry. If one were to abolish the abominable consequences of this arrangement at a stroke, one would destroy the entire agricultural system. The nobility would then have to be compensated for a part of its lost income.

These sentences reveal the dilemma in which the enlightened Frederick found himself: he recognised that the existence of serfdom ran counter to all humanitarian principles, but at the same time he was aware that the implementation of these principles would mean the overthrow of the economic structures and governmental order upon which the nobility depended. *Raison d'état* dictated that Frederick shy away from this course of action; indeed, he could not even consider it without jeopardising the basis of his own power. It was only possible to reduce labour services, not to abolish them, within the limits of the established social order. Joseph II was confronted by exactly the same dilemma. In 1781, however, the Emperor proclaimed the abolition of serfdom in Bohemia, Moravia and Austrian Silesia. Emancipation brought with it a measure of liberalisation and allowed the acquisition of land by the peasantry, but it failed to eradicate *robot*, the serf's compulsory labour. Joseph loved sweeping, general patents, but their impact could be limited in practice. Nevertheless, they demonstrated that he was responding to the call of the Enlightenment to bring about fundamental changes in the eighteenth-century world. Frederick, a generation older and raised in a different governmental tradition, remained more empirical in his general approach. As a result, his attempts to bring his influence to bear on the oppressed condition of the peasantry give the general impression of being a constant search for a practical solution. One such attempt was made as early as 1748, when he issued an instruction to the General Directory to change the unlimited labour services owed by peasants to a specified number of days. Whether this alleviated the peasants' plight to any noticeable degree is doubtful.

On the whole, the King's direct influence was limited to his dealings with the peasants on the royal domain lands. What the nobility did on its own estates was largely beyond his control. He devoted a whole chapter to the peasantry in his Political Testament of 1752 and it begins with the sentence: 'I have moderated the labour services of the peasants', and continues confidently, 'Instead of six days a week as before, they now have to provide only three days compulsory work.' Why, then, did this anger the peasants on noble estates, to the point where in many places they opposed their seigneurial lords? Probably because the nobility resisted the implementation on its own lands of reforms already introduced on the royal domain. Disputes over labour services arose, particularly with the Estates of Pomerania, and continued for decades, extending into the 1770s. The Estates skilfully directed their arguments at the sensitive areas of the Frederician military/political system. Apart from never-ending complaints about the laziness of peasants, who apparently took two-hour naps 'at the first opportunity', assertions were made which could not but disturb the King: the reduction of compulsory service would oblige landlords to employ more servants and labourers, which would lead to the certain ruin of the poorer noble families – exactly the group which was engaged in the service of the state. Then followed the argument which touched upon the very heart of the Prussian military state: if peasant obligations were reduced, the nobility would not be able to spare its sons for the army. This was the thrust of the memorandum from the Pomeranian Estates of 24 May 1751.

The opposition of the provincial Estates to the King's will continued after the beginning of the Seven Years War, a surprising fact bearing in mind the noble officer corps' readiness to fight. In the end, it would appear that Frederick gradually realised he could proceed no further in this matter and limited himself to something of a symbolic act. It is in this light that one must view his sudden attempt in May 1763 to erase the term 'serfdom' from the vocabulary of agrarian society. On 23 May, in Kolberg, he dictated the following sentences in the presence of the Pomeranian Chamber President, von Brenckenhoff: 'Serfdom is to be abolished absolutely and without the slightest objection in the villages owned by the King, his nobility and by the towns.' These words are surely similar to those later employed by Freiherr vom Stein in the October Edict of 1807: '. . . and all those who would oppose it, be brought, by persuasion or force, to aid the implementation of His Royal Highness's idea'. A meeting of the Pomeranian Estates in Stettin, in December 1763, accepted the abolition of serfdom, but refused to sanction any practical concessions, above all the introduction of 'limited or specified obligations'. Frederick II's reforming endeavours were eventually concluded by the Pomeranian Peasant Ordinance of December 1764, although this was little more than a reworking of the 1616 'Peasants, Shepherds and Domestic Servants Decree'. The Ordinance of 1764 merely established that Pomeranian peasants were not serfs or chattels, to be given away or sold, or in any way treated as objects of commercial transactions; their earnings were their own property, to be freely disposed of or inherited, and only the land and farm buildings were owned by the manorial lord. However, the principle that the peasants were tied to the land continued to apply in many areas. Similarly, the Decree of 8 November 1773 for East Prussia and the newly acquired territory of West Prussia, although declaring the condition of serfdom to be obsolete, only served to confirm the continued existence of the practice: the peasants of the demesne 'were under obligation to this or that of our estates' and thus belonged in the same way as servants to noble or other estates 'as *glebae adscripti*'. The question of specified obligations consequently remained open and continued to be so until the final years of Frederick's reign. In 1784, the issue reappeared when the King ordered an inventory of 'all the services, duties and rights' owed by his peasant subjects. Once again, he laid down that specified peasant obligations should replace the unlimited services, in this way improving the serf's lot, but this amelioration was not to be fully implemented during his own lifetime.

In no other area did Prussia's absolute monarch come up against such manifest limitations upon his power as in the attempt to improve the social position of the peasantry, while, at the same time, preserving the interests of the nobility on whom he was dependent. He declared, in his 1752 Political Testament, that the ruler must establish a balance between peasant and nobleman, but this was clearly an impossible task. According to the comments made in 1777, Frederick realised that the only way to bring this matter to a successful conclusion was to compensate the nobility for the material losses they would undoubtedly suffer as a result of a reduction in peasants' services. Under the intellectual and social circumstances of the age, however, this was pure speculation and only the nineteenth century made it possible for it to form the basis of the emancipation of the peasantry.

Frederick undeniably did much for the peasants within his territories. Not only political and material interests, but – unlike most other areas of domestic policy – his own conscience played a part here: slavery was not to be permitted within his possessions. The fact that *raison d'état* pointed in the same direction only served to strengthen his resolve. The peasantry supplied his soldiers and, unlike the nobility, paid taxes. As a result, he sought to guarantee its continued existence and to staunch the flow of noble annexations of peasant land, which were under way in neighbouring territories such as Mecklenburg and Swedish Pomerania. In 1749, therefore, he issued two laws, one for Silesia, the other for the remaining provinces, outlawing noble appropriation of peasant land. This seems to have met with a limited degree of success, although more detailed research remains to be undertaken. The *Allgemeine Landrecht* was subsequently to uphold this peasant code or *Bauernschutz*, although the post-Frederician era placed little emphasis on it. It reads: 'The number of peasant smallholdings is not to be reduced, either by separate or joint appropriation of dwelling and adjoining land' (Vol. VII, Section I, Article 14).

The Seven Years War and its aftermath played a major part in the continuing reduction of peasant smallholdings. In 1764, in order to counteract this trend, Frederick expanded upon the 1749 Ordinance by decreeing that all vacant smallholdings were to be reoccupied within a certain period of time. Progress in this matter, however, was much slower than the King had hoped. Between 1763 and 1779 only 3,539 cottagers were provided with smallholdings in Silesia. Moderately successful attempts were also made after the Seven Years War to improve peasants' inheritance rights. By 1775, all tenant farmers in Silesia owned some sort of hereditary property. It has to be said, however, that the period between Frederick's death and the end of the century saw a marked deterioration in this sphere.

In addition to the measures mentioned above, the King's vigorous efforts to cultivate and settle undeveloped land have also to be remembered. At his instigation, the Netze and Warthe areas were drained, the Oder dammed and the marshlands surrounding it developed. The privileges enjoyed by new settlers there, such as tax concessions for a certain number of years and exemption from military service, helped to raise the status of the peasantry as a whole, although their favourable position could, of course, often lead to tension. Finally, the King was also instrumental in effecting a number of changes and improvements in agricultural production. In the final analysis, it would be wrong to describe Frederick's agrarian policies as *bauernfreundlich* (literally, 'peasant-friendly'). The peasantry to him formed the lowest echelon of the social hierarchy, and his concern lay in maintaining the social status quo while, at the same time, improving peasant productivity. Unlike the initiatives of his contemporary, Charles Frederick, Margrave of Baden, physiocratic ideas played little part in the King's moves towards the abolition of serfdom. The noted physiocrat François Quesnay's concept of a '*monarchie agricole*' failed to exercise any influence over him; indeed, it is uncertain whether he was even aware of its existence. In Frederick's case, his policies could be labelled as agrarian traditionalism, which owed less to economic theory than to *raison d'état*, but in which, nonetheless, traces of physiocratic ideas could be detected. The King, for example, referred to the peasants as 'foster fathers of the state' (*pères nourriciers*), whose existence must not be made any more difficult. 'On the contrary, they must be encouraged so that they work the land well; because this is where the true wealth of the state lies. The soil yields our necessary food, and those who till it are . . . truly the providers for society.'

THE BEGINNINGS OF A MIDDLE CLASS

A Third Estate was gradually added to Prussia's rigid Society of Orders. The *Allgemeine Landrecht* says of this new bourgeoisie: 'The middle class encompasses all inhabitants of the state who by birth belong neither to the nobility nor the peasantry' (Vol. II, Section VIII, Article 1). Within this broad social category, separate distinctions were made for 'independent town-dwelling burghers with civic rights'. Lines of social division between different levels of middle-class status were not drawn: the term '*Bürgertum*' could encompass anyone from the upper echelons of the emerging commercial middle class to civil servants, scholars, and even lowly traders and artisans. Not until 1791/ 92, did the Prussian jurist and co-author of the *Allgemeine Landrecht*, Carl Gottlieb Suarez, attempt to distinguish the varying strata within each Estate according to jobs and professions. The bourgeoisie represented the most complex amalgam, and it ultimately proved impossible for Suarez to reduce it to a common denominator: the bourgeoisie, he wrote, is occupied in business, art and crafts, industry and trade; in addition, he highlighted two 'sub-classes, namely the religious orders, teaching scripture and conducting church services, and civil servants, entrusted with the conduct of military and administrative affairs'. Despite the wide diversity of the middle classes, Prussian political reality meant that birth still determined position, and legal barriers were erected which a bourgeois could not cross.

The exclusively noble composition of the officer corps was only temporarily interrupted by the exigencies of the Seven Years War. Much the same was true of the administration, or at least of its upper echelons. During Frederick's entire reign, the only privy councillor of middle-class descent among the twenty he appointed was Friedrich Gottlieb Michaelis, minister for the Electoral Mark, while only three of all his Chamber Presidents were of bourgeois origins. The King categorically stipulated that the men selected to fill high-ranking posts should come from 'worthy and long-established noble families', since such individuals possess 'natural ability and a capacity for work', conferred by their social origins. Middle-class bureaucrats could only be found in larger numbers among the administrative staff of General Directory Privy Councillors and in the offices of provincial authorities. Records from the year 1770 show that in the provincial governments (*Regierungen*) throughout Prussia, there were 44 bourgeois councillors and only 12 noblemen, while in the War and Domains Chambers (*Kriegs-und Domänenkammern*), 86 were of middle-class and only fourteen of noble descent. Clearly, a stratum of largely middle-class officials was beginning to occupy a central position within the administrative apparatus. Members of this section of the bureaucracy, on the whole, possessed specialist knowledge, diligence, cooperativeness and relevant training and, in time, they began to develop a certain *esprit de corps*. It would be misleading to assume that this group represented nascent bourgeois social consciousness; they showed no signs of aiming for emancipation, or of opposition to the status quo. What these officials displayed was rather a sense of bureaucratic loyalty to the Frederician state system. This was also true of the men in the lower administrative posts, such as the *Steuerräte* (commissioners in charge of urban taxation). In the provinces, the *Landrat*[2] was a Junker, who was both a royal official and a representative of the local nobility, and as such formed an important link between the state headed by the King and the local landowning elite.

The social segregation of nobility and middle class entailed restrictions not only for the bourgeoisie, but also for the nobility. The fact that noble officers were forbidden to socialise with commoners has already been mentioned. Of much greater importance, since it affected society as a whole, were the restrictions placed upon the nobility's right to engage in commercial careers. The *Allgemeine Landrecht* expresses it thus: 'Members of the nobility should not as a rule engage in middle-class occupations, for example trade or the supply of food' (Vol. II, Section IX, Article 76). Such noble abstention from direct involvement in trade or industry was, of course, a feature of European society as a whole and it was, for example, especially marked in Spain. In Prussia, however, it became the social norm and was, moreover, enforced by law. The restrictive legislation was gradually abolished in the course of nineteenth-century reform movements, but the socio-behavioural patterns created by them survived until the downfall of the monarchy and perhaps, in some degree, until 1945. The intention behind Frederick's rigid social policy was entirely to be found in his ideas about the division of functions within the military state, and in his fear that the nobility 'could be distracted from its *métier d'honneur*' – it was reasonable to assume, after all, that certain of its members would apply themselves more diligently to the conduct of trade, than to the pursuit of a military lifestyle. Nevertheless, the *Allgemeine Landrecht* in its wording on this point allowed a certain amount of latitude for a looser interpretation and, in any case, the laws governing noble commercial activities were not always strictly obeyed. Particularly in Silesia, the nobility, influenced by more liberal ideas from Bohemia, engaged in trade and industry on a grand scale, and owned and managed much of the land on which the rich mineral resources of the region were mined. By the end of the eighteenth century, Count Colonna owned the largest private ironworks in Silesia, and several other members of noble families were also involved in the iron industry. On the whole, it seems the limitations placed upon the nobility in Prussia

2. *Landrat* – a local commissioner responsible for the administration of the district or *Kreis*.

did not have the debilitating effects which were to be detected in Spain. The entrepreneurial abilities of the aristocracy, in the core territories at least, were nonetheless underdeveloped and only slowly began to emerge with the introduction of more advanced agricultural techniques during the second half of the eighteenth century.

The laws governing marriages represented a further barrier between nobility and middle class in Frederician Prussia. Unions between members of different orders in society were subject to numerous restrictions. However, in spite of increasingly strict laws against 'unequal and harmful marriages', from the seventeenth century onwards, misalliances between nobles and members of the middle class had become more frequent. Hence Frederick William's Edict of 1739, attempting to restrict such marriages. During the Seven Years War, the economic decline of the nobility and the corresponding increase in the affluence of the middle classes resulted in a further rise in such 'unequal' marriages. Frederick, for his part, frequently accompanied his refusal to grant special dispensations to officers wishing to marry outside their own social stratum with contemptuous and disdainful comments. Eventually, the *Allgemeine Landrecht* gave a more precise definition to what constituted prohibited marriages between 'persons of unequal social standing', and laid down that the nobility was only prohibited from marrying members of the peasantry or lowly townsfolk. Marriages with the 'upper middle classes', on the other hand, were explicitly permitted. Civil servants, with the exception of those in subordinate posts, intellectuals, artists, businessmen and factory owners were all considered to belong to the upper middle class category, as well as 'those accorded the same respect as the aforementioned' – an interesting provision from the perspective of social history, since it occasioned the rise of a Prussian bourgeois–noble middle class without necessitating the creation of a *noblesse de robe*, as had been the case in France. Nor was there a bureaucratic nobility of the kind that existed in Russia, where the purchase of certain civil posts automatically accorded the purchaser noble status. Only rarely, and clearly reluctantly, did Frederick resort to ennoblement. One example was the President of the East Prussian Chamber, Johann Friedrich Domhardt, the son of a tenant farmer on Crown lands. Not until the reign of Frederick's successor was wider use made of this royal prerogative: the number of ennoblements between 1790 and 1806 was as high as 212, among them 89 officers and 68 civil servants.

The stringent legal divisions between social groups were clearly not always strictly observed, as the laws governing marriages and noble property demonstrate. The *Allgemeine Landrecht* succinctly lays down that 'only the nobility is entitled to the possession of noble estates' (Vol. II, Section IX, Article 37). Nevertheless, it does permit the acquisition of such property by persons of middle-class standing provided they obtained a 'special royal dispensation' (Article 51). In this area, too, Frederick proceeded much more reluctantly than would his successor, although it should be noted that he was prepared to make exceptions as a result of the pressures imposed on the nobility by the

Seven Years War. In such cases, he attached certain conditions when granting permission for the sale of noble land to commoners. The new owners were to designate one of their sons for military service, and ownership was never to be transferred to the newly recruited officer, that is, it was not to endanger the supply of new men to the army. In addition, the bourgeois owner was denied the manorial rights usually attached to noble estates. Only a limited shift of ownership towards the middle classes took place in Prussia's provinces. Precise figures do not exist, but it was in no way comparable to the developments which occurred at the peak of late-nineteenth-century industrialisation.

The rigid Prussian social order was, in practice, beginning to attain a somewhat more fluid character. In the first place, the administration's middle ranks developed a 'supra-social', state-orientated service ethic. Though this emerging sense of community was important the traditional barriers between middle class and noble 'servants of the state' remained and must not be overlooked. It was practically impossible for bourgeois officials to be promoted to the top posts. Opposition or, alternatively, simple resignation could easily result from a situation where only noble bureaucrats could strive for promotion. This advantage would obviously give them a different attitude and disposition towards work. More detailed research on this topic certainly would be worthwhile.

The Enlightenment, of course, also contributed in some degree to the lowering of social barriers. It was this philosophical, intellectual movement which took hold of established institutions such as universities, and occasioned the formation of new social organisations such as literary or political societies – some secret, with underground magazines and newspapers. The old Prussian territories possessed three universities: the University of Halle, founded under Frederick III/I, the University of Frankfurt, already substantially run down by the eighteenth century, and the Albertus University at Königsberg. In 1742, the University of Halle attracted the highest number of students, with 1,500 out of a total student population in all Germany of 8,000; this gave it more students than any other German university during the eighteenth century. This was the university preferred by Frederick William I. He not only admired August Hermann Francke, the head and organisational centrepoint of the Pietist Institute at Halle, but also established a training centre there for Prussian bureaucrats. This was to function under the auspices of the law faculty, where a fifth chair was established to promote the study of cameralism. The student population at first consisted largely of noblemen, but gradually the bourgeoisie came to achieve numerical preponderance. From the very beginning, this was a place where people of diverse social backgrounds could meet. The professors at Halle were almost exclusively drawn from the middle class. Its most famous lecturer, the philosopher Christian Wolff, was the son of a tanner from Breslau. He arrived at the university in 1706, was expelled from Prussia in 1723, and brought back by Frederick the Great on his accession. In 1745, he was ennobled, being created a *Reichsfreiherr* (a baron in the Imperial nobility), as the influential jurist, Johann Peter Ludewig, had been twenty-six years earlier. In Christian Thomasius and Christian Wolff, the University of Halle possessed, at different times, two of the most important scholars of the German Enlightenment. Their writings on enlightened natural law theories laid the foundations of the contradictory relationship between absolutism and Enlightenment which Frederick II was to embody. Both had a significant educational impact. Although they did not advocate ideas of middle-class emancipation, their writings were clearly sympathetic to middle-class aspirations.

The University of Königsberg in East Prussia was much older and, on the whole, academically less distinguished than Halle but, situated in a province in which the urban middle class and the rural nobility were much more inter-dependent, it did represent an even greater centre of social integration. Added to this was the presence there of a genius whose effect on the history of Western philosophy was indisputable: Immanuel Kant. Kant was principally influential through his lectures, at which members of all social classes gathered. His social skill enabled him to assemble around his table men from the most diverse walks of life, noble officers and high-ranking bureaucrats, the future provincial minister von Schroetter among them. Through his pupil, Christian Jacob Kraus, who surpassed even his mentor in the impact he had on the public, he influenced the later circle of reformers and, in particular, President Theodor von Schön. The later Frederician era ushered in a period of lively intellectual debate at Königsberg, and it was here that an intellectual stratum, free of social barriers, developed. Its members were eventually to wield direct political power in the reform era at the beginning of the nineteenth century. Some great academic thinkers played a decisive role within it and, for the most part, they stemmed from middle-class or artisan backgrounds: Kant was a saddler's son, Johann Georg Hamann that of a barber-surgeon, while Johann Gottfried Herder's father had originally been a weaver, but had worked himself up to choirmaster and eventually to the position of elementary school teacher. Social barriers, then, could be surmounted through the pursuit of either a university career, as Kant and Wolff had done, through a literary career such as Hamann had chosen, or through theological studies, which Herder followed.

Dining clubs, literary societies and masonic lodges were all eighteenth-century 'intellectual interest groups', which, as a matter of course and necessity, stood above the traditional social divisions. In the capital, Berlin, still as yet without the intellectual focal point of a university, they assumed a particular importance. Here, two clubs, the 'Monday Club' and the 'Wednesday Society', provided a forum in which the social and intellectual aristocracy could mingle. Middle-class members again outnumbered noblemen, although many of the former were holders of state posts, such as Carl Gottlieb Suarez.

One of the fundamental principles governing the proceedings of the 'Wednesday Society' was the strict secrecy surrounding the names of members, who were instead referred to by numbers. Nevertheless, it undoubtedly exercised an influence over the political arena. One of its members, the writer Leopold

Friedrich Günther Goekingk, appointed in 1786 as War and Domains Commissioner in Magdeburg, recalls its meetings: 'I could cite striking examples of ways in which society benefited; I shall only mention one here: it is that the *Allgemeine Landrecht* owes much to it [the Society], since Suarez, who played such a substantial part in drawing it up, clarified many of his ideas [with the help of the Society]'. This could well be an exaggeration, but the Society clearly functioned as a forum for discussion and provided an environment in which enlightened schemes could be produced. Its secrecy, which in May 1800 led to its dissolution, was by no means an indication of political dissent, at most it was to guard against the encroachments of the absolute state which even the *Allgemeine Landrecht* rejected. To this enlightened middle-class stratum, a precursor of the future intelligentsia, Frederick the Great was beyond criticism. Their opinion of the King kindled much controversy and dispute even during his lifetime but, to most of them, he represented a guarantee that it was possible to unite absolutism and Enlightenment in the same person. It was with this in mind that Kant described the Age of Enlightenment as 'Frederick's century'. In the final analysis, however, Frederick's personality stood in the way of a total release of the anti-monarchical forces which would have taken place, had enlightened ideas been pursued to their logical conclusion.

The groups influenced by the Enlightenment formed a proportionately small part of the bourgeoisie, probably smaller even than in other areas of Germany, such as Hamburg, Leipzig or Göttingen. They clearly demonstrate the heterogeneity of the middle classes. Their individual legal positions also differed widely. The *Allgemeine Landrecht* distinguished between 'townspeople of certain standing', those who as a result of their posts, honours or special privileges, were exempted from the jurisdiction of their place of residence, and the so-called '*Schutzverwandte*', town-dwellers who belonged neither to the burghers nor to those who had been exempted. They did not have the right to engage in business or practise a craft, and in some towns, such as Königsberg, the term also encompassed Jews, journeymen, apprentices, all the subservient occupations, indeed, all those belonging to the lowest social strata, among which the relatively few industrial workers could now also be counted (Vol. II, Chapter VIII, Articles 1–5). The legal status of these workers held them apart, and failed to correspond with the concept of determining social standing by birth. As a result, the 'burgher' only existed in a general, even nebulous, sense. The bourgeoisie in Prussia, as in the majority of other German states at this time, was engaged in business and trade on so small a scale that the development of economic conditions akin to those generated by the great international trade and manufacturing centres was all but impossible.

Crafts and trades remained subject to the restrictive practices imposed on them by the guilds, even after Frederick William I's reforms in 1731 had imposed strict state controls on them and the towns in which they operated. Although the *Allgemeine Landrecht* confirmed the rights of the guilds as privileged corporations (Article 191), the monarch retained the sole right to license guilds (Article 182) as well as to introduce new legislation governing their administration; indeed, this clause stipulated that the existing guild law 'be determined and changed by the requirements of the common good'. Such restrictions upon skilled trade corporations were in keeping with the decline of urban self-government. Fuelled by the increasing diversification of skilled crafts, it set in motion a long process of decline for the guilds. In Berlin around 1770, more than 200 trade and craft guilds existed; in Königsberg around 100; and even in small towns, the fragmentation was noticeable. This was by no means an exclusively Prussian development, but one that was taking place across the whole of Germany and whose origins could be traced back to the sixteenth century. The proportion of subsidiary guilds varied, with the textile industry on the whole most strongly represented. These tended to be small workshops with little turnover or profit, and few employees. Gustav Schmoller records 17,249 self-supporting workshops with 12,389 employees in the towns of the Electoral Mark in 1750. This meant an average of 0.718 persons per business, which reveals that many of the craftsmen worked alone. The Berlin employment statistics for the year of Frederick's death are as follows: 7,683 businesses employed 6,014 workers. If one compares these figures with those of 1755 (5,251 businesses with 2,914 employees) or those of 1765, a time of economic crisis following the Seven Years War, when only 3,683 businesses with 3,448 workers were recorded, it becomes clear that not every workshop could afford the luxury of employees and the 1765 figures go as far as to suggest that some formerly self-employed craftsmen were reduced to becoming employees. Economic and social circumstances, therefore, allowed for little freedom of manoeuvre in trade and in manufacturing industries.

Although commerce in Germany as a whole suffered from its geographical isolation from the principal maritime trade routes, this was especially true of Brandenburg-Prussia. Its Baltic ports, Königsberg and Stettin, suffered from the recession in the region's trade; Danzig had not been annexed by the time of Frederick's death in 1786 and would not be acquired until 1793, while access to the North Sea was not secured until 1744 through the acquisition of Emden. The most important centre for trade in Eastern Europe, Leipzig, lay in Saxony, and the Silesian capital, Breslau, which played a significant role in the Austro–Polish transit trade, was badly affected by the imposition of a Prussian transit toll in 1755.

After the acquisition of Silesia, Prussia did, of course, have at its disposal the entire length of the river Oder and, with Magdeburg on the Elbe, it did possess certain advantages, but ultimately these proved negligible and were not sufficient to counterbalance the glaring disadvantages of its geographical position. Magdeburg only enjoyed a temporary boom when the Seven Years War had affected so many other trade routes. As the only larger Prussian town not under foreign occupation, it became, at times, a refuge for the court and the government, while also preserving Prussian trade with Hamburg. Prussia's complete lack of mineral resources and its dependence on agrarian products for the manufacture of trade goods represented major stumbling blocks to a flourishing commercial economy. The export of wool was strictly forbidden after 1718/19, and the attempt to raise silkworms depended on large-scale planting of mulberry trees. Prussia lagged behind neighbouring Saxony in every respect. Factory processing of metals from Saxon mines had begun as early as the sixteenth century; since then, gunpowder factories, gold and silver mines, glassworks, brass, tin and arms factories had all been established. Unlike in Prussia, the foundations for future industrialisation had, therefore, been laid and, to some extent, its associated social changes anticipated. It seems likely that the hoarding of national funds by successive Prussian Kings from Frederick William I onwards, for use on the army and warfare, deprived the state of investment which could otherwise have given much-needed financial aid to economic enterprise.

Such policies, however, did not entirely preclude investment in industry. A characteristic of Prussia's smaller middle-class entrepreneurs was that many reached their positions with state help. Aid was forthcoming in several ways: direct financial assistance to help establish new businesses, protectionist manipulation of foreign trade through import and export restrictions, and the granting of monopolies to certain businesses. The *Lagerhaus* in Berlin, a textile factory producing fine cloth for officers' uniforms founded under Frederick William I, was the prototype of such mercantilist industrial policies. 'By producing everything at home which had previously to be bought in from abroad' (C. Hinrichs), these policies aimed to prevent the drain of hard cash abroad. The *Lagerhaus* was financed by a private entrepreneur, Johann Andreas Krautt, who enjoyed a guaranteed market supplying King and army with his entire output. Since the amount of wool permitted to be exported had been restricted, the raw material for production was much cheaper, and this increased the business's profitability. Krautt, however, was something of an exceptional case: he combined in his person both private enterprise and a position in the state administration, and through his membership of the General Directory was subsequently able to contribute to the banning of wool exports.

The most important beneficiary of the state subsidy programme was the silk industry, which received grants of between 2.5 and 2.8 million thaler, the Electoral Mark alone receiving 1.8 million. The purpose of these subsidies was to stop imports of foreign silk, and to satisfy the demand for luxury goods at home and abroad. Its motives, which ignored the needs of the army, were thus pure mercantilism. The silk industry was personally championed by the King, and it produced outstanding entrepreneurs such as Johann Ernst Gotzkowsky. He had spent his apprenticeship in the *Lagerhaus*, and, upon Frederick's accession in 1740, was employed to develop the manufacturing industries. By 1753, his silk and taffeta factories employed 250 workers. He founded a porcelain factory in Berlin, and during the Russian occupation of the capital in the Seven Years War his private credit contributed considerably towards paying the ransom which the Russian troops demanded. Furthermore, he came to represent the interests of the few velvet-producing firms which, due to a lack of competition, held a type of monopolistic position. After the war, however, he twice found himself in such financial difficulty that even state support failed to prevent his bankruptcy. Nonetheless, Gotzkowsky, with his adventurous, speculative spirit, was an extraordinary personality among the textile entrepreneurs of the Prussian capital.

Berlin did not, however, dominate the silk industry quantitatively or qualitatively. This position was held by a firm founded in 1731 in the Prussian enclave of Krefeld in the Rhineland by the brothers Friedrich and Heinrich von der Leyen. It developed into Prussia's largest manufacturing enterprise and, by 1769, employed around 3,000 people in different factories; by 1786, that figure had risen even higher to 3,400 employees. In 1759, when the territory was occupied by Austria during the Seven Years War, the von der Leyens obtained a monopoly for their business from the 'Imperial Austrian General Administration', and after the war they pursued a totally independent path. They refused to acknowledge the 1766 Berlin silk regulations, claiming that 'they would be impossible to introduce in Krefeld' and that all state intervention would damage their business. What was emerging here was a particular type of entrepreneur in whom, 'to a much greater degree than in most of the Berlin manufacturers, initiative and a willingness to take risks combined with entrepreneurial foresight and skill' (K. Schwieger).

In the core territories around Berlin, where the Prussian metal and armaments industry was concentrated, the most significant manufacturing enterprise was set up by businessmen David Splitgerber and Gottfried Adolph Daun. They were also involved in banking and other financial activities, mostly on behalf of the state, and succeeded in acquiring important metal and armaments factories in Brandenburg under Frederick William I. In 1722, with royal approval, they founded factories in Potsdam and Spandau. As the size of the Prussian army increased sharply under Frederick the Great, their business increased proportionately. By the end of the 1760s, profits had risen to 2.5 million thaler, even after their operations had survived the crisis years of 1763–66. In view of this, it is remarkable to note that the Prussian armaments industry was unable to supply the army's needs in wartime and Prussia was eventually forced to rely on additional arms manufactured in occupied Saxony, where factories in Suhl supplied 20,000 muskets between 1757 and 1762.

The fact that men like Splitgerber, Gotzkowsky and the von der Leyens developed an upper-middle-class self-confidence despite their dependence on state help, has recently been highlighted by East German research. This was a numerically small social group and its freedom of manoeuvre was limited. There were, however, examples of resistance to state direction largely associated with efforts to secure positions of monopoly for the leading businesses. The Magdeburg businessman, Christoph Friedrich Gossler, for example, established a velvet and silk factory in the provinces where he was able to avoid excise duty. He ignored the Magdeburg Chamber's injunctions to cease operating: 'I cannot be limited in any way,' he wrote to the General Directory. It is questionable whether this was a typical contemporary reaction to government policy; it seems rather to have been one of the few isolated cases of opposition. A characteristic of the manufacturing classes in the core territories was that, with only rare exceptions, they failed to constitute a separate social stratum whose influence extended over several generations. This section of society seemed instead to consist of individuals who enjoyed meteoric rises to fame and fortune, but who often plummeted to financial ruin just as rapidly.

The new entrepreneurs generally did not have centralised businesses, but instead divided their operations between several separate factories. Of the 34 enterprises which could boast more than 100 employees around 1770, eighteen were on Crown lands, fourteen of which were situated in Berlin and Potsdam. Only eight of these were centralised manufacturing operations. There were equally few big merchants active in the retail trade in Prussia's few ports. This situation was not comparable to that prevailing in Western Europe. Even Vienna possessed a larger and wealthier sector of businessmen. It must be remembered, moreover, that no clear divisions existed between the various economic activities of entrepreneurs, businessmen and bankers. Splitgerber, for example, was, at times, active in all three spheres of business. The wealthy entrepreneurs, along with intellectuals and civil servants, were, of course, counted among the exempt (that is to say, they were freed from the jurisdiction of their place of residence), but their gradual evolution into an urban patriciate, as had taken place since medieval times in all other European towns with governing councils, failed to occur. The old ruling families and the council oligarchies which they staffed were generally in decline even in the larger towns during the eighteenth century. In the Brandenburg-Prussian territories, their supremacy was undermined by increasingly centralised state and fiscal administration, and their *raison d'être* removed by the appointment of tax inspectors in the localities. G. Schmoller asserts that these royal tax officials 'were vastly more efficient than the families of town burgomasters and senators, who in any case represented anachronistic views of world and state'. Furthermore, he claims that the new breed of civil servants triumphed over the old order 'because they represented greater intelligence and moral strength'. This somewhat pessimistic view of the condition of the towns, as formulated by the doyen of national economic history, must undoubtedly be open to modern revision. What is certain is that the new stratum of middle-class businessmen did leave its mark on the communal traditions of the society which produced it.

Since the Hohenzollern state depended on the constant increase of its population, the fabric of its social structure would clearly undergo constant change. Moreover, rights and privileges accorded to immigrants would create a curious mixture of citizens with widely varying rights. This affected the middle class in two ways: on the one hand, certain particularly sophisticated forms of privilege surpassed even their own positions as exempted citizens; on the other hand, rights against discrimination accorded to French Huguenot refugees and Jews also posed a potential threat to their position. Both immigrant groups have to be considered as members of the middle classes. The emigration of French refugees from France to Prussia was made possible by the Edict of Postsdam, promulgated by the Great Elector in 1685 after the Revocation of the Edict of Nantes. By 1699, 13,847 Huguenots had settled in Brandenburg-Prussia. 5,682 of that number came to Berlin – that is, 41 per cent of all French refugees living in Prussia. By 1724, the French colony in Berlin accounted for 9 per cent of the city's entire population. Large settlements of Huguenots also grew up in other towns, such as Frankfurt-an-der-Oder, Halle and Kolberg.

The French refugees represented a particularly privileged group of immigrants, incorporating members of the nobility as well as of the middle class, urban as well as rural elements, in whom the rights of the exempt were combined with the privileges accorded agrarian colonists. The Edicts of 1709 and 1720 gave them equal legal status with native Prussians as well as enormous advantages facilitating land and house purchases, allowing them exemption from military service and freedom from taxation for fifteen years. The Huguenots, however, constituted a separate section of society for administrative, judicial and educational purposes; the French colony formed an independent body with its own legal system and high court, education programme and separate French Calvinist church administration. Economic integration of this technically and economically advanced population was, of course, the ultimate goal of the favourable treatment which they received. Huguenot economic activity was concentrated in the textile industry, where new techniques were developed and their exemption from membership of guilds or craft organisations allowed for greater economic freedom of movement. In Berlin, a number of French Huguenot families succeeded in rising to upper-middle-class status; among them was that of Karl Stephen Jordan. His family's business had begun with small-scale iron production and after 1700, three consecutive generations ran a factory producing gold, silver and luxury metal goods and were prominent members of the city's financial circles. Huguenots were also involved in the manufacture of silk stockings – indeed the silk trade produced some of their most significant industrialists (for example, the Girards, Michelets, and Baudouins in Berlin). The strong influence of the French at court must not be overlooked either. After the French nobility was granted equal legal status with its Prussian counterpart, it played an active part in court life (for example in the upbringing of the Crown Prince) and in the army. The destabilising effect which these *émigrés* had upon France became a politically and economically stabilising factor in Prussia.

If the Huguenots, with their political, legal and economic advantages, may be seen as one of the most privileged groups of exempted citizens, then the Jews must be regarded as one of the least privileged. In 1750, in Berlin alone they numbered 2,188; in other words, they constituted 1.93 per cent of the city's total population a dramatically smaller proportion than that of the Huguenots. The Prussian state pursued a policy of segregation towards them, while at the same time allowing them a certain freedom of manoeuvre in monetary matters to satisfy its fiscal interests. The *Generalprivileg* of 17 April 1750 incorporated the Jews into the bureaucratic and legal system of the Prussian state, but failed to grant them equal status with other Prussian citizens. The numbers of 'ordinary' exempted Jews (that is, those with the right to pass on their exemption to an heir) was limited to 203, and those with 'extraordinary' exemptions (i.e. those only granted for life) to 63. The state secured its income by levying high taxes on them and introducing a basic, communal liability to pay, which was later extended to cover also bankruptcy and fraud. Jews were forbidden to engage in trades run by guilds, so that their economic base was considerably restricted. They relied largely on commerce, and in certain areas, such as the silver trade, they possessed almost a monopoly. Of the 119 most prominent Jewish traders in Berlin in 1749, 49 were financial dealers, that is, bankers, money-lenders and exchange dealers, and 42 were pawn-brokers. Jews could, however, receive concessions for the 'establishment of certain sorts of factories', of which they took full advantage after the Second Silesian War. Between 1740 and 1753, eight factories were founded by Jews in Berlin. One such founder was the entrepreneur Isaac Benjamin Wulff, who produced cotton and silk goods. Despite the many limitations, Jewish wealth in the capital grew, especially after the Seven Years War, and along with it their cultural integration, as demonstrated, for example, by Moses Mendelssohn.

Though the *Generalprivileg* was introduced during his reign, Frederick II himself showed little respect for the Jews. In both his Political Testaments he spoke of them with disdain, and opposed the tendency in the bureaucracy to support Jews in particular cases or over questions of business. He felt that they 'did not merit any particular favours'. His contempt for the Jewish race was probably influenced by Voltaire's writings, scorning the Jewish religion and its rites. The ideas of tolerance towards the Jews as advocated by Lessing in his *Nathan the Wise* (published in 1780) were probably familiar to him, but seemed to have made little impression to him. It is curious, however, that Mirabeau, on a visit to Sans Souci shortly before Frederick's death, discussed with him Christian Wilhelm Dohm's book *The Improvement of the Civil Status of the Jews* (published in 1784). The content of the conversation, however, unfortunately remains unknown to us.

CHAPTER 3

The Anti-Machiavel *and* Machiavellianism

The rise of a new power within an international state system governed by established, traditional friendships and enmities, in an era of great social and intellectual change; this was the Prussia of Frederick the Great's reign. The problems the King confronted were not only military in nature, those of battles and diplomatic revolutions, but also encompassed a struggle of intellectual forces or, to be more precise, the new emergent ideas concerning state and society. Frederick personified the dichotomy of being, on the one hand, a ruler of the Enlightenment and, on the other, a determined proponent of power politics. The irreconcilability of these two traits within his character, and the permanent inner turmoil which resulted, constitute the basic problem of Frederick's personality.

Frederick was made aware of this inner conflict by his study of the great Renaissance political theorist, Machiavelli. Using the imagery of lion and fox to represent the two essential driving forces of politics, physical strength and cunning, Machiavelli stripped political practice to its barest bones and followed his theories to their logical conclusion. His *Prince* stood in the tradition of medieval 'Mirrors of Princes', and was aimed at dispelling fictitious tales of noble heroism and instead presenting a contemporary view of political reality. Frederick rejected this tale of crime and betrayal in his *Anti-Machiavel*, putting forward instead the moral teachings of an eighteenth-century enlightened monarch.

The background to Frederick's repudiation of Machiavellian ideas is important. In the years prior to his accession, he had already established, at Rheinsberg, a context for all the arts to be displayed, and had promoted a cult of friendship and youth. He himself had experienced the cruel realities of political life at first hand and had meticulously followed the game of power politics over the Jülich-Berg succession question in which Prussia seemed constantly outmanoeuvred. The treatise *Considérations sur l'état présent du corps politique de l'Europe*, produced at the turn of the year 1737/38, was the first result of his observations, as well as a personal contribution to the debate. Already in evidence here was the dichotomy between the real world, where

limitless ambition and the unquenchable thirst of rulers for power and aggrandisement predominated, and that of a world as it should be, governed by benevolent, moderate Kings striving to promote the happiness of their people.
The writings of Voltaire and Fénelon, describing utopian political systems,
provided the yardstick by which Frederick sought to measure the achievements of his own life. While immersed in such enlightened literature, he
received the first chapter in manuscript of Voltaire's *The Century of Louis XIV*
(*Histoire du siècle de Louis XIV*). It was here that he first encountered Machiavelli,
counted among the greatest men of his age. Frederick was filled with indigna-
tion; he was aware of Machiavelli's undoubted talents, he wrote to Voltaire on
31 March 1738, but the Italian should never be entitled to a position reserved
solely for those who had performed virtuous deeds or possessed praiseworthy
abilities. Such a rogue did not belong in the roll-call of eminence which
included Boileau, Colbert and Marshal Luxembourg. It was around this time
that Frederick must have read Amelot de la Houssaye's French translation of
The Prince and first mentioned its author to Voltaire. Although he remained
ignorant of Machiavelli's other works, Frederick's interest in and reaction
to him seems to have been occasioned by the sharp contrast between the
Florentine's theories and those contained in the enlightened literature with
which the King surrounded himself. 'Thoughts rush round and round in my
head, and divine inspiration is needed to disentangle this chaos', Frederick
confessed to Voltaire on 22 March, 1739, after studying Machiavelli's treatise.
As his critical interest in the political theorist grew, the idea of writing a
rejection of Machiavellianism gathered strength. Many remarks indicate that
Voltaire's *Henriade* strengthened his determination, and Frederick resolved
to contrapose Henry IV of France, his ideal monarch, with Cesare Borgia,
Machiavelli's model prince. The *Anti-Machiavel* was his reaction (*une suite*) to
the *Henriade*, he informed Voltaire. Henry IV's nobility of mind provided
him with the sword with which to cut down Cesare Borgia's reputation.
Voltaire, flattered by the compliment the Crown Prince had paid him, spoke
of Frederick's embryonic work as a 'royal catechism', an 'antidote administered by a King'. Such encouragement nurtured Frederick's idealised aspirations
of becoming a ruler of the Enlightenment. His idealism temporarily overshadowed his shrewd grasp of political reality, but it did not entirely obscure
it, as the completed work was to show. Already a sceptic in his early years,
Frederick never lost the ability to curb his imagination. Friedrich Meinecke
suggests that inherent in Frederick was a dualism between Machiavellianism and
anti-Machiavellianism, but this seems too simplistic a hypothesis. Frederick's
anti-Machiavellianism held sway only over the intellectual side of his nature;
his Machiavellianism, on the other hand, was an instinctive ability, permanently at odds with the contemporary ideological forces which fascinated him
but could not always be allowed to influence his actions.

Those who interpreted the *Anti-Machiavel*, published soon after Frederick's
accession, as the deceptive stratagem of a ruler already resolved upon aggressive, expansionistic policies failed to grasp its true meaning. The *Anti-Machiavel*

had two faces. Behind the sparkling, rhetorical condemnation of Machiavelli's corrupt and criminal advice lie certain qualifications and reservations which form the basis of a highly realistic and concrete plan of government. Frederick, the enlightened idealist, commends the person who could banish Machiavellianism from the face of the earth (*détruire entièrement le machiavellisme dans le monde*). He ventures to wake the public from its false illusions of the practice of politics. Politics was nothing more than the combined wisdom of the ruler, not, as widely believed, the domain of villainy and injustice. It was the ruler's task to eliminate falsehood and subterfuge from political agreements and to uphold honour and the rule of law. Order, in other words, was not part of a ruler's inheritance but something which had to be established anew. It would, however, be appropriate for the populace to content itself with its sovereign's efforts to pursue this goal. Those rulers who most distanced themselves from Machiavelli had the greatest chance of success. Not all passages express such scepticism, indeed on several occasions Frederick holds up as attainable the ideal of a Prince imbued with humanitarianism and righteousness. His model here is less Henry IV, and more Fénelon's *Télémaque*, with its portrait of an idealised monarch. It is he who becomes the exemplary ruler to counteract Machiavelli's claims for Cesare Borgia. Télémaque is the classic '*honnête homme*', a man of principles, fairness and justness, the incarnation of all human virtues. Frederick goes so far as to compare him to an angel, consequently characterising Borgia as a demon in order to make the distinction even clearer. This, of course, is purely a literary device. Frederick was quite aware that such analogies stretched the truth beyond its limits. What indeed was virtue? Here a well-developed rationalism can be detected in Frederick's thinking: 'Qui dit la vertu, dit la raison'. Reason invites morality in political acts.

Not without difficulty did Frederick attempt to prove that only an absolute monarch was in a position to guide his state according to the principles of *raison d'état*. Although republicanism had many sympathisers, the early Enlightenment, even Voltaire himself, tended to emphasise the advantages of an enlightened monarchy. Frederick recognised the paradox inherent in the act of a freeborn people subjugating themselves to the rule of a single person, but claims it to be a proven fact that republics were inevitably doomed to failure and would always degenerate into despotism. It would probably be impossible to convince a republican that monarchical institutions were the best form of government unless a King could be found who was prepared to fulfil his duty ('*de remplir son devoir*'); his royal will and power would lend reality to his good intentions. But where was such a phoenix of a King to be found? Frederick, at this point, speaks of a strange 'metaphysical monarchy', a paradise on earth. The reality of despotism transforms this earth to a veritable hell. The author of the *Anti-Machiavel* possessed no experience of government as yet, but already he perceived himself becoming intellectually embroiled in the contradictions inherent in a system of hereditary monarchy. The theory of the '*premier domestique*', the first servant of the state, initially set out at the very beginning of the book, only masks the sharp and irreconcilable contrast between the enlightened law of nature and legitimate monarchy. It would only be acceptable if the ruler took as his most important duty the maintenance of law and order, the well-being of his subjects and the spread of humanitarianism.

Frederick, therefore, even when upholding the principles of enlightened policies against the Machiavellian monster, was no utopian. He emerges as even less of an idealist when one follows the many hidden or even explicit political theories which turned the *Anti-Machiavel* from an idealistic diatribe into something of a political manifesto for the future King of Prussia. This has often been overlooked, a mistake committed by many of Frederick's own contemporaries. In chapter twenty-two, a discussion concerning a ruler's advisers leads Frederick to emphasise his preference for a monarch who sees with his own eyes and holds the reins of government in his own hands, rather than one who allows himself to be led by those who have gained influence over him. On the ruler alone rests the weight of his state, as the world rests on Atlas's shoulders. He deals with internal affairs as he does with external matters. All decrees, laws and edicts emanate from him. In one person he incorporates the roles of supreme judge, commander-in-chief of the armed forces and intendant-general of finance; all that is of significance to the state lies in his grasp. Ministers are only tools in his hands. Frederick's earlier reservations about despotism are at this point forgotten. Without doubt, he is describing here the office of King as he envisaged it for himself.

Frederick's acknowledgement of the rights and duties of a ruler as commander-in-chief is even clearer. Here he agrees wholeheartedly with Machiavelli (*'je me range entièrement du sentiment de Machiavel'*). By the mid-eighteenth century it was by no means the accepted norm for the sovereign to be anything more than the nominal head of the military. The Prussia in which Frederick grew up was an exception to this pattern, although his father's reign witnessed no occasion on which the monarch actually commanded on campaign. Frederick transformed the theory into a personal programme. He demanded not only that the sovereign be present at battles, but also that he himself should lead his men: it was his task to determine the course of the battle and it was his presence that should motivate the rank-and-file. He must set a shining example of how to show disdain in the face of danger and even death, since duty, honour and everlasting glory demanded it. 'What glory awaits the Prince who, with presence of mind, wisdom and valour, protects his state from invasion, triumphs boldly over all his enemies' aggression and, through steadfastness, level-headedness and tactical virtue, asserts himself against unjust attacks.' These sentences do not stem from contemporary experience; nowhere, except perhaps in Charles XII of Sweden, can an example of such a soldier-king be found, not in Louis XIV's France nor in Charles VI's Austria where Prince Eugene of Savoy assumed the role of supreme military leader. Carried along by boundless enthusiasm, Frederick is describing here the blueprint for his own future, and it matters little to him that this means voicing his agreement with Machiavelli.

Such impatient expectation can also be found at other points of his treatise. In the penultimate chapter, the Crown Prince discusses the role played by luck in history and speaks of the two characteristics essential in order to harness luck: bold liveliness (*'vivacité hardie'*) and thoughtful deliberation (*'lenteur circonspecte'*). There are times which lend themselves to the conquistador's quest for glory; such *'hommes hardis et entreprenants'* are born to act and to bring about extraordinary changes in the world. They are fully aware of the risks they run, and they know that fortune favours the brave and that they will not fail and be forgotten.

A close look at the arguments set out in the *Anti-Machiavel* highlights many details of contemporary and future Prussian policies. Thus, Frederick concedes that Machiavelli is right to reject a mercenary army, and argues for a mixture of native and foreign troops if a state does not possess a sufficiently large population to supply the needs of its military forces. He lays down precise rules to maintain the loyalty of unreliable mercenaries and to maintain order, discipline and allegiance. The number of foreigners should not exceed the number of native soldiers. The accumulation of a war treasury was also deemed advisable, as well as the maintenance of strong military discipline. Within this treatise excoriating Machiavellianism, the outlines of the future Prussian military state are clearly discernible.

The ambiguity of the *Anti-Machiavel* becomes even more noticeable when one examines the ethical demands which its author makes, not without pathos, on a number of occasions. This can be demonstrated by the two examples of breach of treaty obligations and just war. In chapter eighteen of *The Prince*, Machiavelli tackles the question of the extent to which a ruler was bound to keep his word. Hardly anywhere else does Frederick show such moral outrage as in his condemnation of Machiavelli for this passage. He describes him as the vilest of human beings engaging in the corruption of virtue. He seeks to prove his moral reprehensibleness, disdain for humanity, lack of intellectual capacity and logical contradictions. Nevertheless, he is ultimately forced to admit that certain difficult situations (*'nécessités fâcheuses'*) at times left the ruler no option but to break his agreements and alliances. In such cases, he must act correctly and inform his allies at once, always provided that the welfare of his subjects and the scale of the emergency left him no alternative.

Soon after his accession, the King, through his invasion of Silesia in the closing months of 1740, was embroiled in European politics and found himself in a situation he had only theoretically described in the *Anti-Machiavel*. Frederick calculated that two things would be in his favour following the death of Charles VI, the last male Habsburg: firstly, that the accession to the throne of a female, Maria Theresa, would, despite its legitimacy, meet with resistance, and force other states such as Bavaria and Saxony to intervene; and, secondly, that the international or, rather, global Anglo–French conflict would draw one of these powers to his side. This assessment proved correct: in June 1741, France concluded an alliance with him, Bavaria made up a third signatory, and Spain subsequently became a fourth. The Silesian conflict grew into a European war fought over Austria's continuing existence. But the expected collapse of the Habsburg Monarchy did not come about. Soon the divergence of aims of Prussia, on the one hand, and France and Bavaria, on the other, became apparent. His aim was the acquisition of Silesia, wrote Frederick in his *History of my own Times (Histoire de mon temps)*, while the allies harboured quite distinct and more far-reaching intentions, above all the destruction of Austria. In his political imagination, Frederick went as far as to suggest that France had wanted to construct four principalities on the ruins of the Habsburg Monarchy, each providing a political balance for the other with France playing the role of arbiter between them. Frederick began his tactical manoeuvring. One questionable step was the secret armistice concluded with Austria at Klein-Schnellendorf and, finally, in June 1742, the dissolution of his alliance with France through the Peace of Breslau, which recognised his acquisition of Silesia.

What had taken place was a blatant breach of a solemn agreement in a treaty, as a result of which Frederick found himself following Machiavellian paths. He suffered heavily for it, as contemporaries were quick to point out. The King's letters to Voltaire sought to quell the storm which his actions had unleashed against him in Paris. Never, he suggested, should the philosopher Voltaire be swayed by public opinion. King and philosopher exchanged verses; Frederick sent the poet a long poem entitled 'The Verdicts which the Public pronounce upon those encumbered with the unhappy task of being Politicians', an attempt to defend the apparent wrongdoings of all politicians, but in reality a defence of his own actions. He repeated his warning against public opinion, responding to appearances and able to indulge in easy, superficial judgements. Above all, he attempted to expose the guiding force behind French policy, the almost ninety-year-old Cardinal Fleury, as the real Machiavellian; he, the King, did not deserve this reproach directed at him from many sides; he was the victim of misinterpretation: '*Tout paraît découvert, Dieu! quel dehors trompeur! Ceux qu'on croit opprimés, sont eux les oppresseurs*' (How we were mistaken by appearances, those who seemed to be the oppressed, turned out to be the oppressors). Earlier while Crown Prince, Frederick had voiced his disdain for Fleury, Machiavelli in 'Roman purple', 'wearing the mitre'; now he saw him at the pinnacle of his evil career which only deserved the words 'deceive the deceivers' ('*trompez les trompeurs*'). It was others, then, who forced him to behave in a Machiavellian way. This continued to be Frederick's decisive argument with which he sought to quieten his own troubled conscience; the decision of 1742 and its repetition by the second peace in 1745 disturbed him more than anything else. The King consequently was not satisfied with justifying himself by merely citing circumstances beyond his control, but sought a systematic solution to the problem: when and under what circumstances is it justifiable to break an agreement?

He sought to answer this question on no fewer than three occasions: in 1742, in the introduction to the first draft of his *Histoire de mon temps*; in 1746, when this work was first revised, and in 1775 in its final version. With each of these forewords, Frederick drew closer to Machiavelli's ideas. In the first edition, a distinction is already drawn between the morality of a private individual and that of a politician, but most decisive is the King's assertion that the principal guiding force of a state is the need for aggrandisement. In the *Anti-Machiavel*, Frederick had still described this as a mistake and cited the example of the Dutch Republic as a strong minor power, comparing it to the backward expanse of Russia. It was much more in the interests of the ruler to increase his population and thus allow his state to flourish. The King's subsequent utterances, however, do not necessarily represent a change of attitude; Frederick is merely seeking to shift the blame by pointing to the other powers' obsessive aggrandisement. He thus conceals the fact that his own need to engage in power politics was only a symptom of an uncompleted phase of state-building.

The second version of the foreword, that of 1746, goes furthest towards defending the breaking of agreements. Following the two successful Silesian Wars and his own resulting neutrality, while the Austrian Succession struggle was still under way, Frederick felt he had reached the apogee of his power. He was now in a position to assert that, in general, it was preferable for a ruler to break his word than to allow his people to be ruined. In the euphoric, power-drunk thinking which these years engendered, Frederick wrote in his Political Testament of 1752: 'Machiavelli claimed that a selfless power standing between two ambitious powers was ultimately doomed to destruction. I am forced to admit that Machiavelli was right.' This decisive argument represented the rehabilitation of the man whom the author of the *Anti-Machiavel* had only a few years earlier described as a monster, the basest and vilest of human beings.

But even this was not the final response to the searching questions posed by the indefatigable Machiavelli: in his later years, following the numerous crises of the Seven Years War, Frederick renewed his attempt to systemise the unpredictability of power politics in the light of his own experiences in the international arena. Once again, he revised the introduction to the *Histoire de mon temps*, and significantly altered its emphasis. Friedrich Meinecke speaks of Frederick's personal progression as a rationalisation rather than a clarification of ethics, and this applies most aptly to the last phase of Frederick's development. Nothing remains vague: moral and ethical transgressions are no longer designated to be extreme measures to meet extreme circumstances, but are clearly justified under certain circumstances and in certain cases which are precisely laid down. Frederick notes: 'The circumstances which permit agreements to be broken are the following: firstly, when an ally fails to fulfil his treaty obligations; secondly, if he plans to deceive and leaves us with no other option but to pre-empt his planned action; thirdly, when a great power exerts its influence over us and forces us to break the contract; and lastly, when the means to continue the war have been exhausted.' The golden rule governing the conduct of all matters of state is always *raison d'état*, and Frederick goes as far as to demand that the ruler was obliged to sacrifice himself for his subjects, which in this instance can only mean that he must sacrifice his good name and reputation. The only pertinent question continues to be: is it better for a state to suffer ruin than for its ruler to break an agreement? Would anyone be so stupid as to hesitate over the answer? Only a sovereign, however, possessed the right to renege on his word, whereas a private individual, responsible only for the misfortune of one person, was not free to act in such a manner.

These arguments, then, could clearly justify all manner of political deceit and, it has to be said, they did. The decisive factor continues to be the distinction between what was understood to have been the interest of the state, public welfare and the commonweal. Frederick's experiences in the Seven Years War, when he himself suffered from the breaking of an agreement, brought about by the fall of William Pitt leading England to abandon its Prussian alliance, inevitably made him more cautious. The conclusions he drew from the course of past events were more pragmatic than normative, and he became more of a sceptic in his view of the world, his friends and his enemies. In his second Political Testament of 1768, which was not permitted to be published until the Hohenzollerns had ceased to rule Germany, this scepticism manifested itself at various points in an indisputably Machiavellian style of thought and argument. 'The ultimate means by which to conceal one's ambition', it is claimed here, 'is to feign peaceful intentions until such a time when it becomes propitious to lay one's cards on the table. All great statesmen have acted in this way.' This advice to feign virtue could have come from *The Prince* itself.

The lessons learned by the King, however, also run as follows: to proceed with the utmost caution and carefully weigh up the interests involved before concluding any alliance. He had already considered alliances to hold little merit in the *Anti-Machiavel*, their only benefit being a reduction in the number of one's enemies. 'One must follow blindly the interests of the state and ally oneself with the power whose interests at that moment correspond most closely with one's own.' This power in the post-Seven Years War period appears to Frederick to have been Russia, with whom he allied himself in 1764, although this alliance did not bring all the expected benefits. At least it secured the gain of West Prussia in the First Partition of Poland, but dependence on a power whose might he had earlier underestimated, came to represent an oppressive burden. To break with Russia was impossible, however attractive a possibility this might have seemed at times, not because moral scruples would not permit it, but because state interest would not allow it. 'Our interests dictate that it is much better to have Russia as an ally than an enemy', the 1768 Testament declares, 'since it could do us much harm from which we would be unable to recover.' In a treatise written in 1776, indeed, the opposite motivation in favour of alliances is voiced, stating that they accorded the allied signatories protection from each other: 'One of the basic rules of statecraft', wrote Frederick, 'dictates that one should seek an alliance with the one neighbouring state capable of dealing one's state the most dangerous blow. Therein lies the reason for Prussia's alliance with Russia . . .'

This, of course, runs counter to Machiavelli's advice which counselled caution in allying with a more powerful neighbour unless an extreme emergency demanded it. The two are, nevertheless, arguing on the same plane. It is no longer a confrontation between morality and calculation, but between calculation and calculation; only different perspectives led to differing conclusions.

In his treatise against *The Prince*, Frederick could make little of the final chapter in which Machiavelli exhorted the Italians to free their lands from barbarians. Instead, Frederick launches upon a discussion of the various means of conducting diplomatic negotiations and the justified reasons for embarking on war. The Crown Prince was here debating the old question of the just war. At that point he could not have been aware that this was to become the central question of his own life, but the intensity with which he deliberated upon this issue demonstrates that it was more than purely theoretical speculation. The chapter contains a number of fundamentally important sentences which highlight the tension between the humanitarian purpose of the state, as advocated by the Enlightenment, and the instruments of power politics with which this goal was to be attained. The peace and happiness of a state were the natural aims of all diplomacy. But this peace, which Frederick equates with the peace of Europe ('*la tranquillité de l'Europe*') depends above all on the maintenance of a balance of power whereby the greater might of one state is counterbalanced by an alliance between the other powers. Were this balance to be disturbed, a great revolution would result and new powers would arise on the ruins of the old states, weakened and powerless through their internal divisions. This concept clearly permitted war as a means to an end, indeed Frederick goes as far as to suggest that 'only a good war provides a lasting peace'. Humanitarianism, happiness and justice appear in the *Anti-Machiavel* as the greatest of virtues, but not as pure pacifism. Peace was the result of political action, not the expression of a cast of mind. Frederick also attempted to erect a framework of possible and permissible actions concerning war, much as he had done with the breaking of agreements. Rather than imagined cases guided by moral principles, these are descriptions of real situations; the fact that he was later to find himself in such situations lends these descriptions, when viewed with hindsight, a certain tension. They must be read with an eye on the King's own political future.

The traditional laws of the just war state that the most legitimate and least avoidable form of conflict was that of a defensive war. One step beyond this is the war occasioned by a ruler's need to defend his rights or claims. Such wars, Frederick argues, serve to maintain a global equilibrium and prevent the enslavement of peoples. The Crown Prince even ventures to argue in favour of aggressive wars when the aggression is seen as a necessary precautionary measure. These are undertaken by monarchs when the great European powers threaten to expand beyond their own borders and swallow up the whole world. Admittedly, this is a vague description of a justified offensive war, but the outlines of a situation in which the author of the *Anti-Machiavel* was to find himself some twenty years later can clearly be detected. The following sentence establishes Frederick's meaning beyond doubt: 'Better, therefore, to take the decision for war while one still has the choice between olive branch and laurels, than to wait until a declaration of war is merely a postponement of eventual enslavement and ruin.' The final form of justified war according to Frederick was that resulting from one's obligations to one's allies – however, he points out that opportunism should dictate whether or not to follow the letter of the alliance. Such a flexible stance would serve the preservation of both one's position and one's security.

This list of justified reasons for war is only an approximation of the traditional law of nations scheme, since it draws less on theoretical form than on practical eventuality. Frederick's enlightened conscience forces him to close the chapter with a warning to Kings to be aware of the pain and suffering occasioned by war. Here we find the sentence: 'Rulers who lead unjust wars are worse than tyrants.' Thus the thread of disputing Machiavelli's work was taken up once again. Frederick's own political interests and instincts led him to be concerned first with the international consequences of great power rivalry and only then with its domestic repercussions.

Among the possible justifications for war in the *Anti-Machiavel*, the maintenance of rights and claims was placed second. This, of course, could be applied directly to the decision to go to war in 1740 following Charles VI's death. In the past, Berlin had harboured hereditary claims upon large areas of Silesia, but during Frederick William's reign these had lain dormant. Prussian policy had instead concentrated upon the claims to the duchies of Jülich and Berg on the Lower Rhine. Under the young King, Silesia returned to the very top of Prussia's list of political priorities, not as a project to be pursued in the future, but as a definite, immediately realisable goal. Now, however, dynastic claims and hereditary rights were not advanced. Frederick instead emphasised the opportunity which presented itself. Initial discussions with his advisors, after news arrived of Charles VI's death, identified Silesia as the best target for Prussian aggrandisement. Frederick's arguments for this annexation rested upon the circumstances which presented themselves (*bienséance*), supported by the strategic and economic advantages which the territories could bring to Prussia, which would gain control over the whole length of the river Oder.

The King was clearly less well informed about the legal basis of Hohenzollern claims to the Silesian lands, and it would appear that these were of little interest to him. Irritated by the efforts of his minister, Podewils, to explain the intricacies of the legal situation, he replied: 'Legal questions are the province of ministers; the time has come to act secretly; orders have already gone out to the troops.' Any discussion of the problems of justifying Prussia's claim before public opinion was not merely postponed but actually prevented, and priority given to military action. The special diplomatic mission which was sent to Vienna, after military operations had begun, was also given no instructions about the legal and treaty basis of Prussia's claim to Silesia. Instead these instructions articulated a quite false concern for the 'genuine well-being of the Austrian Monarchy, now reduced to sad ruins (*des tristes débris*) of its former glory'.

While deliberating on his course of action, the King asked himself the following question, as an exercise in statesmanly sophistry: 'I place before you a problem to solve. When one has the advantage, should one use it or not? I am ready with my troops and everything else; if I do not make use of this, I turn my back on good fortune; if I do, then it will be said that I exploited unfairly the advantage which I had over my neighbour.' According to this, a calculation of one's power before taking political action was alone decisive, the question being simply whether one should enter into negotiations before or after seizure of the disputed territories. The King clearly preferred military action at the outset, something which even Louis XIV with all his ruthlessness had not dared to do, and something which obviously contravened the unwritten code of conduct of his times.

The ultimatum which Frederick presented to Vienna demanded the sanctioning by the Austrian Monarchy of a military annexation which had already taken place. Even in her precarious and weakened situation, it was something which Maria Theresa could not accept. One must not overlook, however, that behind the outward veneer of audacity lay an action of calculated rationality. The idea of destroying the Habsburg Monarchy at a time when it was extremely vulnerable clearly did not occur to Frederick. He had no intention of questioning the Pragmatic Sanction or the young Queen of Hungary's right to succeed to the Austrian throne, he merely wished to realise his own particular rights. The one was so inextricably bound up with the other, however, that such distinctions were forced, and rather appeared a pretext for his true intentions. In the historical sense, the acquisition of Silesia was only one dimension of the general crisis in which Austria became embroiled over the Pragmatic Sanction. The internationalisation of the crisis only subsequently led Frederick to seek rights and motives for the Silesian action in order to present them for foreign consumption. A handwritten mémoire dated 31 December 1740, sent to Prussia's diplomats, was the first attempt to justify before international opinion the Prussian seizure of Silesia.

To view the King of Prussia as unconcerned with right and wrong in this first decisive act of his reign, obscures the tensions inherent in his thoughts and actions. Despite the successes of 1740/41, these events left their mark on him. This is borne out by the care with which he sought to justify his decision to fight in 1756. According to his catalogue of permissible pretexts for war, the Seven Years War was a preventative war. It was better, as he himself said, to anticipate danger than to be taken by surprise (*'praevenire quam praeveniri'*).

Prussia's international position around the middle of the 1750s had changed from that of 1740. What had remained unchanged, however, was the state of cold war between England and France. In May 1756, this was transformed into open conflict by a formal declaration of war as both powers strained for control of North America and India – a conflict with much more far-reaching consequences than the power-political jockeying for position in central Europe.

As it became immersed in this global struggle, Great Britain sought to guarantee the safety of its dynastic salient in Europe, Hanover, through an agreement with Prussia. The resulting convention of Westminster (January 1756) led to the then inconceivable *rapprochement* between the Houses of Habsburg and Bourbon (First Treaty of Versailles, May 1756), which Vienna sought to use not only to regain Silesia, but also to reduce Prussia once again to the status of a second-rate power. Prussia's position was worsened even further by increasing Russian hostility resulting from the advancement of Prussian power towards its Western borders and the threat this posed to its satellite, Poland-Lithuania. The great power on Europe's eastern rim consequently moved closer to the coalition partners and indeed became the driving force behind moves to start hostilities. Only with difficulty were the bellicose ambitions of Empress Elizabeth restrained and military preparations postponed until the following year.

Frederick must indeed have feared this imminent attack by three of the continental great powers, especially since he was prone to interpret all alarming rumours as established fact. Thus he viewed Austro-Russian negotiations as evidence that a treaty had already been signed. It was suspected that Frederick was only looking for a pretext to declare war, the ultimate aim of which was to be the acquisition of Saxony. However, this was clearly not the case. In the seemingly desperate situation of 1756, it was obvious that Frederick would have preferred to avoid war if he had not perceived it as absolutely inevitable. Nevertheless, to view the King as an innocent lamb amongst wolves would also be false. He was not willing to fight a purely defensive war, nor was he satisfied with merely upholding the status quo. He continued to live by the axiom that a war was never justified unless there existed the probability of gaining new lands. This accorded with his character, always prepared for action, determined never to be at a disadvantage and unshakable in his resolve to raise Prussia to great power status. The threat posed by the mighty coalition ranged against him became the occasion, not the pretext, for his offensive against strategically and economically important Saxony. But Frederick's action transformed the loose grouping of great powers into a solid coalition: it transformed the Franco-Austrian treaty into an offensive alliance in May 1757, which Russia subsequently joined. The preventative Prussian action, therefore, had brought about the very thing Frederick had sought to avoid.

But however much developments strengthened Frederick's resolve to act, his actual conduct differed substantially from his actions in 1740. At that time he set little store by right or wrong, but now, in 1756, when once again he broke the peace, he was anxious to appear both to the contemporary world and to posterity as someone whose action had been justified. In order to throw off the yoke of aggressor, he issued a memorandum, originally drawn up in his own hand, laying out his position to those powers uninvolved in the conflict. At its heart was a precise and indisputable definition of an aggressor, a problem which continued to be debated until the Nuremburg trials following the Second World War. There was a distinction between the terms 'aggression' and 'opening of hostilities'. Aggression referred to an act of deliberate breaking of the peace by entering into, for example, offensive alliances with the purpose of creating enemies and forcing war upon them by invading their territory: 'One who can pre-empt such aggression can open hostilities, but is not the aggressor.' This is the very stuff of which disputes concerning the law of nations are composed. Frederick must take his place in the history of these disputes. He cannot be viewed as an isolated case. He merely thought through the norms of behaviour within the European state system to their most radical conclusions.

Did this heightened awareness of justified motives for bellicose action, however, stem from a deeper understanding of the legality of a situation, or was this just another form of Machiavellianism? An analysis of this question must involve a recognition of Frederick's extraordinary interest in clarifying his own legal position prior to opening hostilities. Before he acted, his envoy in Vienna conveyed three questions to the Empress Maria Theresa. In the first, of July 18, the King wondered whether the Austrian military preparations and troop movements in Bohemia and Moravia were aimed at preparing an attack on him. Maria Theresa gave a diplomatically evasive answer. His second, more urgent, question of 2 August demanded an assurance from the Empress that she had no intention of attacking him this year or in future years. Maria Theresa's reply vigorously denied the existence of an Austro-Russian offensive alliance, which Frederick was later to use as a major plank in his own defence against the charge of aggression. His third question, dated 26 August, coincided with the opening of hostilities in Saxony and took the form of an ultimatum to Vienna.

These developments have been much debated, and have been much criticised by historians who have been taken aback by them. From the military standpoint, they have been called 'an inexcusable way to act'. Frederick clearly appreciated the dilemma which confronted him, and did everything in his power not to fuel further the rumours describing him as a violator of the peace. And it was important to him personally that he believed in his own mind that he was not guilty of starting the war. As an advocate of peace, he had to prove to the world and to himself that he would only resort to arms under extreme pressure. He wanted to be sure that on this occasion it was a just war which he had been forced to conduct. At no other time did the opposing positions of two powers about to fight coincide more precisely: Maria Theresa, unshakable in her belief that she possessed the moral right to proceed against the 'wicked man' in Berlin, and Frederick, consumed by the determination not to contravene international law, as he had done in 1740.

The Seven Years War saw Frederick at the pinnacle of his historical renown. Many generations have interpreted this period as if, contrary to the hopes of the French spokesmen for the Enlightenment who, at his accession, had seen in Frederick a Prince of peace from whom the creation of a new humanitarian state could be expected, he entered history as a military hero. He himself contributed much to this image; did he not frequently range himself alongside such military leaders as Caesar, Alexander, Prince Eugene of Savoy or Turenne and claim that the only means of immortality was to clothe oneself in the glorious garb of military success? And no-one can deny that he was a military genius. But the cruel tests which fate decreed he and his subjects were to endure brought about a transformation: in place of glory, such terms as duty, honour and the well-being of the state began to appear. In Frederick's eyes, honour was inextricably bound up with the welfare of his state and with this he took an important step in the history of political thought. Honour could henceforth also mean the subordination of the ruler to the needs of the state. Only when this had been achieved was the King, who had seriously contemplated suicide after the numerous military setbacks, free to act on his own volition. The King was, however, not just identified with the state, as in the absolutism of Louis XIV, but it was expected of him in situations of dire necessity to make all personal sacrifices needed to save his state. Frederick's absolutism was enlightened not only because he pursued his goals rationally and had humanitarian intentions which he attempted, if incompletely, to put into practice at home, but principally because he did not use the state to further his personal aims; on the contrary, he allowed the state to employ him as its servant. Even the General Law Code (*Allgemeine Landrecht*), the legal codification of the Frederician state, gave expression to this 'transformation of the sovereignty of monarchy into the sovereignty of the state'.

The second element in Frederick's transformation during the course of the Seven Years War was his loss of the naiveté which characterised heroes in history. Emperor Marcus Aurelius, who fought great battles and meditated upon the emptiness of life, became his role-model, but it was first and foremost the Stoic philosopher not the military hero who attracted him, especially when luck seemed to have deserted him and he appeared to have lost the game. At times such as these, the Stoic taught him not only to endure but also gave him the strength to reassert himself.

It must not be forgotten, of course, that these transformations also represented immeasurable losses to Frederick's character. The enthusiasm of his period as Crown Prince, which had given rise to the *Anti-Machiavel*, had paled. Although Machiavelli's name was hardly mentioned, the assumption was there that his view of the world, of ingrained and ubiquitous corruption, became more and more an integral part of Frederick's political realism, which came to carry Stoic as well as cynical overtones. During the hopelessness engendered by an exhaustive and never-ending war, he produced, in 1761, 'A Letter concerning the Wickedness of Man', which, although it did not mention Machiavelli's name, was in its analysis of men and their political behaviour in almost complete agreement with the Italian. The Letter is dated 11 November 1761, and written from the Silesian town of Strehlen. It therefore follows the Prussian army's severe setback after the loss of the fortress at Schweidnitz and predates the Russian capture of Kolberg in Pomerania. At this low point of his life, the King meditated upon the corruptible nature of rulers and statesmen, and began by recalling his own intellectual beginnings when, as a naïve young man, unaware of the world and its wickedness, he had been convinced that *homo sapiens* was the best of all forms of life. At that time he was sure he would encounter only virtue and honour, while now he was forced to admit that humans were the cruellest and most bloodthirsty of all God's creations. The world and its inhabitants appear here as Machiavelli had perceived them, and the man who had once denounced Machiavelli for his views, now saw that he had pursued only illusions.

Some years before, in a similarly dire situation, in 1758, the year of the disaster at Hochkirch, Machiavelli's name had appeared once more, although letters or writings hardly ever made any mention of him. In a Letter, Frederick uses a Swiss to express his revulsion at the depravity of mankind. As a Swiss, he was in a unique position to observe the way of the world: 'All these tragic, bloody events are only a piece of theatre to me; Europe is only a magic lantern in my eyes. My only interest is for humanity.' Frederick here was over-whelmed by emotions which recall the idealism of his early years without becoming the guiding force of his actions. They continued to exist in another, internal world in Frederick's split nature, untarnished by the developments in the outside world. In this outside world, the preservation of the state above all else continued to be the first command of government, just as Machiavelli had taught. The idea that world leaders were sensible and their subjects happy was, he wrote, nothing more than a Utopian vision, much like Plato's ideal state.

This was Frederick's final word on the correlation between political ideal-ism and political reality in the interrelationship of states. In his later years, he realised that Machiavelli's view of mankind and its incompatibility with the ideals of the Enlightenment had been proven correct. The duality of his nature, imbued with the whole spectrum of enlightened absolutism, was transferred to the Prussian state upon which he was the most decisive influence. Not only did Frederick as a person have difficulty in escaping the dilemma between power politics and Enlightenment, Prussia itself, at the same time a philo-sophical and a scientific state, carried with it the duality of his legacy. Frederick's interminable balancing act between triumph and destruction was his legacy to future Prusso-German history.

CHAPTER 4

Prussia and Austria

The conquest of Silesia, carried out only a few months after his accession, was undoubtedly the most significant act of Frederick the Great's life. Its importance and repercussions have been analysed for many generations by German and non-German historians. It has been lauded, on the one hand, as the historic moment of Prussia's emergence as a great power and condemned, on the other, as a violently aggressive and morally reprehensible action. However much this event is open to widely divergent interpretations, the facts surrounding it have been established down to the last detail and new discoveries are no longer possible. In Borussian and later German nationalist historiography it has assumed almost legendary status, and it is up to the historian to dispel the myth. The opponents of Prussia and its rise to great power status, be they partisans of an Austrian-centred 'greater Germany' interpretation, or the outraged exponents of morality founded in natural law, saw the events of 1740/ 41 as an act of calculated criminality. Over two hundred years later, after the fall of Prussia and the disappearance of German Silesia, and the rise and fall of a new German dualism which rendered the Prusso-Austrian rivalry redundant, even events which have been thoroughly analysed can be reinterpreted. New questions, which even fifty years ago would not have been asked, have arisen and demand fresh answers. Old interpretations no longer accord with the present, and the demands upon history to legitimate the rights of the Prussian monarchy and the Prusso-German state are irrelevant. No historian would now interpret the past in terms of later events.

Greater historical distance gives rise to questions which, although they may not have been altogether overlooked previously, have not been accorded the historical significance they merited. What was known of the intentions of the young King who acceded to the throne on 31 May 1740? Did his accession herald radical change, as his father's had in 1713? Was the soldier-king to be replaced by a King of enlightenment and philosophy? Voltaire became the mouthpiece of the French Enlightenment, heralding the new ruler as the

'Solomon of the North: a philosopher is to become King, oh, our century certainly wished for such an event but dared not hope that it would come true. My Prince is indeed worthy of reigning over his subjects: he knows how to enlighten them.' Such words were in tune with the expectations of the wider circle of enlightened French intellectuals. Accordingly, Frederick should have begun his reign as a Prince of peace and humanity. But only a fraction of these high expectations was translated into reality. The most spectacular development was clearly the recall of the philosopher Christian Wolff, whom the young King described as 'a conqueror in the land of truth'. The intention to place him at the head of the refounded Berlin Academy was not, however, fulfilled, but Frederick did succeed in securing the French philosopher, Pierre Louis Moreau de Maupertuis, for the post and in acquiring the mathematician Leonard Euler, who was summoned from St Petersburg. Famous scholars were, at that time, almost as free as artists to move wherever they wished. Other developments, too, suggested that the new administration would vigorously pursue its encouragement of the arts and sciences: the plan, soon to be realised, to build a new opera house and engage artists from around the world, for example. Measures such as the abolition of torture and the first judicial reforms all raised expectations of further humanitarian initiatives. The great transformation, however, failed to take place. Frederick's companions from his Rheinsberg days, Dietrich von Keyserlingk and Karl Stephan Jordan, waited in vain for the great roles they had hoped to play. Yet the changes Frederick had introduced were fundamentally superficial. He had long before taken the decision that the importance of developing the power of the state superseded all other considerations. He did not intend to establish new systems as his father had done. Frederick was to build on the military state which Frederick William I had constructed, and to herald the second phase in its development, namely external expansion, with the intention of transforming Prussia into a major power. Voltaire's first visit to Berlin in November 1740, symbolised the meeting of two worlds: the poet saw a ruler who discussed philosophy and the arts, but in reality thought about politics and pursued goals that were shrouded in mystery. The dichotomy inherent in Frederick's character was rarely quite so starkly apparent as at this period.

Not everyone, however, viewed the young ruler with such Voltairian idealism. The more perceptive diplomats who were in a position to observe the King at close quarters long suspected that, although the advancement of the arts and sciences could be anticipated, Frederick's true desire was to achieve glory on the battlefield. On his return to Vienna from Berlin in 1737, an Austrian diplomat explained: 'His ambition is to begin with a great victory.' What really went on in the young King's head can only be surmised from occasional hints which were never precise enough for any definite conclusions to be drawn. The fact that Frederick saw Prussia as an incomplete and insecure state can already be gathered from his letter to Karl Dubislaw von Natzmer, although this was never made public. But in which direction should he expand? Frederick's attack on Silesia in the winter of 1740/41 could not have been foreseen; the Lower Rhenish territories of Jülich and Berg would surely have been a more obvious goal following his father's active efforts to acquire them. Furthermore, although old Prussian legal claims to Silesia had not been abandoned under Frederick William I, they had never been seriously considered to be part of Prussian policy.

Frederick William I's foreign policy was carefully aimed at minimising any risk and concerned itself almost exclusively with securing Prussian rights to the principalities of Jülich-Berg (after 1728, Berg alone), much as the policy of Emperor Charles VI was focused upon securing international guarantees for the Pragmatic Sanction which was to ensure his daughter Maria Theresa's succession. Both cases are examples of the old dynastic politics, the rules of which continued to dominate the international system during the first half of the eighteenth century. By 1737, it was clear that the Prussian King had failed in his enterprise in the Lower Rhine region, an enterprise in which none of the great powers, neither France nor the Empire, had wanted to see him succeed. In February 1738, France, Austria and the Maritime Powers (Britain and the Dutch Republic) agreed that the Palatine claimant should take provisional possession of Berg. Prussia continued to hope for discord between the powers, but eventually had to face the fact that its aspirations were doomed when in January 1739, France and the Emperor agreed to defend the Lower Rhine should Prussia pursue its claims militarily. Finally, the secret agreement which France's leading minister, Cardinal Fleury, concluded with Prussia in April 1739, awarding her the principality of Berg but without the important town of Düsseldorf, was of little real significance.

Crown Prince Frederick, in his last years at Rheinsberg, followed these developments closely and, although Grumbkow, Frederick William's leading advisor, failed to inform him fully of all the details, he became consumed by a feeling of indignant impotence at the apparent squandering of Prussian honour. His dark thoughts about missed opportunities and Prussia's future prospects, however, did not turn into a rebellion against his father; his reproaches were directed largely at Grumbkow, not the King. Nevertheless, by that time he had probably already abandoned hopes of a successful outcome to the affair: 'I can foresee without being a magician that our plan for Jülich-Berg has failed . . .' he wrote to Grumbkow on 20 January 1737. Sudden, decisive military action was required to secure the disputed lands. But how could such action succeed so far from the monarchy's heartlands? Clearly the agreement with France of April 1739, failed to influence Frederick's scepticism over the possibility of winning Berg through negotiation. In his *Memoirs on the History of the House of Brandenburg*, he perceived Frederick William's concessions in the affair as nothing more than signs of waning vitality (*'la perte de son activité'*).

The policies of contemporary states, both great and small, their territorial claims, agreements and disputes, were largely based on rights conferred by inheritance or treaties and often took little account of rational political or even economic utility. The results were widely scattered areas of dynastic rule such as the Holy Roman/German Empire to which the territories of the Prussian

Kings also belonged (with the obvious exception of East Prussia). The German Empire was faced by other great empires which, although stemming from similar dynastic origins, had grown together in the course of the centuries to form more integrated territorial units. The Habsburg Monarchy had significantly strengthened its position as a territorially unified great power by the reincorporation of most of Hungary at the end of the seventeenth century, but nonetheless remained an hermaphrodite with heartlands that sprawled across Central Europe and outlying possessions – on the Upper Rhine, in the Italian Peninsula and in the Southern Netherlands – scattered across Europe. The young Crown Prince undoubtedly took a keen interest in the political machinations of the great powers and, in particular, Prussia's rivalry with Austria. How he was able to do this while subject to the restrictions imposed on him at Küstrin, where all great affairs of state were deliberately withheld from him, can only be explained by Frederick's inborn sense of power and ambition and the early identification of his personal goals with those of the Prussian state. With cold, calculated understanding, he instinctively perceived what *raison d'état* required. Such a realisation was not brought on by the humiliation of his court martial or the horror of witnessing his friend's execution. These experiences only served to awaken inherited instincts. The Crown Prince in the years after Küstrin was not the simple product of his harsh upbringing, but had rather discovered his own character during a period of terrible purgatory.

The first evidence of Frederick's political self-confidence could be found in his letter to von Natzmer in February 1732. It stems from his period of studious contemplation at Rheinsberg and was drafted around the time of the events of 1730/31. Composed as a hypothetical examination of Prussia's peculiar historical situation, it claimed that only two options were open in Berlin's future foreign policy. If it considered the preservation of peace as its greatest priority, Prussia would continue to be a state 'without internal coherence' and, in all probability, fall victim to the predatory intentions of its numerous neighbours. Only a poor statesman, therefore, would recommend a policy of upholding the status quo. As a result, the only viable alternative would be the 'progressive aggrandisement' of the state. Frederick goes on to name the possible targets of such a programme of expansion: Polish Prussia, possession of which would link up Pomerania and East Prussia, thus contributing considerably to the territorial integration of the Hohenzollern lands. Swedish Pomerania and Mecklenburg, that is to say expansion to the north, were also suggested, alongside the traditional aim of acquiring Jülich-Berg in the west. No mention is made of Silesia – as yet, it lay beyond the gaze of the young Crown Prince. Frederick shows himself full of youthful enthusiasm and vigour when contemplating his plans of conquest: 'I stride from state to state, from conquest to conquest and, like Alexander, proudly consider new worlds to conquer.' Such utterances clearly demonstrate that dynastic and hereditary considerations were only of limited importance to him. He spoke of rights only as a politician, in order to preserve established form. This heralded the relative importance of Frederick's motives, proven as fact after 1740.

The Natzmer letter advocates pure Machiavellian policies governed by *raison d'état*: 'political necessity' dictated that Prussia, 'with its peculiar geographical position', acquire the listed provinces. The objective of creating an enlightened, humanitarian state cannot yet be detected. Only traditional utterances are made about the role as ruler of the Christian Prince and the need to encourage and spread the Protestant faith. Echoing the paternalistic style of the Great Elector's government, Frederick writes: 'I wish for the Prussian state to rise from the dust in which it has lain and encourage the Protestant faith to flourish throughout Europe and the Empire so that it will become a refuge for the oppressed, a shelter for the widowed and orphaned, a support for the poor and the scourge of the unjust.' A link is thus forged between the state's internal goals and foreign expansion: only powerful states, Frederick elaborated subsequently, were in a position to do their humanitarian duty.

A widening of the Crown Prince's political vision is apparent in the years after the letter to Natzmer, which had been concerned only with possible territorial gains. In his *Considérations sur l'Etat présent du corps politique de l'Europe* completed in 1738, Frederick analyses the great powers and their policies, the 'necessities' which forced a certain course of action upon them and the actual goals which they pursued. In the years since the War of the Polish Succession (1733–35), Frederick had experienced a growing awareness of the crisis which the whole European system was experiencing: '. . . *le corps politique de l'Europe est dans une situation violente*', he wrote. The balance of power had been disturbed at around the time of the Peace of Utrecht, he thought, and thus the principal means of maintaining order had been removed. Such a highly individual interpretation of events contrives to ignore the peaceful international system which predominated in the mid-1730s, but nevertheless Frederick came to the following conclusion:

> Things cannot stay as they are; they pose great danger. If the statesmanship and wisdom of the European rulers no longer guarantees a balance of power between the great powers, the whole body politic of Europe will feel the repercussions. On the one side there is power, on the other weakness, here the desire to conquer all, there the impotence to prevent it. The most powerful dictate laws, the weaker conform to them. In brief, everything contributes to disorder and confusion. Supreme power is like a raging waterfall. It uproots all and is the cause of the most pernicious of revolutions.

Frederick repeats these thoughts in the twenty-sixth chapter of the *Anti-Machiavel*, but at that point adds that such revolutions would precipitate and facilitate the rise of new monarchies on the ruins of principalities rendered weak and feeble by their divisions.

There is little doubt that the impotent, weak state Frederick described was Prussia itself. Although he only advocated a restoration of the European equilibrium as the essential remedy for Europe's ills, Frederick's true intentions can be detected. Only European disorder and a great crisis would give Prussia the opportunity it needed. He literally wished such a crisis into being. In his

Considérations of 1738, he hints that: 'fate has decreed the moment at which France will carry out its great plans at the expense of the continued existence of the Empire. What situation could be more suited to dominating Europe?' The verdict upon France in these sentences could easily also apply to Prussia, and doubtless the Crown Prince saw Emperor Charles VI's death as the great forthcoming event which would provide him with the opportunity of over-turning the existing European political order and increasing Prussia's power, at a time when Austria languished in a critical state of disarray. One has to understand the entire European situation in order to comprehend Frederick's thoughts. His actions cannot be understood except within this context. The Silesian undertaking of 1740, however curious and provocative it may have been, was only one symptom of a greater upheaval, although it did, of course, have the effect of transforming that upheaval into a serious European crisis. In the eighteenth century, dynastic inheritance determined the fate of great em-pires. The Spanish Succession question, although almost half a century in the past, still cast a shadow over Austrian affairs after the death of the last male Habsburg. The principal aim of Charles VI's policies had been to secure inter-national recognition for the Pragmatic Sanction, and this further highlighted the importance of succession problems. Years before his death, European opinion concurred that his demise followed by Maria Theresa's accession would lead to a critical situation, not only for the Habsburg Monarchy, but also for Europe as a whole. The poor quality of the Austrian army and the chaotic state of Vienna's finances increased the risk, which Prince Eugene of Savoy had hoped to avert by building up military power and financial reserves. France's wish to weaken the Habsburg Monarchy and the continuing claims to the Habsburg crown of the Electors of Bavaria and Saxony, both married to daughters of Emperor Joseph I, seemed likely to bring about some sort of outside intervention, though no-one seemed sure on what scale. In any case, the final decision to go to war was taken not by Cardinal Fleury, though strong pressure was exerted by the anti-Austrian faction under the duc de Belle-Isle, but in Berlin.

Both political calculation and a quest for glory lay behind Frederick's decision in 1740. The King himself mentions the latter as a principal motive on a number of occasions, especially in the *Histoire de mon temps*. Most famous, however, are probably his words to the officers of the Berlin regiment about to embark on the Silesian adventure: 'Depart for your appointment with glory.' The quest for glory – as contemporaries had already established – was a vital driving force in Frederick's character, inspired by the feats of Alexander the Great, Charles XII of Sweden and Eugene of Savoy. The openness with which he admitted this is unsurpassed. Glorious adventures, however, were always held in check by what Frederick determined to be *raison d'état*. The will to increase the power of the state even in the final months of 1740 surpassed the quest for personal glory.

In the period between the Natzmer letter and the Political Testament of 1752, Frederick did not give any further indication of his plans for Prussian aggrandisement. In the final years of Frederick William I's reign, foreign policy centred exclusively on the Jülich-Berg question. The Crown Prince did not criticise this goal, only the methods by which it was pursued; never did he write or speak of possible alternatives, except perhaps when giving heavily veiled hints of the great plans he had decided upon. When the news of the Emperor's death reached him on 26 October, Frederick summoned Field Marshal Count Kurt Christoph von Schwerin and foreign minister Heinrich von Podewils to Rheinsberg for discussions. The product of this meeting was a list of the various foreign policy options open to Prussia. Drawn up by Podewils, it is here that Silesia is first mentioned: '*il faut profiter pour faire l'acquisition de la Silésie*'. It seems inconceivable that this was a spontaneous improvisation on Frederick's part, although not a single word, written or said, prior to this date would indicate anything to the contrary.

Prussian claims to Silesian territory had, in any case, existed for some time and the Duchy was never quite forgotten. Before the battle of the White Mountain in 1620, the Silesian principality of Jägerndorf – which was to remain in Austrian hands after 1742 – had been under Hohenzollern control for over a decade. It then became part of the lands of Bohemia's rebellious nobility, which were divided up after the defeat in 1620. The Prussian demands for the other Silesian principalities of Liegnitz, Brieg and Wohlau stemmed from the Elector Joachim II's alliance with the Piast of Liegnitz. These had been declared void by the King of Bohemia in 1546, but upon the death of the last Duke of Liegnitz, Brieg and Wohlau, the Great Elector had protested against this. When the Empire, threatened simultaneously on two fronts by the French and the Turks in the 1680s, had been forced to ask Brandenburg for help, the latter's reward for its military intervention had been Schwiebus. In accepting, however, the Elector renounced all further claims on Silesian lands. In a secret agreement, meanwhile, Crown Prince Frederick (later Frederick I) had arranged for the return of Schwiebus to the Empire after his father's death, a contract he honoured in 1695. The humiliation caused by this shadowy and unsatisfactory transaction was not to be forgotten. In the early years of the eighteenth century, Berlin reminded Vienna of the Silesian question on a number of occasions, as, for example, at the negotiations surrounding Charles VI's electoral capitulation in 1711, but it was never pursued and always overshadowed by Frederick William I's Lower Rhine ambitions.

Prussian historical writing has greatly exaggerated the importance of a few surviving pieces of evidence concerning Prussia's established quest for Silesian land; in reality, this was no more than one of many such plans and similar demands which littered princely politics. One document, however, stands out from the rest. In 1731 a chance find was made near Spandau of a draft project by the Great Elector for the acquisition of Silesia. Emphasis here was placed more on political than legal arguments. Any guilt about the illegality of conquests was brushed aside, and the importance of not allowing such economic advantages to go unexploited was emphasised. Purely political and strategic reasons in support of the plan were given; only references to 'God's will' and 'freeing His church from the stocks of Popery' indicate another, more traditional, religious motivation. The Great Elector was no longer speaking the language of a timid, minor ruler, able only to envisage the acquisition of new lands through marriage alliances or the traditional processes of inheritance. He was speaking as a powerful politician to whom the aggrandisement of his state had become second nature and whose future conquests were carefully planned, not left to chance.

It was Chamber President von Rochow who, on 1 November 1740, in a letter from Cleves, drew Frederick's attention to the Great Elector's plan. In his reply, Frederick acknowledged that he was already familiar with it; he had probably read it at his father's instigation while still Crown Prince. Significantly, the King was now in complete agreement with the Great Elector's plan to conquer Silesia, in spite of the patent lack of legal justification for such action. In the *Histoire de mon temps*, Silesia's position near the Prussian border is praised and the opportune link between the two territories through the Oder is mentioned. In Podewils' summary of Prussian foreign policy options following Charles VI's death, drawn up at the Rheinsberg meeting with the King and Schwerin, it is suggested that Jülich and Berg be sacrificed for the much richer prize of Silesia, which would not only round out the lands of the Prussian monarchy to form a more unified whole, but also place at the King's disposal the resources of a rich province, well endowed with people and with trade. This, it should be noted, is the only mention of Silesia's economic potential. It was clearly not the lure of increased economic resources, then, which persuaded Frederick, quite capable of including economic factors in his political calculations at other times, in favour of Silesia at the expense of Berg, even though he had first-hand experience of trade with the province during his period at Küstrin. No mention is ever made of the advanced industrialisation of the Lower Rhine and Wupper regions, where, especially during the eighteenth century, a significant iron and cloth industry had emerged. In the second chapter of his *Histoire de mon temps*, Frederick explained his abandonment of the campaign for Berg by claiming that it lay in too difficult a strategic location to attempt a conquest without incurring unacceptably high risks. Nor could Berg, of course, compare in territorial extent with Silesia, being only a tenth of its size. Such considerations may well have crossed Frederick's mind in the years before 1740.

Silesia in Hohenzollern hands could end once and for all Prussia's existence as an hermaphrodite: half Electorate, half kingdom as Frederick himself described its situation at his own accession. The acquisition of Silesia would enlarge and unify the heartlands of the monarchy, while the river Oder, with its entire length now under Prussian control, would serve as an important commercial artery. Such advantages would make all the difference. The modern European great powers had all evolved through a continuing process of territorial consolidation, France as well as Britain. This was not merely a way of enhancing political power; it also facilitated the development of a national consciousness. Germany, on the other hand, was composed of a fragmented series of territories whose very divisions, especially in the southwest, made dependence upon the Habsburgs inevitable. Although Prussia under the Great Elector had begun a process of territorial concentration in the northeast, the programme's success had been limited when compared to the advances made by neighbouring Saxony or Hanover. The impetus behind Prussia's evolution was purely the political ambition of its rulers, and it lacked either the corresponding concern with industrial development or increase in population, or any basis in a unifying national consciousness. The 1740 action, therefore, represents the culmination of a long line of radical decisions, which, although surpassing all previous enterprises in magnitude, was nevertheless not outside the traditions of the Hohenzollern state. Frederick William I, in the Political Testament of 1722 addressed to his son, articulated this tradition: 'The [Great] Elector Frederick William established the territorial basis of our House [of Hohenzollern]; my father added the royal title; I have built up the state machinery and the army. It is your duty, my dear successor, to continue the process which your ancestors have begun and to acquire those lands which God and justice know to be ours by right.'

Although territorial expansion in the age of absolutism was on the whole determined by arguments about hereditary rights, this was not to suggest that these disputes were always resolved by peaceful means. Disputed inheritances formed the basis of many of the great wars of the period, though the rights which were claimed often only served the function of providing a veneer for political ambition. Louis XIV and his advisers developed their own way of advancing France's political ambitions through largely fabricated claims to particular territories. Annexations and wars were clothed in the garb of legal disputes. This method had first been employed in the so-called War of Devolution from 1667 to 1668, in which claims to lands in the Spanish Netherlands were based on the local law of devolution which applied in Brabant. After the death of either the husband or wife of the ruling couple, the remaining spouse became the guardian of that inheritance, while ownership was transferred to the children of that union. This was Louis XIV's justification for his planned annexation of the Spanish Netherlands through his wife, Maria Theresa, the daughter of Philip IV of Spain.

Frederick, in his invasion of Silesia, however, had demonstrated that legal claims mattered less to him than military action. Even Louis XIV himself rarely dared to display such audacious radicalism: his gains in the 1680s by the so-called 'reunions' were supported by legal pretexts. As a result, Frederick's action contravened all contemporary notions of acceptable conduct. His ultimatum, demanding that Vienna sanction already completed territorial robbery, was clearly quite unacceptable to the young Maria Theresa. Frederick's demands were simple blackmail. The King of Prussia believed that he was taking a calculated risk: in the European situation of 1740 one of the two competing superpowers, France or Great Britain, was bound to take his side: 'England and France have fallen out; England would never tolerate French intervention in the affairs of the Empire, and thus each opposing state offers the possibility of a good alliance.' The only advantages which he possessed were an army which his father had built up to number around 80,000 men and a treasury containing 8 million thaler, also inherited from his father – this would be sufficient to undertake a war without having to fall back on foreign subsidies. Contrary to the procedure followed by Louis XIV, the diplomatic preparations for his action were quite inadequate and limited to some tentative enquiries which produced no results. Nonetheless, Frederick knew that Saxony and Bavaria continued to uphold their claims to the Habsburg inheritance. His 'direct action', lacking a legal basis, was to have serious repercussions. In the early negotiations with Vienna, conducted by the Prussian envoy von Borcke and *Oberhofmarschall* Gotter, legal and treaty claims were not mentioned. In the Instruction of 15 November, quite general, even inflammatory motives were given for the invasion of Silesia, such as a concern for the 'true welfare of the sad ruins of the House of Austria'. The lack of legal justification was perceived by the Austrians as a major weakness and exploited to full advantage. The Austrian secretary of state, Johann Christoph von Bartenstein, recorded the last audience he had with the Prussian envoys, and this testifies to the Prussian demands for 'the complete and total cession of all Silesia' ('*cession entière et totale de toute la Silésie*') without supporting these claims with any legal arguments. A little later this record and the refusal of the Austrians to yield was published in the newspapers; the Prussian memorandum of 31 December, containing a detailed explanation of the legal grounds for its claims, did not appear until some time later, by which point Prussian troops had already invaded Silesia.

Reinhold Koser suggests that Prussian diplomacy had committed some serious blunders and argues that a declaration of the old claims by Prussian envoys 'would have made a deep impression'. But such considerations were far from the King's mind at the outset; he had not forgotten them, but merely underestimated their importance. His political realism and inclination for spectacular action did not allow him to consider ancient rights as a possible weapon. When the old Chancellor of the University of Halle, Johann Peter von Ludewig, who had acted as Berlin's publicist when the royal title had been acquired in 1701, offered his services to the King in a letter dated 1 November, and wished to send him a list he had compiled of 'useful details of the pretensions' to the four Silesian principalities, Frederick accepted, but asked him to keep his research secret. Not until 6 January 1741 did the King receive from Podewils the complete treatise entitled 'The legal grounds for the claims of the royal House of Prussia and Brandenburg to the duchies and principalities of Jägerndorf, Liegnitz, Brieg, Wohlau and dependent territories in Silesia in 1740'. This was a laborious document which, precisely because of its length and style could have little effect. It was translated into French and Latin, and distributed through diplomatic channels. The King seemed almost unconcerned with it and does not appear to have pressed for rapid publication. When he first considered the political situation in his '*Idées sur les projets politiques à former au sujet de la mort de l'empereur'*, the question of legality was dismissed in one sentence; clearly the King lacked detailed knowledge. 'Silesia', he wrote, 'is the piece of land to which we are most entitled.' Podewils' tentative attempt to enlighten the King on the complicated legal background to the Prussian claims, was summarily rebuffed. This effectively signalled an end to all public discussion of the legal problems, while priority was given to military action.

This approach continued to govern proceedings. The military occupation of Silesia was already quite far advanced when Frederick sent a handwritten memorandum to Podewils on 29 December, outlining, for the first time, the reasons for the war (*'Raisons qui ont porté le roi à faire entrer ses troupes en Silésie'*). This document, after being thoroughly revised by Podewils, was to form the basis of the *'mémoire'* handed to foreign envoys and eventually published in the London newspapers. It was an extremely belated attempt to justify the Prussian annexation to the international community. Podewils cites the business about Schwiebus, the forced return of which had renewed Prussian claims to the Silesian lands. However, he only touches on the Austrian promise to compensate Brandenburg with a similar tract of land, should Jülich-Berg not be transferred to Prussia, in the Prusso-Austrian agreement of 1728. This was never more than a verbal agreement, Podewils points out. Instead, he emphasises that the King never intended to question the legitimacy of the Pragmatic Sanction, but only wished to realise certain rights he believed to be his. Such a distinction may well have been legally correct, but could not realistically be applied to the political circumstances of the situation. In this sense, the annexation of Silesia was inextricably bound up with the crisis into which the wrangles over the Pragmatic Sanction plunged Austria and from which she was eventually able to emerge having sacrificed Silesia in the process.

'With flags waving and music sounding, I have crossed the Rubicon', Frederick wrote to Podewils on 16 December 1740, following the Prussian entry into Silesia. These words, written during the euphoria of an extraordinary action, not only applied to present events but set the tone for his whole reign. At that moment on 16 December 1740, Frederick's fate was decided, and his historical standing, positive and negative, determined. The English historian G.P. Gooch, in his biography of Frederick, considered the seizure of Silesia and the partition of Poland to have been two of the most sensational crimes of modern history. True, Frederick's method of preferring military to diplomatic means accorded less with the practices of the eighteenth century than with the new principles of the age of Machiavelli. On the other hand, increasing references to *raison d'état* were symptomatic of political changes fostered by the Enlightenment, changes which eventually reached their zenith in the partitions of Poland. The Enlightenment imbued the practice of statecraft with humanitarian principles, the idea of equality before the law and a sense of commonweal, but it also advocated cool rationality and a power-orientated mechanism of action. The latter was clearly, although not exclusively, an important element of Frederician political thought and action. Both the power-orientated and humanitarian aspects of the state are ranged beside each other in Frederick's Prussia. He was convinced that only powerful states were capable of great humanitarian efforts and thus saw it as an unavoidable necessity to transform Prussia into a great power. The radicalism of his action, however, plunged his state and himself into the precarious situation where the danger of destruction cast an ever-present shadow.

FREDERICK IN GREAT POWER POLITICS: THE WAR OF THE
AUSTRIAN SUCCESSION

'Thus the sparks Silesia had ignited were fanned into flames which spread from state to state and soon threatened to engulf the whole of Europe.' With these words Frederick opened the chapter in his *Histoire de mon temps* dealing with the escalation and eventual integration of the Silesian War into the general European crisis brought about by Charles VI's death. The War of the Austrian Succession coincided with and became enmeshed in the global conflict between rival colonial powers, with France and Spain ranged on the one side and Great Britain on the other. The King of Prussia's Silesian undertaking was not, of course, the cause of the great war, merely the critical point at which the general tension erupted into open conflict. Frederick's demands for Silesia did not involve a challenge to the Pragmatic Sanction or Maria Theresa's right of succession; by his action, however, he encouraged those powers who did wish to dispute it. Augustus II of Saxony-Poland (the famous 'Augustus the Strong') and the Elector Charles Albert of Bavaria, both married to daughters of Emperor Joseph I, Charles VI's elder brother, had, upon marriage, abjured all claims to the Austrian inheritance, but the dictates of power politics proved stronger than any legal obligations to observe the Pragmatic Sanction. This provided for the inheritance rights of Charles VI's heirs to take precedence over those of Joseph I. The claimants to the Austrian throne, however, took the opportunity provided by the unstable political situation to try and realise their ambitions. Charles Albert looked to France, without whose support he could achieve nothing; meanwhile, he pressed his claims in Vienna by advancing more and more historical grounds in support of his position. At the same time, the Saxon Elector bided his time. The Spanish Bourbon claims to the Habsburg possessions in Northern Italy were of an entirely different calibre; these had been legally reserved for Bourbon Kings at the time of Charles V's relinquishment of the German parts of the Empire in 1521.

Austria found herself in an extremely precarious situation following Charles VI's death. The succession had been indisputably arranged in favour of the Emperor's eldest daughter, Maria Theresa, wife of the Grand Duke of Tuscany. The manifest weakness of the Habsburg Monarchy in the wake of Prince Eugene's death and the disastrous territorial losses in the war against the Turks required gargantuan efforts on the part of the young ruler to assert herself and save the territorial integrity of the Monarchy. Whether she would succeed was unclear; her political ability and strength of character had not yet been tested. She seemed to possess rather feminine character traits; few expected that she would summon the energy and will-power necessary to reign over a vast empire at such a moment of crisis. She faced, and weathered, the first test of her abilities before the Hungarian Diet, whose military help and loyalty had to be obtained if the Monarchy's continued existence was to be secured. Her success here was due not least to her ability to win people over and secure their respect and sympathy. The threatening European atmosphere following the changes of ruler, first in Prussia, then Austria and finally, after Empress Anna's death, in Russia, was ultimately broken by the emergence of two new figures who towered above the mediocrity of their royal contemporaries. On the one hand was Maria Theresa, her feminine personality governed simultaneously by strong pride and calculating realism; on the other, the King of Prussia, daringly and ambitiously striving towards power and glory, but at the same time able to control those forces within him by an ever-present rationalism. In the years of their youth, both enriched in different ways the ossified routine of late absolutist monarchical institutions. As representatives of their respective states, they faced each other with irreconcilable differences. Maria Theresa transferred this irreconcilability to the person of Frederick himself, referring to him as 'the wicked man in Berlin'. Frederick, however, never spoke without deep respect of 'the Queen of Hungary'. He only displayed personal dislike towards Maria Theresa's son, Joseph II, whose political capability he also refused to acknowledge.

Through these two rulers a dualism of two rival states emerged in German history; it was established by their differing policies, and they were clearly unaware of the historical implications of their actions. Austrian self-confidence and the traditional claims to Imperial rights clearly stood in the path of any division of power within Germany. The Queen of Bohemia and Hungary fought not only for the territorial integrity of her state, but also for the re-establishment of the traditional respect accorded her within the Empire. This she hoped would naturally result from the election of her husband, Francis Stephen of Lorraine, as Emperor. Two of the members of the electoral college, the Electors of Bavaria and Saxony, however, claimed that dignity for themselves and eventually the former was elected. Thus the succession question in Austria was combined with the problem of who would succeed to the Imperial title, and this was ranged alongside the territorial pretensions of Prussia. Frederick never wanted to appear as a contender for the Imperial throne; indeed, he rejected the acquisition of what he considered 'an empty title'. A King of Prussia must rather concentrate on conquering new provinces, the Political Testament of 1752 asserts. 'The sacrifice to vanity is only permitted when the power base has been securely established.'

When, on 24 January 1742, the House of Habsburg lost the Imperial title to the Elector Charles Albert for three years and, in the same year, relinquished all rights to Silesia in the Peace of Breslau of 11 June, the resulting wound was deep indeed. With his Silesian acquisition and possession of the greater part of one of the most important north German rivers, Frederick was nearing his goal of creating a powerful state with territorially unified heartlands, which was separated from eastern Europe by the plains of Bohemia. He moved closer to the core territories of the Austrian Monarchy with the capital, Vienna, without being able to threaten them seriously as long as Moravia stood in his path. His state became the most powerful in northern Germany, was in a position to hold in check his Guelph and Saxon neighbours, and thus created a geographically based antagonism between Prussia and Austria. The threat of a century before, during the Thirty Years War, between the Protestant north and the Catholic south re-emerged. But religious considerations no longer played an important role – the political struggle had long since overtaken them. Nevertheless, they did contribute to the ideological differences in the first German dualism. Silesia, with its mix of different races and religions, was therefore to play a very special role. Of far greater significance, however, was the difference between the two opposing states. Prussia was, in the modern sense, a much more advanced state than the Habsburg Monarchy. It was, of course, still in the process of assimilating its territories, many with their own traditions and structures, but this political and cultural unification had already been set in motion by the centralised administrative system and the large standing army, and in the course of Frederick's reign it was fully accomplished. Prussia appeared to its Austrian opponents principally as a military state, which, due to a lack of resources and crippling poverty, 'began to wage a new type of warfare, the like of which had no equal in the history of war', as a Vienna-inspired pamphlet of 1761 expressed it. It continually strove towards 'aggrandisement at the expense of foreign territories and populations'. This meant the principle prevailed that 'with force one could take all from peaceful states, regardless of religion or international law'. This new way of waging war 'was conducted with such vigour that all parts of the Empire overrun by Prussia are razed to the ground, much like the practice of the Swedish army in the Thirty Years War'. In a memorandum to Field Marshal Daun, Maria Theresa expressed her fear that 'the military basis of government' of Prussia would ultimately pose a grave danger to the whole of Europe.

Was Austro-Prussian dualism, then, principally a competition between the 'military state of Prussia' and the traditional, dynastic state of Austria, whose existence did not need to be justified by a show of power but was based on hereditary rights? Indeed, did Austria represent the very image of a legitimate and righteous power? Certainly contemporary as well as later polemic would have us believe so. Nevertheless, it should not be overlooked that in the power struggle between the two states, it was the internal structure of Prussia which exercised an influence over Austria, not vice versa. The efficiency of the Prussian administrative and military system led the Empress-Queen in 1748 to introduce a comprehensive programme of administrative reform, planned by Graf Friedrich Wilhelm von Haugwitz. It was largely based on the Prussian model and aimed at administrative centralisation as well as a limitation of the power of the provincial Estates. The *Directorium in publicis et cameralibus* gave unity to national political and financial administration and was not dissimilar to Prussia's own General Directory. Its jurisdiction encompassed all of the Monarchy except for Hungary, and reduced the rights of regional Diets to control taxation. The military reforms after 1748, however, were less effective. The establishment of a permanent Council of War in Vienna as the highest military authority only served to increase the cumbersome nature of Austrian warfare and seriously restricted the freedom of manoeuvre of Austrian commanders in the field. It thus served to highlight the ultimate superiority of the Prussian military machine, whose internal tensions between the various commanders never overshadowed the supreme authority and unifying force of the Soldier-King. The Prussian example proved more valuable to Austria in other areas: in May 1770, for example, after the conclusion of the major wars, a recruiting system similar to Prussia's Canton System was introduced. In its wars against Prussia, Austria took decisive steps towards becoming an integrated and unified state. However, it could never become the kind of state embodied in the unity of Prussia, to which the semi-independent position of Hungary was an ever-present obstacle.

The War of the Austrian Succession had been triggered by the Prussian invasion during the winter of 1740/41, despite the fact that the King of Prussia did not question the succession in Vienna. He merely wished to exploit Austria's temporary vulnerability to achieve his limited goal of acquiring Silesia. He waged a regional war, although it will always be viewed as only one dimension of a developing global crisis. Since 1739, an Anglo-Spanish, largely maritime war, known as the 'War of Jenkins' Ear', had been under way over British trading rights with Spanish colonies. France, under Fleury, at first had resisted open intervention, wishing, if at all possible, to avoid war with England, but eventually, in September 1740, shortly before Charles VI's death, a French fleet was dispatched to aid the Spanish cause. It was France, therefore, who played the crucial role of transforming the separate and local conflicts in Silesia and overseas into a continental struggle centred on the Austrian succession. Frederick did not yet have a comprehensive overview of the international situation when he embarked on his Silesian adventure in December 1740, but he was convinced that Anglo-French tensions would provide Prussia with an ally.

But things did not fall into place as easily as he hoped. He was forced to acknowledge that the game of international politics was not played mechanically according to hard and fast rules; there were too many divergent interests for clear-cut decisions to be arrived at easily. British policy concentrated primarily on its maritime and colonial priorities, but it also took account of Hanoverian interests. France's leading minister, Cardinal Fleury, was neither willing to break with Great Britain nor to risk a significant weakening of the Habsburgs. He was faced, however, by a powerful faction led by Marshal Belle-Isle advocating decisive action against Austria in a style reminiscent of the great power-political role of Louis XIV's France. Russia's attitude to the international situation was also unclear in the confusion and political strife which followed Empress Anna's death in October 1740. Russia's foreign policy did not acquire definite direction until the pro-Prussian Count Burkhard Christoph Münnich was toppled in March 1741, and then, in the following December, Peter the Great's daughter, Elizabeth, seized power. The knotty confusion of different and overlapping interests was not untangled until the Prussian army defeated the Imperial Field Marshal Wilhelm Reinhard von Neipperg at Mollwitz on 10 April 1741. This was the young King's first military victory, although he himself played only a minor part. The psychological and political repercussions, meanwhile, far out-weighed the military success. Prussia's adversaries, already moving towards a *rapprochement*, split asunder and in June 1741, France concluded a treaty with Prussia.

By the time the French crossed the Rhine in August, the Bavarian army marched into Upper Austria via Passau and the Spanish navy landed regiments on the Italian coast, Maria Theresa found herself in as desperate a plight as Frederick was himself to experience fifteen years later. The claimants to the Austrian inheritance, Saxony and Bavaria, concluded an agreement on 19 September which included a projected division of the Habsburg spoils between them. Bavarian and French armies continued their advance towards Vienna, but shortly before reaching the capital veered off towards Bohemia. On 26 November they captured Prague, where Charles Albert of Bavaria had himself crowned King of Bohemia. This marked a decisive point in the war, where all the divergent goals of the allies were laid bare. It is unclear whether it was the mistaken opinion of the French, as Frederick later wrote, which led them to fear that with the possible conquest of Vienna the Elector of Bavaria could become overmighty, or the Bavarian fear that Saxony could conquer Bohemia and pre-empt her own desire for these coveted gains. In any case, Frederick now believed the moment to be right to distance himself from these developments and bring peace to Silesia: on 9 October 1741 he concluded a secret armistice with the Austrian commander Neipperg – henceforth known as the Protocol of Klein-Schnellendorf – which granted him Silesia and freed the Austrian troops for the defence of Vienna.

The agreement bound the King to secrecy, which from the outset he must have known that he would break. His promise was soon forgotten and once again he joined the allied cause. For the first time he entered into the murky world of Machiavellian tactics and political unpredictability, the only explanation for which seems to be that he alone pursued a clear goal – the acquisition of Silesia. He made all other considerations secondary to this, while military weakness and lack of political direction ultimately led to the failure of the allied cause. Charles Albert of Bavaria certainly secured election as Emperor on 24 January 1742, but his own lands were lost to Austria when Habsburg troops occupied Munich in February. Frederick was finally persuaded by the Saxons to take part in a campaign to capture Moravia, a strategically important area which protected Vienna to the east and which had always been a stumbling block for him. Here, at Chotusitz in May 1742, he defeated Charles of

Lorraine and, with British mediation, concluded a peace which yielded the whole of Silesia, except for Jägerndorf. The Breslau preliminaries of 11 June were followed on 28 July 1742 by the final peace treaty of Berlin.

The separate Peace of Breslau/Berlin constituted a blatant breach of treaty obligations on Frederick's part. The alliance with France, of course, had already become a considerable burden to him since her military ineptitude had been more of a hindrance than a help. Nevertheless, no amount of logical realism could dispel the King's pangs of moral guilt. At the time of his attack on Silesia, thoughts of injustice were far from his mind, but now, two years later, he was faced by decisions which he had only ever encountered theoretically in the *Anti-Machiavel*. The storm of protest in Paris left him relatively unmoved. To Voltaire he deliberately played down his inner disquiet and in a letter dated 25 July 1742, commented ironically that he compared a treaty to a marriage and believed that when the husband possessed concrete evidence of his wife's infidelity he was quite at liberty to seek a divorce. The true depth of feeling which his decision engendered, however, can be gleaned from the first draft of his introduction to the *Histoire de mon temps*, written in the same year, 1742. It was to be revised twice, in 1746 and 1775. This foreword clearly reveals his frame of mind at the time, having been 'swept into the raging current of great European politics' and placed before the terrible decision 'of whether to sacrifice his people or to break his word'. The art of statecraft, he confessed, was often the very opposite of private morality. 'The morality of rulers was based on the inexorable force of ambition which had to be sacrificed at any price. The history of every state, whether kingdom or republic, supports this theory, and hence political treaties and agreements were just as easily broken as they were concluded. The only difference was that the politics of smaller states tended to be somewhat more timid than that of the larger states.'

Frederick did not aim to defend this kind of statecraft; it had been purely a matter of practice through the ages right up to the present, and he felt himself bound to follow the established practices of rulers. Although he followed custom, his heart was not depraved. Rarely did Frederick comment quite so honestly; one feels that the experiences of the first two years of his reign caused him a great deal of inner turmoil. If the argument that he merely conformed to existing princely practices was correct, then it applied to his actions from the very first hour of his accession, that is even to the time when he lacked any experience of great power politics. What Frederick was proposing was more of a justification to his own conscience as the defender of high ideals, humanitarianism and equity, rather than a justification to his contemporaries and posterity.

The fact that the agreement with Austria was only an interim peace in the struggle over Silesia was hardly surprising. Vienna's determination not to sanction the final abandonment of lands which were valuable economically and served both as geographic barriers for Bohemia and Moravia and as a bridge to Poland, was only to be expected. In the meantime, the War of the

Austrian Succession had assumed quite different dimensions, extending to the New World as well as to areas in the Mediterranean. Silesia was not even at the centre of this war, being merely a peripheral issue, although eventually for Maria Theresa and her advisers it began to symbolise the enduring Austrian will and became a central element in the preservation of the territorial integrity of the Habsburg Monarchy. Frederick rightly viewed the Peace of Breslau as little more than an armistice for the Austrians; indeed, he went as far as evaluating all intelligence from this perspective. To all the political crises which followed his 1740 enterprise, he reacted in the same way: all suspicion became reality, all dangers were painted in the blackest possible colours, spurring him into action. This gained him superiority over his hesitant enemies or allies, but also plunged him into dangerous undertakings which led him to the very edge of destruction. In the years after 1742, he made significant advances in acquiring the art of restraint, an art he had almost forgotten in the victorious euphoria which followed his first conquest. It was clearly very difficult to maintain neutrality in a continuing war being fought over the future shape of Germany and the continued existence of the Habsburg Monarchy. The evershifting power constellations held his continued attention, although frequently he only had fragmentary evidence at his disposal. There were, however, clear signs of power shifts and a general change of direction. Sir Robert Walpole's fall in London in February 1742, and the emergence of a pro-Austrian faction within the British government led by John, Lord Carteret, determined upon military intervention on the continent; Cardinal Fleury's death on 29 January 1743 ended an era of French international politics where for seventeen years the outward semblance of might was mirrored by internal weakness and decay; in Russia the seizure of power by the Empress Elizabeth, led to a change of direction in foreign policy, facilitated by the replacement of pro-Prussian figures such as Count Münnich and their exile to Siberia.

One of the most decisive new developments in continental politics was the appearance of the British 'Pragmatic Army' which on 27 June 1743, defeated the French at Dettingen on the river Main. Once again Bavaria, the possession of Emperor Charles VII, fell into Austrian hands. In this dangerous situation Frederick interpreted his main political goal to be the preservation of the Wittelsbach Imperial crown. In a characteristic memorandum of 27 September 1743, he attempted to analyse the political situation facing him and its possible consequences. He concluded that the paramount objective of his future policy was the absolute necessity of securing European peace on Prussian terms: 'In brief, Prussia must secure a peace on its own terms, firstly that the acquisition of Silesia be guaranteed by all the European powers, secondly to enlist the German Princes and the Empire to her cause, and thirdly to snatch the prize of arranging a peace settlement from the hands of the King of England . . .'. The last point was dictated by the threat of the Pragmatic Army advancing through southern Germany. The first objective, a general guarantee for the possession of Silesia, remained the basis of his policy, which concentrated above all on securing Prussian interests. The second laid the foundation for a political strategy similar to the *Fürstenbund* (League of Princes) of 1785, which sought to balance the absence of an alliance with a European power by a strong Imperial union within Germany.

On both occasions, 1743 and 1785, this resulted in failure. Prussia only became a great power by distancing itself, although never formally, from the Empire; it could never place itself at the head of Imperial politics, whatever form it adopted. This was a contradiction in terms. Ever since Frederick had decided to lend his support to the Wittelsbach Emperor, he had embarked on this course of action. He had to attempt to secure for the increasingly helpless Emperor Charles VII, exiled from his lands and residing in Frankfurt, a secure territorial base which extended beyond Bavaria itself. After hopes of a continued occupation of Bohemia or of other territorial gains were dashed, however, this clearly proved an impossible goal. The *raison d'être* of rulers, as Frederick viewed it, the principle of aggrandisement, could not be practised within the archaic structure of the Empire without destroying it completely. Until 1743 this had been the basis of his policies. By 1744, Frederick's emphasis had shifted to trying to bring about an association of the Circles of the Empire. He attempted to recruit the south German territorial rulers in particular, and combined this idea with the surprising plan of using the association as a means of developing an Imperial army under the permanent leadership of the King of Prussia. The concept had already been outlined in a memorandum of September 1743: France had to be won over to grant subsidies (which were to be in the Emperor's name) to various Imperial rulers, to the Palatinate, Hesse, Württemberg and Gotha. He, the King, could then act as honest broker between the warring factions and force the King of Great Britain and the Queen of Hungary to accept peace terms dictated by him. The Dutch would follow the Empire, and 'the House of Prussia would be the arbiter of an arrangement which would stabilise the situation in Europe for quite some time'. These were nothing more than euphoric hopes, the kind which often clouded the King's judgement. They were not an attempt to secure a reform of the Empire through Prussian hegemony and so analogous to Berlin's German policy in the next century, but merely aimed at securing Prussia's security through the acquisition of Silesia, an impossibility within the framework of traditional Imperial politics. The idea that particular rulers who were to form part of the Imperial army should be subsidised by France was passed over in silence.

It was more Frederick's inner disquiet and impatience than the ostensible goals of his enemies that drove him to seek an alliance with France. On 5 June 1744, his confidant, Count Friedrich Rudolph von Rothenburg, signed the treaty in Paris, the main aim of which was the acquisition of Bohemia for Emperor Charles VII, whose dwindling authority was thus to be restored. Frederick's own objectives were limited to some Moravian and Bohemian border territories. The Second Silesian War, as this episode of the wider War of the Austrian Succession has been labelled, began politically at precisely the moment at which the first had ended. From the Prussian King's point of view the crisis had merely been postponed; the sole benefit the interlude had brought him was a breathing space which allowed him to increase his army to 140,000 men and allow a period of recovery, strengthen his Silesian fortifications and retrain his cavalry following their poor performance against the Austrians. If one can classify any of Frederick's military expeditions as a failure, it must surely have been the opening of this Second Silesian War, although it was the final outcome of this very war which established beyond doubt the glorious military reputation of Prussia's King.

The military struggle of the Second Silesian War was largely characterised by the failure of great plans, rather than by a series of defeats. The core of the new alliance with France, according to Leopold von Ranke, was the plan for a major campaign: 'He lived with new designs constantly on his mind.' To Frederick, military cooperation with the French was of the utmost import-ance, as their intended task was to push back the advancing Austrians as far as Alsace or even the outlying areas of Lorraine and to reconquer Bavaria. These alterations to the military plans were the first result of Frederick's re-entry into the war. He himself was to advance through Saxon territory into Bohe-mia in three columns and to negotiate for troops from the army of the Empire with the ultimate aim of re-establishing the Emperor Charles VII's authority. The advance to Prague succeeded as easily as the rapid capture of the city. After the Prussian army had taken the outlying fortresses of Budweis and Tabor, Bohemia seemed to lie at its feet. Frederick had, thus, 'carried his undertaking to the borders of Austria', and was in a position 'to place a foot on the Austrians' throat'. In other words, a decisive battle would put paid to his Habsburg opponent. Frederick was seldom so determined to fight, indeed lusting after a battle, and seldom had he miscalculated so badly. The great pan-European campaign soon proved to be a chimera. The French and Imper-ial troops never advanced far enough to pose a serious threat to the Austrians. Prince Charles of Lorraine as commander-in-chief of the Habsburg army quickly realised that he had to commit his army against the Prussian forces and take advantage of their exposed position to sever their supply lines. The pro-Habsburg Saxon forces proved an invaluable asset in this. At the moment when Frederick had decided upon battle, his opponent refused to join the fray. Prussia's King had unwittingly fallen into a trap, and found himself in the midst of hostile territory with supplies running out and, equally damaging, with insufficient information about his enemies' movements. The Bohemian adventure of 1744, therefore, ended not with defeat in battle but with a failed campaign: the Prussian army was forced to abandon Bohemia, including Prague. The retreat to Silesia amidst the onset of winter and with insufficient supplies, led to mass desertion and came close to a catastrophe.

Throughout his life the Bohemian campaign remained a trauma of major proportions for Frederick. His newly acquired glorious reputation as military leader and King had been at stake and was nearly lost; his major goals within the German political arena had not been realised: Bohemia remained firmly in Maria Theresa's hands. On 20 January 1745, the unexpected news of Emperor

Charles VII's death dashed all hopes of a non-Habsburg Empire dominated by Prussia and France. Politically and militarily Frederick's principal aim became the preservation of Silesia, where Maria Theresa had already proclaimed that all inhabitants were freed from any obligations to the heretic King. Undoubtedly, however, the experience of 1744 left a lasting effect on Frederick's strategic calculations. In his own writings, he was never as self-critical about any other event as the failed Bohemian campaign. 'No general', he wrote in the *Histoire de mon temps*, 'committed more errors in this campaign than the King.' He goes on to list all of them: the lack of sufficient supplies in the magazines; the faulty assessment of the attitude of Saxony, whose ruler should have been forced to take sides or have his army smashed in battle; the mistaken advance on Budweis and Tabor, although this may have been the brainchild of the French Marshal Belle-Isle. The areas in which the King castigated himself were those in which he praised his opponents, in particular the Austrian General Otto Ferdinand, Count Traun, Prince Charles of Lorraine's adviser, whose conduct he lauded as a masterpiece of warfare, which should be studied and emulated by any soldier who aspired to military success. He concluded with the interesting sentence: 'As the King himself has had to admit, he looked upon this campaign as his school of war and upon Traun as his teacher.'

The King entered the example of the Bohemian campaign of 1744 into his *General Principles of War and their Application to Tactics and the Discipline of Prussian Troops*, composed in 1748 shortly after the formal ending of the Second Silesian War. This discourse is peppered with the traces of experiences learned by the King at that time. In it, all proposed campaigns entailing long advances were deemed 'badly designed'. A practicable plan was to be preferred to a glittering one. 'My experience has shown that Bohemia is easily conquered, but difficult to dominate. Those who wish to subjugate Bohemia will delude themselves each time they take their war there.' The Bohemian experience is dissected down to the last detail of tactical warfare. In the chapter entitled 'War on one's own soil, on neutral territory and on enemy soil', the King returns to the peculiar situation of Bohemia: there, as in Moravia, one must seek to wage a limited war. 'One must never aim to win over the population . . . the landowners are all traitors, however favourably disposed towards you they might appear. The same applies to the clergy and administrators since their interests are inextricably bound up with the House of Austria. Personal interest is always the driving force of men's actions and one can never trust them when their interests do not coincide with one's own.' These may well be the King's superficial observations upon the eighteenth-century Bohemian population, but they were undoubtedly general impressions gained by Frederick during the Second Silesian War. In the *Histoire de mon temps*, he varied these injunctions slightly by warning against religious prejudice which 'could induce in a stupid as well as superstitious people an insurmountable hatred of Prussia'.

The 1744 campaign left a significant imprint on Frederick's future tactical and strategic thinking. The strategic plans of the Seven Years War must always be viewed in the light of the 1744 experience: hence the abstention from advances which would involve the occupation of Prague or Olmütz, an abstention which severely limited Frederick's freedom of manoeuvre but which allowed him to act with incredible speed and decisiveness. In his old age, he once again toyed with great military plans, but these remained theoretical games and were never translated into reality.

The failure of the Bohemian campaign can be ascribed largely to the Austrian command's refusal to give Frederick the opportunity of battle. Its determined conduct of a war of manoeuvre, which made a decisive engagement impossible, was designed to exhaust the King and force him to retreat from Bohemia. Frederick had correctly interpreted the strategy being employed against him and noted it in a historic report: 'The King wishes to engage in battle before his munitions reserves are exhausted. A great victory would be to his advantage, but not to the Austrians and therefore they carefully avoid him.' In the twenty-sixth chapter of the *General Principles*, Frederick reflected upon the political and military functions of battles: 'Battles decide the fate of states', he wrote, 'those who conduct wars bring about such decisions.' But he elaborated on this generalisation by warning military commanders against ever entering into conflict without pursuing an important goal. Were one forced into war, one must accept the consequences of one's mistakes and allow the enemy to dictate the terms for battle. The King continued: 'You see that I do not eulogise my own warfare. Of the five battles into which I delivered my troops, only three had been planned by me.' Frederick here has in mind mainly the campaign of 1745, and specifically mentions the battles of Chotusitz (fought in 1742), Hohenfriedberg and Kesselsdorf; while the battles of Mollwitz (1741) and Soor (1745) had been fought on the initiative of his enemies. Even to examine the proper function of battles was a form of self-criticism, and the King drew up such a list 'so that my officers can learn from my mistakes and at the same time be made aware of the fact that I intend to improve'.

The following list of five valid reasons to engage in battle, however, is not too helpful to an analysis of strategic correlation; rather it was a general description of situations from which various strategic constellations could arise – of which, incidentally, not one applied to Frederick's own position in occupied Bohemia: the attempt to lift the siege of a fortress; the removal of an enemy from a province occupied by him; the advance into enemy territory; the siege of an important town or city and, finally, 'to break the stubbornness of the enemy if he is unwilling to conclude a peace'. The only valid ground rule for his strategic theory was that 'our wars should be kept short and lively', although this was to be totally negated by the Seven Years War. The principle of a limited war was more or less an unwritten law for Prussian warfare. The retreat of 1744 gave Frederick a foretaste of the dangers that lay before him in a long, drawn out conflict: 'A long war', he wrote, 'destroys our discipline bit by bit, depopulates our territory and exhausts our supplies.' According to this theory, the King, after the Bohemian débâcle, must take the initiative in battle. Rarely did he have the freedom of action that presented itself in the spring of 1745, when not only possession of Silesia, but also Prussia's position as a great power was at stake. The letters written from the Silesian headquarters in April and May to Podewils, the rather more cautious foreign minister in Berlin, are filled with almost alarming determination to act: 'I admit to playing a dangerous game, and if all evil in this world takes this opportunity to range against me, I am lost. But I can take no other course of action. Of all the means of proceeding at my disposal in my present situation, a battle is my only option. This course of action will decide the fate of the wounded in a few hours.' Battle was, therefore, not a remedy, but a last resort.

Listening closely to the man who had earlier termed himself a philosopher and who, in a matter of months, lost two of his closest friends (Karl Stephan Jordan on 29 May and August Dietrich, Freiherr von Keyserlingk on 13 August), one can perceive that he had rearranged the order of the values according to which he would act. He still lauded the code of honour of the noble military caste, but now associated it with the self-determination of a state whose creator he saw himself to be and with which he totally identified himself. '*Le salut de la patrie*' and '*la gloire de la maison*' became interchangeable. He believed he had played his part in achieving glory and aggrandisement for his House and dynasty, or at least had done everything to prevent its downfall. His model for such a stance was Maria Theresa: 'that woman did not lose heart despite her desperate situation' when her enemies stood at the gates of Vienna and her most precious provinces had been overrun – an interesting documentation of the similar ethical and political norms of two diametrically opposed characters who were nonetheless both trapped in an eighteenth-century way of thinking. What was missing here in Frederick's first crisis as statesman and military leader was, on the one hand, mention of the term 'duty' and, on the other, an indication of the possible escape that suicide offered in case of great catastrophe. Optimism still predominated in the thirty-three-year-old King; the shadow of death and destruction had not yet fallen on his hopes of attaining glory and success. In the interval between his statements of 1745 and 1759, many ideals would be shattered.

By the spring of 1745, the King of Prussia had not only experienced a disastrous campaign but the overall European situation had deteriorated. Emperor Charles VII's death in January 1745, inaugurated an entirely new era. Vienna's fundamental policy had been that as long as Silesia could not be won back, Bavaria should be conquered as an equivalent. In one stroke, this would destroy both the territorial basis for a Wittelsbach *Imperium* and close the door to any further claimant to the Imperial crown. The price for this was the continuing conflict with France, although it soon became clear that the French war effort was half-hearted, at least in southern Germany. The driving force behind an energetic advance against Austria with Prussian cooperation, Marshal Belle-Isle, had become a prisoner of war in the Hanover area in December 1744. Only Marshal Maurice de Saxe, the pro-Frederician bastard son of

Augustus the Strong, won some important victories against the British on Flanders' battlefields such as that at Fontenoy in May 1745.

In the aftermath of Emperor Charles' death, Viennese foreign policy changed direction and sought a settlement (*Ausgleich*) with Bavaria, which, by the Peace of Füssen of 22 April 1745, thanks to substantial Austrian concessions, secured a return to the status quo of 1741. The young Elector, Maximilian Joseph, was restored to all his lands and, in return, agreed to cast the Bavarian vote for the election as Emperor of Maria Theresa's husband, Grand Duke Francis Stephen of Tuscany. In the great game of power politics, interests and options now became confused, as the global conflict between France, Spain and Great Britain became interwoven with the continental struggle over the survival of the Austrian Monarchy. France was drawn into both spheres of conflict, as was Great Britain, tied by dynastic links to Hanover and threatened both by French advances in the Netherlands and the landing in Scotland of the Young Pretender. Little Prussia could no longer expect foreign aid, and attempted to gain a breathing space by requesting mediation in London and support from Russia. When both had failed, Frederick found himself in a position which left him no option but to resort to arms. He gained a first victory at Hohenfriedberg, in the foothills of the Sudetenland and on the Silesian plains, where he dominated the field against the numerically far superior Austro-Saxon army of Prince Charles of Lorraine on 4 June 1745. This was in reality the first battle in which he had led his men in person. However, it did not bring about a final resolution: Maria Theresa did not abandon the fight; she had long since converted the struggle for Silesia to a more comprehensive plan of aiming for the total destruction of the odious Prussia. Maria Theresa remained firm in her conviction that she was waging a punitive war against a law-breaker and her moral stance was reinforced by the election of her husband as Emperor on 13 September 1745, with the express support of the Electors of Saxony, Bavaria and Hanover.

The victory of Hohenfriedberg, nevertheless, did have its consequences. Britain's George II, facing the domestic difficulties posed by the Jacobite uprising in Scotland, lost interest in participating in an Austro-Prussian war. On 26 August 1745, he concluded a preliminary peace, the Convention of Hanover, with Prussia, which once again confirmed Frederick in possession of Silesia. Great Britain intended to include Austria in the peace talks, but her exhortations fell upon stony ground. Frederick was, therefore, once again forced to take up arms, although his military isolation and dwindling resources made a rapid end to the war imperative. For weeks he remained in 'embarrassing uncertainty'. Military actions became inevitable as hopes of peace evaporated. His mounting impatience, however, did not lead him to a renewed advance on Bohemia; instead, he concentrated his resources on the defence of Silesia and on gaining control of Saxony, on whom only now he formally declared war. Doggedly he pursued the reluctant Count Leopold von Anhalt-Dessau and implored him to engage his army, based as it was in Saxony, 'to go for the throat [of the Saxon troops] and defeat them'. Although he had always deplored the possibility of being forced into battle by the enemy, this fate now awaited him: at Soor on 30 September 1745, he found himself with 22,000 men faced by Charles of Lorraine's Austrian army which outnumbered Prussia's troops by a factor of two to one. However, unfavourable odds allowed his military genius to blossom. He defeated the Austrians through an ability to act swiftly and the disciplined movements of his troops, amidst which the reorganised Prussian cavalry principally excelled. After Leopold of Anhalt-Dessau's victory over the Saxons at Kesselsdorf, the road to the Electorate's capital lay open. There at Christmas 1745, the Second Silesian War was brought to a close by the Peace of Dresden. At the cost of recognising Grand Duke Francis Stephen as Emperor, Prussia's Silesian possessions were guaranteed. Maria Theresa had thus achieved one of the main goals of her policy, namely the recovery of the Imperial dignity for the House of Habsburg, but had failed to secure another, that of regaining Silesia. Since she had already relinquished Bavaria through the Peace of Füssen, she had abandoned all possibility of compensation for the loss of Silesia. Had Maria Theresa followed her own heart, she would never have given up her claim to Silesia, whose value increased steadily in her mind. Her decision was an act of calculated political rationalism and not a sincere renunciation of her right to the disputed territory. Therein lay the seeds of a new war.

What did the Peace of Dresden represent to Frederick II? The *Histoire de mon temps* contains something of a resigned judgement: 'If one evaluates the true worth of events, it must be admitted that in many respects the war led to unnecessary bloodshed, and the string of victories achieved nothing more than confirming Prussia's possession of Silesia.' Had he originally pursued other aims? The claims to Bohemia and Moravia could certainly not be viewed as an objective which would have justified a new war. The intention of securing a firm basis for the non-Habsburg *imperium* of Charles VII under the protection of a hegemonic Prussia seems more plausible. This concept, however, would in all probability have increased the dualism within Germany, not defeated it. It is inconceivable that Charles VII's death alone led to the plan's failure; more probable is that it would in any case have shattered on the rock of the Empire's weakness.

The continuing War of the Austrian Succession, moreover, and the ongoing struggles, until 1748 at least, on the battlefields of western and southern Europe as well as overseas in India and North America demonstrated clearly that the Silesian question, and by extension Prussia, had been relegated to the periphery of European, or indeed global, warfare. It did not have the dimensions of the War of the Spanish Succession or the Seven Years War and was conducted along largely traditional military and political lines. Frederick II resisted all temptation to re-enter the fray, and by the Peace of Aix-la-Chapelle (Aachen) in October 1748, received the guarantee of all the European belligerents for his possession of Silesia and Glatz. Thus the *action d'éclat* of 1740/41 became an internationally guaranteed part of the European territorial balance. It appeared to be the ultimate success for which the King had tirelessly striven.

Frederick, however, remained exposed and vulnerable amidst the rivalries of the great powers, and things did not always go as he wished: old enmities were suddenly toned down and *rapprochements* between former enemies concluded. Frederick's inclination to suspect foul play everywhere was heightened by such developments. In his youth, he had calculated in 1740 that in the global conflict between Britain and France, one of these powers would necessarily be his ally. Now, in the aftermath of the Peace of Aix-la-Chapelle, there developed a distinct, if temporary, *rapprochement* between the two rival powers; both guaranteed Prussia's possession of Silesia. The old system of playing one off against the other was now defunct. Was this in Prussia's interest? Frederick was not placated by the peace and, with the habitual distrust that had become second nature to him, saw his enemies at work everywhere. His representative in Paris, Baron de Chambrier, sent him a report on 20 December 1745, drawing his attention to the last sentence in the record of the Congress of Aix-la-Chapelle to which all the belligerents had lent their signature: 'It has to be realised that it appears as if we have all conducted a war with the sole purpose of increasing the might of the King of Prussia.' The image which foreign contemporaries had of Prussia was anything but favourable. It was seen as unreliable and devious, consumed by unbridled ambition. Was this true? Clearly during the whole of the War of the Austrian Succession, Prussia looked only to its own advantage and thus employed methods which were similar to Machiavelli's own. Frederick had not, however, pursued limitless goals; he had no wish to be the new Alexander the Great. With Prussia's small size and exposed situation, he lacked the basis for such a venture. He wished merely to make Prussia more powerful, and continually shrank back from actions which might have threatened this goal. This was the reason behind what the others had perceived as unreliability and also accounted for his tactical manoeuvring between the great powers. But he was not always a master of Machiavellian artistry, and made very serious mistakes both as statesman and military commander. First he had to experience the purgatory of seeing his state on the edge of destruction before he could fully comprehend the cut-throat nature of the struggle for power amongst the other major states. This test still awaited him.

ON THE EDGE OF DESTRUCTION: THE SEVEN YEARS WAR

1756 – Determining the aggressor

The origins of the Seven Years War were at the centre of a bitter academic controversy in the later nineteenth century over where the responsibility for initiating the war should lie. The debate involved only Prussian historians and was not pursued in the international arena. Even Austrian scholars such as Alfred von Arneth, Maria Theresa's biographer, were not directly involved. At its very heart stood the personality and intentions of Frederick the Great.

Albert Naudé's opinion that the King in 1756 entered into a purely defensive, preventative war, was vigorously opposed by the Göttingen-trained historian Max Lehmann who argued that such theories only perpetuated the Prussian myth of Frederick as the champion of German nationalist policies. Frederick had not begun a defensive war, he maintained, but launched a war of conquest, the plans for which had long been in preparation and the ultimate aim of which had been the acquisition of Saxony. Two offensively inclined powers thus met head on: Prussia and Austria, the latter determined to regain Silesia and destroy Prussia's great power status.

The later-nineteenth-century historical dispute was clearly coloured by strong emotions and a nationalistic identification of Prussian with German policies. Such considerations are no longer applicable today, and the time has come for a comprehensive reassessment of the events of 1756 within their European context. Neither of the two eighteenth-century German great power protagonists exists today; the rivalry between them has ended and the original cause of their dispute, Silesia, has moved into quite different political spheres.

Around the mid-eighteenth century, after Prussia's rise to its somewhat precarious great power status and Russia's entry into the European international system, the system of the Pentarchy had finally been completed. Every major political decision in Europe had to be taken under the watchful eyes of the five great powers and their satellite states. At the time of the War of the Spanish Succession, European politics was still divided into two distinct systems: the struggle over Spain and its Empire in the west, and the Northern War in the north and east remained separate conflicts. However, since Maria Theresa and her Chancellor, Count Wenzel Anton von Kaunitz-Rietberg, had determined upon the reconquest of the lost province of Silesia, Russia's value rose considerably in Vienna's calculations and it came to be seen as a potentially valuable ally. Combined with improved relations with France since 1750, this meant that Austria could complete the encirclement of Prussia. The crisis in central Europe which had facilitated Frederick's seizure of Silesia, not only changed the political balance in that region, but also influenced the situation of the Eastern states. At the same time, England was securing its maritime Empire, and its overseas interests in North America and India gradually began to play a dominant role. The clash in the Ohio valley between the English settlers, advancing westwards, and the French, determined to block their progress, was no isolated colonial conflict but an event fraught with consequences of global proportions. It was here that the European crisis of 1756 had its origins. To provide himself with a political and moral alibi, Frederick never tired of repeating this fact in his treatise of July 1757, entitled *A Vindication of My Political Actions*: 'Everyone is aware', he wrote, 'that the turmoil in which Europe finds itself began in America, where an Anglo-French quarrel over cod-fishing rights and a few remote Canadian territories led to the bloody war which has plunged our part of the world into grief. This war [the American struggle] was so far removed from the possessions of the German rulers that it is difficult to comprehend how a fire in one part of the world can spread rapidly to another. But, thanks to our century's statecraft, there is now no conflict in the world, however small it may be, which, in a very short time, does not threaten to engulf the whole of Christendom and rend it asunder.'

All political dealings were determined by the interaction between the five great powers, their client states and their overseas possessions. However, international relations were not a static system but a fluid one, constantly subject to changing constellations and an ever-shifting balance of power. A perfect equilibrium between two opposing allied groups could only ever exist momentarily while each group sought to gain the upper hand. The struggle to bring Russia into the European political system and to mobilise its considerable armed forces led to a Franco-British competition over the payment of subsidies which was eventually decided in France's favour. Prussia's ability to survive became increasingly dependent upon British subsidies. Changes within traditional alliances, however, could also be brought about by purely political or strategic reasons. Maria Theresa's decision, acting under the advice and influence of Chancellor Kaunitz, to give priority to the reconquest of Silesia, can only be seen in this light. It required that Vienna's foreign policy should seek a new orientation after nearly three centuries of fixed opposition to Bourbon France. The 'Diplomatic Revolution' which in 1756 brought about the *rapprochement* between Vienna and Paris, was in keeping with the new trend of regarding Prussia as the principal enemy. Silesia was not only a buffer zone for Bohemia and Moravia, but could also provide Austria with the strategic bridgehead necessary to exercise an influence over northern and eastern Europe. It was one of the Habsburg Monarchy's most advanced provinces, with a highly developed industry and a sound economy. All this was the Habsburg Monarchy's loss. It was Prussia who now enjoyed the decisive political, strategic and economic advantages conferred by Silesia.

The loss of Silesia, therefore, was not a peripheral problem for Austrian foreign policy but, with its impact on the balance of power, was quite fundamental for the relative standing of continental states. In the words of Kaunitz, it had occasioned 'a change not only in the Austrian, but in the whole European state system'. For this reason the reconquest of Silesia could never be perceived as a mere redrawing of frontiers but as a means by which to weaken Prussia and so reduce the House of Brandenburg to its original second-rank status – 'une petite puissance très secondaire'. These considerations, which formed the basis of Kaunitz's great plan, were combined with what Maria Theresa saw as her moral duty to punish the 'wicked man in Berlin' for overturning the established political order. In instructions to Field Marshal Daun, dating from July 1759, Maria Theresa wrote: 'These and other dire consequences would only be averted by the weakening of the King of Prussia, and there lies the true reason for the present war, fought not only for the reacquisition of Silesia and Glatz, but also in the name of humanity and the maintenance of our Holy [Roman Catholic] religion of which I am practically the only upholder in Germany.' The injection of an ideological dimension into the power struggle with Prussia was a tactic practised with continuing vigour by the Viennese court during the course of the war. In the official 'Views of the [Austrian] State on the Present Prussian War in Germany', published in 1761, Prussia is portrayed as the aggressive originator of 'a completely new kind of warfare, the like of which cannot be found anywhere in the history of war'. This new Prussian way of waging war 'according to which neighbouring neutral states could be forced to supply not only forage and provisions but also all able men and as much money as could possibly be extorted by the severest of means', would reduce the whole Empire to ruins, if Prussia's enemies were to wage war in a similar manner. The weakening and ultimate destruction of Prussian power, therefore, meant the protection of the German Empire and the international state system from the corrupting principle of what was later termed 'militarism'.

The precondition for the success of Kaunitz's great plan to create an alliance directed against the Prussian King was clearly that his potential allies should also feel threatened by Prussian expansion. The most enthusiastic response to Kaunitz's overtures came from the leading Russian minister, A.P. Bestuzhev. A large measure of responsibility for the outbreak of war must, therefore, lie with Russia.

The key to the changing circumstances that ultimately led to war, however, lay in the relationship between Vienna and Paris. The French court had been linked with Prussia in an uneasy alliance, severely strained by the ambiguous policies of the Prussian King and, in any case, due to expire in March 1756. The only benefit to be gained from association with Prussia in French eyes lay in the possibility that Prussia might be willing to attack the British King's Hanoverian territories, in this way partly reducing the pressure upon France in its struggle with Britain on the high seas and in North America. However, this was the very thing Frederick was not prepared to do; he refused to involve himself as some kind of 'Don Quixote' in French squabbles. The ultimate devaluation of the Prussian alliance, however, stemmed from France's need to destroy the traditional Anglo-Austrian alliance and to check the influence of the House of Habsburg. It was primarily this, rather than hostility towards Prussia, which determined French foreign policy and induced France to lend an ear to the overtures from Austria. Vienna and Paris approached the improvement in relations with quite different goals: the Austrians with the intention of gaining an ally in their struggle against Prussia; the French in the hope of preventing Austria intervening on the British side in the colonial struggle with Britain. Having captured Britain's strategically important island stronghold of Minorca in the Mediterranean, the French now felt threatened by the aggressive actions of the British fleet on the Canadian coastline. French commercial shipping was harassed and French warships attacked; border disputes with British colonies in North America intensified. The Anglo-French colonial conflict was transformed into open war in May 1756. Britain, however, seemed more conscious of the fact that this was not just a conflict on the global periphery; it was clearly realised that this was a struggle to determine the future of the world. In Paris, on the other hand, the dispute with London was interpreted as little more than a continuation of the traditional struggle for supremacy as had been the case in the War of the Spanish Succession.

Established traditions and ingrained prejudices in foreign relations cannot, of course, be erased overnight, but have to be gradually overcome. France's change of direction vis-à-vis the Habsburgs was far from being a *fait accompli*, but resulted from Kaunitz's tenacious diplomatic manoeuvring. After the decision to pursue the French had been taken in Vienna in August 1755, he worked hard to gain the support of the influential Marquise de Pompadour as well as Cardinal de Bernis. The French foreign minister, Count Louis Rouillé, hesitated, however, and sent his envoy, the Duc de Nivernais, to Berlin to explore a possible renewal of the alliance. Things were still undecided when Frederick II unwittingly brought about a breakthrough in Paris: his signature of the so-called Convention of Westminster on 16 January 1756, was, according to Kaunitz 'the decisive event in Austria's favour'. This agreement, which obliged the signatories to mutual non-aggression and 'the preservation of peace in Germany', accorded with British needs to secure peace on the continent and ensure the protection of Hanover while embroiled in its maritime and colonial disputes with France. Frederick was principally interested in securing a steadfast alliance partner who would support him against Russia. It seems unlikely that he anticipated initiating a total reversal of alliances. The Anglo-Prussian *rapprochement*, however, angered the French King and his advisers and removed the last obstacle which stood in the way of an alliance with Austria. Having concluded the treaty with London while entering into negotiations with the French envoy immediately afterwards, Frederick came to be seen as duplicitous, a game at which he had already proven himself a master. It was he himself, therefore, who gave the advantage to his diplomatically more skilled opponent, Kaunitz: on 1 May 1756, the first treaty between Paris and Vienna was signed. It was still, to all intents and purposes, a defensive alliance which did not specify that France must abandon its own links with Prussia, but at its core it fulfilled the preconditions for a future offensive coalition in the event that 'one day the peace of Europe should be shattered'. Nevertheless, the divergent starting points of the two powers were clearly visible during the negotiations: Kaunitz's ambassador in Paris, Count Starhemberg, was determined to win his French counterpart over to the Austrian aim of weakening Prussia through the enforced return of Silesia and Glatz, but eventually had to concede that formal French approval could not yet be secured. An equally difficult stage in the negotiations was reached when France demanded the cession of the Austrian Netherlands in return for its subsidies to Austria.

During the age of cabinet politics, foreign policy shifts were brought about by a small circle close to the monarch and every means available in the age of classical diplomacy was employed: intrigue, bribery, deception. Formally, rulers took all the decisions but, on the whole, they were in fact taken by others, the result of personal cabals and intrigues which varied from court to court. Only Frederick ruled as an autocrat, listening to his advisors, but rarely acting upon their recommendations. In Paris, Louis XV's influence was overshadowed by that of the Marquise de Pompadour, while in Vienna, Chancellor Kaunitz laid down the broad lines of policy. The most confusing of situations reigned at the court of St Petersburg, where in the turmoil of numerous court factions Empress Elizabeth attempted to impose her authority on both these and the leading minister, Count A.P. Bestuzhev, not by making rational use of her position of power, but by displays of strong emotion. Russia had long been irritated by Prussian expansion near her western borders and had developed territorial ambitions for eastern and central Europe which fitted in with the offered alliance from Vienna: in return for supporting the Austrian recovery of Silesia, East Prussia was to become part of Russian-dominated Poland; Russia itself would annex the Duchy of Courland and the East Polish territories. Again it was the Anglo-Prussian Convention of Westminster which provided the final impetus needed to drive the Empress into the camp of Prussia's enemies. Shortly after Russia had concluded a subsidy agreement (Convention of St Petersburg, signed in September 1755) with Great Britain which was still to be ratified by the Empress, news of the Convention of Westminster reached St Petersburg. Elizabeth, outraged at Britain's duplicity, quickly agreed to join the Franco-Austrian coalition. In her offer to join the alliance in April 1756, she was prepared to give it an offensive character, something which the First Treaty of Versailles had avoided. Russia, even before it joined the alliance, was the driving force of the moves towards war. It pressed ahead with its military build-up and took the decision to send troops into Livonia, an undertaking which Kaunitz managed only with great difficulty to persuade St Petersburg to postpone until the next year. The Russian troop movements, in any case, had the most serious consequences, since they brought about Frederick's mobilisation in June 1756, having convinced him that war was unavoidable.

How far did Frederick have a comprehensive view of the situation? His own predicament, given the powerful coalition ranged against him, must have seemed quite desperate. In the century of secret politics, the task of gathering news and information fell to the diplomats. Their correspondence, however, was frequently subject to long delays in reaching its destination as well as all sorts of uncertainties, chief among them the possibility of it being monitored or intercepted by a third party. Thus it was customary to have spies in the foreign services of other powers. Prussia successfully followed this practice, and the King devoted a full chapter in his Political Testament of 1752 to these 'poor wretches . . . who are very useful and, like a compass, indicate the direction the mariner must follow if dark clouds on the political horizon obscure his view'. The secretary of the Austrian envoy in Berlin was thus, until his unmasking, in Frederick's employ and furnished the King with secret documents from the Russo-Austrian correspondence. Meanwhile, a clerk in the Saxon cabinet office delivered reports from Vienna and St Petersburg to the Prussian envoy in Dresden. Another important source of information were the dispatches from the Dutch envoy in St Petersburg, van Swart, whose correspondence was opened and scrutinised as it passed through Berlin. The

King rapidly – often too rashly – drew his own conclusions from the news which flowed to him from all these sources; pessimism and mistrust were always more in keeping with his character than brimming optimism. He immediately equated negotiations in progress with treaties already concluded, as in the case of the noted improvement in Austro-Russian relations. Everything which heightened his impatience strengthened his will to act. The decision to act was made before he was fully informed. As a result, attempts have been made to suggest that he was merely seeking a pretext for war, since the decision to fight had long since been taken and its goal had been the conquest of Saxony. But this is clearly too simplified an explanation for Frederick's motivation in going to war. He would undoubtedly have preferred to avoid war in 1756, had he not seen it as inevitable. But if he was to be led down the path to war, he himself wanted to dictate when it was to take place so that his enemies would not have time to align themselves. He considered his opponents' determination to destroy him as a proven fact and there is no doubt that he reckoned on such an eventuality. He was not, however, willing to conduct a purely defensive war; once again the maintenance of the status quo was unimportant to him. The basic principle continued to apply: never to enter into hostilities unless there existed a good chance of making conquests (*'les plus belles apparences à faire des conquêtes'*), as he wrote in November 1755, in his 'Thoughts on and General Rules for War'. It is unclear, however, which conquests he had in mind. He had written extensively on the subject in his Political Testament of 1752, but under the title *'Rêveries politiques'* (Political Pipe Dreams). Saxony, he maintained, would be the most useful acquisition because of its favourable geographical situation, the Elbe and Bohemian border territories serving as valuable buffer zones for the Prussian capital and the Electoral Mark. The considerable economic significance of Saxony, on the other hand, was not mentioned. The next most desirable territories were listed as Polish Prussia (the future West Prussia), and Swedish Pomerania, whose acquisition was to be secured by peaceful means. In his secret instructions to the commander-in-chief in East Prussia, von Lehwaldt, at the outset of the Prussian mobilisation in June 1756, Frederick specified that after his victory over the Russian army the field marshal was to insist on 'possession of the whole of Polish Prussia as an indemnity for the damage wrought by the war'.

Even in a defensive war, plans for conquest were essential for Frederick. This fully accorded with his nature: always prepared for action, constantly superimposing his will on the reality of a situation, arrogantly refusing ever to be at a disadvantage. The threat of a powerful coalition pitted against him provided only the occasion, not the pretext, to put his plans for Saxony into operation. Frederick took the decision to launch a preventative war in the classic sense of the term. On 24 July 1756, he wrote to the British representative in Berlin, Andrew Mitchell, with whom he had been in close contact throughout that summer: 'I have no option but to act first to prevent an attack on me' (*praevenire quam praeveniri*). The date of his decision cannot be clearly established. If the Russian troop movements in June had occasioned the first

Prussian moves towards mobilisation, it was the news of Austrian military dispositions in Bohemia and Moravia which ultimately proved to be the decisive factor.

It is worth comparing the situation in 1756 with that of 1740. In both cases, the King of Prussia was the immediate cause of the war. In 1740, the element of surprise was of primary importance, his action was to precede any negotiation; as yet, no steadfast alliance against him existed. In 1756, the element of surprise was once again employed, but now his opponents had already considered and prepared for the possibility of war. Frederick fell straight into the trap. Prussia's opening of hostilities was a gift for his opponents, headed by Kaunitz, for only now did the allies close ranks against him: the Treaty of Versailles was transformed into an offensive alliance on 1 May 1757, to which Russia became a co-signatory soon afterwards. The King of Prussia had brought about precisely what he had sought to avoid. His actions contained something of the same blindness he had displayed in 1740. His court, his brothers and all his generals except Winterfeldt opposed him. Prince Henry described the King as apparently possessed by the fanatical war-mongering of his adjutant general, Hans Karl von Winterfeldt. Henry, more out of personal inclination than political calculation, bitterly opposed sacrificing the *rapprochement* with France. A report by the veteran foreign minister, Podewils, survives, detailing his meeting with the King on 22 July; in it he confirms that the King's sombre interpretation of his political predicament forced him to act. Podewils, who had already counselled caution in 1740, sought to warn the King of the dangers of prompting both France and Russia into 'fulfilling their defensive obligations'. Instead he advised Frederick to make use of the 'temporarily favourable circumstances' to strengthen the Prussian faction within and outside the Empire and 'perhaps attempt to make a few overtures to France and England to engage in renewed peace negotiations'. This was surely an astute analysis, apparently anticipating that a Prussian attack would occasion the transformation of hitherto defensive treaties into offensive alliances. Would this change have occurred in any case, even if Prussia had remained peaceful? This will remain an imponderable question. Frederick himself rejected such speculative considerations as smacking of 'excessive timidity'. Podewils was abruptly dismissed with the words: '*Adieu, Monsieur de la timide politique*'. Frederick's determination at that moment to go to war was unshakable and no amount of argument could persuade him to abort his plans.

Nevertheless, resolved as he was to break the peace for a second time, certain lessons had been learned from the outbreak of the First Silesian War. Now he attached great importance to appearing to his contemporaries and posterity as the man in the right. He unleashed a veritable propaganda war against Austria, in which all manner of arguments, including an accusation of Habsburg persecution of Protestants, were employed. In order to avoid the odium of being labelled the aggressor, he sought to justify his position in several articles, principally in the great memorandum of August 1756, which was sent to all Prussia's diplomatic representatives and translated into English.

In the critical week prior to the outbreak of war, Frederick did all he could to attach the blame to Austria. It was important to him that '. . . the public . . . should not be impressed by the illusions being propagated by the Viennese court'. In conjunction with this, he sent his three questions to Maria Theresa, conveyed personally to the Empress by his envoy, Joachim Wilhelm von Klinggräffen. The reason for such provocative behaviour was certainly not to obtain favourable or appeasing replies, but to elicit from the Empress statements which could be equated with an admission of guilt. With her proud and dignified reply, however, Maria Theresa forced her opponent into breaking the peace himself. Thus Frederick's tactical intention of placing the Empress in the wrong had failed. The opposing stances of the two monarchs were here clearly highlighted. Maria Theresa, convinced that moral right was on her side, Frederick aware that at least this time he must play according to the rules of international law. In the forthcoming war, only strength of spirit and the tenacity to endure the utmost strain would be important. Both Frederick and Maria Theresa possessed this ability. What eventually decided the outcome of the Seven Years War, however – be it strength of spirit, coincidence, political and military ability, or political constellations, or a strange mixture of all these components – remains still to be seen.

The shifting sands of war

The historical distinctiveness of the Seven Years War does not lie in its length – most other eighteenth-century conflicts spanned longer periods of time. Nor is it to be found in the military or political effort expended or in the material or human losses associated with it; here, too, it did not differ from other conflicts such as the War of the Spanish Succession or the Thirty Years War in particular. On the one hand, the European Seven Years War was a dimension of the global Anglo-French struggle to determine the future of a world which had been shaped by European hands. On the other hand, the continental war was a concentrated struggle fought over a comparatively small area, at the centre of which stood a personality who, although he had taken the initiative, would soon lose the advantage, but continued to retain the ability to react swiftly and thus attempt to diminish the numerical superiority of his opponents. In the historical context, Frederick challenged the traditional powers. He was defending not only Silesia, but also his right to be a member of the charmed circle of great powers. It was he who drew the Russian Empire into the European system and thus expanded it to the east. He revolutionised great power relations and occasioned a metamorphosis of alliances; he polarised the tangled web of states which formed the Holy Roman Empire and transformed the old inter-German confessional rivalry into a new dualism between two competing great powers, something which was to endure until 1866.

Frederick faced a coalition of powers who believed that their combined strength would easily crush their opponent. At the centre of the anti-Prussian alliance was Vienna and its architect, Kaunitz. A master of the diplomatic game, he needed nevertheless to convert his political advantages into allied military success. After Frederick's aggression against Saxony and Austria, he sought to transform the newly established relationship between Vienna and Paris, as laid down by the First Treaty of Versailles, into an offensive alliance. In the resulting Second Treaty, signed on 1 May 1757, France promised to supply an army of 105,000 men as well as substantial subsidies, while Austria recorded that it had at its disposal some 177,000 men. In January 1757, Empress Elizabeth had already promised to mobilise 80,000 men against Prussia whenever necessary. If one adds the 20,000 men which Sweden was obliged by treaty to provide, it becomes clear that the Prussian army, numbering a mere 141,000 men in 1756 and strategically unfavourably deployed, was hopelessly outnumbered. Pure numerical strength, however, did not guarantee automatic victory; ultimately the ability and training of the troops was the decisive factor. And this varied greatly within the coalition. The Austrian army had improved considerably since the end of the War of the Austrian Succession, and the reforms undertaken since 1748 had enhanced both the precision and speed of its capacity to manoeuvre as well as the quality of its armaments and equipment, so that in many respects it rivalled that of Prussia, on whose example the reforms had been modelled. Indeed in its artillery, for example, it exceeded even Prussian standards, although, of course, the quite distinct structure of the Habsburg Monarchy prohibited a complete transformation to a Prussian-style military state. A standing army of 108,000 men was established and its recruitment, formerly carried out by the provincial Estates, taken over by central government. A particularly important part in the Austrian conduct of war was played by the light, irregular troops who, to an extent, broke free from the established conventions of the absolutist standing army and were recruited largely from non-German areas with strong ties to Vienna. The numbers of foreign mercenaries within the rest of the army, moreover, were far fewer than in Prussia.

The Prussian army, meanwhile, had lost none of the strike power and efficiency evident during the Silesian Wars, and had used the intervening years of peace to prepare for the future conflict that was seen as inevitable. It suffered severe losses in the years 1757–59, which eventually forced the King to lower the established requirements for potential new officers. More and more sons of tenant farmers were recruited and the numbers of foreigners were reduced. It is characteristic of the rigours of the Prussian military state and its nobility that during the war even the ranks of commanders and regimental officers were decimated: between 1756 and 1759, no fewer than thirty-three generals were killed in action, among them Field Marshals Schwerin and Keith and the King's close adviser, General von Winterfeldt. On the Austrian side, the important Field Marshal Count von Browne died from his wounds after the battle of Prague, while Field Marshal Count Daun was seriously injured at Torgau in 1760.

When one compares the two principal opponents, it becomes clear that the war was a clash between two different kinds of polity. In the great Memoir, published in 1761 and probably inspired by Kaunitz, Prussia was represented as 'the originator of a new kind of warfare'; its military might was said to be out of proportion to its internal resources and size, necessitating its brutal absorption of the population and property of neutral states to feed its military machine. The danger in Vienna's eyes posed by such warfare lay not only in its threat to the European and German balance of power, but also in the strain it placed on Prussia's opponents to introduce 'similar military forms of government', a process which 'would place an intolerable burden on the whole of Europe' according to Maria Theresa in her instructions to Field Marshal Daun in 1759. Thus the Austro-Prussian contest acquired an ideological dimension, with Austria as the defender of a non-militaristic lifestyle. This impression is strengthened by the differently structured hierarchies of command in both armies. The Austrian commanders were tied completely to political directives from Vienna; here, however, there reigned a tangle of overlapping responsibility which even Kaunitz's reform of the central administration around 1761 failed to eradicate. A slight improvement in the relationship between the army and Vienna's bureaucratic apparatus was brought about when Field Marshal Daun, commander-in-chief since 1758, was made first a minister of state (1760) and then President of the War Council (1762). The cumbersome, sometimes even immobile, nature of the Austrian military machine was, of course, in part due to the complicated command mechanisms, but frequently this was merely cited as an excuse to obscure the procrastination and lack of decision which characterised Daun's leadership.

The King of Prussia, on the other hand, combined in his person both political and military leadership, thus creating a unity of purpose rare in the history of the established European powers. The 1761 Austrian Memoir provides us with an accurate summary of his position: 'Because the King himself commands and does not have to give account of his strategic mistakes to anyone . . . he is able to undertake bolder and more dangerous enterprises, taking risks which a commanding general, dependent on Cabinet orders, would never dare to take.'

In this sense, Frederick appears to have created the very model of an absolutist monarchy – no other state was in a position to replicate his example. 'The King of Prussia possesses, aside from his lust for power and conquest, a great passion and talent for warfare, and thus conducts his wars himself', the 1761 Memoir informs us. What was actually the rule of an absolutist regime, had now become the exception, and Frederick, indeed, personified both the highest form of absolute power as well as its greatest exception. The Prussian army's only leadership problems arose from the fact that although the King was its indisputable commander-in-chief, his forces were, as a rule, divided into several independently operating units. This produced tension and conflict, the most serious example of which was the dispute between the King and his brother, Crown Prince Augustus William, over the retreat from Bohemia after the defeat at Kolin which ended with a complete breach between the brothers. Independent command was also given to Ferdinand of Brunswick and to the King's other brother, Prince Henry. The disputes between the latter and Frederick were often generated by divergent strategic convictions: Henry was tied, much more than the King, to the established conventions of eighteenth-century warfare and also demanded a measure of independence Frederick was not always prepared to give.

An even more unsatisfactory command structure than that of the Austrians existed in Russia where the court had become the playground of factions and opportunists following the succession disputes. The Russian high command was characterised by frequent changes of personnel and, although Frederick had underestimated the military quality of the Russian soldiers, their numbers constantly replenishable from an inexhaustible reservoir of serfs, the leading Russian officers were simply not equal to the demands of the situation. The newly established secret War Council failed to issue unambiguous orders to its commander-in-chief, whose authority was in any case seriously undermined by the frequency and ease with which he could be replaced. Uncertainty and inactivity among troop commanders resulted. Although the Russo-Austrian treaty of January 1757 clearly specified that there should be military cooperation between the two powers, this was never fully effective and always short-lived. Only this allowed Frederick to survive such catastrophes as that at Kunersdorf in 1759.

The assistance provided by France also failed to live up to Kaunitz's expectations. The French did, of course, supply the promised 110,000 men and were indeed able to achieve a considerable amount of success at the beginning of the conflict. However, the internal fabric of the French army and especially its officer corps, which was experiencing a crisis at the very highest levels was incapable of bearing the strain of a war on two fronts, overseas and on the continent. Army appointments and promotions depended upon noble birth and favour at court, not military ability; by the later-eighteenth century French absolutism, with its nobility rigidly frozen into courtly society, could no longer produce military successes of the kind Louis XIV's Turenne had achieved. The advantages its armies had initially gained in northwest Germany were, therefore, soon lost.

Prussia was thus less threatened by the mighty coalition than might have been supposed, since the allied superiority of numbers belied the coalition's heterogeneity and its members' divergent political interests. The threat lay instead in the uncertainty of the military goals in the four or five theatres of operations. Frederick attempted to cut the Gordian knot before his opponents could field their combined fighting strength by taking sudden preventative action within an economically and numerically supportable framework. This led to the questionable decision to conquer Saxony, the Prussian occupation of which began the war at the end of August 1756. Frederick was not satisfied with half measures, and exploited the Electorate's financial and military resources to such an extent that it caused an international sensation in a century used to victors reaping their spoils from the vanquished and not from a country nominally neutral. Of its total income from taxation of six million thaler,

Saxony was forced to pay Prussia five million per annum during the occupation; even the monies which had formerly been employed for the upkeep of the opulent court of Dresden were mercilessly redirected to the support of the Prussian military state. The most draconian measure, however, was the forced enlistment into the Prussian army of the Saxon troops which had surrendered at Pirna: over 18,000 men were recruited in this way and only officers had the option of refusal. As in many other instances, the King's violent action had far overstepped the boundaries of established contemporary practice. In the event he failed to profit from it; many of those forcibly drafted later deserted and formed the core of a Saxon army in exile. This episode suggests that the armies of the late eighteenth century were not entirely characterised by a mercenary mentality, but also by an embryonic national sentiment, something which applied not least to the Prussian army itself.

It has often been said that Prussia's action against formally neutral Saxony destroyed Frederick's moral and political reputation in much the same way as disregard for Belgian neutrality in 1914 severely damaged the position of the German Empire. Its contemporary effect was indeed similar, although the theory and practice of international law were, of course, much more standardised in the twentieth century than in the eighteenth. The King, however, felt the same need to justify his actions against Saxony as he had done in his relations with Austria. He did not shy away from forcefully acquiring the Saxon archives and searching for proof of the undoubtedly questionable activities of Saxony, under the direction of Count Brühl, in its relations with the great powers. The documents which had been seized formed the basis of several *apologias*, the last of which, published in October 1756, was formulated by Ewald Friedrich von Hertzberg, who was later to become Prussia's foreign minister. Only one goal eluded Frederick in his 1756 campaign: he had planned to take possession of at least northern Bohemia to serve as a strategic base for further operations in the future. He had failed in this aim, despite his victory at Lobositz on 1 October over the Austrian army sent to relieve occupied Saxony. The 'aligning of the chess pieces', as Frederick referred to the military events of 1756, did not produce the desired outcome.

Everything now depended on the next move in the game. Who would make it and where? As far as Prussia's strategy was concerned, much was to be said for remaining in its newly won 'protected central position' by the river Elbe and waiting to see what its opponents would do. This accorded with Austrian tactical plans which counted on some form of French assistance in the forthcoming offensive. The initial Austrian campaign was to be directed at Saxony. But Frederick's mentality, together with the reasons why he had launched the war, would not permit him to hand over the initiative. He carefully analysed the situation and all its possibilities in his 'Consideration of Various Projects' and began a written debate on the subject with Field Marshal Schwerin and General von Winterfeldt. It was Winterfeldt who was the principal advocate of the view that a surprise attack on the enemy should be made before any French intervention took place: 'It would deal the unsuspecting

enemy the most mighty of thunderbolts and thus reduce all to fear and confusion', he wrote. The King agreed in principle with this notion ('the project
is admirable', he noted on 21 March), improved on its strategic feasibility and
made it his own. Four Prussian columns advanced into Bohemia on 18–22
April 1757 and forced the surprised Austrians to retreat as far as Prague, where
both armies met on 6 May. The battle of Prague proved a decisive victory for
Frederick, but at the price of heavy losses, including Field Marshal Schwerin.
The King was, however, only able to encircle the fortified city loosely, not
subject it to a full-scale siege, and he was in no position to prevent Field
Marshal Daun's concentration of strong Austrian contingents on the upper
reaches of the Vltava (Moldau) in Bohemia. The decisive battle, the one,
destructive blow against enemy forces of which he had dreamed, had not been
achieved. The newly won positions in Bohemia were lost a few weeks later,
on 18 June, when Frederick suffered a severe defeat at the hands of the Austrians
under Daun at Kolin. The encirclement of Prague had to be lifted, and the
wholescale withdrawal from Bohemia and Moravia initiated. 'Finally Phaeton
has fallen', wrote Prince Henry, who had only followed his brother into the
war with grave misgivings and grudging loyalty. Indeed, Kolin marked a
decisive turning point in the war: as the battle of the Marne in 1914 and the
1941 battle outside the gates of Moscow would do, it occasioned the transformation of a short war into a drawn out war of attrition.

The King was well aware of the dangers inherent in this change. In his
General Principles of War, an educational treatise for his officers drawn up in
1748, he wrote: 'Our wars must be short and lively because it is not to our
advantage to conduct a drawn out struggle, since such a conflict would lower
our admirable standards of discipline, depopulate our state and exhaust our
resources.' This was the ground rule by which a materially and numerically
inferior state such as Prussia had to survive, and the strategy Frederick advocated anticipated the twentieth-century '*Blitzkrieg*'. The application of this
principle, however, failed in 1757. What would take its place? Shortly before
the outbreak of war, Frederick had considered this possibility in his *Thoughts
and General Rules of War* of 1755, differentiating between successful early campaigns which would have a decisive effect on the whole war, and later campaigns within the framework of a protracted struggle; for the latter it was
obviously impossible to lay down general rules except that one should attempt
to maintain one's base of operations and make no further advances. Ultimately,
this aptly described the Prussian King's strategic conduct for the remainder of
the war. His main aim was to preserve his position in Saxony and Silesia,
although with the course of time, this would become increasingly difficult.

In pursuing his goal, Frederick reaped the advantages of a strategy of interior lines, but these were not sufficient to allow him to fend off constantly
mounting dangers. Chief among these was his numerical inferiority in the
face of his opponents, especially when their forces were united. Frederick was
particularly vulnerable on the fronts in the Lusatia and Oder regions where
Austro-Russian forces could unite against him. On several occasions, he failed

to prevent Austro-Russian military cooperation and eventually had to pay heavily with the devastating defeat at Kunersdorf in August 1759, which plunged him to the very edge of catastrophe. A potential danger lay also, of course, in the creation of a united Franco-Austrian force, but despite the treaty between Vienna and Paris, this did not immediately materialise. The probable exhaustion of Prussia's financial and human resources was an additional and permanent risk throughout the conduct of a long war. It was on this that Austrian policy particularly pinned its hopes. In an official report from the Viennese court published in 1761 amidst general fatigue among the allies and a wavering of commitment to the coalition, this seemed the only hope to which Austria could cling. Its own impotence, however, was betrayed by the fact that after five exhausting years of war, it had been unable to crush its weaker Prussian enemy.

To Frederick, the Seven Years War was a constant balancing act on the edge of the abyss, 'a tightrope walk' as he himself frequently called it. Crisis followed crisis, and at stake was not only military victory but the continued existence of Prussia itself. Following his retreat from Bohemia, pressure was heaped upon the King from all sides. Russia invaded East Prussia which, in January 1758, Frederick forfeited for the remainder of the war. The Swedes, allied to France since March 1757, advanced on Pomerania. France occupied the whole of northwest Germany and by a neutrality Convention of Kloster-Seven, concluded on 8 September 1757, effectively neutralised Hanover and the defensive 'army of observation' under the Duke of Cumberland, established to protect it. In January 1757, the Diet at Regensburg had voted to enter the war against Prussia, and Imperial troops now combined with the French army in an eastward push through central Germany. This desperate situation forced Frederick to develop a defensive strategy based upon lightning operational speed, striking first at one then another of his most threatening opponents. Battles were forced upon him by the enemy armies. His freedom of decision had run out at Prague and Kolin, and the crisis between 1757 and 1759, in which he reached the pinnacle of his strategic genius, was nothing less than a terrible struggle for survival. Despite prodigious feats such as the successful attacks on his numerically superior opponents at Rossbach near the Saale on 5 November 1757, and at Leuthen near Lissa on 5 December 1757, the fact remained that he was only ever able to achieve partial success, never total victory. Rossbach was fought to free his rear for an attack on the Austrians in Silesia, which had fallen almost completely into their hands. His success at Leuthen, probably the most remarkable demonstration of Frederick's skills as a military commander, restored Prussian control over Silesia, which once again reverted to its role of an integral element in Prussian operations. The structure of the Prussian state, the political circumstances of a war fought on several fronts and Frederick's own temperament and strength of will all lent themselves to decisions being sought in battle. But slow-moving supplies and the restrictions upon the army's freedom of manoeuvre, imposed by the fact that it largely consisted of conscripted mercenaries prone to desertion, as well as Frederick's ever-increasing numerical inferiority, forced him to adopt a defensive strategy. Frederick's disadvantages, however, were certainly compensated for by the increasing loyalty of his officer corps which probably lent the Prussian army much greater strike power than other absolutist armies generally possessed. Ultimately, of course, one must not forget that Frederick's powerful personal charisma acted as a significant integrating force and he employed it to good effect as, for example, in the speech to his officers before the battle of Leuthen.

The temporary improvement in Prussia's prospects influenced the global struggle even more than previously. In London, William Pitt resolved to increase his support for the Prussian military state and employ it as a continental bastion against France. The Convention of Kloster-Seven, which had handed over northwest Germany to France and necessitated Frederick's military intervention at Rossbach, was annulled. The disbanded army of observation was revived, strengthened by a British contingent and placed under the able command of Prince Ferdinand of Brunswick, who eventually succeeded in forcing the French army back behind the Rhine. Following the temporary respite this produced, the main focus of the war again shifted to the area between the rivers Elbe and Oder. Here a new situation had arisen, occasioned by the Russian advance towards the Electoral Mark and Silesia following its occupation of East Prussia. In spite of his limited room for manoeuvre, the King of Prussia once again seized the initiative, captured the Austrian fortress of Schweidnitz and advanced towards Moravia with the ultimate aim of capturing Olmütz. In his earlier strategic calculations, Frederick had attached great importance to Moravia since its proximity to Vienna made it a particularly vulnerable region of the Habsburg Monarchy. Bearing in mind Prussia's relative weakness, it was, of course, inconceivable to have ever considered marching on Vienna itself; Frederick's principal aim was probably to draw upon himself the Austrians under Daun in order to prevent their linking up with the Russian troops, to defeat the former in battle and then turn his attention to the latter. In the event, however, this plan failed hopelessly. A shortage of munitions and supplies contributed substantially to an early lifting of the siege of Olmütz and although Daun, nearing the besieged fortress, failed to take advantage of the situation to deal the final decisive blow to the retreating Prussian army, the abortive undertaking, even without defeat in battle, was a strategic disaster for Frederick.

Olmütz taught him that he was no longer in a position to engage in major offensive operations. Furthermore, his area of campaigning was now even more confined by the Russian army's approach to the line of the Oder. Frederick, believing himself safe from Austrian intervention, undertook the arduous march through the Oder-Warthe region to meet the advancing Russian troops to prevent them advancing into the heartlands of the Electoral Mark. At the battle of Zorndorf on 25 August 1758, after a considerable struggle and heavy losses on both sides, he forced the Russian army under General Fermor to retreat. The initial danger of a combined Russo-Austrian force thus seemed to have been averted; Frederick, however, made the fatal mistake of underestimating the tenacity and steadfastness of the Russian peasant army whose future deployment was to prove almost catastrophic for him. Only its withdrawal from the war would finally bring about his deliverance. Restlessly, he operated with his main army between the Elbe and Oder in the hope of containing the Austrians and preventing them from uniting with the Russians. At Hochkirch on 13 October 1758, however, Daun launched a surprise night attack against him and, aided considerably by Frederick's imprudent choice of camp, won his second decisive victory after Kolin. Thoughtlessness was clearly also one of the King's character traits; in many ways, it was the essential corollary of his boldness. It often caused the fruits of victory to be snatched from his grasp, although, fortunately for him, his opponents frequently lacked the necessary resolution and cohesion to capitalise on their successes.

The need to conduct an all-round defence of an ever-decreasing theatre of operations determined Frederick's position at the beginning of 1759, a year which was to produce his most disastrous setbacks and defeats. Prussia consisted, more than ever, only of the territory its army could defend. In the final days of 1758, Frederick took stock of his situation and concluded that his experiences could only be useful if they were thoroughly examined: 'What use is life if one only vegetates?'. As a result, he wrote *Reflections on Certain Changes in the Art of Warfare*, in the hope that 'careful examination of our enemies' systems and the obstacles they place in our way would produce suitable means with which to overcome them'. These reflections represent both a decisive change of Frederician strategy as well as evidence of unashamed self-criticism. The King reminded his officers of the method he himself had formerly employed in order to stand firm against the colossus 'which threatened to crush me'. Only the mistakes of his enemies, however, had allowed him to employ it: 'Their sluggish reluctance ever to seize the opportunity and their general inertia made my alertness useful.' But he could not continue to set such an example in the future. A helmsman who follows the moods of the wind more than the direction of his compass should never be allowed to act as a role model. Frederick listed the incredible progress the Austrians had made during the war; of all his opponents, their advances in the art of warfare had been the most significant. Did this mean, however, that their troops had become invincible? 'By no means! That is something I shall never concede. However, I would not advise anyone to engage rashly an army with so many advantages.' Frederick instead emphasised the importance of capitalising on the enemy's mistakes, learning to recognise his weaknesses and emulating his strengths. Large, decisive battles which would decide the fate of states, nevertheless, were now beyond Prussia's capabilities, Frederick was forced to admit. It was thus necessary to destroy the enemy in different, more limited ways. Only when Frederick admitted this to himself, did he become fully aware of the gravity of his situation: 'The entire weight of Europe is bearing down upon us. Our army has to be constantly on the move, defending a border here, rushing to the aid of a province there. We are forced to follow the paths our enemies map out for us, rather than dictating them, and have to gear our campaigns to accord with theirs.' Such insight was essentially an admission that his previous strategy had failed. The only possible way out would be to lure the enemy into the open and defeat him there, an undertaking which could only be attempted in Lower Silesia, on Frederick's own soil. The King admitted that this presented a terrible prospect, but stressed that it was his only option. He left open the question of whether he would, in fact, resort to this plan and consoled himself with the thought that until then his salvation had always been the 'incredible blunders' committed by his enemies. This gave rise to hope, but also to resignation. These insights were the only fruit 'which the last campaign has borne'. The year 1759 was to prove, however, that his predicament could become even bleaker. He would be driven to the point where even the limited courage detectable in his desperation at the end of 1758 would desert him.

Frederick's immediate strategic goal was to prevent the amalgamation of the Russian army, stationed near the Oder, with the Austrian corps under the inventive and able General Gideon Ernst von Laudon. As a result of a series of mistakes by subordinate Prussian commanders, however, success eluded him. His attack upon the numerically far superior allied forces to the east of the Oder near Frankfurt resulted, on 12 August 1759, in the most decisive defeat he had ever suffered. The battle of Kunersdorf decimated his army, leaving him with a mere 10,000 men and only fifty large guns. His losses, numbering some 19,000 men, surpassed even those of the allies. It was the moment of his deepest crisis; indeed, he needed several days to recover from the shock. Then, on 1 September, he announced to Prince Henry 'the miracle of the House of Brandenburg . . . this time the enemy could have crossed the Oder and, with a second battle, concluded the war; instead, however, he marched from Müllrose to Lieberose'. This 'miracle' had been the product of the Russian commander Saltykov's refusal to join his exhausted army with the Austrians for the final push to Berlin advocated by Laudon. The repercussions of the disaster at Kunersdorf were thus limited to the loss of Dresden, which was to remain in Austrian hands until the end of the war. The remaining campaigns, fought amidst material and personal exhaustion as well as mounting war-weariness on all sides, centred on the struggle for Silesia and Saxony. Frederick experienced further setbacks, such as the Prussian general Friedrich August von Finck's capitulation at Maxen on 20 November 1759. Neither the victory at Liegnitz on 15 August 1760, nor that at Torgau on 3 November 1760, improved Prussia's situation. Ultimately, Frederick was unable to prevent the occupation of Berlin between 8 and 12 October 1760 by Russian, Austrian and Saxon troops. The occupation was not only of symbolic importance to the allies, but also a blow to Prussia's munitions industry concentrated in its capital. The Russians destroyed the Royal Canon Works as well as most of the gunpowder factories, although the *Lagerhaus*, the important textile factory, remained unscathed.

The final phase of this drawn out war was increasingly characterised by the numerical superiority of the Russo-Austrian forces. Saxony was largely under Daun's control, while in central Silesia, the Russian army under Buturlin joined with Laudon's Austrian contingent. Hemmed in from all sides and with only limited resources at his disposal, Frederick was unable to retain the initiative and instead followed a traditional strategy and avoided provoking attacks by his opponents. Typical of Frederick's situation in the latter part of the war was the time he spent besieged in the fortified camp of Bunzelwitz outside the fortress of Schweidnitz between 20 August and 10 September 1761. Surrounded by overwhelmingly superior forces, he lived with the constant fear that a shattering enemy attack was imminent. A mere 55,000 Prussian troops faced 65,000 Russians and 75,000 Austrians. Having failed to prevent a Russo-Austrian combination Frederick had sought to hold his position at Schweidnitz, make use of the fortress's munitions store and possibly repel an attack on Breslau. The camp at Bunzelwitz, later to become a symbol of steadfastness in an almost hopeless situation, was in reality no more than a skilful move in the cunning game of strategic manoeuvring. Whereas aggressive tactics had been open to him earlier, the King was now restricted to more cautious moves against an enemy about whose intentions he was completely in the dark. Despite some skilful operations, however, Schweidnitz was ultimately lost, as was Kolberg in Pomerania which, after surviving several attempts to besiege it into submission, finally fell into Russian hands. In his own account of the Seven Years War, Frederick used the bleakest of language to describe his predicament: 'The army had to defend itself against the Austrians facing it and the Russians at its back. Supply lines between Berlin and Breslau were in constant danger of being cut. But the situation became completely desperate after the fall of Kolberg. With the approach of spring, the Russians, now unhindered, were free to besiege Stettin or even bring Berlin and the entire Electoral Mark under their control.' But, on the King's own admission, the situation 'only appeared to be lost'. In matters of such great importance, steadfastness was everything, enabling 'one to overcome all adversity and imminent danger'.

Frederick's gloomy words, of course, could merely have been a literary device employed to prepare the reader for the subsequent turn of events. In one sense, it contained an element of truth: the war had indeed reached its final stage, since all its participants had, for varying reasons, become anxious for an end to the fighting. Austria displayed the most obvious signs of fatigue. Its resources were all but exhausted; the state debt had risen from 49 million gulden in 1756 to 136 million gulden, while the annual income amounted to no more than 24 million gulden. Under the pressure of such severe financial difficulties, economies were implemented in the 1760 campaign, and in 1761, against vigorous opposition from the military, the Emperor and the Crown Prince, Maria Theresa sanctioned a reduction of troop numbers and the dissolution of two companies within each regiment. This was thought to be a reasonable risk to take in view of the not altogether unlikely possibility of

Frederick's imminent ruin from exhaustion. It was estimated that he could safely be left to a lingering 'death from emaciation'. Despite troop reductions, however, hopes of regaining Silesia and Glatz remained and the necessary military preparations were made to give Austria a favourable bargaining position at the forthcoming peace negotiations. Preparations for this had begun as early as summer 1759. Prussia, however, sought to obscure the scale of its exhaustion. Its only salvation lay in collaboration with Great Britain, and all moves towards a separate peace between Paris and London had to be prevented. As the defeats of 1759 (Kunersdorf and Maxen) lowered Prussia's political standing, England's star was rising as a result of its victories in Canada, particularly the capture of Quebec. France was driven into a corner by the British successes and began to entertain the idea of relieving the pressure by concluding a peace with Prussia. Voltaire was employed as mediator, but was as unsuccessful in this as he had been in his earlier diplomatic undertakings. All the powers involved had a hand in the diplomatic game, which ran concurrently with the continuing military struggle. Frederick had no option but to pin all his hopes on diplomacy. He even formulated grandiose plans of territorial exchanges in Prussia's favour, doubtless aware that 'if the worst came to the worst . . . things could only be returned to the *status quo ante bellum*'. What at this point was still described as the worst possible scenario, soon emerged as the best that could probably be salvaged from the war. Maintaining the status quo undoubtedly became the guiding force behind the King's diplomacy. It was a principle which was unflinchingly adhered to and, aided by some unexpected developments, eventually met with success.

The first significant peace initiative was taken jointly by England and Prussia. Pitt, under considerable domestic pressure, was behind the Anglo-Prussian proposal of peace delivered to France and the two imperial powers at Ryswijk. Dated 25 November 1760, it was principally an invitation to form a peace congress. Although France was prepared to consider the offer, Kaunitz, despite Austria's financial plight, rejected it out of hand. Empress Elizabeth's continued military assistance had already been bought on 1 April 1760, in an agreement which guaranteed East Prussia to Russia, and Austria seemed determined to continue the struggle. Hopes of peace were thus soon dashed, although in March 1761, efforts continued to be made to arrange a peace congress at Augsburg. It was clear, however, that the divergent aims of the opposing powers were as irreconcilable as ever. Frederick clung to his demand for a return to the 1756 *status quo ante bellum*, while the allies insisted on a guarantee of their present territorial assets: in which case, the whole of East Prussia, Glatz, parts of Silesia and Pomerania as well as Cleves and Mark would have been lost to Prussia. In the summer of 1761, this was still an unthinkable basis for negotiation for Frederick, however desperate his situation may have been at the time.

France continued to face the dilemma of simultaneously waging a colonial war in North America and India and a continental war in northwestern Germany. The heavy losses and defeats incurred overseas – Montreal, its last bastion in Canada, Madras, Pondicherry – had, of course, progressively weakened its position vis-à-vis England, but somewhat paradoxically also led to an increased effort to win ground in Germany. The final French offensive in Hanover and Westphalia, however, met with staunch resistance from Ferdinand of Brunswick's mobile Anglo-Prussian force and had to be abandoned. In any case, internal developments in the great powers on the European periphery, England and Russia, were considerably more important. These were to prove that the outcome of the Seven Years War could not be decided on the battlefield. As the military deadlock in central and eastern Europe continued and permanent stalemate threatened, events in North America, on the high seas, and even in western Germany, assumed a new importance. Spain's entry into the war, moreover, significantly widened the area of conflict. In view of the *rapprochement* between the Bourbon courts of Paris and Madrid, Pitt's foreign policy had sought to avoid incurring Spanish hostility at all costs. His fall from power, however, was followed by the appointment of George III's favourite, Lord Bute. He lacked his predecessor's considerable ability and energy, which even Frederick of Prussia had acknowledged by describing Pitt as a 'truly Roman character'. The British people's desire for peace, however, necessitated a change of government in October 1761. Bute did not immediately withdraw from the alliance with Prussia, but his actions left little doubt that he had in fact abandoned his ally. It also seemed likely that the Anglo-Prussian subsidy treaty, due to run out in December 1761, would not be renewed. It became clear that Bute sought a *rapprochement* with Austria and attempted to persuade the King of Prussia that he, too, should sacrifice his lands for the sake of peace with Vienna. Frederick , of course, refused, but the situation was desperate and the pressure on him to comply enormous.

Suddenly, he was heartened by extraordinary news from St Petersburg: on 5 January 1762, Empress Elizabeth had died. Brushing aside all *raison d'état*, it was she who had pursued Frederick with passionate personal hatred. Her successor, the Grand Duke Peter (who became Emperor as Peter III), on the other hand, was a fervent admirer of the King of Prussia. In an absolute monarchy, a change of sovereign could influence that state's foreign policy to a much greater extent than would have been possible in other political systems. The resulting transformation in Russo-Prussian relations, however, was far more radical than could have been anticipated: Peter III not only concluded a rapid peace with Prussia (5 May) but, on 19 June 1762, also entered into an alliance with her. Such a momentous change in policy doubtless stemmed solely from Peter III's fascination with Frederick, since the only advantage Russia could hope to gain from the union would be Prussian support in its dispute with Denmark over Schleswig, which the ducal House of Holstein (of which Russia's ruler was a member) sought to annex. In the maelstrom of the new great power constellations, war-weary Sweden, too, concluded peace with Prussia on 22 May with a treaty based on the territorial position of 1720. 'Thank heaven, our backs are freed', Frederick wrote to Prince Henry upon hearing the news of the Empress Elizabeth's death. These words continued to ring true even after Peter's death, since his wife and successor, Catherine, while abandoning the active pro-Prussian initiatives launched by her husband, at least confirmed the Russo-Prussian peace treaty.

Ultimately the political developments in western and eastern Europe in the final stages of the Seven Years War transformed the military situation. In the west, the Anglo-French conflict threatened to engulf the whole continent, following Spain's entry into the war and its invasion of Portugal; in the east, all the belligerents were now exhausted. Frederick's illusory hopes of an Ottoman attack failed to materialise, and instead the theatre of operations contracted to its original proportions. Frederick himself won a significant victory on 21 July 1762, at Burkersdorf in Silesia; while his brother Henry succeeded in crushing Austrian and Imperial troops at Freiberg in Saxony. These final battles considerably improved Prussia's negotiating position at the forthcoming peace talks which were now inevitable. These were eventually conducted separately. In Paris on 10 February 1763, peace was concluded between Great Britain, Spain and France, and a treaty signed whereby Great Britain gained Canada, Florida and the areas west of the Mississippi, while France retained its dominant position in the West Indies. These gains – less than the fallen Pitt would have demanded – were to determine the history of the following century. By comparison, the results of the Peace of Hubertusburg, concluded five days later at a Saxon hunting lodge, between Austria, Prussia and Saxony seemed positively inconsequential: the status quo, which the earlier treaties of Breslau and Dresden had established, was guaranteed; Silesia as well as Glatz, which, to the last, Austrian diplomacy had sought to regain, remained in Prussian hands, and Saxony's existing borders were guaranteed.

Victory without gain

What are we now to make of the words Frederick used in his address to his officers in 1755? 'Each war which fails to lead to conquest weakens the victor and debilitates the state. One must, therefore, seek never to enter into hostilities which do not present the possibility of conquest. This immediately determines the type of war: it makes it an offensive war. . . .' Had his original intention been the conquest of Saxony or West Prussia, which only with difficulty can be said to have been the case, he had clearly failed. Was he now the great loser, returning to a ruined Prussia, bled dry by its great human losses? His thoughts at the end of the war are contained in the final section of his *Histoire de la guerre de sept ans* (*History of the Seven Years War*): 'Is it not remarkable', he wrote, 'that all cunning and might is so often duped by unexpected developments or fateful blows? Does it not seem as if a mysterious force is contemptuously playing games with the plans of men? At the beginning of a war, does not every sensible person expect its outcome to be different? Who would have thought that Prussia could withstand an attack from the mighty league of Austria, Russia, France, Sweden and the entire Holy Roman Empire, with the omnipresent threat of destruction which this confrontation entailed, and emerge from the war without any territorial losses?' These lines, of course, obscure the fact that Frederick himself harboured serious doubts as to Prussia's chances of survival, and ignore considerable economic and demographic losses.

If one is inclined to view the Seven Years War as a Prussian success, one has to measure success and failure in war by a different yardstick. Prussia, at the beginning of Frederick's reign, was a military state without a natural territorial, demographic or economic base. The seizure of Silesia, with its highly advanced economy and strategic importance, was a step on the road to acquiring a sufficient basis for its militarisation and, by extension, its safety. But the Habsburg Monarchy was not prepared to acknowledge this loss, since Vienna perceived it as the occasion for a great shift in the European power constellation, and one which would confer upon Prussia a much more prominent position in the hierarchy of states. Everyone clamoured for proof of the durability of Prussia's new status, hoping that the events of 1740 and their consequences could be reversed. The novice great power was to be subjected to a test, and failure to pass it would once again mean relegation to the political second division.

If one views matters in this light, then the Seven Years War was a war of revenge in which the hitherto dominant power in central Europe had met its match. By 1763, Prussian great power status had been established beyond question. Leopold von Ranke, in his essay on the great powers, put it like this: 'If the measure of a great power is its ability to survive the combined attack of other powers, then Frederick had achieved this position for Prussia.' Certainly, its long term effects are undeniable. It was the first time since Henry the Lionheart, that a lesser German Prince had challenged the Emperor with such explosive consequences.

Prussia's extraordinary survival, of course, begs the question as to how and under what circumstances such a feat was achieved. However, this one question only opens the door to a number of unanswered questions. How could a single human being withstand the extreme physical and mental pressures to which Frederick was subjected? Where and how did he find the officers, soldiers, civil servants and friends willing, if at times reluctantly, to do his bidding? Was it chance that saved him from the worst of fates? These problems constantly occupied the King himself. Among the factors which allowed Prussia to survive, not least was Frederick's own heroism as well as his remarkable, ever-changing and adaptable nature. His ability 'to keep up his morale' was crucial, according to Ranke. He contends that Frederick's resilience stemmed not only from his military genius, but also from an 'internal, moral and spiritual strength'. As Jacob Burckhardt says, 'the fate of peoples and states, and the direction of whole civilisations could depend upon the ability of one person to withstand extreme mental pressure at certain times. All central European history since has been affected by Frederick the Great's ability to do this from 1759 to 1763.' Burckhardt's words come close to a psychological analysis. Real strength of character, however, can surely also be attributed to Maria Theresa, permanently confident that morality was on her side. Thomas Mann, in an essay published in 1915, simplified the problem of 'Frederick and the Great Coalition', and spoke of the King's 'almost superhuman nervous strength', which, to Mann, had assumed almost demonic overtones: 'One might perceive him to have been some kind of goblin, engendering universal hate and distaste, leading the world a merry dance like an androgynous troll who failed to be exhausted by the death of millions of people.'

Frederick's ability, nevertheless, only provides part of the answer. He himself was aware of this. His constant preoccupation with the reasons for his own survival is well documented. An important source is the King's letters to his sister, Wilhelmina of Bayreuth, which continued until her death on the day of the battle of Hochkirch; another is his correspondence with the Marquis d'Argens. Thirdly, there are the memoirs of Henri de Catt which, although somewhat distorted by a certain amount of literary licence, give an accurate account of the King's state of mind by recording conversations with him from March 1758 to July 1760. Finally, Frederick's own, frequently dilletantish, poetry and philosophy allow the observer a glimpse of his inner self. The latter undoubtedly served as a welcome distraction from the shock and strain of war. All these sources point to the fact that the magic word 'glory' had lost its appeal for Frederick. Mention was briefly made of it at the beginning of the war, but subsequently abandoned. It is replaced by terms such as 'duty' and talk of 'the honour and well-being of the state'. 'I think of the state, not glory', he wrote to d'Argens on 20 August 1759. Honour was the maxim by which a King must live and which must, ipso facto, be equated with the well-being of the state. 'I have allowed myself as King to think like a monarch, and have made it my basic conviction that a Prince's good name (*"la réputation"*) must be dearer to him than life itself', Frederick wrote to Wilhelmina on 13 July 1757. His reference to a box that would end all suffering sounds as if he fought a constant battle within himself not to commit suicide; but a ruler was not the master of his own destiny, he was not free to act as an ordinary person without responsibility. Hence the end of his letter to Earl Marshal George Keith:

'Que s'il sauve l'état, quitte de son emploi
Il pourra disposer la liberté de soi.'

(If one is to serve the state and perform one's duty correctly, one must forsake one's individual liberty.)

The natural, almost instinctive, identification of self with state was, of course, absolutism in its purest form; but now the term no longer possessed the naiveté with which it may have been tinged in the age of Louis XIV, and instead contained an understanding that a time of great crisis necessitated great personal sacrifice. Enlightened it was not, rather a form of puritan asceticism in the Prussian tradition. Duty, in Frederick's case, could be interpreted as the preparedness to do everything to preserve the state and save it from ruin.

This principle merged with the demands of honour, which, by this time, had replaced the quest for glory. Frederick's very personal interpretation of duty and honour, therefore, formed the core of his aristocratic philosophy.

At no stage of Frederick's life was this philosophy, demanding lightning reaction to changing circumstances more manifest than in the Seven Years War. His was a very human tragedy, as his poetry bears witness. The man who was exposed to the shifting sands of war and who recognised the futility of all human plans, could not perceive his role in world history: 'I know not my destiny. Where do I come from? Where am I? Where am I going?', he asked in a letter to Keith in September 1758. 'We are but the puppets of an invisible power and act without knowing what we are doing', he wrote to d'Argens on 8 June 1762. The old problem of predestinarianism, which had earlier preoccupied him in his youth, surfaced once again, and Frederick enquired in a letter to d'Argens on 13 May 1761: 'Does predestination exist or not?' He admitted that he did not have an answer. 'Philosophy, my dear friend, eases the pain of past and future suffering, but on the present it has no effect', d'Argens was told in a letter dated 19 July 1757. Philosophy contained no activating forces for the campaigning military leader, nor, however, did it debilitate him. Ultimately, Frederick could only give way to cynicism, as in a letter to his brother, Henry, written on 15 November 1761: 'Life for you has been but a school for death.'

Only at one point can a link between Frederick's military planning and military writings be established: he was aware of the importance of chance in war. In the *General Principles of War* of 1748, he cautioned his generals never to rely on continuing good fortune or to become complacent in the face of success. 'We should think much more on the fact that, with our limited wisdom and care, we are often the chess pieces of fate.' In his great ode '*Sur le Hasard*', composed in September 1757, for his sister, Amalie, chance (*le hasard*) is the great determining force of world history. The fates of such as Catherine II and the Marquise de Pompadour, who had risen to positions of great power from relatively humble beginnings, are cited as proof. Chance or fortune were not metaphysical concepts for Frederick, but arose simply from the inability of human reason to light the darkness which had spread into certain corners of the world. On two occasions, at least, Frederick himself experienced chance as a favourable factor in the war: the first time was after the catastrophe of Kunersdorf when the opposing armies failed to deal him the final blow. At the time, he even described it as a miracle. The second occasion was the death of Empress Elizabeth in January, 1762, which removed all anxieties in his rear. 'How great is the game of chance! It mocks the haughty wisdom of mortals, preserves the hopes of one and dashes those of another.'

But did the game of chance really decide the outcome of the Seven Years War? Was it the King's steadfastness which gave chance the opportunity to preserve Prussia from ruin? One can clearly not expect too much from un-known forces and the heroism of a single man. Nevertheless, an explanation is clearly needed why a fragile, and in many ways incomplete, state survived the ultimate test of strength. In the age of absolutism, states threatened from abroad often also fell prey to internal turmoil, such as the Dutch Republic after the French invasion of 1672, and Sweden after Charles XII's death. External danger fanned the flames of internal discontent. What was the reaction in Prussia? If one considers, first of all, the King's immediate family, it becomes clear that right from the start, the war met with vehement resistance. From the outset, the King's brothers, Augustus William and Henry, firmly opposed the very idea of war. In the grave crises which followed, especially after the defeats at Kolin in 1757 and Kunersdorf in 1759 as well as Finck's capitulation at Maxen in the same year, Prince Henry's opposition was such as to send him into fits of passionate, spiteful anger, an example of which was his comment about Phaeton's fall in his letter to Amalia. According to de Catt, Henry had vigorously protested to his brother about the planned dispatch of a regiment to Maxen and warned his brother that he must take upon himself responsibility for the disaster which would consequently befall the state. After the expected catastrophe had descended upon the Prussian corps, the Prince vented his anger by noting on a report from Frederick: 'the King has plunged us into this terrible war and only the bravery of the generals and soldiers can extricate us from it. Since the day my forces became embroiled in it, nothing but disorder and misfortune have befallen us. All my efforts in this campaign and the luck that was on my side, all has been lost through Frederick.' All has been lost through Frederick – this was not only an expression of Henry's outrage and wounded pride, but an opinion prevalent in the army as a whole. In an anonymous letter, sent to Henry by his brother, Ferdinand, the King is accused of rashly squandering lives without achieving any goal. Henry's conduct of the war, on the other hand, is given the highest praise.

Was this a half-hearted attempt to incite Prince Henry to rebel? Had the brothers not already agreed that the King was in the process of destroying the state? If such thoughts ever surfaced, they were never transformed into concrete plans. Never, regardless of the crisis facing them, was the loyalty of the royal Princes to the reigning monarch in question. To protest openly about the King was against their upbringing, although Henry seems to have had the chance to do so. Nearing a nervous breakdown after the heavy blow of Kunersdorf, Frederick had made his brother *generalissimo* of the army, reflecting '. . . it will be impossible to right this misfortune; instead what my brother commands will be done'. The document in which Frederick gave these orders has not survived; it can, therefore, never be proven conclusively to have existed. In any case, even if it had, it is virtually certain that Henry would not have misused it to place himself in the saddle. In the minds of both brothers, the principle of primogeniture ranked above all other personal or dynastic ambition. Augustus William's son was and remained Crown Prince. Even to consider the violent transfers of political authority which took place in contemporary Russia was utterly foreign to Prince Henry. The most radical action he felt able to take was to resign from the army on two occasions and withdraw his services from the war. Ultimately redeployed as commander-in-chief in Saxony in April 1761, he emerged victorious at Freiberg on 29 October 1762.

The royal dynasty, despite its outrage and anger, never represented so serious a source of opposition as to endanger the King. It was already too closely bound to the Prussian ethos of *raison d'état*. A break in the line of succession would have destroyed the very foundations upon which the monarchy rested. The emergent institutionalisation and incorporation into the state machinery of the royal family also began to encompass the aristocracy. Already by the early eighteenth century, the time of rebellion under noble leadership had passed, although the aristocracy had not yet grown into its later, pivotal role within the state. Frederick William I had regarded the older, 'turbulent' families of the Mark with the deepest of mistrust, and consequently forced the sons of Junkers into cadet schools in Berlin, so that they would eventually become officers in the army. Under his successor, Frederick II, the nobility, with its highly developed *esprit de corps* and strict code of honour, gradually came to form the backbone of the officer corps. At its peak, the proportion of noble officers was as high as 90 per cent. In Pomerania by 1724, the landed aristocracy were, almost without exception, former or active officers; in the Electoral Mark, it was 68 per cent and in East Prussia, 60 per cent.

Under Frederick William I, aristocratic enlistment into the army had been principally the result of political and social necessity, whereas his son began to speak of the aristocratic and ethical principles of noble participation: it was imperative that the nobility retain its 'honneur', the loss of which would make continued personal and family survival impossible. In a state constantly prepared for war, the 1752 Political Testament asserted, a nobleman was the ideal military leader. Indeed, the Prussian nobility was to prove its worth in the Frederician wars and in the Seven Years War especially. Its losses, even in the highest echelons, were considerable and eventually forced desperate measures such as the admission of commoners into officer ranks. In the final analysis, the King's calculations were correct: the aristocratic principle of honour not only remained a steadfast political ideal, but also formed the glue which bound together not only the officer corps but the whole fabric of the state at a time when it was threatened from all sides. A noble ethic became the ethic of the state. It was a matter of *raison d'état* to preserve intact the honour of the state. Matters of state were ultimately determined not according to enlightened principles of reason, but according to feudal codes of honour. The King, of course, provided frequent occasion for strong criticism and opposition, especially from the younger officers, if de Catt is to be believed; these never developed, however, to the point where orders were disobeyed or full-scale mutiny was imminent. Nevertheless, although the military leadership was predominantly aristocratic, one must not overlook the fact that the Cantonal System encompassed the sons of peasant farmers who served side-by-side with foreign mercenaries, both constant sources of dissent and incitement to desertion. This exposed a great chasm in the Prussian military state. The officers' code of honour did not apply to the ordinary soldier, whose service depended upon his total subjugation to brutally harsh orders. One might, therefore, expect the enlisted man to display, if not revolutionary tendencies, at least a certain obstinacy in the face of discipline.

The emergent middle class was totally divorced from this hierarchical agrarian society; indeed, it failed even to provide a focus of intellectual opposition during the war. Support and criticism seemed more or less to balance each other out. The Church lent the King strong support, especially in the dark days of the war, and its ministers lauded his name in their sermons. The effect on one group of Prussian poets was the desired one. Karl Wilhelm Ramler, Ewald von Kleist, himself doomed to become a victim of the war, and Johann Wilhelm Ludwig Gleim made the King's cause their own. Gleim's 'War and Victory Songs of a Prussian Grenadier' (1758), for example, sought to hit a traditional, folkloric note.

Undercurrents not only of opposition, but open defiance, on the other hand, could be detected in the capital. According to a report from Andrew Mitchell, three weeks after Frederick's return to Berlin in 1763, certain street signs had posters pinned to them depicting the King as a tyrant who deserved the fate of Russia's Peter III. The origin of these posters, however, was not traced, and the King was not informed of the matter. It is interesting to consider the opinion of the sharply critical royal observer, Christian Garve, in his 'Fragments of a Portrayal of the Mind, Character and Government of Frederick II', on the limited degree of internal cohesion within Prussian society after Frederick's death. 'Never before has a ruler', he wrote, 'laid himself so open to the judgement of his subjects.' 'Not only the strength of the military ruled out any thoughts of dissent among his subjects, but also the natural inclination to peaceful obedience of the inhabitants of both his established and newly acquired provinces, their love of peaceful pursuits and the lack of a common, unifying force, apart from their subjugation to the same monarch; all this guaranteed Frederick immunity from potentially damaging literary attacks, designed to damage his reputation.' Garve's analysis, its implied criticism and, at the same time, its admiration clearly detectable, is one of the most precise characterisations of the psyche of the Frederician state itself, with all its robustness as well as its passive acceptance.

The mood in the country and, indeed, the strength of loyalty to the Prussian state, of course, varied from region to region. Surprisingly, weakening support for the Crown was not only to be detected in the new provinces of East Friesland and Silesia, but also in the Hohenzollern heartland of East Prussia. The Kingdom, occupied by the Russians from January 1758 until the end of the war, displayed a remarkable ability to adapt to the changing circumstances. After Elizabeth declared East Prussia a Russian possession in a patent of 31 December 1757, and its capital, Königsberg, was occupied on 21 January 1758, those remaining administrators together with the provincial Estates swore an oath of allegiance to the Russian ruler. The conduct of the East Prussian nobility deeply angered Frederick, who never again visited the province. In his Political Testament of 1768, he wrote: 'I had every reason to be displeased with the East Prussian aristocracy in the last war. Its inclination was to be more Russian than Prussian, and, incidentally, it was capable of all the misdeeds which one attributes to the Poles.'

In Silesia, only assimilated by Prussia in 1742, the situation was slightly different. In a province where a large proportion of the population was Protestant and had been subject to considerable pressure from Vienna while under Austrian rule, confessional differences became polarised and were transferred to either Austrian or Prussian sympathies. Silesian Protestants welcomed Frederick in 1740, but the Breslau merchant classes, for instance, maintained a certain reserve, probably due to economic considerations. The Catholic clergy and its flock unreservedly took the Austrian side, and supported Vienna both openly and secretly in both Silesian Wars. In Upper Silesia, Catholicism predominated and its aristocracy continued into the 1760s also to hold land in Habsburg territory, i.e. in Bohemia and Moravia. Political changes such as those of 1742 could not, of course, take place entirely smoothly. Silesians felt oppressed by the heavy demands of the Prussian army; instead of 4,000 soldiers, 40,000 were now stationed within its borders. The loss of its traditional markets plunged the Silesian linen industry into a severe crisis from which it was never fully able to recover. A willingness to return to the Austrian fold seemed to be emerging and, if allowed to grow, could seriously endanger Prussia's conduct of the Seven Years War. However, in spite of some isolated, if spectacular, cases of Silesian collusion with Austria, the population as a whole remained passively quiet. The fact that the province did not remain under enemy occupation for any length of time may also have helped. When the Empress Queen announced her recapture of the lost lands after the seizure of Breslau in September 1757, the willingness of the local administrators to take an oath of allegiance only superficially resembled the East Prussian case. Reassimilation into Austria would doubtless have taken place without difficulty, since the full integration of Silesia into the Prussian state did not take place until after the Seven Years War. However, Silesia ultimately contributed little or nothing to the efforts of its former Austrian rulers in the fighting after 1756. In his 1768 Political Testament, Frederick deals leniently with them, but gives detailed instructions as to how to deal with people suspected of being Austrian agents 'as soon as war seems a possibility'. If one adds to this the uncertain situation in the scattered Prussian possessions on the Lower Rhine, largely occupied by France during the war, or the territory of East Friesland, one has a sum of Prussia's most vulnerable areas. Nevertheless, a process of internal disintegration cannot be said to have taken place during the Seven Years War. As long as its army existed, the Prussian state could survive.

In his own account, Frederick puts forward three reasons why the anticipated defeat of Prussia failed to materialise:

1. Lack of agreement and harmony between the alliance powers; the divergence of their individual interests prevented them from agreeing on numerous plans of operation; in particular, the low level of cooperation

between Russian and Austrian generals, who often shied away from working together at precisely the point at which the destruction of Prussia would have been possible.

2. The Austrian court's cunning and misconceived statecraft which pushed the most difficult and dangerous military undertakings onto its allies, so that, by the end of the war, its army was more numerous and in better condition than those of the other powers. Herein lies the reason for the Austrian command's excessive caution. Ultimately, the price was several missed opportunities to deal the final blow to a Prussia on its knees and close to destruction.

3. The death of Empress Elizabeth who took the Austrian alliance with her to the grave; the subsequent withdrawal of the Russians from the war; Peter III's swift conclusion of an alliance with Prussia and the dispatch of a Russian corps to assist Prussian forces in Silesia.

The arguments advanced by Frederick require further examination. Up to the moment of Elizabeth's death, Prussia had survived undefeated. Why? Frederick cites a lack of agreement and a failure of cooperation among the great powers as the principal reason. This, of course, applies to most coalitions, even those who were eventually victorious; it must, therefore, have been a higher degree of differences that divided the anti-Prussian alliance than, for example, had existed during the War of the Spanish Succession. At that time, England and Austria shared the common interest of preventing a union between France and Spain. The moment an Austro-Spanish *rapprochement* was inevitable after Charles VI's accession, the coalition and its joint ventures were moribund. When, after the battle of Kunersdorf, the Prussian position to the east of the Oder seemed finally to be about to collapse, Russia's foreign policy ceased to be interested in conducting an offensive war and determined to leave such campaigning to Austria. Saltykov's hesitation to join in a push to Berlin, therefore, accorded fully with the St Petersburg's new line. The aim of destroying Prussia appeared to be of secondary importance and it has to be asked whether this was actually Russia's intention. Frederick, then, had clearly not fully analysed the political background to the 'low level of cooperation'. His second point was an attempt, employing rational thought, to explain the structural weakness of the Austrian command. But his claims cannot be substantiated. Daun's hesitant conduct during the last two years of the war was fully in tune with the demands of the situation; Austria was not prepared to risk the forces necessary for the decisive blow against Prussia without Russian assistance.

In any case, however persuasive arguments of structural and political weakness in a coalition may be, the inescapable conclusion remains that the 'miracle of the House of Brandenburg' was brought about by Frederick's own genius. Aided only by a British army operating in North Germany he succeeded in sustaining a determined resistance against a coalition of three great powers and their satellites, a feat many contemporaries believed impossible. His superiority, especially in the face of Prussia's principal opponent, Austria, which committed all its available resources to regain Silesia, lay in the fact that in his person, he united both political and military leadership. Frederick II must be described as a militarist, but one whose military actions were always determined by political goals. These objectives clearly underwent a change in the course of the war: in the early phase, his aim was still territorial gain, principally Saxony and perhaps Northern Bohemia and West Prussia, and his strategy was drawn up accordingly. By the end of 1757, however, the preservation of Prussia's territorial integrity determined his military plans. This meant adapting his strategy to encompass purely defensive action, with the ultimate aim of preventing his opponents' military cooperation through a series of single, sharp blows. The battles of Rossbach and Leuthen were particularly representative of this new kind of *Blitzkrieg* strategy. With these battles, Frederick reached the height of his popularity: Rossbach was celebrated not only as a victory over the Imperial army, but also over France, and Leuthen was fêted for being the result of remarkable military leadership in spite of his army's extreme weakness and exhaustion. In the concluding years of the war, the King increasingly lost the power to deal such blows and attempted instead to survive by means of shrewd tactical manoeuvres.

The principal advantage Frederick had over his opponents, aside from the benefits conferred by his strategy of interior lines, was Prussia's unified political and military leadership. Not only had they to agree on a command strategy within the coalition, but also had to bridge the gap between the military and political conduct of the war within their individual states. In Austria, it was primarily the political leadership under Kaunitz which held the military reins. Frederick's position as Soldier-King was based on his authority as absolute monarch. His rise could not, of course, be compared to, say, Napoleon's; but his charismatic leadership won him respect and glory which transcended the traditional position of a King. His charisma was not always in evidence, but at moments such as the battle of Leuthen, his military genius shone through. In his address to his officers before the battle, the King offered those who did not wish to follow him their freedom, and then announced the penalties regiments would incur should they fail in the attack. Herein lay the foundations of his authority: the combination of charisma and traditional royal power. In the hours before Leuthen, the former was clearly in the ascendant. Without doubt, no contemporary parallel existed among his opponents. Maria Theresa surpassed Frederick in her humanity and uprightness; she was popular and, even in difficult moments such as her appeal for help to the Hungarian Diet in September 1741, could always resort to the emotive power of words. But, ultimately, she lacked the charisma of Frederick II. Moreover, her most able military commanders, Count Leopold Daun, the victor of Kolin and Hochkirch, and Gideon Ernst von Laudon, the instigator of the Prussian defeat at Kunersdorf and captor of the fortress at Schweidnitz, did not measure up to Frederick's standards. The French army was now but a pale shadow of its former self and the leadership of commanders such as Soubise or Broglie possessed none of the greatness of Turenne or even Maurice de Saxe. Of the Russian commanders – Fermor, Saltykov, Buturlin or Chernyshev – not one rose above mediocrity and, in any case, all were further handicapped by frequent political interference.

In the Seven Years War, Frederick II of Prussia reached the pinnacle of his historical importance. He entered the realms of history, not as the patron of a humanitarian state structure, but as the supreme example of a military leader. If this is to demonstrate his limitations, it must not be forgotten that he continued to live according to the ideals of his youth in a dream world he entered before his battles and at moments of great crisis. The title 'the Great' was not awarded him because he increased the power of his state, but because he was prepared to accept the consequences of his 'youthful prank' in 1740 and would never take a backward step. His appointment with glory demanded a life of stoic existence. His exemplar was Marcus Aurelius, the Roman Emperor who was both successful military leader and philosopher contemplating the futility of life. Frederick II was not suited to being a national hero – any kind of national German feeling was alien to him. At most, the preservation and consolidation of the Prussian state sowed the seeds of Prussia's national development in the next century. The Seven Years War earned the King popularity for his defeat of the French at Rossbach. But his admirers failed to see that among the defeated at Rossbach was also the Imperial army, and its defeat would ultimately speed the destruction of the old German Empire. When Goethe, in his essay *Dichtung und Wahrheit* ('Poetry and Truth'), wrote that Frederick the Great's deeds in the war fuelled the development of German literature, he may well have been right. The Germans now had a King who far surpassed the mediocrity of public life and his fellow German rulers.

Frederick returned to Berlin after six years, not as a triumphant victor, but a man broken in body and soul. Now someone who had passed the zenith of his life, he felt foreign in the familiar surroundings and regretted the high price of war. He mourned not only the heavy Prussian losses but also, on a more personal level, those close to him who had died in or during the fighting: the many friends, his mother, and his beloved sister, Wilhelmina, who had passed away on the very day of Hochkirch. Was it not also depressing to have returned only as a semi-victor, who had merely saved the state from ruin, not enriched it with further acquisitions? The old maxim never to conduct a war unless there existed the possibility of gains now seemed hollow. If he truly felt his constantly reiterated desire to serve the state and its people, then it must have been painful indeed to see the many wounds inflicted by the war. The King estimated the dead to number some 180,000, which, according to today's research, seems to be fairly accurate. Throughout Prussia, the war years saw a dramatic decline in population: in the Electoral Mark, the population between 1756 and 1763 dropped by 57,000 people, similar figures were recorded in the New Mark, while in Pomerania the decline was by 72,000, in East Prussia by around 90,000 and in Silesia by about 46,000. The sum total of these areas alone, therefore, was something in the order of 300,000 people; for the whole of Prussia, the figure has been estimated to have been around 400,000. These were considerable losses in an age in which demographic resources were central to the social and economic well-being of a state. Across large tracts of Prussia, thousands of homes were devastated and cities partly destroyed, Küstrin being an example. Added to this was the tremendous burden of indebtedness which hung over the towns and the rural estates, following their subjection to heavy wartime taxation and the confiscation of their goods by occupying forces. The capital itself was forced to make many sacrifices. During the course of the war, prices had risen to exorbitant levels and devaluation further increased the difficulties. In 1763, the cost of living reached an all-time high, while the overall economic crisis was intensified by a pan-European depression which had originated in the Netherlands, but soon came to encompass Hamburg and Berlin.

Only one state had suffered more from the war than Prussia: Saxony. Occupied by Prussian forces as early as autumn 1756, it subsequently became an indispensible part of the Prussian supply and financial base as well as an important area for recruitment. Saxony's contributions to the Prussian war effort are estimated to have been around 40 to 50 million thaler. The material damage suffered by Saxony surpassed even that of Prussia: a large number of cities, such as Zittau, Wittenberg and Dresden were partly or completely destroyed, indeed, the devastation caused by the Prussian bombardment of Dresden had been unequalled in its history.

Central Europe was the principal theatre of war after 1756 but, surprisingly, the peace settlement of 1763 made no significant alterations to the area's existing political geography. Even Saxony emerged intact, its territorial integrity guaranteed. The rise of Prussia had not yet allowed it to break free from the confines of territorial compactness. It could be argued that Great Britain was the real victor of the Seven Years War with its further gains in North America and that, by extension, this would open a new chapter in Europe's history in which disputes would be fought on a much wider, global scale, relegating Prussia to the periphery of events between 1763 and 1772. Frederick failed to recognise the implications of these developments. The occasional references to Great Britain, in his *History of the Seven Years War* or the Political Testament of 1768, are sceptical and contradictory, and reflected his belief that England's hour of glory had passed. Frederick admitted, however, that it had given rise to a genius in the form of William Pitt, and the latter's ability to conduct affairs in an intellectually superior manner was acknowledged by the King.

If one considers the origins of the war, it becomes clear that its political inception did not lie in the Anglo-Prussian Convention of Westminster, but in the reversal of alliances which made possible the Franco-Austrian *rapprochement*. This agreement, concluded in spring 1756 and later joined by Russia, brought none of the signatories any success. Kaunitz's great plan had failed: Silesia remained in Prussian hands and Prussia's rise to the status of Germany's second great power was not halted. These events mapped out the contours of central European politics for over a century, despite a temporary interruption during the Napoleonic era. The eventual fall of Austria was not, however, immediately recognisable though the financial consequences of the struggle were severe and affected not merely the rest of Maria Theresa's reign, but that of Joseph II as well. Indeed, Frederick in his 1768 Testament, presents a somewhat flattering portrait of Maria Theresa, her personality and her state. The ultimate loser of the 1756 alliance was France, whose European political decline continued after the Peace of Versailles in 1783 and whose progression towards 1789 was inescapable. Frederick, in his historical essays, deemed it to have been a serious mistake for the French to have become enmeshed in the German struggle. They had taken the wrong path and became 'involved in something which was none of their concern. Until then, they had been a supreme maritime power, surpassing even Britain; as soon as their attention was distracted by the continental war, and their financial resources, which could otherwise have been employed to increase the fleet, drained by their armies in Germany, the death knell of their seaborne might was sounded. The English thus gained the upper hand and remained dominant in all parts of the globe.'

CHAPTER 5

Russia – a dangerous neighbour

In seizing Silesia, Frederick had taken a fundamental decision: Prussia's expansion programme would be directed towards the east; not the west, where only its scattered possessions on the Lower Rhine were located. The principal Prussian territories of Brandenburg, Pomerania and East Prussia were all crucial regions within eastern and central European politics, and had been wrested largely from Sweden, Poland and Austria. In many ways Prussia's territorial disposition dictated the direction in which expansion must lie. Sweden and Poland, still a threat at the time of the Great Elector, had since fallen into decline and the resultant power vacuum had been filled by the westward thrust of Russia, recently reinvigorated by Peter the Great. Few contemporaries recognised the significance of this, despite the fact that in 1735 during the War of the Polish Succession, Russian troops had advanced as far as the western border regions of Germany. No other state must have felt the threat of this new power more than Prussia with its East Prussian salient and widespread political and economic interests in eastern Europe. Under Frederick William I, a rather volatile but productive relationship between the two states developed. Similarities in the internal structures of both powers as well as the personal inclinations of the two rulers contributed to a mutual recognition of each other's spheres of interest, and some agreements were concluded. Frederick William and Peter met on several occasions, the last time in Berlin in 1717. Frederick was then five and may well have remembered the meeting, although no evidence of this has survived. The memoirs of his sister, Wilhelmina of Bayreuth, on the other hand, contain a vivid account of the Tsar's visit. She provides a malicious, mocking description of the Tsar's 'barbarian court', the unsightly appearance of the Tsarina, whom she thought could be compared to a German comedienne, and of the curious incidents which punctuated the meeting.

Twenty years later, on 6 March 1737 in his correspondence with Voltaire, Crown Prince Frederick discussed Peter the Great, concluding that he thought him to be the only truly educated great ruler 'of our times' ('*de nos jours*'). In order to have been an example to other monarchs, however, he would have to have had a less barbaric and cruel upbringing than the one he had received in a country where unlimited authority found expression only in brutality. Voltaire agreed, but his praise of Peter was tempered by the fact that although he thought him an admirable ruler, as a human being he found him difficult to like. The debate continued on several other occasions. After receiving the assessment of Johann Gotthilf Vockerodt, a Prussian Secretary at the St Petersburg embassy, on 13 November 1737, however, Frederick was ultimately forced to revise his opinion and admit that his high regard for Tsar Peter could not be sustained. He acknowledged that he had created a *'fantôme héroïque'*. At most, Peter was 'a great man . . . in the real world'.

It is characteristic of Frederick that his acquaintance with Russia should be through the person of the great Tsar; he had little knowledge of actual conditions in Russia. This ignorance continued for some time. In all his other analyses of great power politics, Frederick's calculations were based on an assessment of each state's interests; Russian politics, on the other hand, he deemed to be determined by the whims of a single individual. In the Political Testament of 1752, he emphasised that Russia must never be numbered among 'our real enemies'. 'There are no areas of dispute between her and Prussia. Only chance could turn her into a foe. A corrupt minister in the pay of Austria and England has laboured to find a pretext for antagonism between our two courts. The fall of this minister must occasion a return to the natural way of things.' The minister in question was A.P. Bestuzhev-Riumin, Russian chancellor from 1744 until 1758. Such oversimplified personalisation of policy initiatives, elsewhere determined by interests of state, reflected Frederick's conviction that the distinctive structure of the Russian Empire required such an approach to the conduct of its foreign policy. The King of Prussia only acquired a clear understanding of this after his bitter experiences in the Seven Years War. In the 1768 Testament, the Russian government's great splendour (*'grand éclat'*) was said to occasion disquiet abroad and internal intrigue 'as in every other court in Europe'. The fact that the measure of confusion and intrigue surpassed that of other courts is highlighted by mention of the Russian Empress's pangs of conscience about her crime, a direct reference to Catherine's part in the murder of her husband, Peter III, in 1762. These *'vices intérieurs'* predominated to an extent unusual even in eighteenth-century Europe. They led to constant uncertainty surrounding the succession and became an irritant in the conduct of the foreign policy of this massive empire. In his *Histoire de mon temps*, Frederick recounts one of the many *coups d'état* which rocked Russia during the eighteenth century. In this case, it was the seizure of power by his future foe Elizabeth, with the help of the Preobrashinski Regiment in 1741. 'Undertakings, which in all other states would seem fantastic, are possible in Russia. It is an affront to the spirit of nations. The Russians, like other peoples, are constantly dissatisfied with the present and hope for everything in the future.' In Frederick's mind, such fickleness applied especially to the Russians. From the very outset, he had a highly unfavourable opinion of them. It was the haughty view of a ruler indebted to western Enlightenment ideas, demonstrating his disdain for the lack of education and the immorality of an underdeveloped nation. 'The Russians are characterised by a mixture of distrust and villainy; they are lazy but self-centred; they are given to emulation but have no talent to produce their own initiatives.' Thus the 1775 version, in which, surprisingly, the wording is much stronger than it had been in 1746, in spite of the King's acquaintance in the interim with the Russian peasant army's powerful fighting strength.

Frederick, nevertheless, recognised the potential threat posed by the Russia that had been reinvigorated by Peter the Great. As early as 1746, he wrote in the *Histoire de mon temps* that since Charles XII's death, the accession of Augustus the Strong in Poland and General Münnich's victories over the Turks (Frederick calls him the Russian Prince Eugene), Russia had truly become the 'arbiter of the north'. Why was Russia's novel power, which seemed to him to have emerged from nothing (*'sortir du néant'*), so daunting? In the first place, its greatest advantage was that of size, which it made it unassailable: 'They [the Russians] were so terrible that no-one who attempted to attack could win; in order to penetrate and face the enemy, one would have to pursue a scorched earth policy; if attacked by them, everything could then be lost, even if one confined oneself to a defensive war.' When he wrote, Frederick's observations were not based on personal experience, but he astutely attributed Russia's military advantage to the numbers of Tartars, Cossacks and Calmucks in its army. In the absolutist standing armies of the day, these men would have been termed light troops and thought to be of limited military value. Frederick accorded 'these vagabond hordes of pillagers and arsonists', capable of razing the most prosperous provinces to the ground, a disproportionate amount of importance within the Russian army. He thought the military threat so great that all Russia's neighbours avoided contact with it or, conversely, concluded protective alliances with it. Prussia, or at least its eastern provinces, could, of course, be numbered among Russia's neighbours and this would explain why Frederick developed the outlines of his Russian policy at an early stage. He later expanded it to encompass the principle of concluding alliances, since a basic rule of statecraft was 'to seek an alliance with those of one's neighbours capable of delivering the most dangerous of blows', as he wrote in 1776, in a treatise entitled *An Analysis of the Prussian Government and the Principles upon which it rests, along with some Political Observations.*

Frederick's view of Russia in the first decade and a half after his own accession differed little from the negative opinion he was to hold in the later phase of his reign, by which time he had come into military and diplomatic contact with it. The view conjured up almost became a stereotype, even during the years when Voltaire still pursued Russian themes and sought close links with Catherine II. Such prejudice cannot have been engendered purely by the reports of Prussian envoys in St Petersburg; it had more fundamental origins and, to an extent, perhaps stemmed from deep-rooted fear. Frederick was one of the first to recognise the momentous implications of increased Russian power for western and central European politics. In the 1768 Political Testament, he highlighted the importance not of its geographical extent, but the size of its population. The nine million inhabitants in 1768,[1] he speculated, were bound to increase and Russia would emerge as the most dangerous power in Europe as soon as it had brought a proportion of its undeveloped land under cultivation. He attempted even more precise projections: in ten years, the Russian population would have increased by 1,060,000 and would continue to rise over the following thirty to forty years. The conclusion which the King drew from his analysis is surprising and perhaps even self-critical: how mad and blind must Europe be to contribute to the rise of a people which would one day be its undoing? Was that intended to include himself and Prussia? All calculations about Russia produced nightmarish visions and only served to highlight Prussia's small size and vulnerability. This had been the case long before the Seven Years War proved the point, and was even more of a truism thereafter.

Frederick's ideas about Russian power did not in practice affect his policies in the early years of his reign. The political constellation of fundamental importance to him was the Franco-British relationship, and he assumed that this rivalry would automatically provide him with an ally. His attack on the Habsburg province of Silesia, however, affected eastern not western spheres of power. Russia was at that point convulsed by the great upheavals associated with a disputed succession. One consequence of Peter the Great's 1722 Succession Law, which allowed the ruling monarch to name his heir, was that the succession was constantly at the mercy of factional strife at the Russian court. In a *coup d'état* on 5 December 1741, Peter the Great's daughter, Elizabeth, seized power, effectively ending the epoch of 'German rule' which had begun with the accession of Anna in 1730. Surrounded by ever-changing advisers, the most prominent and long-standing of whom was A.P. Bestuzhev-Riumin, the Empress Elizabeth was to determine the fate of this massive empire for over two decades (1741–62). During the Elizabethan period, foreign policy was undoubtedly dictated not only by *raison d'état*, but also by intrigues, changing whims and bribery. Russian absolutism was at the mercy of court factions and favourites. Since its acquisition of Silesia, Prussia was regarded as an obstacle to Russia's unlimited control of Poland and the Baltic coastline. Frederick's enhanced international position proved disconcerting to Russian statesmen, not only because of its territorial expansion, but also because of Berlin's close ties with France, whose influence in Poland was an irritant. Would Prussia become part of France's eastern European barrier, based on the twin pillars of Sweden and Poland? In an informative memorandum of September 1744, Vice-Chancellor Michail Voronzov summarised Russian fears occasioned by 'extensive Prussian policy plans'; here, apart from 'French and Prussian incitement in Poland', mention is made of possible links with the Ottoman Empire. If Russia's relationship with Prussia had long wavered

---

1. This was, in fact, a considerable underestimate. Russia's population in 1762 was at least 23 million.

between *rapprochement* and enmity, under Empress Elizabeth, the latter came to predominate to the point where between 1746 and 1756 vociferous calls for war could be heard in St Petersburg.

For a time, the possibility of *rapprochement* continued to exist. When in the summer of 1743 one of the many changes of personnel in St Petersburg resulted in the temporary disgrace of the Bestuzhev brothers, Frederick seized the opportunity to conclude an alliance. Although it contained no concrete assurances, above all no guarantees for Silesia, it strengthened Prussia's position vis-à-vis the western powers. Hence, Frederick's note to his foreign minister Podewils on 21 August: 'Once we have hooked firmly onto St Petersburg, we will be able to have a louder voice in Europe.' However, even this limited gain was temporary; only a few years later, in the months during which Frederick emerged victorious from the Second Silesian War following his subjection of Saxony, a fundamental change occurred in the Russian capital: in June 1746, Elizabeth concluded a defensive alliance with Maria Theresa, aimed principally against Prussia. In the fourth secret article, it was agreed that Austria's claim to Silesia and Glatz would be upheld and, in the case of a Prussian attack on Russia or Poland, the allies would support each other with 30,000 men initially, and double that number thereafter.

The assurances which underpinned this agreement, nevertheless, were less significant than Empress Elizabeth's fundamental shift of position. She was to be unswerving in her pursuit of this new policy, that of opposition to Prussia. Her diplomatic strategy aimed ultimately to surround Russia with a line of more or less dependent satellites. Frederick commented on this system in his Second Political Testament, remarking that luckily it precluded any new conquests, and sought only to subjugate and dominate the more vulnerable Kings of Sweden, Denmark and Poland. Areas of conflict, however, could still arise. Sweden's remaining German possessions in Western Pomerania bordered on Prussian territory, while Poland's West Prussian territories blocked the way to East Prussia. Throughout these regions, Prussian and Russian interests collided, as long as Russia clung to a system of maintaining dependent states on its frontiers. Frederick's success in the Second Silesian War also proved a source of unease for the Russian leadership. The latter thought him capable of marching towards Russian spheres of influence, even of subjugating the Polish throne. At the St Petersburg court he was seen as the second Charles XII. Wiser than the Swedish King, however, Frederick avoided this strategy by concluding a peace with Austria in Dresden in December 1745. The War of the Austrian Succession, meanwhile, continued apace. For the second time that century, in December 1747, Russian troops mobilised and moved westwards, their movements apprehensively monitored by Frederick. Without intervening in the fray, they succeeded in restoring the peace in Europe and equilibrium on the Rhine. The event was of chiefly symbolic significance and demonstrated the immense change the European state system had undergone.

Russia carried substantially greater weight at the outset and during the course of the Seven Years War than it had in the 1740s. This was undoubtedly true for the beginning of the war, its decisive turning point and its culmination. As it led France to join with Austria, so the Anglo-Prussian Convention of Westminster (January 1756) occasioned a change of policy in St Petersburg, now directed against Prussia. The Empress Elizabeth was about to ratify an Anglo-Russian subsidy treaty when news of the Convention of Westminster reached her. She was outraged at what she regarded as British duplicity and felt betrayed by her new British ally. Anti-Prussian sentiment began to dominate at court and, as is often the case when insecurity dictates action, led to hasty and incautious decisions. Pressure was brought to bear on Vienna and Paris, and troops deployed to advance from Livonia. Only with difficulty did Kaunitz manage to secure agreement from the Russian government to postpone the attack until the following year.

The King of Prussia was to remain ignorant of these developments. Even in his retrospective account of the Seven Years War, he continued to believe that Russia had been a reluctant partner in the coalition. Frederick saw the danger posed by Russia, without recognising its cause. Bestuzhev's motives were indeed difficult to establish. State and personal interest and advantage were inextricably linked in his person; hence the decision-making process was fundamentally different from that of calculated rationality of action prevalent in Kaunitz's Austria. But in as tense a situation as that of 1756, irrational action often starts the ball rolling. In the summer of that year, the Russian initiative though called off after Austria's diplomatic intervention, set in motion a corresponding mobilisation in Prussia. Russian policy, with all its confusing aspects, must, therefore, bear considerable responsibility for the outbreak of the Seven Years War. All surviving sources confirm the shocking blow which Russian military preparations delivered to Frederick II. On June 23, he gave Field Marshal von Lehwaldt, commander-in-chief of the regiments stationed in East Prussia, comprehensive instructions and virtually unlimited authority. Frederick's explanation was that he believed Russia to have thrown in her lot with Austria and 'with her would form a dangerous partnership.' Frederick was in fact badly informed on Russian policy since diplomatic relations with St Petersburg had been broken off five years earlier, and news could only be gleaned by opening foreign diplomatic correspondence passing through Berlin. As a result, he mistakenly assumed that a firm Russo-Austrian offensive alliance already existed; when Maria Theresa vigorously denied this, he merely substituted the word '*rapprochement*' for alliance. Russia's unilateral action in early summer 1756, nevertheless, was a storm warning; in February 1757, the two Imperial powers did, indeed, seal their alliance, leaving Prussia threatened first by a war on three fronts, then, after Sweden's entry into the coalition, on four.

In an evaluation of Russia's overall military contribution to the Seven Years War, it becomes clear that in comparison to Austria it was, in many ways, second-rate. Despite the faults inherent in its military machine, its achievements were, nonetheless, more important than Frederick had anticipated. Initially, he had seriously underestimated the Russian army, and only later came to make a more accurate assessment. He expressed respect for the rank-and-file which included no mercenaries and was levied exclusively from the estates of the aristocratic officer corps. His opinion of the Russian command, however, was far more critical. Its principal weakness was its dependence upon a divided political leadership in St Petersburg. Under Empress Elizabeth, a military council was set up, but it was paralysed by the opposing court factions which staffed it and issued constantly changing plans and orders. The commanding officers' ability to take their own decisions was extremely limited, while their inherent passivity narrowed freedom of action even further. In five years of campaigning, none of the four commanders-in-chief – Apraxin, Fermor, Saltykov and Buturlin – was able personally to take any decisions of importance. East Prussia, whose defencelessness due to its geographical isolation should have permitted an effortless Russian conquest, was not captured until the second attempt early in 1758. It was treated as an incorporated Russian province whose possession Austria guaranteed in a treaty concluded on 1 April 1760. Strategically and politically there now seemed no problems in this region.

The same could not be said, however, for the front near the river Oder, where Russian troops had been stationed since spring 1758. Their strategic brief was twofold: to push forward into the Prussian heartlands, if possible as far as Berlin, and always to operate in conjunction with the Austrians under Daun and Laudon in Silesia and Saxony, and the Swedes in Western Pomerania. Twice the Russians faced their opponents in battle: on 25 August 1758, at Zorndorf under Fermor and on 12 August 1759, at Kunersdorf under Saltykov, this time united with the Austrian contingent under Laudon. The outcomes of these battles were very different – Zorndorf, despite heavy losses, could be seen as a Prussian victory, while Kunersdorf was the greatest defeat ever suffered by the Prussian King. Yet on both occasions and especially after Kunersdorf, a final push into the opponent's heartlands could have ended the war. However, as Fermor remained immobile after Zorndorf and Frederick's withdrawal, so, too, Saltykov and Daun decided against pursuing the remnants of the Prussian army after Kunersdorf. This failure can be ascribed to several factors, not least the differences between the coalition partners. In any case, what was described by the King of Prussia as the 'miracle of the House of Brandenburg', was the result of quite banal reasons. Frederick's salvation was due to his Russian opponents' unwillingness to take risks and their rivalry with their Austrian partners. Saltykov therefore reported that he must conserve his forces, as Daun had done with his throughout the summer. The cumbersome Russian transport system, moreover, made the army dependent to a large extent on magazines for its provisions and hence unable to move freely. Russia's strategic objectives, therefore, remained unchanged when in September 1760, Saltykov was replaced by Alexander Buturlin, although the latter's incompetence compounded the existing shortcomings and weaknesses, in spite of the temporary capture of Berlin at the beginning of October. When in the summer of 1761, the great strategic goal of uniting Russian and Austrian troops under Laudon in Silesia was achieved, the Russians refused for the third time to undertake a final decisive battle jointly with the Austrians against the numerically far inferior Prussian King encamped near the fortress of Schweidnitz, and instead proceeded to withdraw. The last great opportunity of defeating the Prussian military machine had been thrown away, shortly before Empress Elizabeth's death was to bring about a turning point in Russian policy.

The question, therefore, remains: why did Frederick the Great emerge from the Seven Years War with an almost traumatic fear of Russia, in spite of the fact that the latter had clearly shown itself incapable of decisive military action in the war? Frederick voiced his concern about an emerging Russian superpower on several occasions in his Political Testament of 1768, and herein must lie his justification for the Prusso-Russian alliance of 1764. Above all, the argument recurs that it was impossible to attack Russia because of its vastness. Even more important to Frederick was the size of the Russian population and its potential to increase which could transform Russia into Europe's most dangerous power. 'All that can be said with certainty about this vast empire is that, according to the usual course of things, it will constantly increase in size.' This argument, however, cannot be substantiated by experiences during the war. Russian troop numbers were by no means larger than those of other states and, when compared to the size of the population, were indeed rather small. Fermor advanced on East Prussia with 34,000 men in 1758 and in late summer the same year deployed 66,000 men on the Oder front. At Kunersdorf, Russian forces numbered around 40,000 with the addition of another 10,000 so-called irregular troops. The Russian army was further strengthened by 18,000–19,000 Austrians, while the Prussians numbered only 53,000. This could hardly be described as numerical steamroller tactics. Transport and supply lines were, in any case, totally inadequate for such a strategy. Frederick's fear of Russia was not the result of personal experience; it was a nightmarish vision, not without an element of truth, but one which, at the time of writing, did not apply to the present but to the future. As he was confined to a small, cramped state, a certain amount of jealousy of his neighbour's huge dimensions and the fact that it all lay before him beyond reach and beyond attack could also have contributed.

Frederick the Great's relationship with Russia in the Seven Years War was not decided on the battlefield. On 5 January 1762, Empress Elizabeth died and her nephew, the Duke of Holstein-Gottorp, succeeded her as Tsar Peter III. He was among the most ardent of Frederick's admirers, a man whose blind adoration superseded all *raison d'état* and whose highly personal actions would significantly affect the course of great power politics. Unlike Joseph II, who always knew precisely how to differentiate between the interests of the state and personal admiration for the King of Prussia, Peter III was the architect of his own destruction. His obsession with the Prussian model undermined his position and robbed him of sympathisers. Following his overthrow [July], his wife Catherine did not overturn the peace settlement which he had concluded with Prussia, but effectively terminated the Russo-Prussian alliance.

What consequences did the changes in Russia hold for Prussia? It was certainly in the political interests of the Empress Catherine II to uphold the peace with Prussia; a continuation of the war would have hindered the internal stabilisation which her insecure position made essential. The loss of Russia's only war gain, East Prussia, seemed a small price to pay. It was a particular moral victory for Frederick to see a return to the territorial *status quo ante bellum* which the peace with Russia envisaged and which could be seen as a model for forthcoming general peace negotiations. This had been the very demand he had clung to steadfastly, even in the darkest hours of the war. Its achievement meant the realisation of his vision: the elevation of Prussia to great power status. At first, Frederick reacted to Russia's break with her coalition partners with caution and sober scepticism. After news of the Empress Elizabeth's death reached him, he wrote to his minister, Count Finckenstein: 'A great event which will perhaps have a slight impact.' To Prince Ferdinand of Brunswick, however, he was more enthusiastic: 'The sky begins to brighten. Let us have faith.' In Britain, in October 1761, a few months before the Empress's death, William Pitt had been replaced by the Earl of Bute who made it an integral part of his policy to dissolve the Prussian alliance. As far as their implications for Prussia were concerned, Frederick clearly felt that events in Britain and Russia cancelled each other out and merely saw in them further proof of the unpredictability of international developments. 'Kaunitz could not have foreseen the events in Russia', d'Argens – to whom the King revealed his innermost thoughts – was informed, 'and all that has taken place in England could not have been part of my political calculations.'

Russia had been the most unpredictable power in the war; it is somewhat surprising, then, that shortly after the peace treaty had been signed, Frederick should choose his former enemy as an alliance partner. The decision had been a difficult one, he confirmed later, and perhaps out of a sense of guilt sought to justify it to himself and his successor in the 1768 Political Testament. The only advantage for Frederick of the Russo-Prussian defensive alliance concluded on 11 April 1764, was a Russian guarantee for his possession of Silesia; otherwise it totally tied his hands in Poland, where the two states' interests would clash in the future. In a number of secret articles, he agreed to assist Russia in suppressing any attempts to alter the status quo in Poland, especially changes which might establish a hereditary monarchy there, and to support the Russian policy of allowing religious dissidents in Poland freedom to practise their faith. Most importantly, he promised to support the election as King of Poland of the Empress's favourite, Stanislas Poniatowski, who was the figurehead of the pro-Russian faction, the Czartoryski. Russia could continue to do with Poland as it wished. But did this accord with Prussian interests? Had the aggrandisement of Prussia not been blocked at the very point deemed most important in all of Frederick's political designs since the letter to Natzmer written when he was Crown Prince – the acquisition of Polish Prussia? It was mentioned in the Second Political Testament: after citing his designs upon

Saxony which were always a priority, he again speaks of '*la Prusse polonaise et Danzig*'. The latter's acquisition would be most advantageous, he states further on, since the state which controlled the course of the river Vistula and the city of Danzig had more power over Poland than its own King. Admittedly, his Polish plans are relegated to a chapter in the Testament entitled '*Rêves et projets chimériques*'. But despite the opposition it would occasion from Russia, Frederick could not afford to sacrifice so significant a component of his irreversible plan to transform Prussia into a great power.

For the moment, however, such projects had to be shelved since in Frederick's opinion political necessity ('*l'intérêt de l'état*') demanded alliance with St Petersburg. In his justification, only occasional mention was made of the deep-seated fears and anxieties which underpinned Russo-Prussian relations from early 1762. In order to understand the changing circumstances for Prussia occasioned by the rise of Russia, one has to piece together scant available evidence from widely scattered sources. In contrast to the situation in the nineteenth century, Russia was in fact nowhere Prussia's immediate neighbour, but its advance to the Baltic coastline and the establishment of a form of suzerainty over the Duchy of Courland began to threaten East Prussia in particular, as the Seven Years War would demonstrate. Poland's increasingly obvious status as a Russian satellite must also have exerted constant pressure, further increased when the acquisition of Silesia more than doubled the length of the Prusso-Polish border. Any consolidation of Russian influence over Poland was, therefore, definitely not in Prussia's interest. As Frederick explained in the Political Testament, however, the alliance must be viewed among those measures which cannot be fully condoned because they do not entirely accord with Prussian interests. But, in his defence, he added that one should consider the implications for Prussia had Russia instead decided to ally with Austria. The King of Prussia always intended the alliance to be a preventative measure designed to prevent an alliance between the two Imperial powers, just as Bismarck a century later intended the lines to St Petersburg to remain open, blocking a Franco-Russian *rapprochement*. In the event, both initiatives ended in failure; the 'nightmare vision of alliances' remained a reality for both statesmen and dictated the direction of their subsequent policies. In the 1768 Testament, Frederick's only certainty about the future was that Russia 'would keep increasing in size'. At the same time he thought it obvious that Poland's powerful neighbours would agree 'to partition these spoils'. It would not be entirely inconsistent with Frederick's Machiavellian principles, therefore, to suggest that the alliance was a means of preventing his exclusion from any settlement of the Polish question. 'Political wisdom consists of waiting for the opportunity, assessing the political situation and using it to best advantage.'

When this principle is applied to the Russian alliance, however, it becomes clear that far from bringing any benefits, it severely constrained Frederick's freedom of action. In time, his own attitude to it became increasingly sceptical. It brought 'neither gain nor loss', he wrote to Count Solms, his envoy in Russia in 1767. The possibility of future advantage could not be ruled out, he continued, but up to this point Russia alone had profited, particularly because the alliance facilitated the realisation of its Polish aspirations. Frederick's gaze was still on Poland, then, but this was precisely where he was blocked. It was an insoluble problem from which only *rapprochement* with Austria could eventually provide an escape. The '*rêveries*' [pipe-dreams] chapter in the 1768 Testament indicates that Frederick had considered the possibility: 'Perhaps Russia's immense expansion will, in time, force a coming together of Prussia and Austria for a joint endeavour to curb the dangerous ambitions of this vast empire.'

Where did Frederick fear Russian expansion most? In the year he composed the Second Political Testament, his thoughts undoubtedly centred on Poland. Undaunted by her own origins in a minor German principality, it was here that Empress Catherine steadfastly sought to continue the programme of political expansion launched by Peter the Great. She became embroiled in a lasting conflict with Polish nationalist and Catholic groups who had united to form the Confederation of Bar as a means of defending Poland's Catholic faith and political independence. This was the first military confrontation between the Polish independence movement and Russian imperialism in a long line of disputes stretching back over hundreds of years. But Catherine's plans went even further: in August 1768, Russian troops crossed the Turkish border in pursuit of forces from the Confederation which had arisen in Podolia. In the same way that Peter I had already achieved the breakthrough to the Baltic, this event marked the beginning of Russia's great expansion towards the Black Sea. Even before the outbreak of fighting with the Confederates, Prussia sought to insure against the need for her own military intervention on behalf of the dissidents. A secret agreement of April 1767 limited her obligation to diversionary tactics, possibly directed against the Austrian heartlands, should a Russo-Austrian confrontation arise. When the Turkish imbroglio, however, severely strained Russia's military commitments in Poland, the Russian foreign minister Nikita Panin, and the President of her War Council, Zachary Czernyshev, requested Prussian aid to subdue the Commonwealth ('*à tenir en respect la Grande Pologne*'). It was an open invitation to become caught up in the Russo-Polish confusion, and Frederick resolutely rejected the request, claiming that the treaty of 1764 only obliged him to pay a subsidy of 400,000 rubles in the event of a war with the Ottoman Empire. There was no binding treaty obligation, he insisted, for becoming involved in the dispute over the Polish dissidents. Fearing an escalation of the situation, Frederick then aimed to dampen down the flames of conflict in southeastern Europe. Thirty years earlier, he would undoubtedly have taken advantage of Russia's predicament to seize some Polish territory. But this was no longer the old King's political style, although it was probably not moral scruples which held him back.

Frederick now continued to pursue his Russian policy on two separate levels. He explored all possibilities which would enable him to escape any potentially dangerous obligations arising out of the alliance with St Petersburg but, at the same time, sought to safeguard it to avoid complete isolation and perhaps still reap some benefits from it in the future. Behind these concurrent diplomatic endeavours lay the constant threat of an overmighty Russia exerting increasing pressure on Europe and Prussia in particular. This situation was to dictate Russo-Austrian relations for the next century, since Prussia alone was powerless to resist being swamped by its powerful neighbour. In his relations with Catherine and Panin, Frederick was never quite sure of Russia's intentions. He could never fathom the Empress's character; like many contemporaries, he found it hard to understand how the daughter of a German count and Prussian general could immerse herself so completely in all things Russian and encourage its expansion with such vigour. Even in an age when countless noblemen and generals were uprooted and forced to adjust to alien political environments, such assimilation was extraordinary. Frederick, who had only met Catherine as a young girl, failed to grasp her enormous abilities. In the 1768 Testament, she was portrayed as the focus of court intrigue, surrounded by favourites and lovers, and held to have been undoubtedly responsible for her husband, Peter III's, death. Her soul, the King thought, was torn by remorse for the crime she had committed. Unlike Maria Theresa, for whom he had high praise, Frederick never uttered a complimentary word about her. Indeed the somewhat pathetic style of his letters to the Russian Empress could be interpreted as hinting at ridicule. Kaunitz's report to the Empress-Queen of the meeting at Neustadt in Moravia in September 1770, mentions Frederick's derisory assessment of Catherine. The King is said to have described her as exceptionally haughty, ambitious and vain; as a result, she was difficult to handle, which, being a woman, was in any case only to be expected. He thought it impossible to speak to her as one would to a minister and bemoaned the care needed to avoid provoking her. At one point, Frederick declared that the Empress's ambition was directly responsible for Russia's menacing policies. He realised, however, that she alone was not responsible for the potential threat posed by Russia; the danger ultimately lay in the empire's vastness, its inaccessibility and the size of its population. Convinced that nothing would reverse this trend, he conceded that alliance with Russia was unavoidable. 'Our interests demand adherence, even a strengthening of the Russian alliance', the Political Testament tells us. 'It is better to have Russia as an ally than an enemy, since she could do untold damage while we would be powerless to resist.'

Despite his misgivings, then, Frederick sought not only to maintain but actually to strengthen the alliance with St Petersburg. Russian politicians interpreted Frederick's efforts as a sign of weakness and in the negotiations attempted to impose obligations on Prussia which would transform the defensive alliance into an offensive one. The talks were, therefore, long and drawn out. Prussia used this time to pursue its own aims. The King was determined to probe whether Russia was prepared to pay a higher price for Prussian cooperation and, with all his Machiavellian skill, aimed to have the Polish partition plans included in the discussions. In a letter dated 2 February 1769, to Count Solms, his representative in St Petersburg, he mentions a proposition supposedly put before him by the Danish diplomat, Count Lynar, which he thought sufficiently interesting to transform the face of European politics at a stroke. As a reward for Austro-Prussian support against the Ottoman Empire, Russia should force its satellite, Poland, to cede Zips, Lemberg and the surrounding areas to Austria, while Polish Prussia, including Ermland and a protectorate over Danzig, would go to Prussia. Russia would then be free to absorb the remaining parts of Poland to defray the costs of the war. These gains would eliminate political rivalry. Frederick, who in all probability had concocted the plan himself, called it 'seductive'. Solms was left to decide whether or not to put it to Panin. It was no more than an exploratory gesture by the King which his envoy, too, concluded was not yet solid enough for diplomatic use.

Much has been done to play down this episode so that it would not be seen as the opening move in the partition of Poland. Strictly speaking, of course, it was not, since Frederick's plan had little impact in St Petersburg. Russia already possessed more land than it was able to administer, Panin explained to Solms. However, the Russian minister's words sounded somewhat hollow in the light of his counter proposals envisaging a complete redrawing of the map. As the Ottoman Empire had only been able to sustain itself for so long because of the rivalries and divisions among the Christian powers, he suggested an alliance of the three Eastern powers to deal the death blow. Constantinople and its provinces would be left to Russia and transformed into the heart of a new state. It was, of course, impossible for Frederick to agree to the plan since it would have involved him in a war which he sought to prevent with all the means at his disposal.

Mention of Panin's designs for a '*réunion avec la Russe et la maison d' Autriche*' led to an immediate withdrawal of Lynar's project. As was typical of the changed style of Frederick's later diplomacy, Prussia shifted to a completely different approach. Between 25 and 28 August 1769, a series of meetings took place between Frederick the Great and Joseph II at the town of Neiße in Silesia. The Emperor for his part hoped to secure an unconditional promise of neutrality should the tension, particularly in eastern Europe, lead to open conflict. The terms of the Russo-Prussian alliance, of course, did not allow Frederick to give such an undertaking since, in some circumstances, he would be obliged to attack certain Austrian territories. The King, therefore, limited his promise of neutrality to the event of an Anglo-French war. But what was his own political programme whose merits he wished to persuade the Emperor to accept? Joseph's personal notes of their discussions suggest that Prussia's King sought to turn his Austrian guests against Russia. 'He wants to teach us to fear the Russians.' 'He constantly seeks to instil in us a sense of unease about the Russians, their occupation of Azov and their wish for toleration towards the dissidents.' 'After dinner, he pressed me again on the Russians and told me that all Europe must take up arms to contain this power for she will absorb it all.' 'In time, not you or I but Europe as a whole must hold these people in check. The Turks don't even compare to them.' Frederick's remarks were presumably aimed at recruiting Austria for a joint undertaking against a power threatening the peace of Europe. But Joseph declined. On 27 August, the Emperor noted: 'The more he wishes to alarm us about the Russians, the calmer I become, and finally said to him: Sire, in the event of a major war, you will form the "Avant-garde" and we can, therefore, sleep peacefully as we are sure you will achieve all you hope to against the Russians', and added irritably: 'Come now, Sire, you need this alliance with Russia, we do not; but the price you must pay for it is high and often uncomfortable.' Attempts to frighten Austria had clearly failed. Kaunitz commented that Frederick probably feared the Russians less than he claimed and in truth sought only to prevent his own isolation in case Vienna should attempt to wean Russia away from Prussia. His failure at Neiße left the King with little choice but to agree to an extension of the Russian alliance. The only gain was a guarantee for the return of the Margravates of Ansbach and Bayreuth when, on 27 October 1769, the treaty was formally renewed.

The alliance, by this time, formed one of the preconditions for the partition of Poland. An awareness of the complicated tangle of political forces at play in eastern Europe, from Sweden to the Black Sea, is crucial to understanding this event. It was one move in a great chess game marking the end of an era in which legal rights and dynastic inheritance claims had dictated political strategy. Although old rules and practices were not entirely abandoned, the diplomatic actions of the great eastern powers were henceforth dictated purely by territorial demands created by the requirements of the political equilibrium. The term 'balance of power' lost its defensive purpose of safeguarding against the emergence of a single, hegemonic state. It became a widely cited concept employed to justify one's own expansion to keep pace with the other powers. This was certainly Frederick's interpretation of events and a theme he returned to time and again in his political writings: as he saw it, the only remaining balancing factor would be the powers' ability to establish mutually acceptable borders. Poland proved the most extreme example of this. Such political rationalism owed no little debt to the intellectual currents of the Enlightenment. The instigators of partition politics – Frederick II, Catherine II and Joseph II – after all, all owed a debt to the Enlightenment. Their action could be misinterpreted as paradoxical if one considered only the moral, humanitarian dimensions of enlightened thought without its related rationalisation of the concept of *raison d'état*. It marked a break with traditional ideas of divinely ordained, dynastic legitimacy still prevalent in the early eighteenth century and to which Maria Theresa still tended to incline. Questions of dynastic legitimacy were in any case soon to become important again, in central Europe at least. The greater precision of central European succession laws preserved those states from the fate of the elective monarchy of Poland or the non-Christian Ottoman Empire where the great powers' dreams of unlimited conquest were free to unfold.

The debate surrounding the First Polish Partition has, until recently, been dominated by a search for those responsible, leading to different interpretations depending on the political view point of the analyst. It can, however, only be fully understood if viewed as a great power game in which all three eastern monarchies participated. Whoever initiated the project was not necessarily the architect of the ultimate partition plan. Poland, riven by internal division and civil war, and governed since 1764 by a Russian *protégé*, Stanislas Poniatowski, practically invited its more powerful neighbours to cross its borders. In the summer of 1769, Austria took possession of Polish Zips, after Poniatowski had sought to protect the region from the Polish Confederation. In July 1770, further areas were occupied. These events on the periphery of the Polish civil war initially had limited territorial objectives and were hardly noted. In autumn 1770, Prussia, too, began to run a cordon through West Prussia, ostensibly as a precautionary measure to contain the plague, but in reality to secure a connection with East Prussia. The Austrian action did not assume political importance until Prince Henry's first visit to Russia in the winter of 1769/70.

Henry had long tried to persuade his brother to engage in further conquest and argued for the acquisition of more Baltic territory to make Prussia master of the entire coastline. The principal aim of his visit, therefore, was to prepare the ground for his brother's annexation of West Prussia. In the course of an audience with the Empress, Austria's action on Poland's southern border was mentioned and Catherine asked: 'But why doesn't everyone make a grab for it?' Henry somewhat reticently replied that his brother's cordon across Poland should not be equated with an occupation. Smiling, the Empress asked: 'But why not occupy?' Her minister, Count Czernyshev, repeated the question, adding more specifically: 'Why not annex the bishopric of Ermland?.' At the time, Frederick had not yet decided on a definite political plan for the acquisition of Polish Prussia, and was disturbed by the idea that an expansion of Prussia might bring about a corresponding expansion of Russia. He held that it would be an unforgivable mistake to contribute to the aggrandisement of a power which would become a dangerous neighbour to all of Europe. To his mind, the re-establishment of peace between Russia and the Ottoman Empire was much more of a priority; the conflict imposed on Prussia undesirably high financial commitments and might widen into a general war at any moment.

The King's reticence is surprising in the light of his 1732 letter to Natzmer, where he expressed the view that Polish Prussia was a vital element in Prussia's rise to great power status. By 1752, however, the King's opinion seems to have shifted and the first Political Testament dismissed the province's acquisition by force of arms as unnecessary. On a number of occasions, Frederick cited Victor Amadeus of Savoy-Sardinia's words that Lombardy should be consumed leaf by leaf like an artichoke, and used the analogy to apply to Poland. He suggested that one ought to make use of the factional strife which inevitably follows the death of a King and, as one's price for neutrality, acquire a town here, a province there until everything had been assimilated. Danzig would have to wait until last, since the loss of such an economically significant port would occasion 'a great outcry' from the Poles. At least on the last point, the King proceeded according to plan. But was the main reason for his calculations not fear of Russia? Was this not what led him to advise his successor to avoid war with Russia as long as his honour would permit? The 1768 Testament openly admits that any attempt to appropriate Polish Prussia would meet with the most vehement opposition from Russia. Would it not be more advisable, therefore, to aim for assimilation by negotiation, piece by piece (*'par négociation, morceau par morceau'*) instead of by conquest? Here once again the artichoke principle is to be seen. The opportunity to acquire parts of Polish Prussia is no longer viewed as something which would follow in the wake of electoral confusion and factional strife, but would present itself at times when Russia was in urgent need of Prussian help (*'pourrait avoir un besoin de notre assistance'*). One could then expect her to agree to the cession of Thorn and Elbing which would establish a link between Pomerania and the Vistula. On the next occasion, another piece could be acquired. Again, Danzig would have to wait *'pour la fin de l'opération'*. In other words, Russia held the key to the acquisition of West Prussia. This was precisely the premise on which the King proceeded in the early 1770s, by which time Russia was indisputably master of Poland. He would not act until he was sure that a Prussian intervention would not jeopardise his relationship with St Petersburg and that Russia would participate in the action.

Such cooperation was far from a foregone conclusion as long as Panin, a staunch opponent of military action in Poland, directed Russian foreign policy. Panin stood *'pour la tranquillité et la paix'*, Henry wrote from St Petersburg on 11 January 1770. On his return to Berlin a month later (17 February), Henry succeeded in persuading his brother to change his Russian policy in the light of the new information from St Petersburg. On 20 February, the King wrote to Solms of the need for 'equal gains for all of Poland's neighbours' (*'un agrandissement égal pour tous les voisins de la Pologne'*). For the first time, Austria's occupation of Zips was cited as justification for the partition of Poland. It could not be preserved intact after the Austrians had seized a piece. The emphasis must now lie in preventing a post-partition shift in the Austro-Prussian balance of power. 'Since its preservation is important to me and of acute interest to the Russian court', there was, therefore, 'no other means of preserving the equilibrium than to follow the example set by Vienna.' The Poles alone had the right to protest, but had themselves thrown this away by their behaviour. They could not prevent the re-establishment of peace by the great powers, for once acting together. The cries of protest would, in any case, 'dissipate' and become 'a powerless lament', Frederick wrote cynically to his minister, Count Finckenstein. These lines contain more than a formula for attaining political goals; they demonstrate that the Machiavellianism inherent in all of Frederick's earlier foreign policy calculations had now evolved into a new kind of political arithmetic. The expansion of one power must not disturb the balance of power between the rest; a balance could only be maintained by the aggrandisement of all.

Such calculations could certainly be reckoned to meet with Austrian favour. Kaunitz's perception of what constituted the preservation of the balance of power, however, differed from that of the King of Prussia. He saw Poland as last on the agenda for Vienna's share of this mutual aggrandisement; Austria should instead receive Glatz and parts of Silesia as compensation for Prussian gains in Polish Prussia. The proposition was, of course, indignantly rejected by Frederick. Kaunitz then raised even more comprehensive plans, encompassing not only partition of Poland, but also the Ottoman Empire. He examined all possibilities, including the Russian idea of an independent state comprising the European parts of the Ottoman Empire with its capital in Constantinople; herein lay the germ of Russia's subsequent grand plan for a revived 'Greek Empire'. But any Russian expansion in southeast Europe inevitably posed a threat to the Hungarian parts of the Habsburg Monarchy. Austrian policy, therefore, vehemently opposed Russian plans to occupy Moldavia and Wallachia.

Although Kaunitz's precise political calculations agreed in principle, if not in their ultimate goals, with those of Frederick, other minds were involved in the decision-making process: the young Joseph II's imagination led him to speculate on plans for expansion of a magnitude comparable only with Catherine's imperial projects. These, however, were doomed to remain mere schemes as long as his mother was alive. While Maria Theresa, morally outraged by the partition proposals, resisted until the last moment, Joseph actively supported the venture. When faced by the decision, the Empress-Queen argued that 'the easiest option would be to participate in Poland's partition. But what right do we have to rob the innocent we have always sought to defend and protect . . . the motive of avoiding isolation among the other powers does not suffice to warrant an unjust usurpation . . .' Maria Theresa's stance was the exact antithesis of that expressed in Frederick's *Anti-Machiavel*, where it was argued that the ethics of *raison d'état* were irreconcilable with private morality. From the very beginning of his reign, Frederick had accepted this as political reality. Although Maria Theresa attempted to resist the inevitable demands of *raison d'état*, she ultimately found it impossible.

Frederick's breach of international law in 1740 and his breaking of treaty obligations in 1742 were not entirely without repercussions. In 1756, he did everything in his power to appear before the world (and himself) as justified in his action; now, however, on the eve of his participation in the division of Polish territory, his need for legal justification had once again diminished. Although he asked his foreign ministers, Finckenstein and Hertzberg, to submit grounds for Prussia's Polish pretensions in February 1771, their only reply was that this was the 'most useful acquisition' and that his claims were 'the most applicable'. Precise historical rights to West Prussia were only later advanced in the Patent of Seizure (18 September 1772) and in an elaborate discourse by Hertzberg. The ministers' thoughts accorded entirely with the King's own. The only problem Frederick could foresee lay in the Protestant acquisition of a Catholic bishopric (Ermland). In February 1772, the Convention for the Partition of Poland was first signed only by Russia and Prussia, and finally, in August, by Austria as well. In his memoirs, Frederick describes the period from 1763 to 1772 under the heading of 'Preservation of Peace'; but the guiding force of these years for him was clearly the maintenance of a balance of power through '*agrandissement égal*'. This had been the added new dimension in the great powers' decision to dispose so ruthlessly of the kingdom of Poland. Under pressure from the three eastern powers, the Polish Diet had little choice but to submit and voted to do so in September 1773.

The partition agreement apportioned Ermland, Marienburg, Kulm and Pomerelia to Prussia, but not the valuable towns of Danzig and Thorn. The territorial gains only amounted to 660 square miles, as opposed to Russia's 1,700 and Austria's 1,500 square miles.[2] Although at first glance it was not an equitable division, Prussia did gain a bridge to East Prussia as well as control of the river Vistula, and thus made the most advantageous gains. It was said that the lion's share had gone to Austria with her acquisition of Galicia, but the inescapable fact emerged that the integration of West Prussia into Prussia was by far more significant than Galicia into Austria, since the latter province was always to remain on the periphery of the Monarchy.

Assessments of the First Polish Partition have always been controversial. Moral outrage voiced by Anglo-Saxon historians like Macaulay and G.P. Gooch was countered by Prussian apologists who argued that the power constellation in the early 1770s made partition inevitable: 'a masterstroke of Frederician diplomacy', Otto Hintze called it. Ranke, however, did see the change in international politics occasioned by the events of 1772. 'At first sight, it broke all the accepted and contractual laws on which European states rested; it shook the foundations on which their safety depended.' The First Polish Partition could thus be seen as the initial step towards the great changes in the map of Europe which were to follow in the wake of the French Revolution. Such suggestions or scruples, however, were alien to Frederick; his calculations were based on the balance of power as each situation demanded. 'Partition had to take place in order to avoid a general war', he wrote in his *Memoirs from the Peace of Hubertusburg to the end of the Polish Partition*.

The acquisition of West Prussia proved the only substantial gain to be made from the Russian alliance which Frederick once declared brought him neither loss nor gain ('*ni perte ni profit*'). What motives, then, did the King have for clinging to the partnership with Russia? Its primary function seemed to be to prevent the nightmare vision of an Austro-Russian *rapprochement*, something which, as he wrote to Prince Henry in November 1776, Frederick feared more than anything. The real test whether the Russian alliance was more than a protective alignment for Prussia came during the Austro-Prussian conflict over Bavaria, which Austria had seized as compensation for Silesia. Russia ultimately

---

2. These figures are given in German miles. A modern estimate is that Prussia secured 36,000 square kilometres of new territory, Austria 83,000 and Russia 92,000.

refused to lend military aid to its alliance partner, preferring the diplomatic role. 'All has suddenly changed', Frederick observed. Russian diplomacy had succeeded in evading its treaty obligations and in creating for itself the role of mediator between the two German powers, eventually acting as guarantor of the Peace of Teschen, concluded on 13 May 1779. These developments were ultimately contrary to Prussian interests. They marked an improvement in relations between Vienna and St Petersburg, piloted and encouraged by Count Potemkin, and culminated in the summit conference between Joseph II and Empress Catherine at Mohilev in June 1780. Joseph aimed to damage, and if possible destroy, the Prussian alliance; Catherine hoped for Austrian support in driving the Turks from Europe and the eventual destruction of the Ottoman Empire. The meeting passed with neither side laying all its cards on the table; this was not done until an exchange of letters between the Emperor and Empress two years later. In these, Catherine revealed her plans to transform the Greek Empire with its capital, Constantinople, into a Russian secundogeniture and to establish a second kingdom of Dacia encompassing Bessarabia, Moldavia and Wallachia, as a Russian buffer state. She also submitted candidates for the newly created thrones for Joseph's approval. In his reply, Joseph made similarly grandiose demands. He made claims, amongst others, on parts of Serbia, Bosnia and Herzegovina, the Venetian hinterland, Istria and Dalmatia; his plans, of course, primarily envisaged the acquisition of Bavaria and the destruction of Prussia's great power status. Catherine and Joseph finally agreed, if only in an exchange of letters, on mutual cooperation in case of war with the Ottoman Empire. Should either Austria or Russia be attacked during the course of this war by a third power – which could only have meant Prussia – it would be taken as the *casus foederis*, that is to say, it would make the alliance operative. In fact, it marked the end of the Russo-Prussian alliance.

Frederick was not familiar with the details of this exchange, but was fully aware of its existence and its implications. The only suitable partner for a defensive alliance was France, which had been Austria's ally since 1756 and, in the years immediately prior to the Revolution, faced crippling financial debts and was hardly in a position to be of real help should the situation deteriorate. The King – like most of his contemporaries – failed to recognise that Europe was on the brink of an immense political upheaval; all he could see was how small Prussia seemed in comparison to the real great powers. It was in these last years that, with his usual sense of irony, Frederick, in conversation with Marchese Lucchesini, suggested heraldic devices for the great European states: thundering Jupiter for Austria, the 'pirate captain', Mercury, for England, the Star of Venus for France and 'for us the Monkey, since we ape the great powers without being one ourselves'. In an analysis of the political state of Europe, written in May 1782, Frederick remarks: 'Since the Emperor's *rapprochement* with Russia, Prussia can no longer count on its alliance with Empress Catherine.' This he viewed as an ominous development for Prussia; in a reversal of his earlier opinion, he now considered Austria his most dangerous neighbour. In a dire warning to his successor, he cautioned against sleepy idleness which 'Joseph would take advantage of, I can foresee, until within thirty years neither Prussia nor the House of Brandenburg will exist'. The final consequence of losing his Russian alliance partner, then, was renewed fear of his Austrian opponent – from his early Silesian adventure, he had come full circle. Should the Emperor have designs against Prussia, Frederick now faced him alone.

CHAPTER 6

Prussia and the Holy Roman Empire: from the Imperial Ban to the League of Princes

As Elector of Brandenburg, Frederick belonged to the elite group of Imperial Princes whose task it was to elect the Emperor. Since the time of the Golden Bull, these rulers had enjoyed special political privileges which greatly enhanced their monarchical rights. By the eighteenth century, these had undoubtedly been overtaken by events, but nevertheless they served to strengthen and accelerate the ambitions of Hohenzollern rulers at an early stage. When the Duchy of Prussia (that is to say, East Prussia) the former, secularised state of the Teutonic Order, was acquired by the Electors of Brandenburg in 1618, the newly formed state, which also included Cleves on the Lower Rhine, was no longer seen as a mere component of the Empire but, after the Duchy's independence from the King of Poland was secured in 1660, an independent sovereign state. Although this status applied only to East Prussia, not Brandenburg, the question of internal and external sovereignty became blurred as the Great Elector strove to weld his scattered territories into a homogeneous power base. Although he acted without regard for Emperor or Empire, the Elector thought of himself as first and foremost a Prince of the Empire. The issue of Prussia's external sovereignty was not raised again until Elector Frederick III aimed to transform his state into a monarchy. Following the Emperor's acknowledgement of the Elector's new royal status on 16 November 1700, the Empire held suzerainty over Prussia in name only: in the same agreement, the Elector proclaimed his political and military independence. Frederick the Great judged the action of the first Prussian King in securing a royal title to be a diversionary tactic intended to camouflage his inability to attain a position of real power. However, he recognised the event's important repercussions. 'What was originally an act of vanity, proved ultimately to have been a political masterstroke', he wrote in his *History of the House of Brandenburg*. His grandfather's achievement, he admitted, provided the impetus to complete the foundations for the breakthrough to great power status.

As the provinces of the Prussian monarchy were gradually united, a result above all of Frederick William I's administrative reforms, an awareness of the need for complete political independence grew. In Frederick William's time it was still compatible with loyalty to the Emperor, but during his successor's reign it was transformed into indifference and, ultimately, enmity. Frederick II's reasons probably stemmed initially more from a Voltairian distaste for archaic, anachronistic medievalism and the dominance of superstition and the priesthood than from sound political motives. Only slowly was his prejudice replaced by political calculation. At that point the Empire was transformed into a field of operations for attempted or actual shifts of power in which Austria and Prussia faced each other as opponents of equal rank. It is interesting to note Frederick's treatment of the Empire in his Political Testaments. In both, it is designated an independent power among European states, but clearly distinguishable from the great powers among which Austria and Prussia were numbered. In the 1752 Testament, Frederick only reluctantly admits that the 'anachronistic and bizarre political composition of the Empire' is still sustainable. The Empire survived solely 'because of the rivalries of the princes of the Empire and of neighbouring powers' and was constantly exposed to a process of assimilation whereby the smaller rulers and Imperial cities were at the mercy of the more powerful ones. The Emperor's power, he speculated, would steadily decrease. By 1768, with the experience of the Seven Years War behind him, it was stated more confidently that the growth of Imperial power had been stemmed since the Peace of Westphalia and was held in check by Austria's rivalry with Prussia.

It is clear, then, that the King saw in the Holy Roman Empire neither a subordinate nor an equal power, but a passive system of smaller states incapable of unified decision-making, from which two European great powers emerged. Frederick never made a serious attempt to destroy this system or to distance himself from it; instead he exploited it for his own purposes. His relations with the Empire were more contradictory than those with any other European power. His Imperial policy wholly lacked any sense of Imperial German patriotism: it served Prussian *raison d'état* exclusively. No other prince of the Empire had ever gone as far. Precisely for this reason, it seems almost certain that Frederick never aimed to acquire the Imperial title himself. The theoretical possibility did exist after Emperor Charles VI's death in October 1740. At the end of this month, Voltaire wrote to the King: 'You are on the point of either electing or becoming an Emperor. It would be entirely apt for one who possessed the character of a Titus, Trajan, Antonius and Julian to ascend the throne.' This was more than idle flattery since other men close to Frederick, such as Prince Leopold of Anhalt-Dessau and even his usually cautious minister, Podewils, were thinking along similar lines. Frederick never answered Voltaire. When the letter reached him, the King was in the midst of preparations for his Silesian adventure. Not until the 1752 Testament did he give his reasons for rejecting such a proposal: a King of Prussia should rather strive to conquer a province than adorn himself with empty titles. 'Your primary task', he urged his successor, 'is to lead the state to the peak of its power, the ideal vision of which I have described to you. Only when you have secured a lasting power base can you abandon yourself to vanity.' Unlike the monarchical title of 1701, also purely a product of vanity, the Imperial title failed to hold for him the stimulus of political greatness. His newly founded state based on real power had no need for decoration with a title which brought no authority, but required its holder to have an established power base.

These were the conclusions Frederick drew in 1752 from the failed Imperial aspirations of the Bavarian Emperor, Charles VII, with whose election and support he had been closely involved. In the first phase of his Imperial politics, Frederick assumed the highly paradoxical role of protector of a powerless non-Habsburg *Imperium* for whose creation he was partly responsible and whose role was principally to provide an alternative to the Habsburg Maria Theresa. The King used the most diverse and often contradictory methods to imbue the new Empire with power and authority. At first he supported the great projects to partition Austria put forward by Saxony and Bavaria, and sought to secure Bohemia for the Wittelsbach Emperor, who had already sent an army to occupy it with French help. The combination of Bohemia and Bavaria would have provided a sufficient power base for Frederick's Imperial candidate, the Wittelsbach Elector. When the course of the war put an end to such far-reaching territorial changes, the King of Prussia withdrew in order to preserve his Silesian gains. He did not, however, altogether abandon plans to secure a territorial base for the unhappy Charles VII, who by now had been driven from his own territories and established a provisional Imperial residence in Frankfurt. Even before the Peace of Breslau, the Prussian ministry raised the suggestion of secularising certain bishoprics like Eichstädt, Freising, Regensburg, Augsburg and Salzburg with the aim of expanding the Emperor's Bavarian domain. The leaking of this proposal occasioned a storm of protest, including from the Pope himself; it demonstrated the fundamental, almost sacred religious prerequisites upon which the old Empire rested. Frederick, a quintessential product of the Enlightenment, had little appreciation of such things. In the eleventh chapter of his *Anti-Machiavel* he delivered a damning critique of ecclesiastical principalities, but admitted in the first Political Testament that the time when these could be secularised had passed. Such moves would be opposed by the Pope and all Catholics, and no Catholic ruler would, in any case, want to acquire them. This, of course, was an exact description of events: Emperor Charles VII himself refused to accept the Greek gifts offered him, although accused of initially seeking to acquire them. Ultimately the secularisation plans only served to strengthen the moral position of the Habsburgs, whose protection the ecclesiastical principalities, already traditionally Vienna's clients, now sought.

Frederick was unfortunate in the unfamiliar world of Imperial politics. He was either too far ahead of his time, as with the secularisation project, or fumbled with worn-out ideas like the reorganisation of the Imperial army. With the help of an association of the Circles of the Empire, this ostensibly neutral army was to provide the King of Prussia, as he himself later admitted, with the opportunity of becoming lieutenant-general in perpetuity of Imperial troops. This kind of Imperial reform would have lent predominance to the Prussian military state and established a kind of 'hereditary position of major-domo'. 'But the plan failed', according to the *Histoire de mon temps*, 'because of the Imperial Princes' servile fear of the House of Austria'; in other words, because of the established dependence of the smaller German territories on Vienna's hegemony within the Empire, thought to be easier to bear than that of Prussia, behind which French diplomacy might well be lurking. The King did indeed assume that French help, at least in the form of subsidies, would be forthcoming. There was no other way: an anti-Habsburg *Imperium* under Prussian protection was impossible without shaking the old Empire to its very foundations. The conflict between Austria and the aspirant great power, Prussia, had to be carried out on the European stage. The Empire remained on the periphery and only assumed a predominant position in the final years of Frederick's life when Prussia had exhausted the possibilities for other alliances. The army project was only of passing interest. The King soon abandoned his Imperial political plans, many of which began to seem fantastic, and contented himself with possession of Silesia, leaving the Empire, after the hapless Charles VII's death on 20 January 1745, to the Habsburgs. In September 1745, the Grand Duke of Tuscany, Maria Theresa's husband, was elected as Charles VII's successor. Although Frederick initially greeted it with protests, he eventually acknowledged the election in the Peace of Dresden on 25 December 1745, after Maria Theresa had again confirmed his possession of Silesia.

Thus ended an inherently contradictory phase of Frederick II's Imperial policies. A state whose sophisticated political structure had long outgrown Imperial tutelage and which functioned as a European power in its own right, only using the *Imperium* as a means of promoting its own power, was intrinsically such a paradoxical scenario that it was never seriously pursued by Frederick. As a proponent of the Enlightenment, as a Protestant ruler and as the head of an administratively and militarily streamlined state – for any one of these reasons, the King of Prussia was more suited to the role of rebel who broke the Imperial chains, as Henry the Lionheart had done. However little the Empire and his own position as an Elector meant to Frederick, his aggression in the early 1740s and attacks on Saxony and Bohemia in 1756–57 provided Vienna with a welcome pretext for strengthening Imperial ties and attempting to gather as many Protestant Electors into its clientage network as possible. On 14 September 1756, a decree reached the Imperial Diet in Ratisbon accusing the King of Prussia of 'an attack on the Empire' and warned Electors that a 'similar rape' of their own territory was always possible. The King himself received an Imperial reprimand, urging him to refrain from 'hostile anti-Imperialism and insurrection against us and the Empire', while Prussia's generals, colonels and other commanding officers were freed from their oaths and duties to the Empire.

The next Imperial Diet, on 17 January 1757, was urged to defend the Empire and its laws against the turbulent prince, and the *Reichsexecution* against Prussia was issued on 31 January. As in 1866, it was to be a civil war in which the two most powerful German states confronted each other. It seems unlikely that Frederick viewed these developments as more than Habsburg irritation on the periphery of the main political and military events of the day. The provocative stubbornness of Frederick's representative in Ratisbon, Erich Cristoph von Plotho, only served to highlight Prussian confidence before the defeat at Kolin. It was a significant setback which nullified the great plan of a decisive victory. Even Plotho felt the wind in his face. The frequently delayed mobilisation of the Imperial army now took place. Frederick reacted by declaring that for his part the 'Imperial throne stood vacant and that the Emperor was unfit for his responsibilities'. By then, Kolin had been put behind him, and the great victories of Rossbach, in which, along with the French, the Imperial army had been thoroughly beaten, and of Leuthen were fresh in his mind. To contemporaries, Rossbach was principally a victory over the French who comprised three-quarters of the army, and German patriotism heralded the victor. This national euphoria can only be viewed against the backdrop of nearly a century of French military superiority which had its origins in the days of Louis XIV. However, the fact that Rossbach was also a catastrophic defeat for the Imperial army did not escape popular attention and several folk songs pouring scorn on the Imperial as well as the French army survive. The structural weaknesses of the Imperial army were so blatant that there was little prospect of its regeneration. Badly led by its commanding officer, the Austrian Field Marshal Prince Joseph Friedrich von Sachsen-Hildburghausen, it displayed all the disadvantages of a composite army, consisting of many units of varying sizes, and lacked any trace of homogeneity or cohesion in practice: the Swabian Circle contained no fewer than 95 towns and 189 separate contingents. Compared to a military state such as Prussia, the Imperial army was at a hopeless disadvantage. Its failure can also partly be attributed to open sympathy for Prussia among the Protestant Princes. In his description of Rossbach in the *History of the Seven Years War* Frederick barely mentions the Imperial troops. Instead he speaks almost exclusively of the French army under Prince Soubise. When he juxtaposes 'German calm' with 'French foolhardiness and boastfulness', he is describing Prussian troops. The impression one is left with is that he sought to identify himself with the German cause; was he not the powerful rebel who had defeated the Imperial army?

The defeat at Rossbach emasculated the Empire, and although its army continued to participate in the war it could no longer function as a politically independent power. After the conclusion of the Seven Years War, Frederick the Great lost almost all interest in Imperial politics while Kaunitz used the post-war years to strengthen Vienna's influence within the Empire using the traditional tool of creating clients among the Catholic princes.

The growth of Prussian power, however, also had its limits. From the 1770s it became normal to speak of a balance of power within Germany in the context of the greater European equilibrium. This could only be interpreted as a dualism of political might within Germany; alongside the *Imperium* claimed as a hereditary possession by Austria, Prussia had risen to create a kind of rival

Imperium. In the 1768 Testament, this concept was first described: a balance of the two great powers ensured the maintenance of the privileges, possessions and freedom of those rulers who had formerly stood in danger of being swamped by the Empire. Since the Peace of Westphalia, the Empire's power had been curtailed, and it continued to be held in check by Austria's rivalry with Prussia. 'In the last war, the Emperor did not dare impose his will on myself, the King of England or the other rulers in our faction, however much he may have wanted to do so.' It was, therefore, seen as Prussia's duty to establish and maintain a counterbalance within the Empire; this meant in effect, holding the Emperor's despotism (to which Frederick refers constantly) in check. Prussia should thus have a right of veto within Imperial matters. All this implied a defensive role, but also required the necessary territorial and military base to lend Prussia the authority to carry out her task. No less a person than Kaunitz spoke of the King of Prussia's 'military state' based on the 'poaching of hard-working labourers from other Imperial lands' and forcing his neighbours to maintain their troops in such a condition as to withstand at least the initial onslaught. Here the open wound of Imperial politics was visibly exposed: instead of a uniform, hierarchical system headed by the Emperor, a dualism threatened where the two most powerful Imperial states found themselves in a constant struggle for influence over the Empire and the territories which made it up.

There is little doubt that such rivalry ran counter to the interests of the King of Prussia, who understood a balance of power to mean curtailing the traditional sphere of influence over the Catholic princes and allowing Prussia to play the role of 'guardian of the Imperial constitution' by holding in check Austria's power. Habsburg policy – and particularly Joseph II's expansionist inclinations – played unwillingly into Frederick's hands by constantly striving for compensation for Silesia. This was not only to make up for Austria's territorial losses, but also to expand her sphere of influence within Imperial politics. Frederick waged a propaganda war against such claims using the key words of 'Imperial despotism' and 'preservation of the Imperial constitution' and it was not without success among the various smaller rulers within the Empire, already intimidated by some of Joseph II's measures.

In the second half of the eighteenth century, several cases of disputed inheritance threatened to break 'asunder the internal cohesion of the Empire' (K.O. von Aretin). The Margraviate of Ansbach and Bayreuth, the Electorate of Bavaria and the Electoral Palatinate were all governed by rulers who lacked legitimate heirs. The power-political circumstances of the Houses of Wittelsbach and Hohenzollern could change overnight, and the unification of all Wittelsbach possessions under one ruler became a distinct possibility. It could establish a new Wittelsbach *Imperium*, founded on a considerably larger power base and strengthened by the support of Prussia or even France, which would pose a substantial threat to Habsburg Austria. However, all this remained pure speculation; events, in reality, followed a totally different direction. It was Vienna which saw in the great game of inheritance disputes its long-awaited chance to acquire Bavaria in exchange for the Austrian Netherlands. Its pretensions were based on highly questionable claims to the Straubing region in Lower Bavaria. The negotiations with the Bavarian heir, the Elector Palatine Charles Theodore, begun before the sudden death of the last Bavarian Wittelsbach, Maximilian III, in December 1777, were a supreme example of the dynastic chess game. Spurred on by Charles Theodore's reluctance to accept the Munich inheritance and his ambitions to construct a monarchy on the Lower Rhine by combining Berg, the Palatinate and the Austrian Netherlands, as well as by Joseph II's burning ambition to widen his Austrian power base within the Empire, the negotiations were nonetheless doomed to failure. Unlike the eager Charles Theodore, the next male relative, the Duke Charles Augustus of Zweibrücken, encouraged and supported by Prussia, refused even to enter into talks. Joseph, hoping to escape the effects of a military clash with Prussia, now brought the Ansbach-Bayreuth succession question into play and in return offered Frederick a guarantee for the Prussian succession in the Franconian Margraviates. The two, however, were hardly of comparable bargaining weight. Moreover, Prussia's dynastic claims in Franconia were far stronger than Austria's to the Bavarian lands. Against the advice of his brother, Henry, Frederick now decided to oppose directly the Emperor's plans, which, in effect, meant that for the fourth time Prussia was committing itself to war with Austria. The Empire, which Maria Theresa had called upon to act as arbiter, was powerless to act. Frederick's claim to defend the Empire stemmed from a need to ensure his own survival, and the preservation of its internal balance of power precluded any expansion of Austria's power base in Germany. In his history of the 1770s, written in the King's old age, he claimed that Bavaria had been a strategically pivotal area from which the whole of southern Germany, including Alsace and Lorraine, could be controlled. He accused Joseph II of attempting to make himself master of the Empire and of aiming to become 'mightier than all the monarchs of Europe'.

For the time being, Prussia did not stand alone as long as Russia was still formally her ally, although military assistance could not be expected. In the peace settlement concluded at Teschen on 13 May 1779, which brought to an end the War of Bavarian Succession and secured Bavaria's independence, Frederick successfully established Russia in the place of Sweden as a guarantor of the Empire and its constitution. The resulting increase in Prussia's political standing in Europe, however, was more symbolic than real. Apart from guaranteeing the status quo within the Empire, the peace brought Prussia recognition of her right to succeed in the principalities of Ansbach and Bayreuth, though this did not take place until 1791.

The War of Bavarian Succession was only a pale shadow of the earlier Silesian Wars, and Prussia's notably outdated army and leadership were juxtaposed with Joseph II's youthful, rapid actions such as his advance into Bavaria. However, although Joseph undoubtedly sought to imitate Frederick the Great, he failed to reach his model's former brilliance. His instability and lack of self-control, more evident after his mother's death in 1780, made

Austrian policy less predictable. Although Frederick failed to distinguish in his historical writings between the Emperor's impetuous behaviour and Kaunitz's more calculated conduct, his political calculations had to take it into account. This was especially so in Imperial politics where Joseph's behaviour was alienating his traditional support among Catholic and ecclesiastical territories. In Frederick's last years, then, Joseph played directly into his hands. The King could once again appear as the protector of the Empire against an Emperor who sought to go beyond the political settlement established at the Peace of Westphalia.

The War of Bavarian Succession clearly demonstrated that the dualism of its two principal powers had become the dominant factor within Imperial politics; in the Silesian Wars and the Seven Years War, Prussia had still been jockeying for equal rank. As a result, the smaller and medium-sized territories of the Empire felt a growing disquiet. They attempted, through closer links, to form a third power, a development which stretched forward into the nineteenth century but never came to fruition. Plans for a 'League of Princes' (*Fürstenbund*) were first developed among the minor German rulers: by Charles Augustus of Weimar, Francis of Anhalt-Dessau and Charles Frederick of Baden. They were joined, under pressure from his minister Christian von Hohenfels, by Charles Augustus of Zweibrücken, the next heir to the House of Wittelsbach. Apart from a natural desire for self-preservation, the plan stemmed from a genuine spirit of Imperial patriotism, which Joseph II's programme of modernising reforms seemed more and more to obscure. In Frederick II's Prussia, there was no room for it in any case. The driving force was initially Charles Frederick of Baden's leading minister, William von Edelsheim, who in November 1783 produced a memorandum outlining plans for a League of Princes, guaranteed by Prussia, but excluding both Austria and Prussia from membership. At its core was a guarantee of existing borders, but it also advanced reforming schemes for a combined army. Frederick was at first unaware of such projects; his interest was only awakened when Joseph, offering tempting financial incentives, renewed his attempt to win the heavily indebted Duke of Zweibrücken to his objective of exchanging Wittelsbach territory for the Austrian Netherlands. Frederick, however, had no need to intervene directly in order to destroy the project. It was Charles Augustus's minister, Hohenfels, possibly encouraged by Prussian money, who persuaded the Duke not to sign the proposed contract. French displeasure at Joseph's risky proposal also clearly played a part. On 6 January 1785, Louis XVI wrote to his brother-in-law asserting that Bavaria's future should not be decided except in consultation with the King of Prussia.

However little Frederick was informed about the details of these developments – he saw things not as an Imperial ruler, but in the general framework of European politics – his vision was bleak. Since the mid-point of his life, the decisive year of 1756, he was plagued by anxiety over the continued existence of Prussia, of whose relative weakness he was constantly aware. The inner disquiet which marked his final years, however, was of a more personal nature.

He was troubled by anxieties about Prussia's future under a weaker successor. Was it possible to secure this future? In his writings of these final years, words of resignation can occasionally be found: the best that could be done in the present situation was 'not to budge and wait until [potentially propitious] events unfold in Europe'. These words applied ultimately to great power politics which, according to Frederick, had, since the Peace of Teschen, deteriorated 'into chaos'. The Emperor, who attributed the failure of his Bavarian plans in 1778–79 to strong Russo-Prussian ties, had proceeded to destroy Frederick's Russian alignment for him, substituting his own alliance with Empress Catherine, secretly concluded in the summer of 1781. 'For the time being, I cannot count on Russia', wrote Frederick, although a formal alliance between Potsdam and St Petersburg continued to exist. France's star had sunk so low that alliance with her could not be more than 'a last resort'. In England, the new Whig administration under Charles James Fox 'had not yet found its feet' and, at that point, he would, therefore, not 'enter into any major negotiations'.

Frederick's own words indicated that a League of Princes presented the last and only possibility. It has, therefore, been seen as an admission of the lack of alternatives in foreign policy. A return to the blinkered world of Imperial politics and to an association with those who had formerly been his bitter enemies could not be a means of extricating himself from the complexities of the European power system, but it could establish peace in Prussia's immediate surrounding area and form a counterweight to increasing Imperial power. This would explain the essentially defensive nature of Frederick the Great's League of Princes. It was rumoured that secret talks concerning the possible resurrection of a Wittelsbach *Imperium* took place prior to the League's formation. Hohenfels was thought to have entered into negotiations in Berlin with the Prussian foreign ministers, Finckenstein and Hertzberg. The result had been a secret clause in the treaty establishing the League designed to ensure the Duke of Zweibrücken's election as Emperor after his accession in Munich. This plan, if indeed it existed, was nullified by the longevity of the Bavarian Elector, Charles Theodore; he did not die until 1799, thereby surviving the Emperor Joseph II by nine years. A repeat of the unsuccessful attempt to establish a Wittelsbach Imperial House would undoubtedly have had a firmer territorial base than in 1742, with the combination of Bavaria and the Palatinate, but – as under Charles VII – would have been no more than provocation of Austria. In any case, against the contemporary background of the French Revolution and the upheavals it occasioned in Europe it began, in time, to seem an anachronistic undertaking.

The plan principally bore the imprint of one Prussian foreign minister, Hertzberg; whether it ever received Frederick's blessing is extremely doubtful. The King's League of Princes aimed at containment, not confrontation, its goal was not subversion but the preservation of the 'Imperial fabric'. Once the Bavarian exchange plan could visibly be seen to have failed, Frederick outlined the 'League of German Princes' project in a memorandum sent to

Finckenstein and Hertzberg on 24 October 1784. It began with the important statement that such a League was not to have any offensive characteristics, but should be formed with the sole purpose of 'preserving the rights and freedom of the German Princes, regardless of religion'. His own objective was to prevent 'an ambitious and predatory Emperor from destroying the German Imperial framework by his piecemeal destruction'. The disruption of Austro-Imperial policy was, therefore, the principal motive for the League's inception; it was Prussian *raison d'état* in the garb of conservative Imperial politics. This was wholly in accordance with the membership initially envisaged by Frederick. The Elector of Hanover was simultaneously King of Great Britain; his participation would represent the welcome support of the British Empire for Frederick's European political manoeuvring. The Elector of Saxony, who could only be persuaded to join under duress, was crucial because of the location of his territories. Throughout the Silesian Wars, Saxony always acted as a buffer zone against Austria and each time Frederick used every means at his disposal to gain control over it. Prussia's trump card was played on 18 October 1785, when it was revealed that the Imperial Archchancellor, the Archbishop-Elector of Mainz, Frederick Charles von Erthal, had been persuaded to join. His willingness had been occasioned by the Emperor's division of the Austrian diocese, although it proved impossible to increase significantly the participation of ecclesiastical rulers. A dozen of the smaller secular rulers joined, nevertheless, among them those with entirely different motives. Charles Augustus of Weimar, the Margrave of Baden and the Duke of Zweibrücken all entertained distinctly imperialist sympathies. These were clearly doomed to disappointment under Prussia's auspices. The League, however, stood little chance without Prussian great power support.

The League of Princes, officially formed on 23 July 1785 as an association of the three Electoral Houses of Saxony, Brandenburg and Hanover, followed Prussian lines and proclaimed its aim to be 'the constitutional preservation of the German Imperial system, its laws and freedom'. This was purely a declaration which sought to uphold laws which were not directly threatened by the Emperor's policies. It did, however, touch a nerve of Josephinian politics when the 'constant activity and continued existence' of the Regensburg Imperial Diet was demanded, while the assertion that 'no reforms, unauthorised interference or autocratic impositions' would be tolerated clearly had the Emperor's conduct in mind. In case of an exchange or occupation of Bavaria or 'other enterprises contrary to the Imperial constitution', each signatory to the alliance would supply 15,000 men. Could the fulfilment of such a commitment, however, really be envisaged in the light of the half-hearted support it received, with Saxony alone among the larger states joining?

If one compares the final text with Frederick's first draft produced in October 1784, with its strong language and intellectual precision, it becomes clear that little of the King's original wording remained. It was much more the administrative language of Hertzberg, whom the King had charged with 'polishing' his draft. The result was more a translation of a political programme into an antiquated declaration of rights.

How far one can speculate on the political impact of the League of Princes is almost a hypothetical question in view of its short-lived existence. It certainly caused some confusion among Austrian political circles and probably prevented the Bavarian exchange plan being pursued further. For Prussia, it was a source of security during the years of international tension, which would follow Frederick the Great's death. In the longer term, the League, even had it survived, could never have protected Prussia from the fate which befell it twenty years later.

The League's strongest impact must, therefore, be seen in the emotions and political sympathies it engendered. It holds a special place in the complicated history of the development of German national consciousness. Nascent nationalism could already be detected in the eighteenth century, when tidal waves of publicity from governments and courts in the form of treatises and flysheets began to sweep over the public. Political and legal controversies, only familiar to a limited few, were publicly aired. In due course Frederick learned to use this important tool and by the outbreak of the Seven Years War was in full command of it. In his final years he had at his disposal the able help of foreign minister Hertzberg whose numerous treatises, including those from the era of Frederick William II, were later published in several volumes. All these articles were officially sponsored, such as those by the Prussian diplomat Christian Wilhelm von Dohm; they advanced political points of view and legal arguments but hardly had an impact beyond the narrow sphere of elite political circles. The same applied to the treatises published in Vienna. They were no more than exercises for political experts, semi-public discussions of which even the interested few took little notice. Nevertheless, events themselves came to capture the public's imagination. If during his lifetime Frederick ever engendered feelings of nationalism, it was firstly after Rossbach, and then with the formation of the League of Princes. To a large degree, the League was responsible for a fusion of the surviving Imperial patriotism of the smaller territories with emerging bourgeois-intellectual national consciousness. It was Frederick who finally brought about the amalgamation of the two forces. His deeds awoke a German self-consciousness as yet lacking in political definition. This function of a national Frederician myth, of the ruler who, instead of the powerless and faded *Imperium*, sought to regenerate the Empire, was never as potent as in the years of the League of Princes. The vision was, of course, more image than reality; and it had less to do with the person of Frederick the Great himself than the stimulus he proved to be for the German public.

The euphoria achieved by the time of the League's formation can be measured by the corresponding disappointment which set in after the King's death and dashed hopes of a continuation of the union. The conviction that Frederick's heirs failed in their duty to carry through the true purpose of the League of

Princes as a vehicle for national reform prevailed until the nationalist movement gathered momentum in the mid-nineteenth century. The historian Adolf Schmidt, a former member of the Frankfurt National Assembly, published his book *Prussia's German Policy* in 1850. The true purpose of the League, he wrote, was 'to replace the Empire and construct a new Germany under Prussian leadership'. The 1785 League of Princes, therefore, contributed significantly to the creation of a German nationalist Frederician myth, far removed from the reality of Frederick's own policies.

CHAPTER 7

The Frederician state: the theory and practice of government

The controversy surrounding the concept of 'Enlightened Absolutism', its meaning, basis in theory and applicability in practice, has given rise to a mountain of academic literature. The actual term was never employed in the eighteenth century and was the product of nineteenth-century attempts to categorise history. But is it really a historically viable concept? Does it not combine two fundamentally irreconcilable elements? Or does it describe genuine attempts by absolute monarchies to put the Enlightenment into practice? Or was it no more than an endeavour 'to rationalise the accepted actions of an absolutist Prince' (V. Sellin)? All these opinions have been put forward at various times, but only on one point is there overwhelming consensus. Frederick the Great is viewed almost universally as the archetypal proponent of Enlightened Absolutism. This would indicate that his example contributed considerably to the establishment of the term; not, of course, in the sense that he described himself as an Enlightened Absolutist, but by the definition he gave to his role, the political landmarks he set and, to a lesser degree, the practical legacy of his reign. Both he and his system of government must be seen within the context of his time. He undoubtedly left a mark on the eighteenth century, but he was also shaped by it. This was precisely what Kant meant when he described the Age of Enlightenment as the century of Frederick.

Eighteenth-century ideas about the state are well documented and clearly exercised an influence on political action; however, in order to reach a deeper understanding of Frederick, one must attempt to analyse his own words and establish what the Enlightenment and the absolutist system meant to him. Here, of course, one comes up against the inescapable fact that Frederick's numerous statements are complex and multi-layered, and must be divided into different categories. Naturally predisposed to reflect on his role, he produced much theoretical analysis of the basis of his power and of the duties of a ruler, as well as more general reflections on the role of the state. The Political Testaments of 1752 and 1768 come closer to the reality of political action and must be seen as part theoretical reflection and part instruction for his successor. In the final analysis, the clearest record of the day-to-day practice of government is provided by the mass of Frederick's political correspondence, decrees and legislation. Although these different sources do not always agree, they do provide the key to interpreting the nature of Frederician government. A comparison of one of his earliest theoretical writings, the *Anti-Machiavel*, composed in 1739–40, with one of his final essays, the *Essai sur les formes de gouvernement et sur les devoirs des souverains* (*Essay on the Forms of Government and on the Duties of Rulers*) of 1777, makes clear that in both works Frederick the Great was influenced by the political thought of the Enlightenment. The *Anti-Machiavel* was written with the vision of an enlightened monarchy in mind, of the kind described by Voltaire in the *Henriade* and by Fénelon in *Télémaque*. Monarchy was the best form of government provided the King fulfilled his duty. Since this was by no means always the case, Frederick called his ideal a 'metaphysical monarchy' while condemning despotism as 'a veritable hell'.

Even the enlightened idealism of the young Frederick, however, was tempered by remarkable political realism – to the extent that many passages of the *Anti-Machiavel* appeared as a major programme of Prussian government. The tension between the two spheres of influence, the philosophical and the pragmatic, continued throughout the King's life. His inherent sense of power was strengthened, and progressively rationalised, subjected more to practical reality than theoretical ideas. Eventually the King even concerned himself with the question of how his position as monarch could be legitimised. Although the *Anti-Machiavel* does debate the merits of republicanism, it dismisses it as a form of government flawed in its internal structure and doomed to revert to despotism. But was this empirical statement sufficient to justify the legitimacy of monarchical rule? It surely had to be proven that monarchical government was conducted according to the will of those over whom it governed. Here the fashionable philosophical concept of the social contract proved helpful. In his 1777 treatise, the King elaborates: the upholding of laws was the only reason to elect a ruling élite, 'here lies the true origin of sovereign power'. Soon after this, the King describes himself on no fewer than six occasions as the first servant of the state. This role therefore stemmed from the social contract between a ruler and his subjects, not from one-sided usurpation. In the same vein, the parlement of Paris had argued against Louis XV at the beginning of the century that the King was merely 'the first and sovereign magistrate in this state'. In Frederician Prussia, it was no longer the Estates, but the people as a whole on whom the legitimacy of monarchical power was based.

This was certainly a complete transformation of attitudes concerning the origins of monarchy, hitherto based on dynastic right and religious sanction. Ultimately, neither a social contract interpretation nor Hobbes' theory of an irreversible grant of sovereignty by the people to their ruler predominated, but Rousseau's revolutionary, democratic idea of the general will (*volonté générale*). Though Frederick was always aware of the pitfalls of a system of government which rested upon natural law doctrines, his main argument against the critics of monarchical government and the defenders of the rights of subjects was the structural weakness of elective systems as demonstrated in Germany's bishoprics, in Poland and 'even in Rome'. Frederick's later political writings demonstrate a constant concern to preserve the institution of monarchy by reminding rulers to look to their consciences. But did this suffice? 'We would wish', we read at the end of his essay on forms of government and monarchical duty, 'that this feeble attempt could nurture rulers like Marcus Aurelius. This would be the greatest reward imaginable and would also ensure the preservation of mankind.' The preservation of mankind – it was more than the survival of the ruler alone which preoccupied the King in his old age. His concern was for the preservation of monarchical forms of government in general, since to him these alone represented a guarantee of continuity.

In his 1777 treatise, Frederick defends absolute monarchy by claiming that its authority was limited by the existence not merely of representative institutions but also by ministerial power. Ministers were a source of confusion, since their constant replacement left little time to allow plans to reach fruition. The minister was not master of the state and therefore did not have its true well-being at heart. King and people, however, formed a single body; the monarch who rules is to his state as a head is to the body, he has to see, think and act for the general public in order to attain for it every desirable advantage. Frederick defends an autocratic form of monarchy, and is clearly aware of the threat posed by over-powerful ministers, as was particularly the case in France. The new forms of monarchy limited by parliament evolving, for example, in Great Britain during the eighteenth century, are only touched on in one sentence: England, he declares, should be prepared for the fate which befell the Roman Republic 'when the Lower House no longer has the nation's interests at heart and prefers to give way to the shameful corruption which undermines it'. It is curious to reflect, then, that the British system alone withstood the crisis which befell the continental monarchies.

One characteristic element in Frederick's interpretation of political absolutism was his claim while still Crown Prince to be more than a nominal commander-in-chief of the army. In the twelfth chapter of the *Anti-Machiavel* he argues that it is of the utmost importance to the defence of the realm for the monarch to lead the army in person. Although this principle had been followed by Louis XIV, there are few other eighteenth-century examples of this practice – with the exception of Sweden's Charles XII and Russia's Peter the Great. The ruler, Frederick believed, should give the orders and determine the course of the battle, 'he will demonstrate how victory will constantly crown his endeavours, how with wisdom he harnesses luck and provides a shining example of how fearlessly one can face danger and even death when duty, honour and eternal glory demand it.' In 1739, these were still empty phrases, but it was soon to become clear how Frederick interpreted such statements. The absolutist ruler was also to be his own commander-in-chief – a principle followed only by the King of Prussia among the leading powers of the Frederician era and one of which he alone was capable. This form of military absolutism had little to do with the Enlightenment unless the uniting of civil and military leadership permitted a more completely rational line of conduct to be pursued. Frederick returned to this point in his 1752 Political Testament, with the experience of two wars. He uses the example of the Dutch failure in 1672 to resist the French invasion and then the Republic's recovery under William III to demonstrate the importance, especially for an emerging power, of a ruler who is also leader of the army. The justification for his own ability to combine both roles stemmed not from the two successful military ventures he had undertaken but from his own military training as a youth.

Let us return, however, to the Enlightenment. If one examines the effect of the King's acceptance of natural law theory on the practice of his statecraft, it is clear that this influence was incomplete. The transformation of the monarch ruling by divine right into a secular head of state was never totally successful. Neither Frederick nor the other Enlightened Absolutists became bourgeois monarchs; they rather transformed a state of courtly ceremony and hierarchy into a state with a military hierarchy, alongside which an intellectual élite developed quite separately. Frederick's undisputed charisma distanced him from other men and did not encourage familiarity. The King was not like others, but a loner who was isolated by his genius. His system was not transferable; it was inextricably bound up with his own person. He was an autocrat not only in a political, but also in a highly personal sense.

The attempt to apply enlightened principles within a state governed autocratically and within an overwhelmingly feudal social structure obviously could not be completely successful, though some success was achieved. The King's indifference to the Church and his attitude to religion were much in the spirit of the Enlightenment. The usual strict application of the principle of *cuius regio, eius religio*, established in Imperial law, forbade any digression from the Lutheranism of the majority of Prussia's inhabitants, though its ruling house remained Calvinist. Prussia was characterised by the toleration which existed because of the two Protestant faiths. Frederick therefore held it to be without consequence whether the ruler had any religious conviction or not, as he made clear in the 1752 Political Testament. To him, the various religions were 'a fabulous system which is more or less preposterous'. Religious toleration therefore did not stem from any fundamental conviction but from expediency, although at times – as in 1777 – he claimed that the ruler had no right to dictate the beliefs of his subjects. With the well-known words 'all religions must be tolerated, and government must only guard against one faith damaging the other, since here everyone must find happiness in his own way', he certainly expressed a basic conviction, but this was an isolated example. He failed to issue a Patent of Toleration to provide the basis for his religious policy – as Joseph II had done as part of his programme of enlightened reform on 13 October 1781. Moreover, in the same way that Protestants in Austria were denied full citizenship, Catholics in Prussia fared no better. This was based upon sound political arguments. The largest group of Catholics was located in Silesia, and a number of its clerics showed open sympathy with Austria during the Silesian Wars. Breslau, indeed, was deemed by Frederick in 1752 to exhibit a fanatical bias (*partialité fanatique*) in favour of Maria Theresa. As a result, he saw to it that when ecclesiastical vacancies occurred they were filled by 'peaceful-minded men'. Although he declared: 'I am neutral between Rome and Geneva', he could not permit neutrality between Berlin and Vienna. *Raison d'état*, in any case, was the governing precept and *raison d'état* dictated toleration. The King reiterated this with considerable conviction in 1777 in his *Essay on the Forms of Government and the Duties of Rulers*, in which he declared that toleration was so advantageous for the community that it was 'the foundation of the state's happiness'.

Frederick's pragmatic approach in religious matters contrasted dramatically with Joseph II's systematic radicalism and stemmed both from tactical calculation and personal indifference. Can one detect the same indifference in his attitude to the law? Although the King by the grace of God was absolute in the sense of *legibus solutus*, he was bound by the dictates of natural law which had been created by God. Once divine right was abolished, natural law, as dictated by reason, remained. In his 1749 treatise *Reasons to Implement or Abolish Laws*, Frederick discussed the historical role of laws as a consequence of Montesquieu's *Spirit of the Laws* published in the previous year. In the *Anti-Machiavel*, the law and administration of justice are defined as being the foundation of a ruler's greatness. He must never discard this basis of his power. But did the laws either of Prussia or the Empire accord with the laws and principles of reason? And do they guarantee that the law corresponded with natural justice? At first the King contented himself with introducing a single reform, which in the spirit of the times he perceived to be the most urgent: on 3 June 1740 he abolished torture, and later, in 1755, removed the final exceptions – cases of suspected high treason or mass murder – as well. This was a humanitarian action for which he had first declared his support in the *Anti-Machiavel*. Subsequently, in 1749, he declared torture a custom 'which was a disgrace to Christian and cultured people, and was useless as well as cruel'. He did not, however, tackle the fundamental judicial defects, particularly the diversity of the legal systems to be found within the Prussian state. This was not tackled until in May 1746 he received the *Privilegium de non appellando* (the right to stop appeals going to the Imperial Courts) for the Hohenzollern provinces formerly subject to the laws of the Empire and therefore acquired complete sovereignty over them.

With the appointment of Samuel von Cocceji as Great Chancellor in 1747, a thorough reorganisation of the administration of justice and of the body of laws was begun, with the aim less of fundamental reform than of unifying Prussian law. This was successfully accomplished for all parts of the monarchy, including Silesia, with the exception of the territory of East Prussia. By abolishing the numerous high courts in the individual provinces, the influence of the Estates was curtailed, so that the judicial reform programme also became a dimension of absolutist state reform. Cocceji was a proponent of natural law doctrines and launched the first Frederician attempt to codify civil law, the *Corpus Juris Fredericianum* in 1749 and 1751 – but it remained incomplete. Frederick gave the reform his blessing in his treatise *Reasons to Implement or Abolish Laws* in which he praised highly the Chancellor's 'wisdom'. These were reflections, strongly influenced by Montesquieu, about the links between laws, and the spirit of the people and different forms of government. The King believed the Prussian criminal law to have achieved a middle way between leniency and severity and therefore to have come as close to 'natural justice' as possible. He noted that a complete code of law was 'a masterpiece of human reason in the field of statecraft'. But such completeness he judged to be beyond human competence. The Enlightenment, nonetheless, had provided the impulse to the Frederician state to strive for such precision in the codification of its laws. Several decades were to pass, however, before the next steps towards this goal were taken.

It was a single case, that of the Miller Arnold, which forced a dramatic and arbitrary intervention from the King; Arnold claimed that he had been deprived of his mill by a local nobleman and then denied legal redress by the local authorities of the New Mark. He and his wife appealed directly to the King who intervened on very questionable legal grounds and restored the mill. The case led to the imprisonment of seven judges, and also brought about the fall of the Great Chancellor Joseph von Fürst, who had stood in the way of fundamental judicial reform. The cabinet order of 14 April 1780 promoted Johann Heinrich Carmer, head of several *Regierungen* (provincial courts) with the title of Minister of Justice in Silesia, to be Great Chancellor and charged him with the task of completing the reform of the legal system; this was to be the most significant achievement of Enlightened Absolutism in Prussia. In the April 1780 cabinet order, drawn up by Carl Gottlieb Suarez, the great project of drawing up a new law code was almost hidden behind the other tasks, such as a revision of legal procedure, and the scale of the undertaking was not yet recognised. The cabinet order noted that the legal codes and customs varied considerably from province to province. Since the provincial statutes and customs were limited to 'only certain instances and contained no uniform or complete rules of law', the Justinian *Corpus Juris* had been adopted, as in many other European states, some centuries before. The authority of Roman law, however, had since been shattered, and 'was shot through with contradictions'. These arguments fuelled the efforts to protect the new law code from all sides and at the same time to establish the basis on which the new laws were to be fashioned. A new Prussian law code was to be drawn up, one which would leave both the laws of individual provinces and Roman law untouched. It took almost a decade and a half to complete this task, and the *Allgemeine Landrecht für die Preußischen Staaten* (the General Law Code of the Prussian Territories) of 1794 faithfully mirrored Frederician Prussia, with all its contradictions: between absolutism and human rights, between the principle of equality and corporate privilege.

The new Law Code was not guided, however, by any enlightened concept of society. A much more powerful influence was the traditional hierarchy of the Society of Orders. Hence the three Estates – peasants, middle class, and nobility – were portrayed as distinct groups whose birth determined their various social and political functions. Thus the peasantry was defined as all inhabitants of the countryside 'engaged in the direct working of the land or involved in agriculture' (Vol. II, Section 7, Paragraph 1). The definition of the middle classes, however, was not determined by their social function but by the fact that 'according to their birth they could not be classed as belonging either to the nobility or the peasantry, and are not subsequently assimilated by either' (Section 8, Paragraph 1). The functional duties of the nobility, however, were emphasised: 'The nobility, as the First Estate, is responsible for the defence of the state, the upholding of its dignity abroad and the maintenance of the fabric of its internal cohesion' (Section 9, Paragraph 1). The fact that nobility was determined purely by birth was made clear in the second sentence: 'Only those born to the aristocracy or those who inherited land and title will be counted among the noble Estate.' The attempts to define the nature and duties of the Estates within society and state highlighted the tensions among the different authors of the new General Law Code. The almost simultaneous drawing up of a law code in Josephinian Austria invites comparison: the authors of the *Allgemeines Bürgerliches Gesetzbuch* (Civil Law Code) of 1811, led by Franz Alois von Zeiler, declared themselves fundamentally more in favour of a middle-class society in the modern sense and of equality 'as the inescapable basis of the community of the state', while leaving the hierarchy of the Society of Orders in place.

The obstacles to implementing social reforms in the middle-class spirit of the Enlightenment whilst restricted by a society riddled with corporate privilege were not only theoretical in nature. Although the Enlightenment called for dignity and respect for people at all levels of society and Frederick had declared himself to be a follower of its humanitarian ideals, he failed to raise the legal and social position of the East Elbian serfs to a humane level. The need for reform in this sphere arose not only out of humanitarian considerations, but also the state's need to preserve the peasant as a soldier and taxpayer. In contrast to Joseph II, Frederick was not influenced at all by physiocratic ideas. The King's efforts, initially in Pomerania, to abolish serfdom ended only in an argument about the different degrees of servitude. Serfdom could be abolished only in Silesia and West and East Prussia, and then solely on royal domains. The King's account of these disputes in the *Essay on the Forms of Government and the Duties of Rulers* of 1777 was tinged by deep resignation. Here he frankly acknowledged the economic necessity of serfdom in all its forms: 'If one were to abolish these abhorrent practices at a stroke, one would ruin agriculture. The nobility would then have to be compensated for a part of its losses.' Joseph II, whose reforms for a time were a great deal more radical and included the abolition of serfdom on noble estates in 1781, failed in a much more spectacular fashion.

Although the King's theoretical writings on the nature of monarchical authority are revealing, the Political Testaments of 1752 and 1768 are of far greater importance, since they summarised practical policy and contained guidance for the future. They included analyses of domestic as well as foreign policy, although the latter was examined much more frequently than the former. Here Frederick also set out his attitude to absolutism. It is useful to compare his principles of an absolute monarchy with the reality of the Frederician constitution and administration. In the first Political Testament, the question is posed: 'should a sovereign rule himself?' The question here was not the reasons for the right to absolute monarchical self-government but its utility. Frederick's response was that it was essential for a state like Prussia. Here as elsewhere his argument centred almost exclusively on the disadvantages of ministerial government. Autocracy, however, conferred not only privileges, but duties, which were more important. This accorded with Frederick's probably erroneous opinion that monarchical rule was only threatened by the incompetence, lack of education, laziness and stupidity of the sovereign, not by republican movements or the demands of rising new classes within society. The only safeguard of monarchical rule is therefore the acceptance of the monarch's duty as the first servant of the state. Autocracy required ability – this was absolutism's dilemma. Louis XV, whose example was immediately before Frederick's eyes, decided to rule in person after Cardinal Fleury's death, but his 'indolence and carelessness made him unfit for it'. In such cases if the successor was unsuitable for his office there was no way out and, although Frederick secretly feared this to be so with his own heir, the principle of the Prussian King's duty to strive for absolute authority remained inviolate.

This did not, of course, mean that Prussia's ruler had to concern himself with every detail, but only that, with the help of his ministers, he must deal personally with the most important matters. Frederick provided a short and considerably simplified description of the Prussian administrative hierarchy. The General Directory appears solely as a body which supervised the finances; although its departments were, in fact, responsible for the implementation of policy, any mention of institutions not representative of the entire state was to be avoided. Absolutism required above all the concentration of the state's power at its head. 'A well-managed government must have as coherent an administrative system as a philosophical framework. All measures must be well thought through and must direct finances, politics and the army towards a single goal: namely the strengthening of the state and the growth of its power.' Such a system, however, can only come from one head, and therefore that must be the ruler, according to the 1752 Testament. This defined the areas which the King reserved solely for himself: 'Everything to do with war, I have always tackled myself; since I held it to be my duty to be commander-in-chief of the army and inspector of the forces,' he wrote in 1768. By the same token, the most important matters in foreign policy, negotiations with the great powers, the conclusion of treaties, the inevitable political intrigues and everything which concerned the state's principal interests fell upon the

King's shoulders, although he could consult with the *Kabinettsministerium*, the body formally responsible for foreign affairs.

The absolute monarch's principal roles, according to Frederick, were to be commander of the army and director of foreign policy. But here, too, he was no more able to act without assistance than in the internal government of the state, with its multitude of administrative, social and economic problems, where detailed knowledge as well as consideration of regional differences were of the utmost importance. Within the domestic sphere the ruler's dependence upon subordinates to provide constant information and supervision was undoubtedly far greater. A prerequisite of absolutism was therefore a complicated process of decision-making. Whilst in Austria Maria Theresa formulated policy in committees such as the *Staatsrat* ('Council of State') set up in 1761, Frederick the Great prided himself in 1768 on never having held a council of ministers. Nothing, in his opinion, could have been more damaging. It was impossible that several heads could deal in a uniform fashion with so many different interests and strive towards a common goal. The verbal debate and often fiercely divergent opinions only clouded the issue, while secrecy, vital in all discussions, could never be fully guaranteed with so many privy to the details of policy. Such words do not stem so much out of a systematic vision of absolute rule as out of the incredible confidence of a ruler who, since his youth, had had to assert himself against powerful forces.

Frederick did not discuss policy with his ministers, but employed a method of written communication earlier practised by his father. Every day the ministers of the General Directory – itself organised on collegiate principles – the Department of Justice and the *Kabinettsministerium* sent detailed reports to the King about matters requiring a decision from him. The Political Testament of 1752 provided the following account: 'In disputed or difficult cases the minister himself would set out the arguments for and against [in a written submission]. In this way the ruler was enabled to take a decision at first glance, providing that he takes the trouble to read carefully and understand the matters before him.' The royal decision would then appear in the form of a cabinet order. It has been established that in the second half of Frederick's reign up to twelve such cabinet orders (which then became law) were issued each day. In the years between 1728 and 1795, their total number rose from 300 to 400,000.

The most important role in the administration of the state was consequently played by the royal *Kabinett* and its confidential secretaries, above all August Friedrich Eichel. His influence extended far beyond the formal boundaries of his post, and until his death in 1768 he had the complete trust of his master. After the Seven Years War, the *Kabinett* (the secretaries and officials who surrounded the King and provided essential scribal services) acquired more and more business at the expense of the General Directory. The number of *Kabinett* secretaries doubled after 1768 from three to six – a sure sign of an increased workload. A tendency towards greater departmentalisation was apparent and became more pronounced after Frederick's death. The department for foreign affairs, particularly during the Frederician era, developed naturally into a Cabinet ministry with a wide sphere of influence. Where foreign policy was concerned, the King's will was unquestionably dominant, but in all other areas of policy the monarch's role in practice should not be exaggerated. Absolutism reached its limits as soon as it became entangled in the thicket of administrative detail, despite the King's attempts to secure an overview through his inspections (*revues*) on his regular journeys. The gulf between the ruler and the administrative machinery had nonetheless grown considerably. The 'omnipresent King' was seldom a reality, however remarkable the King's memory and knowledge of his staff.

The royal autocracy which took the form of government from the King's Cabinet, was clearly unusually efficient under Frederick the Great, at least in the first half of his reign. In the long term, however, it was not suited to controlling the expanding apparatus of the state. It required the development of a comprehensive administrative state with a bureaucracy, which would carry out the King's wishes, but also develop initiatives of its own. It has been argued by Hans Rosenberg that this bureaucracy succeeded in transforming the safeguards and checks introduced by the King, such as the civil service commissions (*Oberexaminationskommissionen*) established in 1770, into convenient mechanisms for its own purposes and turning them into 'instruments of corporate autonomy and hierarchical autocracy'. The bureaucracy supposedly controlled the key administrative appointments through an extensive system of patronage and in this way seriously undermined royal autocracy. These arguments are clearly exaggerated: as far as the higher bureaucracy, described in the General Law Code as 'servants of the state', was concerned, the only corporate element which existed was that of a noble corporation. Within the *esprit de corps* of the officer corps, any corporate elements were inconsistent with officers' ambitions and the high degree of competition for advancement. The Presidents of the twelve War and Domain Chambers (the heads of the actual provincial governments) in 1779 were almost all of noble birth. Only the East Prussian President of the Chambers of Königsberg, Gumbinnen and Marienwerder, Johann Friedrich Domhardt, was a commoner, and he was subsequently ennobled. On the other hand, middle-class heads were to be found in the provincial Chambers. Advancement to President, however, usually came about from the post of *Landrat* (local commissioner or councillor) rather than from the ranks of the officials in the provincial Chambers. The *Landrat*, although a royal civil servant, was at the same time allied to the local nobility and frequently drawn from its ranks. Since the nomination of leading bureaucrats as a rule stemmed from suggestions made by the General Directory, the higher bureaucracy itself selected its leading officials and thus guaranteed its own preservation. All the ruler should do, as the Political Testament of 1768 expressed it, was to fill the provincial Chambers with good Presidents, and to give them the necessary authority to keep their subordinates in check and to remove officials incapable of discharging the functions of their post or doing harm through greed or self-interest. These are simply general moral precepts; a system could not be detected in all this.

The widespread *ancien régime* practice of selling offices, which contributed considerably to the fiscal needs of many states, was at certain periods not unimportant in Brandenburg-Prussia, particularly under the Great Elector, though it never reached the scale it did in France. Under Frederick the Great it was attacked vigorously and with considerable success, though the impact of this campaign was least in the western provinces. The most energetic onslaught upon venality of office in the legal system was undertaken by Cocceji's judicial reforms during the 1740s. The introduction of examinations established norms of professional competence in the appointment of judges. There was, however, one example of venality in Brandenburg-Prussia. Leases for royal domains were sold to the highest bidder. Although the leaseholder functioned as a local official, these leases cannot be compared with other state posts. An important point of social history was that the owners of these leases were predominantly middle class. The King aimed to make the bureaucracy a self-perpetuating organism, in which posts were earned through merit rather than simply being inherited. In a General Directory directive, dated 26 December 1746, the bureaucracy is described as 'a good nursery of able people trained for their posts from an early stage', and the reality was not too far removed from the King's vision. The only obvious problem remained the neglect of non-noble candidates for appointment and the tension created by this situation.

Unlike other European states, no corrupt system of sinecures developed in Prussia. The bureaucracy remained on the whole not only willing but also able. A high turnover of posts was apparent in provincial government; unsuitable officials were sometimes removed by the King's disapproval and censure. It is clear that many unjust and arbitrary decisions were taken. In his old age, Frederick, with his increasing disdain for mankind, had few illusions about the qualities of his civil servants. 'To imagine,' he wrote in 1752, 'that all two legged-beings without feathers are honourable men would be to deceive oneself like an idiot.' Army officers who transferred to civil posts and were appointed Presidents were viewed more favourably. 'Officers [the King wrote] know how to obey and to secure obedience and if they are tested, they see to the task themselves and are more reliable than the others.' This statement could lead to the erroneous view that the King preferred army officers as Chamber Presidents; in fact only four out of a total of 41 Presidents were officers. Civilian administrators overwhelmingly predominated, a fact to which the numerous wars and the heavy losses which resulted within the officer corps no doubt contributed. The most successful Presidents, Domhardt among them, distinguished themselves more by personal initiative and at times by open opposition than by military-style obedience. Only one former officer, Friedrich Wilhelm von der Schulenburg-Kehnert, was promoted to be a minister of state from the ranks of the Chamber Presidents.

If one examines the Political Testaments as a whole, it becomes clear that they are more a statement of absolutism than Enlightened Absolutism, and more precisely they are a record of the King's autocracy. The extent of this autocracy, and its limitations, are only hinted at. From these hints one has to attempt to reconstruct the administrative system in all its detail. This can only be done successfully through an examination of the major documents produced by the day-to-day operation of government. A good example would be the 'Renewed Instruction for the General Directory' dated 20 May 1748. Here Frederick built on one of his father's most important political creations: the General Directory. This had been established by Frederick William I in December 1722 through an Instruction which proved to be a milestone in Prussia's administrative absolutism with its intention to force all leading groups within society into the service of the state. Frederick changed none of the principles of his predecessor. He confirmed, among other things, the distinctive functional dichotomy of this central institution whose four departments were at some time responsible for the individual parts of the monarchy – apart from Silesia – as well as for particular departmental matters. Frederick left this system untouched, but throughout the course of his reign added another four departments to the General Directory, all of which functioned according to strict principles of departmentalisation as *Realdepartements* for the state. The Fifth Department, responsible for commerce and manufacturing, was added as early as 1740.

Although the authority of the General Directory was extended into new areas of policy, its importance failed to increase and its competence was clearly compromised by its size. The King always mistrusted it, perhaps because of its collegial structure, and this suspicion certainly lay behind his Instruction of 1748. In it, he spoke of the negligent habits into which the General Directory had fallen; it was necessary 'to awake it from its slumber, remind it anew of its duties and animate it into showing its awareness of these duties by more diligent and honest work than has hitherto been apparent'. The extent to which disagreement and rivalry dominated the bureaucracy is apparent when, in the Instruction, the King remarks that his greatest displeasure is occasioned by the fact 'that amongst the ministers a form of hatred, animosity and *esprit de parti* seems to have crept in'. It was important, however, 'in so respected a bureau that all personal animosities should be put to one side and nothing else be thought of or worked towards than the welfare and best interests of the state'. The Instruction was clearly designed to enable the King to regain firm control over the General Directory. He states that, like his father, he himself would become President, reiterates the detailed responsibilities of each Department and refers to ability and experience as necessary prerequisites in appointments to posts. The prospective incumbents, moreover, had to be of Prussian birth and of the Protestant faith. He would personally oversee the daily duties of the officials and threatens severe punishment in cases of absence or breach of confidentiality. Two fundamental maxims of orthodox mercantilism were stressed: the need, firstly, to attract money from abroad, 'this will happen through commerce'; and secondly, to prevent an unnecessary flow of cash out of Prussia, 'and this will be brought about by developing the manufacturing industry'.

One looks in vain through this document to find evidence of the influence of enlightened ideas. The Instruction of 1748 embodied the principles, based only on utility and economic efficiency, of Frederick William I's harsh, military, bureaucratic state, which his son has adopted. Even the article about the 'preservation of one's vassals' with its demands to limit dues imposed upon the peasantry could already be found in Frederick William I's Instruction and was only lightly influenced by the spirit of the Enlightenment – with its argument 'that the happiness of the sovereign depended mainly on the welfare of his subjects'. In an additional section concerning the individual War and Domain Chambers, however, a different tone can be detected. Here an appeal is made to 'sensible people, whose love of humanity had not wholly vanished' and to 'enormous and quite Egyptian forms of labour-services common in many places', which are pilloried and described as 'more unbearable than slavery itself'. Frederick had, in those early days, not yet reached the high degree of resignation apparent in his theoretical treatise, the *Essay on the Forms of Government and the Duties of Rulers* of 1777. As a rule, however, pure utility and practicality dominated the administrative documents of Frederick's reign.

One goal above all played a decisive role in the King's policy: the creation of a unified Prussian state, a task begun by the Great Elector, was continued with renewed vigour. This objective not only involved institutional and administrative changes, but also necessitated a shift in consciousness which was brought about by the political and military achievements of the Frederician monarchy. Frederick therefore began with the army. He had taken a great deal of trouble during the first two Silesian Wars, as he explained in the Political Testament of 1752, to drum into all officers, regardless of the province from which they came, that they represented Prussia, and that all the Hohenzollern territories, even if geographically separate, formed a unified whole (*un corps ensemble*). By the end of Frederick's reign, this sense of a national consciousness had been established among the upper strata of the state administration, the army and the intelligentsia, not least because of the events of the Seven Years War. The greatest resistance to the changes, however, came from the nobility in the individual provinces. The Great Elector had earlier broken their political power during the seventeenth century, but had left their social privileges intact. Frederick William I created a central administration responsible for the collection of urban and rural taxation, respectively the Excise and Contribution, without allowing the Estates of the various provinces any share in their collection. In most European polities, such as the Habsburg Monarchy, the provincial nobleman was, to varying degrees, involved in the collection of taxes, and even in the 'Prussian lands', according to the *Allgemeine Landrecht* (General Law Code) the practice had not been fully eradicated.

Frederick proceeded along the path mapped out for him by his predecessors and set out to limit the last remnant of corporate, noble power, the *Landtage der Ritterschaften* (Assemblies of Nobility). After his accession, he accepted the gravamen of the provincial Estates without ever bothering to answer them, on a journey to receive the homage of his subjects. These complaints tended to concern their military cantonal obligations, demands for the reconfirmation of their privileges and of the power of the *Landtage* (provincial assemblies). The most substantial demands were made by Cleves and Mark, where the Estates had resisted especially fiercely under the Great Elector. Here the corporate bodies, with their separate chambers for the nobility and the townspeople, retained important powers and they submitted a list of 38 grievances, among them a demand for the re-establishment of the *Indignatsrecht* (the so-called 'Law of the Native Born' which reserved posts in the provincial administration to those born or naturalised in that territory). Moreover, they still retained the right to approve new taxes and participate in drawing up new laws. Throughout the Prussian territories, corporate privileges were rights which had to be defended against the centralised state and its bureaucracy, for example the provincial administrative institutions of the War and Domain Chambers.

The quality of Prussia's bureaucratic state apparatus clearly far surpassed that of the Habsburg Monarchy, even after Haugwitz's reforms after 1748 substantially limited the power of the territorial Estates in finance and government. The three-tier administrative system – General Directory, War and Domain Chambers, local commissioners (*Landräte*) – was gradually introduced into the whole monarchy, beginning with the Electoral Mark. Corporate bodies such as the Assemblies of the Estates (*Ständelandtage*) were not formally abolished but were simply never summoned again. Disputes continued over other matters. The Pomeranian Estates, for instance, refused for decades to limit the dues owed by the better-off peasants and merely agreed to the abolition of the term 'serfdom'. In those provinces in which the Great Elector had already encountered greatest resistance, in East Prussia, Cleves and Mark, dualistic forms of government, in which the territorial Estates continued to play a role, persisted longest, as they did in East Friesland, acquired in 1744. In an edict dated 22 August 1752, the system of *Landräte* which already existed in Brandenburg was introduced into East Friesland, but the right of the local community to nominate them was preserved. Cleves-Mark was the most stubborn pocket of resistance; corporate rights were so entrenched that, even under Frederick William I, tax assessments continued to be carried out by the local administration of the Estates. Not until February 1753 was the *Landrat* system introduced by cabinet order; the Estates attempted to undermine it by obstructive practices and made little use of their continuing right to nominate candidates for appointment. This, in effect, meant self-emasculation. In complete contrast, the Estates and their subordinate agencies in Guelders retained their powers and their role in government. The joint administrative college in which the Estates participated, was confirmed by royal cabinet order in its function as immediately subordinate to the General Directory and its administrative authority was equivalent to that of the War and Domain Chambers. The attempt by the Pomeranian Estates to implement a similar arrangement – that is, to preserve the independence of the leader of the local Estates from the authority of the Stettin War and Domain Chamber – failed.

In the latter years of Frederick's reign, pressure for increased participation by these bodies once again increased, as it did in many other German states in

the final decades of the eighteenth century. This only became politically significant in the 1780s when the provincial assemblies in the Prussian core territories,
summoning up their traditional privileges, demanded a voice in the judicial
reforms which, with their aim of establishing a uniform code of law, threatened
to encroach on established provincial rights. In the spring of 1783 the representative of the local Estates protested against the judicial reforms in the
Electoral and New Mark and 'that a new code of law, about which we have
not been consulted, is to appear'. It was thus clear that fundamental reform of
the state could never be harnessed to the old, dualistic system with all its
special interests and provincial loyalties. Reform of local government in town
and country demanded new institutions such as those vom Stein attempted to
introduce through his urban reforms at the beginning of the nineteenth century. The unified Prussia was an artificial construction which did not assimil-
ate the provincial corporate bodies. Frederick the Great failed to destroy these
completely, but managed to nudge them gently towards obsolescence. In
1741, for instance, in response to a complaint from the financial administration of the Estates in Silesia, the King issued a statement that the services of
'the hitherto established practices and in particular the General Taxation Office
of the honourable nobles and Estates are no longer needed'. In his Political
Testaments, the King at times exaggerated the regional diversity of his provinces and their nobilities, but he used this as a pretext to impress upon the élite
that 'all provinces, even if geographically separate, form a single unified state'.

The Enlightenment as the realisation of human rights and humanitarian
sentiments again had little impact on all this. The more one examines the details
of Frederick the Great's internal policies, the stronger becomes the impression
that their principal aim was the strengthening of the state and the creation of
a society moulded by the state. The General Law Code still showed the evidence of these changes to the social structure and how the functions of those born
into corporate bodies were transformed into the tasks of professional and political groups. It has, therefore, been argued by Volker Sellin 'that Enlightened
Absolutism in Prussia meant not only individual, isolated reforms inspired by
enlightened philosophy, but a primary aim to shape the state and its institutions into a rational system; only that which ran counter to the efficiency and
logic of the system was abolished; only that which furthered [these aims] was
introduced'. Enlightenment was therefore to be equated with rationalisation
or, to use a term more familiar today, modernisation. Such a verdict, however, is only half the story. The strengthening of the state by means of rationalisation was clearly one dimension of the Enlightenment to Frederick – as it
was to Joseph II and Catherine II – but the King's original, enlightened idealism was based on the idea that the state had a higher purpose in promoting
equality, humanitarianism and happiness. It is possible that this idealism con-
flicted with a stronger will for power and in time evaporated. Had Frederick
grown up exclusively within the confines of Frederick William I's state and
been untouched by the ideas of the French *philosophes*, he would not have
been as conscious of the internal contradictions within himself. He did not

want to dispel these tensions, but to turn this into a productive antithesis which constantly drove him to reflect upon his actions. He was thus not an ordinary exponent of power politics with a medium-sized state, but a philosopher for whom the power he held was a constant intellectual problem. Precisely because of this, he was an Enlightened Absolutist monarch.

CAMERALISM AND MERCANTILISM

Most of Frederick II's practical policies were reasoned out theoretically. This was as much a reflection of the dichotomy within his inner self as a radical consequence of the external pressures to which all of his actions were subject. His real motives, moreover, were not always apparent in the decisions he took. He reached a plethora of small decisions on economic matters and left a corresponding amount of paperwork on the subject, more than survives in any other field, with the possible exception of foreign policy and warfare; paradoxically, however, he left next to nothing on the theoretical issues of economic policy. There is a range of documents on his political philosophy, his thoughts on particular forms of government, international relations, war and peace, but nothing on the general principles of the economy. We cannot be certain that he was even familiar with contemporary and earlier economic theory, such as the writings of Johann Joachim Becher or Johann Heinrich Gottlob von Justi for example. A rich crop of economic literature existed in Prussia, most of which was opposed to the ideas of the physiocrats. It is possible that the King assimilated something of its content through economic experts in his administration or from more general philosophical works. He would certainly not have been able to define the theoretical differences between mercantilism, physiocracy, fiscalism or cameralism and relied exclusively on practical utility, which alone to him was important.

Economic options always depended on a subjective assessment of their aims. Mercantilism clearly proves this point. It was originally adopted as part of the process of state building which, along with state control of the army and administration, also included the economy. This would mean that economic activity was to be directed by the state with the aim of increasing its power. Later this attitude was qualified: not only was the state to gain from the profits of mercantilist ventures, but also its citizens, principally its townsfolk, merchants and manufacturers. The historical prerequisite of an agrarian infrastructure would form a basis on which to develop an industrial and commercial economic system. Fiscalism, wrongly seen as synonymous with mercantilism, was primarily an endeavour to increase the state's revenue even at the cost of economically damaging objectives and prohibitive means such as artificially high and unproductive taxes. It is precisely these drawbacks which cameralism, the central European variant of western European mercantilism, strove to avoid. The considerable number of German cameralists – Johann Joachim Becher, Veit Ludwig von Seckendorff, Johann Heinrich Gottlob von Justi, Joseph von Sonnenfels – argued that state power rested upon its promotion of the welfare and prosperity of the individual citizen and that these goals had to be mutually compatible.

Frederick the Great examined this central problem in his 1768 Political Testament. He questioned the function of taxation: 'Should the good of the state or that of the individual take precedence, and what decision should one come to? My answer is: the state is composed of many private individuals, and the good of the sovereign is synonymous with that of his subjects. Each private individual must contribute to the costs of the state, but he should not have to share half his income with the sovereign. In a well-managed state, peasant, town-dweller and nobleman should all retain the majority of his income and contribute only a part to the state.' Did Frederick really act according to these principles? In general, his economic policies were not determined by purely fiscal calculations; to him their ultimate aim was indisputably to increase the state's power and above all its military strength. He clearly stated this in other parts of the Political Testament, although almost always linked with the idea that this would also serve the good of the people. The security of the state is equated with the welfare of the subject. In the later 'Reflections on the Prussian Financial Administration', written in 1784, the national treasury's annual surplus is justified by the argument that 'the poor people are spared taxes which an incompetent sovereign would heap upon them in times of war'. Here is evidence of the almost desperate struggle to reconcile the King's preoccupation with national security with the original vision of the state's humanitarian purpose. The aims of Frederick's economic policies were not, therefore, fiscal in the strictest sense, but they were ultimately geared to the interests of the state. As always, the King was divided: his policies in practice were often rather different from his views in theory.

The unfavourable economic preconditions to be found in Prussia must be born in mind. Brandenburg-Prussia was not a territorially unified state. Its provinces were scattered across the whole of northern Germany from the Rhine to the river Memel, and only the central heartlands (Brandenburg and Pomerania) formed a comparatively compact block which was expanded southeastwards by the acquisition of Silesia. Was it feasible under such circumstances to conduct a uniform economic policy, especially since the separate but highly productive western territories differed completely in structure from the core provinces? The Great Elector had attempted to promote the political homogeneity of his rudimentary centralised state, together with unity in the economic sphere, by means of a uniform taxation system whose principles were based on the example of the Dutch Republic. Frederick William I built on this and strove to unite his territories administratively, or at least to introduce uniform principles of government, with central responsibility for the range of activities covered by the term 'police' (*Polizei*): roads, weights and measures, colonisation policies and laws on Jews, grain provision and magazines throughout the Prussian provinces. A customs union was still far from his thoughts, and tariff barriers continued to separate the individual territories. Frederick William I's fiscal policies aimed primarily to maximise income from taxation, which was essential if the army were to be built up and a war chest (*Staatsschatz*) created to support it. He adhered to the mercantilist principle of preventing revenue flowing out of the country, by promoting domestic production and erecting protective barriers, in order to increase expenditure on the army and to build up a national treasure for military purposes. His encouragement of the manufacturing industries largely served the same purpose. The profits generated by the establishment of the *Lagerhaus*, the great Berlin state enterprise, for example, were employed to maintain the military orphanage in Potsdam. The exclusively military aims of all Frederick William's economic undertakings lent a distinctive character to his cameralism. Nevertheless, its effects went far beyond purely military benefits: an effectively organised state administration, internal colonisation and an increase in population were its wider consequences.

Frederick II first encountered his father's cameralist system during his time at Küstrin. He was made to learn its very basic workings since, according to his father's educational methods, he was to understand it from the example of details; its larger aims were not disclosed to him. His cameralist mentor, Chamber Director Christoph Werner Hille, however, did enlighten him on occasion about broader economic matters. Hille had earlier published a treatise in 1725 in which he advocated an economic system based upon trade. It is impossible to say how much of this was retained by the Crown Prince. His few early statements on economic matters, such as those to be found in the *Anti-Machiavel*, give little away. Nevertheless, they do portray a peculiar mixture of opinions, in part following the tradition established by his father, but also going far beyond Frederick William's narrow horizons. The strength of a state, Frederick wrote, does not lie in the expansion of its borders, but in an increased population. Similar arguments had been advanced by Frederick William I, but the author of the *Anti-Machiavel* could support his case with examples which did not exist in his father's time. He used the example of the Dutch Republic to demonstrate that a small state could rank second only to the great powers and support an army of 100,000 men. In the thirteenth chapter, on the other hand, he cites the relative weakness of the vast Russian Empire, whose wealth, military strength and financial power all lagged far behind the Dutch Republic. It is clear, then, that military power rather than economic strength was uppermost in the Crown Prince's mind, despite the Dutch example which combined both. It cannot be said, however, that he was to follow the logic of such arguments and pursue conquests solely for the increases in population which these would yield. Although his efforts to promote demographic growth were far more successful than those of his Hohenzollern predecessors, Prussia's increased population during his reign was to a large extent the consequence of his territorial gains, and these were undertaken with different motives in mind.

There are other parts of the *Anti-Machiavel* which reveal Frederick's intentions. In chapter sixteen, he advances an unusual argument justifying the luxury of a great national treasure for sizeable empires, but rejecting it as an option for smaller states. For the larger states, he wrote, it represented the same 'as the function of the heart for the human body, pumping blood through the main arteries to the outermost limbs from where the smaller veins redirect it back to the heart, forming a renewing circulation for the whole organism'. To a smaller state, on the other hand, the same luxury would be a curse: 'inhabitants [would be] ruined by the expenditure, and since more money would flow out of the country than could be made up for by cash coming in, the fragile body [of the state] would eventually wither and perish of emaciation'. It was not difficult to find such examples among the small German states, but in which category was Prussia? The answer would clearly determine her economic policies. In contrast to Frederick I's Prussia, Frederick William I's state was not one in which luxury was promoted. Frederick II, however, refused to follow his father's austerity completely, and in certain dimensions of his policies towards manufacturing a new era could be detected, in which the demand for luxury items was beginning to be met. This can be seen, for example, in the King's promotion of silk production. The *Anti-Machiavel* anticipated the importance manufacturing industries would assume. Frederick proclaimed them to be 'most useful and profitable for the state. Moreover, they meet the basic needs of the inhabitants as well as their taste for luxury, and our neighbours contribute towards them; they prevent money from flowing out of the country and provide the state with revenue for the sale of goods [to neighbours].' This was a considerable divergence from the protectionism practised by Frederick William I: in this early treatise, Frederick clearly advocates promoting manufacture and trade beyond national boundaries. Later, in the 1768 Political Testament, he devoted a special section to emphasising the drawbacks of luxury, which seemed to him somewhat contagious: 'Once luxury takes a hold within a state, no-one wants to spend less than his neighbour.' A man's reputation is then determined by expenditure he undertakes. 'Let us remain frugal and preserve our nobility and our good attributes or, if you like, our German virtues . . .' Here we find one of the rare occasions on which the King deigned to praise the German way of life.

Did Frederick keep his word? One of the first decisions he took as a young King was to establish a Fifth Department of the General Directory on 27 June 1740, to be responsible for 'commerce and manufacturing'. In the Instruction to its Director, the minister of state, Samuel von Marschall, three tasks were laid down for the new department: '1. to improve existing factories; 2. to introduce new manufacturing industries; 3. to attract [to Prussia] as many foreigners of all kinds of background, character and type as possible.' Though this initiative was unexpected, its importance must not be exaggerated – Frederick was only following precedents established by other German rulers. His goals, moreover, were limited: canvas production, which hitherto had failed to meet demand, was to be increased and the new factories were to produce very high-quality consumer goods largely for export. Details about the kinds of people to be attracted to Prussia were more precise: they were to be those capable of establishing and running sugar refineries or paper factories, or simply 'wealthy people' willing to invest their capital; they must be granted 'favourable conditions', financial incentives and freedom of religion. These ideas were not particularly original, and their importance lies rather in the way in which they reveal the depth of Frederick's knowledge, something he had undoubtedly acquired in Rheinsberg. In several respects these ideas went beyond his father's economic principles, as the following years would show even more clearly. In a lengthy treatise dated October 1749, entitled 'General Commercial Ideas for this Country', and addressed to Marschall's associate and successor, the Swiss Johann Rudolf Fäsch, he distinguishes between two types of factories: 'those which could process raw materials found at home, and those which had to import them. The first type is, of course, preferable, but the second also has merit since it can help to attract workers, which is a great benefit.' A few years later, the major chapter on finance in the 1752 Political Testament lays out, albeit somewhat unsystematically, Frederick's economic programme with all its benefits and admitted shortcomings. The encouragement which it was proposed to give to Prussia's manufacturing industries and an increase in excise revenues were once again declared to be its aims. The production of wool could not be made any more efficient; it was clearly the most natural of Prussia's industries since its raw material was one of the country's main products. The promotion of the silk industry was a project close to the King's heart. He pinned great hopes on the cultivation of mulberry trees, he wrote, although aware of the disadvantages of the cold climate. The silk industry generated large sums of money, he went on, such as the premiums paid to merchants selling Prussian fabrics abroad. Ailing factories are identified as being those producing sewing needles and good-quality paper and those reprinting books. The armaments industry, strangely enough, is not mentioned at all, although the success of the army, of course, was dependent upon it operating efficiently.

The Political Testaments of 1752 and 1768 provide perhaps the fullest exposition of the King's economic programme. In these writings, Frederick's opinions are clearly set out. They reveal that the King was an empiricist who was quite independent of received wisdom. He was not, however, ignorant of cameralism's theoretical principles, though it is impossible to establish precisely the authors or the texts which he read. A wide range of cameralist publications appeared in Prussia, among them the works of Johann Christoph Schöllmer, Karl Friedrich von Beneckendorf, Johann Friedrich Förster, Johann Peter Süssmilch and the most prominent of all, Johann Heinrich Gottlob von Justi. The King himself contributed to the latter's tragic fate. Justi, born in Thuringia in 1720, led the life of an independent writer, not attached to any university, and worked in the administration of a number of states, among them Austria and Saxony. From 1760 onwards he is believed to have lived in Berlin. One of his final works, dealing with financial systems and written in 1766, was dedicated to Frederick the Great, as a mark of his considerable respect for the King. This was not, however, entirely reciprocated, since Justi's views were based on Montesquieu's teachings, which advocated a constitutional monarchy along British lines. In 1765, the King appointed Justi as head of the mining authority (*Berghauptmann*) and superintendent of glass and steel factories, with privileges which allowed him a certain amount of independence from the state bureaucracy. He eventually came into conflict with the latter and was accused of misappropriating government funds. In 1768, he was arrested and imprisoned in Küstrin, where he died three years later. The King himself had ordered his arrest, but it is not clear why he was treated quite so harshly. Justi was certainly no martyr for his ideas; he was always careful in his writings not to criticise directly the Prussian system, with which he was, in fact, in agreement on many points. He was anything but an agitator, far removed from the later French Enlightenment which so incensed Frederick. Justi rejected the concepts of popular sovereignty and the right of resistance. Nevertheless, he opposed certain Frederician practices such as the building up of a war-chest and the increase in the Excise. Frederick specifically rejected Justi's arguments against hoarding a state treasure – that it removed cash from circulation, thus weakening trade and lowering living standards throughout his territories – in his 1768 Testament. The explanation for the King's treatment of Justi, however, did not lie in ideological differences. It must rather be sought in Frederick's anger with an individual who was undoubtedly capable of being irritating, and whose efficiency, moreover, was being compromised by his increasing blindness. As a cameralist theorist with experience of the world and a practical disposition, Justi would have been an ideal conversational partner for Frederick. But apart from his own unsuitability for such a role – exactly that assumed by his pupil Joseph von Sonnenfels in Vienna – the King himself sought far less contact with economists than he did with philosophers or writers. At times it even seemed as if Frederick had a particularly low opinion of the advice of intellectuals from the middle class. Thus one can hardly speak of Justi's influence on Prussia's economic and social policy.

Frederick's basic beliefs were, however, undoubtedly cameralist in spirit, even if he was unacquainted with the detail of cameralist teachings. He was more far-sighted than his father and recognised the commercial and maritime mercantilism practised by Britain and the Dutch Republic to be a font of true wealth. From the very beginning, however, he knew that Prussia could not compete with these countries. This was acknowledged in the Political Testament of 1768. He never forgot that the economy was affected both by external circumstances and by the inherited or historically conditioned mentality of the people, their disposition for or against trade and industry and the necessity of an established group of businessmen and manufacturers within society willing to take risks. Frederick's opinion of Prussia and its inhabitants in this respect was highly critical: 'Our people are backward and lazy,' he wrote, 'The government continually battles against these two national vices; everyone follows the habits of their fathers. Little reading is done and scant interest paid to practices elsewhere, and any innovation is unsettling.' All these were characteristics of an agrarian society in which the tenant farmer continued to predominate. Frederick was always conscious of living in a poor state which lacked many of the preconditions, and perhaps even the strength, for great economic enterprise or participation in international trade. These views betray a resignation in the King which was similar to his attitude towards the enormous expansion of the Russian Empire. This he confronted with an almost fatalistic awareness of the limitations upon his own power. It must be noted, on the other hand, that the motives which underpinned the Frederician policies of conquest, which were to strengthen Prussia so considerably, were not economic, but the product of the political will of a state which rested upon a military nobility.

Ultimately, the only yardstick by which Frederick's economic policies can be measured is their impact in practice. The concept of a favourable balance of trade, together with mercantilist principles, produced firstly a programme designed to promote indigenous production with the aim of transforming an agrarian country into an industrialised power. Secondly, the importation of any goods which could be produced at home was prohibited, and these restrictions became more and more rigorous in the post-war era after 1763. Thirdly, and finally, internal colonisation policies involved the acquisition and settlement of hitherto uncultivated areas. Frederician policies therefore contributed to a considerable increase in agrarian output, although the King only rarely took heed of the general interest in new agricultural methods. The involvement of Frederick himself in agrarian matters was rare and mostly unsuccessful. A case in point was the abolition in January 1750 of common land which at the time was widely believed to be an obstacle to increased production. Each change met with the obstacles inherent in the rigid social order which prevailed in the countryside. Although agricultural output contributed considerably to Prussia's gross national product, Frederick shrank from any vigorous efforts to improve conditions as soon as he came up against the barriers of the social status quo. Occasionally, he made suggestions designed to improve agrarian productivity and increase the food supply. The most famous initiative was his 1764 directive forcing peasants to grow potatoes. It was only adhered to with great reluctance and suspicion, and not until the period of famine in the early 1770s did the rural population become aware of its advantages. Another example of the King's personal involvement was his introduction of Spanish merino sheep in 1748 in order to increase wool production.

In addition, Brandenburg-Prussia possessed few of the natural resources essential to develop manufacturing. Some mineral deposits could be found in its western enclaves, but they were of little significance to the Prussian economy as a whole. In Upper Silesia, mines and iron foundries were not established until the final years of Frederick's reign. The existing production of wool and linen in the central regions of Brandenburg and Magdeburg formed the basis for an increased output of these two commodities. Frederick William I had encouraged it in every way. In 1719, the export of wool was forbidden and state-run wool stores established, with the aim of avoiding a rise in the price of this crucial raw material. The *Lagerhaus* in Berlin, the great royal cloth factory, had earlier been founded at the very beginning of Frederick William I's reign. It was initially intended to supply only the army, but subsequently began to produce for civilian consumption as well. From that point onwards the cloth industry flourished but, despite the addition of the efficient Silesian industry, it failed to meet domestic demand or, at times, even the requirements of the fast-growing army.

In his first Political Testament, Frederick the Great devoted only a few lines to wool manufacturing: it could not be improved, and the only thing to be done was 'to encourage it further'. This was clearly an off-hand remark which was probably influenced by Frederick's preference for the textile industry, especially silk, which was promoted by all manner of state inducements – export premiums, tax exemption, high import duties, and ultimately, the complete prohibition of silk imports in 1756 for all areas east of the river Elbe. This also affected silkworm breeding and the plantation of mulberry trees, for which climatic conditions were far from ideal. Apart from the products of the Krefeld family, the von der Leyen, the quality and quantity of whose output surpassed all others in the central regions of the monarchy, Prussia's silk production was dominated by one man – Johann Ernst Gotzkowsky. He was one of the few important Prussian entrepreneurs of his time who managed to establish a monopolistic position for his own and a number of smaller factories. A separate treasury, the *Seidenmanufakturkasse* (literally, 'treasury for silk manufacturing'), was established to provide state subsidies, which sought to encourage both mulberry tree plantations and silk factories. Expenditure on silk factories reached its peak in 1748 and 1768–69, while sums spent on mulberry tree plantations increased considerably during the final decade of Frederick's reign. A total of 1.6 million thaler is reputed to have been invested in silk manufacturing. To his last days, the King followed the progress of mulberry tree cultivation with particular interest. Indeed, one of his final cabinet orders concerned a mulberry tree plantation in Zossen which, he was 'displeased' to have been informed, had perished.

Frederick's efforts to promote the silk industry had a wider importance: they aimed to encourage the production of what was principally a luxury product. Did he believe his own argument that Prussia was now one of the great powers for whom luxury had an invigorating and not a ruinous effect? It is certainly questionable whether the silk industry responded in the way which was intended, and the sums invested in it could clearly have been applied more profitably in other sectors of the Prussian economy. While the silk industry catered for the needs of a relatively small social élite, the cotton industry grew to mass production levels, threatening both the established wool and linen industries and bringing about a complete change in the demand for clothing. Frederick William I had attempted to avert these developments with a rigorous ban on cotton imports in 1721. Frederick lifted this prohibition only in order to permit the establishment of Prussian cotton factories. By 1763, ten already existed in Berlin and by the end of the century, despite little state support, the number of cotton looms exceeded those in the wool factories. This new textile industry aimed, to a much higher degree than the silk or velvet manufacturers, at mass consumerism in foreign markets. One of its agents openly defended the principle of free competition against state monopolies, principally the Berlin *Lagerhaus*. However much Frederick in theory disliked monopolies, in practice they dominated the Prussian economy. Whole areas such as the sale of wood or tobacco were state monopolies, while the same privileges were given to certain private enterprises such as sugar production, established in the Prussian capital by David Splitgerber between 1749 and 1754, or the handful of businesses which held the monopoly for velvet production.

It is often assumed that the war and armaments industry must have played a dominant role in the economy of a military state such as Prussia. This was, however, only partly true, and the major area of production for the army was the cloth industry, led by the *Lagerhaus*, which met its demand for clothing and uniforms. The greatest expenditure on the army was for pay and provisions. A contemporary survey for the years 1756–60 revealed that the cost of the war, including bread and food, weapons and munitions of all kinds, uniforms and leather goods, together amounted to only 13 per cent of total expenditure. This would imply that compared to more modern, fully mechanised armies, there was little demand for weapons and technical equipment. Eighteenth-century warfare was indeed less sophisticated and relied heavily on the use of cold steel. The growing importance of the artillery, which Frederick viewed with a mixture of frustration and mistrust but was forced to embrace because of Austrian superiority, signified the first major breakthrough of modern technological weaponry and increased the army's dependence on industrial production. This, particularly during the Seven Years War, became something of a bottleneck for Prussian warfare.

Prussia's armaments' industry, scarcely developed by Frederick William I, was still in its infancy at Frederick II's accession. The limited number of small-scale producers, however, had been supplemented before 1740 by two new manufacturing operations: a gunpowder works and a gun factory were established near the capital. But their production fell far short of the requirements of the King's constantly expanding army. From the beginning of its expansion, the Prussian army was forced to purchase its munitions from abroad. This contradicted both the dictates of mercantilism and ideas about the balance of trade, but neither Frederick William nor his son ever made the efforts needed to close the gap. The obstacles to the development of an indigenous armaments industry were, of course, considerable and included a lack of skilled labour as well as a total absence of raw materials, above all iron. The company of Splitgerber and Daun, founded in 1712, became the middle man and commissioning agent for munitions imported from abroad and continued to hold this position under Frederick the Great. The state itself did not want to be responsible for weapon procurement, which demanded technological advances, and the task was left to a company striving for high profits, although Frederick William I originally only guaranteed a commission of 2 per cent.

Splitgerber and Daun eventually added entrepreneurial ventures, such as leasing the new gun factory, to their intermediate trading role.

Frederick William went on to set up a further armaments factory, the *Königliche Gießhaus* or Royal Foundry, where guns and artillery could be cast. In 1741, Frederick II attempted to convert a second foundry in Breslau to artillery production, though with only moderate success. It has always been difficult to establish how Prussia managed to obtain replacements for its field guns during the Seven Years War. According to contemporary figures for the individual battles, losses of artillery were extremely high and new supplies limited. The cast iron guns used especially in fortresses were imported from Sweden by Splitgerber and Daun, while some 1,500 cannons, including howitzers and mortars, were cast in Prussia itself between 1741 and 1762. One must also assume that a large part of the artillery captured by the victor of each battle could be redeployed and this was, in many cases, something from which the Prussian army benefited. An even greater problem was the supply of munitions, cannons and bombs, which under Frederick William were bought largely from Holland, but still had to be acquired from abroad during the Silesian Wars. It is surprising then that the King, after the establishment of new ironworks in Upper Silesia during the first half of the 1750s, instructed his Silesian minister in 1756 that 'bombs should not be continually cast' and munitions orders should be met only 'incidentally and when necessary'.

The enduring impression is that the production of munitions was considered to be an arcane art. Warfare during the absolutist era was certainly envisaged more in terms of human numbers than in the strength of the armies' technical arms. This was clearly true of Frederick II, perhaps more so than many of his contemporaries. The armaments industry was a rather alien element in the Prussian economy, both where domestic production and foreign imports were concerned. Not one syllable was devoted to it in the sections on fiscal policy in the Political Testaments. And although in the military sections detailed information is given on the army's demand for weaponry, munitions and equipment, no mention is made of how these were to be produced. One fortress, which served as an arsenal, was described in the following terms: 'The army needs 8,000 hundredweight of powder, several million ready and loaded cartridges, 30–40 pontoons with carriages, 15–20,000 guns, saddlecloths, saddles, pistols, sabres, harnesses, belts, ammunition pouches, etc., so that all the army's requirements in the field are met.' The King omitted to mention where all this was to come from; instead, he merely addresses the question of paying for these munitions and equipment. Towards the end of the military section of the Political Testament, in a part entitled 'Speculations on future developments', some mention is made of measures to be taken to improve the army. Here the King envisaged encouraging saltpetre factories, increasing the number of gunpowder factories as well as bomb and ball foundries, and extending the production capabilities of munitions factories to the point where they are able to supply 20,000 guns, 10,000 swords and 4,000 sabres annually. But these were almost incidental thoughts and clearly failed to arouse Frederick's interest. In the 1768 Testament, following the experiences of the Seven Years War, all that is recorded is a planned increase of annual gunpowder production from 4,000 hundredweight to 6,000!

The manufacturing industry in Frederician Prussia was, overall, quite underdeveloped and unevenly distributed. The industrially advanced capital Berlin, which by the end of Frederick's reign produced a third of all Prussian manufactured goods, had to be placed alongside the diversity of the western provinces and the predominantly agrarian central and eastern territories, while mining and smelting were still in their infancy and only blossomed in the King's final years under the guidance of Friedrich Anton von Heinitz. A country with such diverse economic components lacked the historic infrastructure of its western European neighbours essential to become a model mercantilist state. Nevertheless, it not only strove vigorously to increase its industrial output and lessen its dependence upon foreign imports, but also to strengthen its internal markets by erecting protectionist barriers. This meant creating a homogeneous economic unit out of the prevailing political, economic and territorial diversity, reinforced as it was by internal customs barriers between provinces. Such unification was initially limited to the territorially unified core provinces of Brandenburg, Pomerania, Magdeburg and Halberstadt. In his 1752 Political Testament, Frederick describes them as 'the heart of the state'; they were the only areas which could be protected militarily. Silesia was gradually integrated into the economic core and in 1747 its internal customs barriers were removed. East Prussia, however, was not fully integrated until as late as 1780. The first pan-Prussian tariff legislation (which included Silesia but only applied in limited form to the western enclaves) was the so-called *Deklarationspatent* (Customs Duties Patent) of 14 April 1766. It established new rates for the Excise, which took account of social considerations. Accordingly the grain duty was abolished, while that for wine, beer, brandy and meat was raised. A further increase on all wines, liqueurs and coffee was imposed in 1772, and the tax was raised once more for wines from the Rhineland in November 1785. The psychological impact of these rigid measures, designed to reduce and even prevent consumption of popular luxury goods, was exacerbated by the overbearing actions of the administration, which put a considerable strain on the financial policy of the later Frederician period. Despite Mirabeau's homage to the efficiency of the Prussian monarchy, the collection and administration of indirect taxes and customs duties was transferred on 14 July 1766 to the so-called '*Regie*', a group of French officials under the direction of La Haye de Launay. This did not introduce wholesale tax farming along French lines, but took the form of a contractual lease in which the agents responsible for administering the tax were rewarded by high pay and a share of the profits. The collection of taxation by foreign functionaries was, in practice, to arouse widespread suspicion and unrest.

The introduction of the *Regie*, which was the most decisive development in later Frederician financial policy, must not be viewed as an isolated measure but understood in the context of the grave economic crisis which followed the

Seven Years War. At the same time as the state's demand for revenue grew (to finance the reconstruction of provinces devastated by the fighting and the rebuilding and strengthening of the army), receipts from the excise declined, adding to the general shortage of money. There were several reasons for this, including the partial reversal of a devaluation carried out during the war. This was finally abandoned completely by the Mint Edicts of May 1763 and March 1764, which imposed a painful restoration of sound currency and fixed the rates at which depreciated coins would be accepted. If, as the King claimed in the 1768 Testament, the introduction of the *Regie* was a direct consequence of reduced Excise revenues then the reasons for this initiative were primarily fiscal. Nevertheless, it must also be seen as a consequence of the economic crisis which exacerbated the war's devastating consequences for a broad section of Prussia's population. The recession began with the spectacular collapse of banks on the Amsterdam money market, the most important in Europe. Amsterdam had been used as the principal clearing house for Britain's subsidies to Prussia, and the origin of the economic crisis lay in the exchange dealings which, after the colonial and continental wars had been concluded by the peace treaties of Paris and Hubertusburg, fully highlighted the large and burdensome debts taken on as a result of borrowing during the course of the struggle. The growing integration of international money markets during the war meant the crisis soon engulfed the banking and merchant communities of Hamburg and eventually spread to Prussia, already suffering from the aftermath of the fighting. Here it led to the ruin of substantial companies, principally the firm of Gotzkowsky, whose recovery the King himself tried, but ultimately failed, to promote. Frederick found the causes of the crisis incomprehensible. He had no previous experience or frame of reference to help him understand why the bankruptcies had occurred. He blamed them on the failure and even the ill-will of the Prussian merchant community whom he suspected of complicity with his civil servants, in whom his trust had been severely shaken. All this contributed to the decisions he was now to take.

In economic crises such as these, particularly during the seventeenth and eighteenth centuries, dubious speculators often flourished. This was certainly the case in Prussia: the King, ultimately powerless and lacking confidence in his own officials and the Prussian business community, fell prey to the projects of adventurers like Antonio di Calzabigi, a banker from Livorno. It is a measure of the King's state of mind and his uncertainty in economic matters that Voltaire's conversational partner should associate with such a man. It was Calzabigi who put forward the not unreasonable plan of establishing a new bank. This new institution, however, was not only to engage in financial transactions, but to become a sort of holding company for a variety of monopolistic trading ventures such as the Silesian linen trade. The plan came to nothing, partly because the necessary investments did not materialise and partly because the whole undertaking met with vehement resistance from businessmen and entrepreneurs, many of whom were themselves on the brink of bankruptcy. In June 1765, however, a 'Giro Discount and Credit Bank' was founded in Berlin, with strong financial support from the state. At first it failed to acquire any credit because of the mistakes and transgressions of its first directors, Calzabigi among them. Only after several reorganisations and changes of personnel was the bank given the right to issue notes, became the bank of issue for all coins, and started to prosper. In the eighteen years between 1767/8 and 1785/6 its profits, paid to the state, increased tenfold. Under the name 'Prussian State Bank for Overseas Trade' which it acquired in 1772, it remained in existence until the end of the Prussian state.

The establishment of the *Regie* took place against a background of depressed financial and economic conditions. Frederick's appointment of French financial officials was a genuine attempt to bring about an improvement in the public finances. What use was it, however, to fix new tariffs for the customs and excise when these did not include the trade in manufactured goods and when the duties were in any case circumvented by black market activities? A high degree of mistrust was often a guiding force behind Frederick's economic policies and so it was in this case. He believed that, when new duties were introduced, the experienced French financial officials would eliminate tax avoidance. Even if this had been the case, one inevitable consequence was to alienate the population from the government, which had a more serious impact on the integration of a protean state such as Prussia than within a larger and relatively consolidated polity. The real burdens associated with the *Regie* scheme were the price of the return which it yielded. The initiative produced a surplus, over the twenty-one years of its operation (1766–86) of 2.3 million thaler, around 100,000 thaler annually. At the same time, however, the King's own popularity and the further unification of the Prussian territories were adversely affected. Though Frederick was not indifferent to the tangible loss of authority, not until 1783 did he react and considerably limit the number of officials involved in the *Regie*. The structure of a purely bureaucratic state, meanwhile, continued to be mingled with organisations which were leased out: aside from the *Regie's* administration of the Excise, in 1766 the postal service and the General Tobacco Administration both became independent and, in 1781, the State Coffee Monopoly, employing 200 invalids as controllers, the so-called 'coffee sniffers', whose job was to search out coffee which had been smuggled; and finally a State Lottery. These authorities were initially staffed by Frenchmen, but were eventually leased out to native officials. The trade in salt remained a royal monopoly.

The growing trend of assimilating increasingly wide sectors of the economy and placing them under direct state control corresponded with the development of a country increasingly closed to the outside. A phase of high tolls was almost always followed by import prohibitions for various manufactured and hand-produced goods to the point where, in 1786, foreign products were almost completely excluded from the Prussian marketplace. At the same time, the wave of export prohibitions, begun by Frederick William I's ban on wool exports, continued apace with a ban in 1765 on grain exports and an embargo on potato exports in 1771. This was to secure the country's basic food requirements as well as to protect its few natural resources. The storage of grain, initially begun for military purposes in 1746, could be used to ease demand in years of poor harvests such as 1771 and 1772. The state's almost complete control of the economy also performed a social function: through its taxation and grain storage policies as well as its controls upon exports, the cost of living was kept reasonably low. However, it prevented the development of a free market economy and of a commercial middle class. As a result, neither Prussia's officials nor its middle class accepted the King's economic policy unquestion-ingly. A critical report by the Secret Finance Secretary Erhard Ursinus of the Fifth Department submitted on 26 September 1766 was symptomatic of the mood among both government officials and the business community. An inquiry into the state of the economy had been ordered, against the back-ground of this dissatisfaction and the post-war depression. Ursinus's report was highly critical of royal economic policy and specifically of the promotion of the velvet and silk industries, whose products were often of poor quality yet 40–75 per cent more expensive than foreign equivalents. It also censured the various monopolies, which were deemed 'highly damaging to general trade', and particularly the General Tobacco Monopoly which caused 'the greatest of hardships'. The King reacted angrily. Ursinus, after the revelation that he had accepted bribes and favours from the business community, was imprisoned in Spandau for a year. The King was particularly riled by collaboration between officials and businessmen; such an alliance could grow into a dangerous opposi-tion. However, it never came to anything. Isolated entrepreneurs such as the Magdeburg businessman Christoph Friedrich Gossler opposed the privileges enjoyed by silk and velvet factories in Berlin and Potsdam, set up a rival business producing velvet and silk and spoke out against the prevailing policy, but such initiatives were rare. After the economic recovery during the later 1770s, the relationship between the state and business community improved, and the government's erstwhile opponents lost their *raison d'être*.

The pursuit of protectionism accompanied by rigid autarky involved a series of risks and undesirable consequences for the Frederician monarchy, and while some of these were increased, others were diminished by the conquest of Silesia. The annexed province with its linen production was a prosperous exporter and this improved Prussia's balance of trade. It was also, however, the region crossed by transit trade from Bohemia to Poland and was a barrier between the Habsburg Monarchy and Saxony, and their trading partners fur-ther east. The province was crucial to economic relations between the two parts of the Saxon-Polish composite monarchy by virtue of its geographical location, yet on the other hand Silesia was cut off from its established markets in Bohemia and Moravia. Prusso-Saxon political relations first reached a low point during the Second Silesian War when Saxony, earlier a member of the anti-Austrian coalition, changed sides. Simultaneously, economic relations became extremely strained, and the weapons of commercial warfare were certainly employed for political ends. The geographic dovetailing of Saxony and Prussia allowed obstacles to be placed in the way of transit trade: the

Electorate revived an old privilege to charge a toll called the *Straßenzwang* (literally the 'route levy') on all Prussian goods which passed through its territory. Prussia answered in 1747 with a similar levy on all traffic along the river Elbe. Tensions rose during the period which preceded the outbreak of the Seven Years War. Prussia demanded high transit tolls for all routes through the provinces of Magdeburg and Halberstadt, to which Saxony replied on 13 May 1755 by prohibiting the import of various Prussian goods. At the end of the same year, a trade agreement seemed near, but Frederick broke off the negotiations at the end of April 1756. He refused to include Silesia in the discussions, while the Saxon delegation was particularly interested in removing the Silesian customs barriers. The failure of these talks clearly reflected the considerable deterioration in political relations between the two states at this time. Peaceful commercial relations were not even restored after the Seven Years War, which had so devastated Saxony. Embittered by his failure to annex the Electorate, Frederick would not conclude any agreement, convinced that the exclusion of Saxon products was preferable for Prussia to a commercial treaty which regulated the flow of goods.

Silesia's economic relationship with the Habsburg Monarchy was also disrupted by the Prussian annexation, and a customs war broke out in 1753. Its causes were rather different than in the case of the conflict with Saxony. Prussia wished to preserve Silesia's Austrian market, while Austria aimed to sever all economic links with its erstwhile province and to protect itself from foreign imports. On 1 April 1753, in Bohemia, Moravia and the rump of Austrian Silesia, customs duties of up to 130 per cent were placed upon most textile products, colonial goods and sea-fish. In the following year, the Archduchy of Austria and even the Kingdom of Hungary were brought within this tariff system. In retaliation Prussia imposed tolls on Austrian and Hungarian wines, and subsequently on all goods from the Habsburg lands. These disputes immediately preceded the outbreak of war, and one could ask if they were not simply a prelude to the fighting. It was a characteristic of the eighteenth century that trade disputes might develop into political conflicts, although commercial clashes could also exist independently. Vienna's commercial policy therefore assumed Silesia's loss to be permanent, while its political strategy gave priority to the province's recovery.

Prussia's acquisition of Silesia was of more than purely territorial or political significance, and had important economic and geostrategic repercussions. The province's geographical position meant that the Prussian monarchy acquired control over the first of the great rivers of northern Germany, the Oder, almost from its source right to its mouth on the Baltic Sea, and thereby secured one of the region's most important trading arteries. The potential benefits were considerable: trade could flourish both to the east along the river Vistula and down the Oder to the port of Stettin. On the river Elbe Prussia's only involvement was its customs barrier at Magdeburg. After the King's visit there in 1747, all ships coming from the upper reaches of the Elbe in Saxony were forced to unload their cargoes and transfer them to Magdeburg vessels for transport to Hamburg. Hamburg was a principal target of Prussia's commercial policy, since at this period it was one of a handful of German cities involved in overseas trade. Prussia hoped to redirect this commerce to its own ships and trading companies and into its own ports. Though the means by which this could be accomplished were limited, at least Prussia's network of inland waterways could be expanded. In addition, meandering river routes could be shortened. Thus the large curve of the lower Havel was shortened by the construction of the Plauensche canal during the first years of Frederick's reign, while the Finow canal between the Havel and the Oder, decaying since the Thirty Years War, was renewed. Together these improvements created a much shorter link between the port of Stettin and the city of Magdeburg on the Elbe. Stettin was separated from the Baltic Sea by the Haff and ships leaving the port had to pass through Swedish waters. Here the mouth of the Oder, the Swine, was made navigable and a harbour was established at Swinemünde in 1747. Favourable circumstances for the expansion of navigation on the Oder appeared to exist, but the high tolls and rivalries between the Oder towns of Stettin and Frankfurt constituted an enormous obstacle. Only the intervention of the King could overcome these short-sighted local interests. In 1752, the 'pacification' or levelling of all tolls on the Elbe and Oder was implemented. As a result, shipping on the Oder increased considerably and Pomeranian ships supplanted those from Hamburg, though not completely. The attempt to redirect grain transport from Poland to the Oder failed. The Oder could never compete with the river Vistula and the port of Danzig. Stettin was not the great port Prussia needed while Emden (in East Friesland), despite its proximity to the North Sea, was far removed from the monarchy's heartlands and therefore was neglected.

The Frederician state's contribution to the development of internal river communications was praiseworthy, but its neglect of the road system was even more apparent. To complete the picture of a military state in constant readiness against attack on several fronts it was necessary to have an efficient network of roads, as was usual from the period of the Roman Empire to that of Napoleon. Although Frederick speaks in his Political Testament of developing canals, he does not mention roads. Even in his writings on military theory, they are rarely mentioned and are treated almost as a natural phenomenon exactly like hills and valleys. Their condition depended upon the time of year: in the spring and autumn, roads which were poor, rutted and muddy had to be taken into account during military manoeuvres. That is all the information one receives in the 1777 treatise *On Military Manoeuvres and the Points to be noted during them*. Here we have a strange gap in Frederick the Great's military thought. This may explain the fact that for all its endurance and speed, the Frederician army's manoeuvres were always undertaken within a relatively limited area and never depended on foreign roads in the way that the Napoleonic army was to do. Frederick rejected nothing more vehemently than a military enterprise which took him too far from his starting point. The great warning against such undertakings had always been Charles XII.

Cameralist ideas particularly emphasised the importance of demographic growth. Behind the belief in the need to increase one's population lay the conviction that more people would result in the production of more goods and articles of value, that the state's military potential would be enhanced and that the number of inhabitants constituted the most important factor in its power. All cameralist writers agreed on this point. Johann Heinrich Gottlob von Justi in his 1755 treatise on economic policy even goes as far as to state that no viable reason exists 'to place a ceiling on the number of people'. The Prussian cleric Johann Peter Süssmilch saw in a large population the key to the promotion of general happiness. An increasing population is here viewed as the prerequisite for an industrious society, whose needs were constantly growing. It was the essential duty of all rulers to promote demographic expansion. This meant 'foreigners, if one needs them, [could be] encouraged by reasonable inducements'. 'Every new subject is a new conquest.' The Austrian cameralist Joseph von Sonnenfels also believed that growth in population would bring with it improvements in 'common benefits like security and a more comfortable life'. This is still quite some distance from the gloomy prognostications which Thomas Malthus was to make at the end of the eighteenth century concerning unrestrained demographic growth.

Demographic theories corresponded with eighteenth-century reality: after a period of stagnation and even decline which followed the great European wars of the previous century, these decades saw a considerable increase in population levels. Between 1700 and 1800, Europe's population grew from 118 million to 178 million inhabitants; that of England from 7.5 million in 1750 to 9.5 million in 1801; that of France between 1715 and 1785 from 18 to 26 million. This upward trend also extended to the German lands, although here the considerable losses of the Thirty Years War were not made good until the middle of the eighteenth century. This was true for Brandenburg-Prussia as well, although growth depended not only upon natural regeneration but also to a considerable extent on an influx of foreign settlers. This resulted from a deliberate, and partly forced, immigration policy of the kind which was also pursued by Russia's Catherine II and Austria's Maria Theresa and Joseph II. Colonisation was a cornerstone of the economic and social policy of these three continental great powers. They sought to channel the surplus population of pre-industrial Europe into the not yet fully developed regions of central and eastern Europe. In absolute monarchies population policies took the form of state-sponsored colonisation.

Population growth was nowhere so central an issue as in Prussia – as it had been ever since the days of the Great Elector. It received increased impetus first under Frederick William I and then Frederick the Great, who followed his predecessors' example in seeking to enhance the limited potential of his territories by encouraging immigration of both urban artisans and peasants into the countryside. One important way in which this policy was pursued was through invitations to those suffering persecution on account of their religious beliefs. Two such groups were particularly significant. Firstly, there were the French Huguenot refugees whom the Great Elector encouraged to come to Brandenburg by means of the Edict of Potsdam in 1685. This led to an influx of around 20,000 Huguenots, who were to have the strongest socio-political influence – other than in England and Holland – in the Hohenzollern territories since they concentrated their efforts fully on their new homeland. They were followed under Frederick William I by around 15,000 exiles from Salzburg, who after 1732 repopulated the eastern regions of East Prussia whose population had been decimated by the plague of 1709–10. With them, the shift of emphasis towards peasant colonisation became clear, a change which became apparent under Frederick William I.

Frederick II's efforts to make Prussia a great power not merely by territorial conquests but also by encouraging the immigration of new subjects was firmly within an established Hohenzollern tradition. Increasing the numbers of Prussian subjects was as important a means of aggrandisement as extending Prussia's borders. In keeping with the mercantilist ideas prevalent at the time, 'professionals' or skilled workers from other states were especially prized, in order to build up new manufacturing industries. The Prussian practice of bringing in such skilled labour from abroad therefore was first and foremost mercantilist economic policy, and only secondly immigration policy in the strict sense of the term. In the Political Testament of 1752, Frederick provides an explanation of this, using the example of wool-spinners. The King had heard that Prussia's wool manufacturers bemoaned the lack of spinners and therefore had the work done in Saxony 'so that each year a great quantity of spun wool came into the country from Saxony'. He found out that around 60,000 Saxons found employment in the wool-spinning workshops there. He took immediate measures to find spinners and attract colonists from Saxony, Poland and Mecklenburg and to settle them in various regions of Prussia. With an annual quota of 1,000 families, the target of 60,000 would be achieved in only twelve years. Even if this figure was never attained – and the King was given to euphoric speculation – the link between mercantilist and demographic object-ives is clearly apparent. Frederick generally followed this goal, although he often contented himself with placing 'professionals' in the right area. The skilled labourers, principally from Lyon and Geneva, who staffed his principal interest, the silk industry, performed their tasks but were not permanent employees and drifted back to their home regions. Most immigrants were Frenchmen, not merely those drawn from the ranks of religious refugees but also other incomers who worked in other branches of manufacturing, notably the leather and hat industries. The craftsmen who founded the first knife and scissor works came from neighbouring German territories. Without foreign labour, German and non-German, and the technical knowledge this brought, Prussian manufacturing would never have reached the level it did during the Frederician era: in 1785, Hertzberg rated it fourth behind France, England and the Dutch Republic.

Prussia's industrial policy, and the foundation and expansion of factories to which it led, brought about an increase in urban population. Rural repopulation was an integral part both of agrarian policy and of wider state policy, together with all its side effects. The political goal of repopulation is easily discernible, at times appearing to be an end in itself: the quantitative increase of the population was more important than anything else. Frederick himself presents us with a considerable amount of evidence for this, and his writings on economic matters very much echoed the ideas of the cameralists. The King, however, did not wholly embrace the theory that it was preferable to increase one's population through internal colonisation rather than by means of territorial conquest. Brandenburg-Prussia and its neighbouring territories were poor, having been further devastated and impoverished by the Thirty Years War. Colonisation here pursued certain distinct goals such as regaining productive land through direct action, above all by means of irrigation. The section entitled 'What still has to be done' in the first Political Testament begins with the sentences: 'Pomerania must be viewed as half uncultivated. In . . . Western and Eastern Pomerania . . . there still remains a great deal of marshland to be drained before one can colonise it with 100,000 souls.' Colonisation and agrarian improvements went hand in hand. In eighteenth-century Europe as a whole, agriculture was entering a period of change during which traditional methods were replaced by new techniques which would increase crop yields and improve food production. The population of eastern and central Europe had been severely depleted by a series of natural disasters. The position was similar in Russia, Hungary and throughout northeastern Europe where the Thirty Years War had wrought particular devastation. Added to this was the destruction caused by the Seven Years War in the Prussian heartlands and in Saxony. This allowed the policies of colonisation and repopulation to appear to be a period of restoration and recovery, the *rétablissement* which from 1763 had entered its second phase, the first having been the East Prussian *rétablissement* under Frederick William I.

Frederician colonisation was a state enterprise. It presupposed that the state had land at its disposal and was free to determine its use. This broadly accorded with the facts of Prussian landownership, since about a third of Prussia was royal domain and was administered by the treasury. Most of this was to be found in the Hohenzollern heartlands, and least in Silesia. In the hitherto uncultivated areas bordering Prussia's streams and rivers, near the Oder, Warthe and Netze, state improvement and colonisation projects took little notice of ownership and simply appropriated lands not already under state control. Private landowners had to hand over to the treasury between a third and one half of all lands which had been reclaimed for cultivation, thus opening up areas for colonisation. From the very beginning, Frederick showed an exceptional interest in colonisation and land reclamation; it was here that his desire to improve conditions for his subjects, which had so often been overshadowed by other priorities, came into play. Hence in the early years of his reign, dominated as these were by diplomacy and war, only individual and small-scale measures were taken. This situation changed only during the decade between the wars of the 1740s and the conflict after 1756. Then larger enterprises were undertaken, principal among them the cultivation of the great Oder marshlands. Regular floods caused havoc here to an area of between 10 and 12 German square miles, and the region around Lebus in the vicinity of Frankfurt-an-der-Oder had already frustrated Frederick William I's attempts to make it cultivatable. Frederick II continued these efforts, and himself played a considerable part. He set up an Oder Building Commission headed by minister of state Samuel von Marschall and staffed, among others, by a Dutch hydraulic engineer from Haarlem. The Commission was instructed to devise a system to stem the current, to redirect it into different, specially constructed basins and to build strong dams to contain these. It was a project characterised by scientific precision: on 8 July 1747, a special barge was sent down the Oder to take all the requisite measurements and make the necessary calculations. One of the team was a mathematician and member of the Berlin Academy, Leonard Euler – one of the first instances where theoretical and practical thinking was united in the King's statecraft. The project was beset by enormous technical difficulties and the number of workers employed, whom the King envisaged as future colonists, comfortably exceeded one thousand. In the end, several hundred soldiers from a nearby regiment also had to be recruited. When it was finally completed in 1753, the King uttered the memorable words: 'Here I have conquered a province in peacetime'; 200,000 *morgen* of land had been dammed. In total, 1,200 families were settled in 43 newly founded colonies which were divided into royal, noble and municipal villages.

The whole exercise was in stark contrast to the King's military conquests during previous years which had gained him fame and glory in a much more conspicuous way. Did his personal involvement through royal orders, encouragement and criticism stem from an inner need for self-justification? Later projects such as the draining of the Netze marshland from 1763 to 1767 and the reclamation of almost 100,000 *morgen* in the marshes around the river Warthe from 1765, for which plans were submitted by the most active individual in this field, the administrator Franz Balthasar von Brenckenhoff, a financial councillor, marked the second phase of such policies of improvement. A large-scale improvement project of 11 October 1774 included a kind of land reclamation plan for the entire monarchy, which since 1772 had included West Prussia.

The reclamation of land was everywhere followed by colonisation. Wherever favourable conditions seemed to exist, Frederick publicised his open-door policy. Agencies were to be found in Amsterdam, Frankfurt-am-Main, Regensburg, Geneva and Hamburg which were in direct competition with groups advertising opportunities to emigrate to Europe's overseas colonies. Military and civil priorities also merged: from 1769 the promotion of colonisation opportunities was given to the army, which only reluctantly took on this task. In cases of groups of settlers from one particular area, so-called social contracts were sometimes concluded by which whole colonies were bound to work the land; this practice had begun under Frederick William I. Such was the case with the Swiss who colonised East Prussia in 1729 and with the refugees from Salzburg, and later with the colonists from Nassau and the Palatinate during Frederick the Great's reign. The French communities such as the Huguenots enjoyed a special status. In these villages, no property could be transferred to other foreign immigrants.

The largest proportion of the colonists who were recruited, moreover, consisted of single families who lacked a common origin or cast of mind and – to the irritation and outrage of the Prussian bureaucracy – contained a large number of totally unsuitable candidates, adventurers and fortune hunters who tended to vanish if conditions proved unfavourable. This in its turn angered the King, who viewed it as nothing less than desertion, and in cases where the fugitives were captured severe fines were imposed. His father had even decreed the penalty of death by hanging in such cases, although no instances of actual executions are known. Other states sought to protect themselves from immigrants of this kind, individuals fleeing from states where they had been colonists, as Austria did in an Edict of July 1768. Other rulers, such as those of Hesse-Kassel, Trier and the Palatinate, followed suit. Much more effective in the race to repopulate was the widespread practice of attracting new colonists by means of offering incentives which, of course, only the larger powers could afford. Thus the Empress Maria Theresa issued a colonisation patent in 1755 for colonists from Further Austria who settled in the Batschka. Catherine II published her great manifesto to attract foreign colonists on 3 August 1763, an initiative which was later to produce the so-called Volga German settlements. Joseph II followed in September 1782 with his colonisation patent for German colonists in Hungary, Galicia and Lodomeria. These appeals were all very similar in as far as they all promised much the same benefits. In Prussia, these were first laid down under Frederick William I, and then granted by Frederick the Great in a series of edicts, the earliest in 1741 and 1747, and the last in April 1769 and 1770. By these patents the colonists on the royal domain were accorded the status of hereditary peasants (*Erbzinsleute*) and therefore had greater rights than the majority of peasants. They were exempt from military conscription for three generations, were freed from performing all labour services and enjoyed fiscal privileges such as exemption from direct taxation for a number of years. Guarantees of religious freedom were contained in all the monarchs' patents, and expressly so in those of Maria Theresa and her son. Repopulation in the cameralist sense was here also seen as an aid to development.

As far as the origins of the colonists were concerned, the King particularly welcomed foreigners. The term 'foreigner', however, was by no means a synonym for non-German. It simply meant anyone who lived outside the Hohenzollern lands, and most Prussian colonists tended to come from neighbouring areas such as Bohemia, Saxony and Mecklenburg, together with many Germans from Poland. Of those who came from further afield, only the numbers of colonists from the Palatinate and Württemberg were of any significance.

Over a century ago, Max Beheim-Schwarzbach painstakingly calculated approximate numbers of colonists and settlements, and his researches continue to form the basis of our figures today. Without taking into account the municipal villages, the number of newly founded villages was around 1,500 in which dwelt 57,475 families (that is to say, approximately 250,000 people). The numbers in the municipal settlements were estimated by Beheim-Schwarzbach to be around 100,000. These numbers were considerable, even when compared to Catherine II's repopulation of the Volga, which was estimated at 8,000 families with 29,000 people, or those of Maria Theresa and Joseph II in Hungary. The Theresian colonisation of the Banat up to 1770 was estimated at 10,000 German families with around 40,000 people, while the Josephinian settlement of the Batschka, principally between 1784 and 1787, involved around 3,050 families. This clearly highlights the progress made by Prussia in this 'new phase of mercantilist rural development', especially when one considers the relationship between geographic area and the number of inhabitants. 'Prussia in the eighteenth century', wrote Gustav Schmoller, 'was the poorest of the major states, which proportionately had the greatest rate of population growth.' One implication of Beheim-Schwarzbach's researches is that 10 per cent of Prussia's inhabitants in 1786 were either colonists or the descendants of colonists who had arrived in the Hohenzollern lands since 1640.

Since the final decades of the nineteenth century, German historical scholarship has extensively studied the colonisation policies of eighteenth-century Prussian Kings. This may result, on the one hand, from an effort to prove a continuous tradition of German eastern colonisation, and on the other from an attempt to represent Frederick not as a conqueror and military leader, a Caesar or Alexander, but as a peaceful monarch bent upon reclaiming land. In fact the King was both, and internal and external conquest served an identical purpose: the increase of the state's power: 'Political and social order, improved food supply and population growth are actually only different dimensions of the same process' (G. Mackenroth).

CHAPTER 8

Soldier-King

Frederick II's renown was based above all on his ability as a military leader. In Clausewitz's great work *On War* (1827) he appears alongside Julius Caesar, Gustavus Adolphus, and Charles XII exclusively as a soldier and commander. That this was only one dimension of a multifaceted personality, whose contradictory whole was made up of quite disparate elements, is often overlooked. Frederick's military role can only be understood in terms of the way he united in his own person war and politics, military and philosophical intelligence, and an ability for both practical action and theoretical reflection. In the vision the King himself had of a good military leader, these prerequisites always were inextricably bound together. 'Whoever believes that a general needs only courage, is very wrong', he wrote in 1770 in the *Principles of Military Camps and Tactics*. 'Courage is of course an important quality, but he has to possess other abilities. A general determined to preserve order and discipline among his troops deserves praise, but this would not suffice at a time of war because in everything he does he needs good judgement. How can he attain this, however, if he lacks knowledge and ability?' According to Frederick, this resulted from historical developments. Since the invention of gunpowder, the system of mutual destruction had completely changed and war had assumed a totally different form. 'Force of numbers, the mainstay of the heroes of old, no longer counts. Cunning triumphs over force, skill over bravery. The head of the army commander exercises more influence over the success of his campaign than the arms of his soldiers. Intelligence shows courage the way, bravery is saved until the execution of the task.' These propositions, written in 1758, are part of a study of Charles XII who seemed to be an exception to the rule. He owed nothing to artfulness and everything to nature, as Frederick wrote during the Seven Years War. But was it not this very thing which plunged Sweden's King into misfortune? Since Charles XII was more brave than skilful, more active than clever, more a slave to his passions than was good for him, according to Frederick one should only follow his example with caution. The example of the Swedish ruler should rather be an opportunity to impress upon young people 'that bravery is nothing without wisdom and that a calculating head ultimately triumphs over daring boldness'. Thus Charles XII, whom Frederick secretly admired but who also represented a warning of the possibility of his own downfall, failed to pass the ultimate test of great military leadership. He serves to confirm the view that the conduct of war was a matter of intelligence and education, and could not be left to 'courage' alone.

This conviction had been instilled in Frederick after the first two Silesian Wars, and in the late 1740s he sought to lay it down in an 'Instruction' to his generals which eventually grew into a kind of textbook on war. In its final edition, printed in the winter of 1752–53, it was given the title *The General Principles of War applied to Tactics and the Discipline of Prussian Troops*. It contained a chapter devoted to 'The Talents a General must possess'. Here the conduct of war was likened to the highest of intellectual exercises. 'A complete general', one reads, 'is an *être de raison*' [that is to say, is governed by reason alone], a Platonic Republic, the *centrum gravitas* of philosophers, the philosophers' stone of the alchemists. Such perfection is by no means compatible with human nature. At the same time, however, the awareness of our own incompleteness should not prevent us from inventing complete role models, so that generous souls are animated to emulate them out of a principle of honour and try to come close to their exemplar while not being able to achieve complete perfection. Only the great examples, the great prototypes, attract people and when heroes such as Eugene, Condé, Turenne or Caesar demand our admiration, why should a whole, a composite incorporating all their varying qualities, not inspire us? In other words, the conduct of war is a task demanding unattainable heights of philosophical perfection, but one can learn from the example of the great strategists, whose individual qualities can be assembled into one ideal. It is this ideal the King is trying to instil into his generals in the *General Principles of War* by listing the talents a commander must possess. He speaks of contradictory qualities: dissimulation and openness, mildness and severity, always distrustful and constantly calm, protective of the soldiers out of humanitarian concern while at the same time willing to expend their blood, and so forth. But then comes the decisive sentence: 'The main task of a general is his work in the Cabinet, that is to plan projects, combine ideas . . .' What Frederick so admired in Prince Eugene, 'the greatest military hero of our century' as he called him in 1775 in his *Reflections on Projects of Campaign*, was his ability to plan great campaigns, that is his ability to be intellectually creative. Here this is cited as the principal task of the military leader. The King issued such lectures to an officer corps many of whose members had a pitifully low level of education. These ideas were formulated in as clear a form as possible, written by a man who in his youth was already convinced that the conduct of war was an art which required the highest degree of intellectual application. The application of empirically orientated reason, rather than humanitarian principles, was thus the Enlightenment's contribution to the science of warfare. Almost nowhere is the ethical validity of war discussed. A war is good (*bonum*) – presumably meaning justified – we read in the Political Testament of 1768 when it serves to 'uphold respect for the state, preserves its security, provides aid to its allies or stems the ambitious intentions of a ruler seeking to make gains which would be detrimental to your own interests'. Whether the war is aggressive or defensive is of secondary importance, except in the specific circumstances of 1740 and 1756.

If war was an art, it could only be learned by studying the great examples in history. This had been borne out by Frederick's own experience. He read everything there was on the subject. By this, he meant works of military history in which campaigns were described, such as descriptions of the wars of Turenne, Prince Eugene, Charles XII or the works of the Marquis de Feuquières. Frederick himself wrote introductions to extracts from the masters of military theory such as Jean Charles de Folard or the Marquis de Quincy, the author of the *Histoire militaire du règne de Louis le Grand*. In these introductions, he represented the role of theory as a possible means of improving situations which arose in practice. He equated the art of war with any other art which required to be studied thoroughly. Caesar's *Commentaries* were no longer applicable, he felt; only with Turenne had the art of war been revived. Frederick agreed with the widely held view that war had only really begun again with the armies of the seventeenth and eighteenth centuries, and that this was more than mere blind strength and force of numbers. Only since then, wrote Frederick in his essay on Charles XII, did the head of the commander do more to bring about a successful outcome than the arms of his soldiers. In reality, it was not until the seventeenth century that the history of war could yield practical examples of warfare since the material conditions were identical or broadly similar. In the final analysis, only that commanded his interest. A theory of war for its own sake was of no value to him. He was far removed from Clausewitz's penetrating theoretical examination of the nature of war.

Unlike Charles XII, a military role was not a natural one for Frederick. Rather, his harsh upbringing forced it upon him and perhaps awakened hidden instincts in him. He only really encountered the full reality of war as a young ruler who had brought it upon himself. His participation in the unsuccessful campaign led by Prince Eugene – now a shadow of the commander he had once been – on the Upper Rhine in 1734 was of little importance. Frederick, raised in his father's military state, had experience of manoeuvres and military exercises, but had only come close to actual fighting and campaigning through his studies. Through these he came to know the military leaders of previous generations who were to become his models. Turenne, Condé, Luxembourg, the most important military figures in Louis XIV's state, which through his contact with Voltaire seemed very real to him; then there was Prince Eugene of Savoy, the creator of Austrian great power status and an admired master of ambitious military plans; and finally the glittering figure of the King of Sweden, Charles XII, who fascinated him and who provided a constant example by which to measure his own life and to try to predict his future. The 'Phoenix of the North' who lost his glory and became Don Quixote was the ultimate warning of the fate which awaited any general lacking theoretical education; it was this education Frederick hoped to acquire for himself.

It is interesting to note that in one respect, Frederick failed to acknowledge Charles XII's position as a historical figure. With the single possible exception of Russia's Peter the Great, the King of Sweden was in his century the only reigning monarch who not only commanded his army in person but actually led his troops into battle: exactly as Frederick demanded in the *Anti-Machiavel*. This call was also made to himself, a prediction of his intention after his accession. In the *Anti-Machiavel*, it appears as a kind of duty incumbent upon sovereign rulers, although one which was dependent upon the personal aptitude of the monarch in question. If this was lacking, as was often the case, the exercise of command could only lead to disaster. If a monarch was not a born soldier, he should follow the advice of knowledgeable generals, of whom there were always some in the army; under no circumstances should he allow himself to be dictated to by a council of ministers, as Chapter XII of the *Anti-Machiavel* makes clear. The Crown Prince was quite clear that this principle would apply to himself and, long before his steadfastness and ability as a commander were tested, he was resolved to unite in his own person both military leadership and the direction of state politics.

One of his first acts as King was to assume the full authority of a ruler, which precluded any competitive authorities from functioning. Military councils, such as the one which Field Marshal Prince Leopold von Anhalt-Dessau had attempted to establish under Frederick's father, were therefore out of the question. This did not mean, of course, that the King was not open to the influence of military advisers, as was especially the case with the advice of his *aide-de-camp*, Hans Karl von Winterfeldt, in the run-up to the Seven Years War. In a state as geographically diverse as Prussia, moreover, it was impossible during wartime, with so many fronts and so many enemies, to uphold strictly the principle of undivided high command. However much he disliked the idea of a council of war, delegation of authority emerged as an inescapable necessity. This was particularly the case during the Seven Years War, when East Prussia, cut off geographically from the rest of the Hohenzollern monarchy, came under the command of Field Marshal Hans von Lehwaldt. Frederick transferred to him the 'authority, which I myself would have if I were there'. Quite different was the situation in the west, where Prince Ferdinand of Brunswick, the King's brother-in-law, was given command of the combined armies in November 1757 at the request of Britain's George II. With troops from seven different states, he successfully defended western Germany, especially Hanover, in glorious campaigns against numerically far superior French troops and therefore provided valuable protection for Prussia's western flank. Ferdinand, a Prussian field marshal whose military education was similar to Frederick's own, conformed to the King's general strategic plan, but did so with increasing independence as a military commander in his own right.

Even more problematical was Frederick's relationship with his brother, Henry, who was highly sceptical about royal strategy and a sharp critic of the

King. Nevertheless, he never openly defied his brother. Frederick initially transferred to him command of the second army in the main theatre of war in Saxony in March 1758, then subsequently entrusted him with operations on the eastern front against the Russians. He was given wide-ranging powers and retained command, with only short breaks, until the conclusion of the fighting. Disagreements and conflicts arose out of this situation, concerning both single decisions and more fundamental questions of political and military strategy. The roots of these quarrels lay deep in the self-confidence of the younger brother, who felt intellectually superior to the reigning monarch and commander-in-chief but was aware that he could never hope to replace him. On one occasion it briefly seemed that such an opportunity had presented itself: after Frederick's severe physical and psychological breakdown following the shattering defeat at Russian hands in the battle of Kunersdorf on 12 August 1759, he appointed his brother 'Generalissimo of the Army'. ('The orders of my brother must be followed.') This order was lost and never reached Prince Henry, but the King expressly mentions it in other instructions. All the indications point towards the conclusion that Frederick had seriously considered abdication or even suicide for several days. However, ultimately no crisis for the Prussian monarchy materialised out of the personal crisis which the King underwent, as he wrote to his brother on 16 August: 'I will support the state as is my duty.'

The critical position of 1759 makes clear that what was at issue in Frederick's case was not merely the King's administrative power but what can only be described as his charismatic authority. 'The charismatic hero', we read in Max Weber's *Economy and Society*, 'does not exercise his authority like a bureaucratic function with orders and statutes, nor like a patriarchal power based on inherited custom and feudal homage, but he wins and retains it by proving his strength through his actions. He must perform heroic deeds if he wants to be a military leader.' Frederick did not possess this prerequisite of charisma until he emerged victorious from an unconventional war which had been conducted in contravention of all the established rules of eighteenth-century warfare. This was not to be until the end of the Second Silesian War, after the battles of Soor and Hohenfriedberg. The charismatic authority of Frederick the Great, as he was now called, also had an effect on his military opponents who, as the Austrian commander, Daun, confirmed, frequently dared not attack despite enjoying a numerical superiority. Even after the severe setback of Kolin, the King's charisma remained undamaged and came into play in the battle at Leuthen in December 1757. In his speech to the officers before the battle, he appealed not only for obedience but voluntary allegiance. In the critical period from 1758 onwards, particularly after the catastrophe of Kunersdorf, Frederick could no longer sustain the myth of a great commander and only damaged his reputation further by making inexcusably bad decisions as he did at Hochkirch on 14 October 1758 and before Maxen on 20 November 1759.

What then took the place of these victories, however, was an unusual moral resilience, which itself contained charismatic elements, and this reinforced his inherited authority as Prussia's ruler. Even 'a charismatic hero' could, according to Max Weber, take 'discipline' into his service, however incompatible such charisma was with rational discipline. In view of the composition of the Prussian army, which like other forces of the absolutist period contained a large proportion of mercenaries (some of whom were forcibly enrolled in Prussian regiments after their own armies had been defeated), discipline was of the utmost importance. That element of national enthusiasm, later described by campaign theorists of the French revolutionary age as the motor of armies, was still lacking under Frederick and could be glimpsed only in the officers' *esprit de corps* and their patriotic oath of honour. The Frederician army was no longer the peasant army of the Thirty Years War and not yet the mass army of the *levée en masse* with its revolutionary *élan*, but an army composed of mercenaries and conscripted peasants under the King's command. His charismatic aura could therefore only have a limited range of effectiveness as a result of the army's heterogeneous composition. In the Seven Years War, the number of native Prussian soldiers increased and came to share a sense of belonging to their own country as personified by the King. There are examples, as at the battle of Leuthen, where this was also to be found among the rank-and-file. However, side by side with them stood the mass desertions of mercenaries, a phenomenon which increased in the War of the Bavarian Succession and which could never be eradicated. Over such men, the King's charisma clearly held no sway. In the autobiography of Ulrich Bräker, a Swiss press-ganged into the Prussian army who deserted at the battle of Lobositz, the King is at one point described as 'the just Frederick'; of greater significance, however, is the angry outburst: 'The King alone is King, his generals, colonels, majors are themselves his servants – and we, oh! we – the mercenary dogs of war to be dispensed with in times of peace, and stabbed and shot to death in times of war.'

When the King wrote that a general's principal task was always carried out at his desk, the impression is given that the army of absolutist Prussia already displayed the division – characteristic of the nineteenth and twentieth centuries – between the centres of command, which were removed from the front, and the fighting troops – a division which was evident in the wars waged by Helmuth von Moltke. But things had not developed as far as that in the standing army of the absolutist era. Living standards, moreover, were precisely graded according to rank and status. The generals and other senior officers travelled in the complete luxury and comfort of Rococo society which considerably hindered the army's mobility: this was especially true in the eighteenth-century French army. The Prussian army differed significantly from the situation in other armies, although ranks were distinguished by their equipment and their quarters. The spartan lifestyle adopted by the Swedish forces under Charles XII, to which the King subjected himself, also prevailed in the Prussian army at times of emergency. In the fortified camp at Bunzelwitz in August 1761, Frederick the Great slept on some hay under open skies, as he explained in a letter to the Marquis d'Argens ('as the Russians and Austrians are blockading the royal camp'). The letter makes clear, however, that this was an exception, whereas with Charles XII it was a permanent way of life. Frederick nevertheless had to content himself with basic quarters as in the winter of 1759–60 in the Erzgebirge mountains; Henri de Catt informs us that in these weeks he suffered great physical hardships, but sought to overcome them by writing even more. The King's response to pain and deprivation could not be described as stoic calmness but rather as nervous pessimism, although this did not paralyse his ability to act. One of the characteristics of the Prussian army's leadership system was that its upper echelons were exposed to constant danger which led to great losses among its generals. The King himself also entered the fray in many battles, in the process risking his own life. During the battle of Torgau (5 November 1760), he was hit in the chest by a musket ball, but his winter clothes lessened the impact and partly deflected the ball from his body. Frederick was briefly knocked unconscious and collapsed. Such dangers could at any time usher in a crisis for the whole state, whose existence was linked to the sovereign's survival. Frederick sought to provide for such an eventuality by making several emergency wills in the field, as on 22 August 1758, three days before the battle of Zorndorf, in this case entitled 'Order to my generals of the army as to their conduct in case I am shot dead'. It contained a curious mixture of military instructions for the present and fundamental political decisions such as the order to swear in the heir to the throne immediately and to follow the orders of Prince Henry 'as well as those of the reigning monarch'. A similar crisis occurred after the battle of Kunersdorf, although we have no authentic evidence for this. The possibility that the King might die in battle was the ultimate consequence of his military autocracy but signified a constant test for the stability of the Frederician state. In order to safeguard against any negative consequences the King, despite his lack of belief in the abilities of his successor, never missed an opportunity to stress the strict adherence to the norms of succession through male primogeniture.

Legends have been built up around Frederick as a military leader; he became a myth on which the Prussian army existed until the end of the Hohenzollern monarchy. In a scholarly analysis of his strategy written after the foundation of the German Empire and the victory over France in which Moltke's strategic planning triumphed, Frederick the Great's decision to seek battle was found to be at the heart of his strategic planning. The important military writer, Theodor von Bernhardi, in his book published in 1881 and entitled *Frederick the Great as Military Commander*, puts forward the thesis that all Frederick's battles were designed to be decisive, in a way which anticipated Napoleon. In this, according to Bernhardi, he was 'far ahead of his time' since on the whole his contemporaries viewed the option of battle only as a final resort. The King 'soon freed himself from the chains of accepted thought and recognised the true nature of war. Alone among his contemporaries he knew . . . that the destruction of enemy forces was the only decisive way to win a war and that every advantage won without a decisive victory in battle was only conditional and insecure.' Prince Henry is cited as support for this theory: 'My brother always wanted to fight, that was his entire military art!' Bernhardi's book is pervaded by the self-confidence of the era of Moltke and Bismarck, in which the Prussian army was seen as the fundamental security of the new Empire and Moltke's strategy had led to the great victories of Königgrätz and Sedan. Its arguments, however, were not entirely upheld by the more detailed studies of Frederician warfare undertaken under the aegis of the historical section of the German General Staff.

The term 'strategy of destruction', pre-eminent in the nineteenth-century heroic view of Frederick, led the military historian Hans Delbrück to begin a controversy which has gradually sucked in all scholars who study the era of Frederick the Great. Delbrück disputed the validity of the term 'strategy of destruction'. The King, he argued, must be seen in terms of the eighteenth century and should therefore be described as a representative of the strategy of exhaustion in which battle, rather than something to be avoided, could be in certain circumstances a desirable goal. It is unimportant here to go into the various arguments Delbrück raised to counter the increasingly dogmatic assertions of scholars such as Otto Hintze and Reinhold Koser. On the whole, it remained a fruitless debate even if Delbrück succeeded in revealing the way in which Frederick remained rooted in eighteenth-century military thinking. He never intended to diminish the King's greatness, merely to strip away the layers of myth and reveal the true historical figure.

It is curious that this controversy developed at such a late point, when Clausewitz in his great work *On War* had already established the groundwork for an understanding of Frederick. Clausewitz stressed the importance of distinguishing between the different political reasons for war: either the destruction of the enemy, in order to destroy him politically, or the securing of some territorial gains. The different political goals produced different ways of waging war. This is precisely what Clausewitz clarified in his analysis of Frederick's strategy during the Seven Years War. In Chapter VIII of Book VIII of *On War*, from the opening campaign of 1757 to the fortified camp at Bunzelwitz, he portrays how each strategic decision was dependent on the changing military situation. The war ultimately 'became quite a different one'. The final strategy was only based on gaining time and preserving those lands the King still possessed. What Clausewitz styled as 'absolute war' was now a distant prospect, since the destruction of the enemy was no longer possible. Winning time and regaining strength for a 'subordinate aim' (Book VII, Chapter III) replaced the 'principal aim', strategy is no longer purely military, it is a function of political goals. The campaign of 1760 appears as 'a true example of strategic mastery' (Book III, Chapter I), 'just sufficient to achieve its aim'. Clausewitz counts Frederick among 'the three new Alexanders' of the modern period, alongside Gustavus Adolphus and Charles XII. They all attempted 'to found great monarchies from small states by means of powerful and total war'. However, their efforts met with 'only partial success' since they could not rise above the political equilibrium of Europe. 'The political interests, friendships and enmities had evolved into such a finely tuned system that no cannon could be fired in Europe without all the chancelleries becoming involved.' The interconnection of the state system together with its structure, which constantly aimed at a balance of power, made it impossible for Frederick to break free and to raise himself above it as Napoleon was able to do. With 'his destructive energy' Napoleon came closest to total war and Clausewitz calls him 'the very god of war' (Book VII, Chapter III). In comparison with him, what remained for Frederick was to take 'pride in a glorious fall' (Book VII, Chapter IV), a curious term by which Clausewitz must have meant the catastrophe which was to befall the entire Frederician state in 1806.

Clausewitz's interpretation incorporates elements both of the heroic view of Frederick, which he could never fully abandon, and a recognition of the limitations of the King's policy and strategy within the context of Europe's eighteenth century. Moreover, these are not judged to be incompatible opposites nor forces within a system of dual polarity. What emerges is more a strategy bound by political necessity and prevailing power constellations. Clausewitz's image of Frederick, which was built up almost without reference to the King's own writings, can be completed by comparing the practice of Frederician warfare with the theoretical works which he produced. First one must cite Frederick's view on the great plan for war which dominates his writings. In 1775, a decade and more after the Seven Years War, he dedicated a whole treatise to campaign plans (*projets de campagne*). The question of the validity of such schemes and how they were to be put into operation concerned him throughout his life, but at all times he clung to the belief that campaign plans must have an offensive character. In *The Thoughts and Rules for War* written in 1755 (that is to say, before the Seven Years War) the term 'offensive' was linked with the justified aim of new conquest. In the *General Principles of War* which was written even earlier, more careful emphasis was laid on the circumstances of the moment and the number of enemy troops before embarking on such campaigns. The fact that Frederick was preparing for all eventualities in the tense situation before the Seven Years War is clear from another part of the 1755 treatise, in which we find the following striking analysis. It is necessary to 'distinguish between plans drawn up at the beginning of the war and those which take shape after a few campaigns. The first, if well executed, can decide the whole war, if you employ all the advantages over your enemy which your army, the timing or a position which you have gained initially give you. The second is dependent upon so many circumstances that it is impossible to lay down general rules, other than that you should seek to preserve your base of operations and not to advance too far . . .'

These sentences, penned in the year before the outbreak of the momentous Seven Years War, sound like a prognosis for the course of this most difficult of Frederick II's military struggles. Indeed, the initial campaign of 1757 in Bohemia and Moravia was the King's only significant military undertaking which was conducted according to a great plan. This plan for a coordinated offensive into Bohemia was the product of intensive correspondence between the King, and Field Marshal Schwerin and Lieutenant General Winterfeldt, which developed into a memorandum listing the various options entitled 'Conjectures on Various Projects'. In many ways similar to Moltke's famous 1866 campaign (although this had the advantage of greater mobility as a result of technological innovations), it advocated an invasion by separate battalions and their ultimate concentration in one battle, perhaps at Prague. For this decisive battle which was to determine the fate of the war, Frederick set the highest standards. He compared it to the day of Pharsalus, the victory over Pompey in 48 BC which established Caesar's power. The plan failed on the one hand because of the unexpected withdrawal into Prague of the Austrians under Prince Charles of Lorraine and, on the other, because of the defeat at Kolin suffered by Frederick at the hands of the Austrian relief army commanded by Daun. This transformed the character of the war: what was to be a decisive, one-off battle with important political consequences turned into a protracted, all-consuming struggle for the course of which it was impossible to establish 'any hard and fast rules'. There was, in effect, no alternative to the basic Prussian rule of warfare that 'our wars must be short and lively, since it does not suit us to drag out such things'.

This outcome was clearly something which affected Frederick deeply. Great campaign plans and their failure was a topic he could never abandon after 1763. He dealt with it in his 1768 Political Testament, tending towards a certain scepticism when commenting on the outcome of battles. The campaign of 1757 served as an example of the possible success it could have brought had it succeeded. Later on, in the treatise of 1775, the wisdom of hindsight was brought to bear on great campaign plans and a number of hypothetical possibilities examined. One example was an offensive alliance of Prussia, Austria, the Empire, England and the Dutch Republic combined in a war against France; a second was another Prussian war against Austria in which the lessons of 1744 and 1757 have been learned: the surest means of securing the conquest of Bohemia was to take the war to the Danube – precisely what Frederick had sought to avoid in his earlier campaigns and dared not do in 1778 during the War of the Bavarian Succession. 'Thus Vienna is forced to pull back its main forces from Bohemia and the army seeking to invade there then has the opportunity of implementing its plan.' These are, of course, simply intellectual exercises. But at the same time surely they reveal the King's disappointment that he had never achieved the decisive victory? Frederick seeks to console himself and at the same time justify his own actions with the thought that no man had ever existed whose plans have all succeeded. 'But if you make only small plans, you will always be only a mediocre figure. However, should two out of ten great undertakings succeed, your name will be immortal.' To support this theory, Frederick recalls the career of Prince Eugene, who succeeded in winning decisive battles in war: Turin (1706), Blenheim (1704) and Belgrade (1717) 'which decided the fate of thrones and peoples'. Yet he, too, could not escape failure such as the abortive attempt in 1702 to capture Cremona where the entire French high command was stationed.

Nevertheless, Eugene remained 'the model of a great commander' who always kept the most important issues in view. He operated within a much larger geographical circumference and therefore enjoyed a freedom of manoeuvre denied to the King of Prussia. Frederick, after all, was hemmed in on all sides and was forced to operate in an extremely confined space. This may have contributed to the admiration bordering upon jealousy with which Frederick always wrote about Prince Eugene.

Eugene never had to risk all by operating too far from his own territory and sources of supply. According to Frederick, in the campaigns the Prince conducted from Hungary, he could always rely on the Danube as a supply route, something which his successors to their detriment failed to do in the Turkish War of 1737–39. At this point, too, one senses the King's recollection of his own experiences: in the campaign of 1741, which he himself had brought about through his invasion of Silesia, the French had advanced as far as Linz and, according to Frederick, missed the opportunity to strike towards Vienna in order to dictate terms to Austria. Instead, for no obvious purpose, they marched into Bohemia. In this way the King sought to demonstrate the consequences of ill-laid plans.

Eugene's campaign plans were based as a rule on the military superiority which the Prince enjoyed, and were therefore offensive in nature. There is no doubt that this was an unfulfilled dream of Frederick's. But after the débâcle of 1757 no other opportunity presented itself to allow him to plan a great offensive campaign. The advance to Olmütz in 1758 was also limited in its aims. He now had to develop plans for defensive warfare in which he had to assume numerically superior opponents and his own considerable inferiority. Or were the military actions of the Prussian King from 1758 to 1759 a series of improvisations which had the sole aim of preserving his operational base, an interpretation which would accord exactly with Clausewitz's interpretation? Of course, the term 'campaign plan' can only be loosely applied to describe the basis of the operations conducted by the King after 1758. He had lost the initiative and was obliged to react to his opponents' initiatives. The King nevertheless endeavoured to establish clearly which form of warfare remained a possibility for him: the first time in a treatise dated 27 December 1758, and later in the second part of his discourse on campaign plans of 1775. The 1758 piece, written in the midst of war, put forward ideas about actions forced upon a commander by his enemies. They betray numerous insecurities and are marked by an impression that the state's very survival was at stake. The first conclusion drawn from the changed situation was therefore 'never to allow oneself to be forced into battle', and another lesson was to seek to destroy one's enemy by small-scale actions. 'The means to the end are irrelevant, provided one only retains the upper hand.' This also meant taking into account when planning one's own loss of initiative: 'We are forced to accept the dictates of our enemies, rather than to give them, and have to gear our operations to theirs.'

What was in 1758 an uncertain insight in a game of chance, was transformed by his reflections during the post-war period into rules which, two decades before, Frederick would have believed impossible. The eighteen instructions on conducting a defensive war contained in the treatise of 1775 are the result of an *ex post facto* overcoming of the strategic problems which faced him during the second, far more difficult phase of the Seven Years War. It is fundamentally an attempt to categorise improvisations. Here we find sentences such as: 'Aim to risk everything to gain the offensive. Notch up many small successes, the sum of which will equate with one great victory. Seek to gain the respect of your enemy and contain him through fear of your armaments. Use guile, subterfuge and false information to bring about the happy moment when the damage he inflicted on you can be paid back with interest. Always look out for new means and ways to retain your position. Change your methods to deceive the enemy. You will often be forced to conduct a phoney war. Whenever possible attack the enemy when he is divided, but don't allow yourself to become involved in a full-scale battle since your weakness would make you inferior. With time, that is all one could expect from the most skilled of generals.' What is described here is nothing less than the tactical finesse through which Frederick the Great survived the Seven Years War; here it is important to distinguish between the King's advice for an offensive and that for a defensive war. No longer is there any mention of a great campaign plan, one of the first prerequisites for an offensive war, but rather many pieces of advice, the sum of which form a whole, in an attempt to circumvent the art of improvisation or, in Moltke's words, 'a system of makeshift'. Much of this was similar to the strategy of manoeuvre or of exhaustion, as it was later to be called, but all these ideas do not constitute an overarching theoretical system. Frederick hardly mentions any rule of defensive warfare which he had not broken by his own conduct. If one considers the campaigns of 1760 and 1761, the King weakened the main army by dispatching troops to other fronts. At Liegnitz and Torgau, he engaged in full-scale battles, sustaining heavy losses. By setting up camp at Bunzelwitz he had chosen a location which was easily surrounded – all these were decisions against which subsequently he expressly warned. In the latter phase of the Seven Years War one can no longer speak of planned campaigns and it is difficult to claim that they were 'an artful work of strategic mastery', as Clausewitz had done. That is not to diminish the genius of improvisation in a situation which was all but hopeless. This was the source of Frederick's greatness.

It can be called a strategy of exhaustion in the sense that it was a strategy which sought constantly to combat one's own exhaustion and one which was dependent on conserving strength to wear down the enemy. If one compares the principal proponents of the strategy of exhaustion, the Austrian field marshal Leopold Joseph Maria von Daun and Frederick's brother, Prince Henry, one can detect very few differences in the basic principles employed but more a distinction in the level of tension and nervous energy. As a personality,

Daun was much more complacent, a source of permanent irritation in Vienna because of his inactivity, above all after the battle of Kunersdorf in 1759 when everyone expected an advance on Berlin. Nevertheless, Daun's tactics were well thought out: he loved to establish himself in secure places which were difficult to attack, and whose capture would involve heavy losses and was hardly worthwhile. Thus in the final campaign of the war, he occupied a fortress near the Austrian-held Schweidnitz from which he gradually retreated onto the heights near Burkersdorf. Against all expectation, Frederick attacked here, captured the Austrian defences and forced Daun to abandon his position near Schweidnitz and to retreat in the direction of Bohemia. In the previous year, 1761, Frederick had similarly fortified himself close to Schweidnitz, at Bunzelwitz, in the face of a vastly superior army consisting of the combined Austrian and Russian forces under Laudon and Buturlin. Frederick only averted an attack through his unexpected and undetected withdrawal. On that occasion it was not Daun but Laudon, the far more enterprising general and in many ways as able a commander as Frederick, who shrank from engaging in battle with only the Austrian army and lacking Russian assistance.

The similarity in Austrian and Prussian strategy and tactics was undoubtedly due to the way in which each side studied and assimilated the other's methods. Frederick adopted many of Daun's tactics, which he described in the preface to *The History of the Seven Years War* as 'indisputably good'. Early on he recognised the weakness of the Prussian cavalry when compared to its Austrian counterpart and above all the superiority of the Habsburg artillery. He admired the 'mighty [Austrian] artillery' in his musings on tactics of 1758, and as late as 1782 issued instructions for the new weapons. He had no way of recognising that the increased use of artillery was the first step on the road to a technological war, but he had always displayed a certain distaste for it. Not by chance was the social status of the artillery officer corps far below that of officers from 'traditional' arms of the service, that is to say the infantry and cavalry.

The fact that in the critical situation at Burkersdorf, Frederick was prepared to risk an attack is proof of his constant readiness to break the defensive position imposed upon him at the first opportunity. This was characteristic of his strategic conduct of the war and one which emerged in disputes with his brother Henry. It was particularly clear in 1760. Then, shortly before the battle of Liegnitz, he failed to convince his brother of the need to attempt an '*affaire décisive*'. This not merely involved differences of temperament and contrasting political perspectives upon the war, but also fundamental differences over strategy. They 'argued over questions of overall strategy at a time when both were so completely at the mercy of events as to give only limited freedom to their choices' (Chester V. Easum). Henry was in command of an army which, with the Austrians under Laudon at its rear, observed the Russian troops and through clever manoeuvring prevented their union with Laudon's army. Frederick, who sought to gain time with a victory in Silesia, pressed for a concentration of the two Prussian armies so that together they could engage in a decisive battle against the Austrians. The King used emotive language to win Henry over to his plan ('I beseech you once more in the name of God') but the Prince considered it a disastrous mistake. 'To concentrate against only one enemy means to give the other foe a completely free hand,' he wrote to the King on 18 August. This led to a temporary breach between the brothers. Henry withdrew from his command because of illness. Both men were in their own way correct. The abandonment of the eastern front allowed Russian troops to capture Berlin but Frederick, who had retreated to Saxony because of the threat to the capital and whose proximity eventually persuaded the Russians to withdraw from Berlin, won a victory at Torgau over Daun on 3 November 1760 in a terrible battle which, despite enormous Prussian losses, proved not to be the '*affaire décisive*' for which the King had hoped.

In the brothers' disputes, theoretical and strategic concepts played a greater role for Henry than the manoeuvres of Frederick and Daun in Silesia could take account of. Moreover, if one examines Prince Henry's performance in the war, it can be seen that the brothers' differences ultimately rested more on divergent assessments of a seemingly hopeless situation than on fundamental differences. One can no more deny the Prince's ability and will to seek decisions in battle than Frederick's capacity for all kinds of manoeuvres during the struggle. It should also be noted that the King possessed greater strength of will – Jacob Burckhardt called it 'strength of the soul' – and without his brother's steadfastness, Prince Henry would long ago have abandoned the fray. Therefore Prussia ultimately survived the crisis because of Frederick – despite the mistakes of which his brother often wrongly accused him. One has to ask whether on the Austrian side, where a similar conflict was under way between Daun and Laudon, it was not Daun's tenacity bordering on sluggishness which formed the firm basis for Laudon's activities and whether the latter's impetuous temperament was suited to stand alone against Frederick.

Let us return once more to Frederick's advice for the conduct of a defensive war and compare it to Clausewitz's analysis of the Seven Years War. This comparison makes clear that the latter had a much clearer understanding of the principal prerequisites of conducting defensive warfare with weakened forces. Frederick at best gives us a 'theory of practice' which he himself only followed to a limited extent; Clausewitz by contrast sought to build this analysis into a general theory. For the King, defensive war was a necessity imposed upon him; Clausewitz was convinced in principle of its greater effectiveness. Frederick fails to explain what the advantages of operations conducted on interior lines are, whereas Clausewitz discusses the 'benefits of short lines'. He also appreciates more clearly the operational goal which the King must pursue in order to survive: this, apart from winning time, was 'to preserve what he still owned' and thus he became 'progressively more economical with land' (that is to say, he had to preserve his operational base in Saxony, Silesia and Pomerania). If this failed, theoretically there was only one way out – which Clausewitz perceived only after the disaster of 1806. In a memorandum written between 1807 and 1808, we read these lines: 'My idea is that one should sacrifice a state which it is no longer possible to defend in order to save the army . . . An army which in a wide and varied theatre of war (and such is Germany) has nothing to defend but its own security and exists only for its own survival, is twice or three times as powerful as an army which has to protect a state and, worst of all, has to defend this region or that. When the Prussian army cannot be bound to the state without going down with it, and the fall of the state is inevitable then it seems to me to be wiser to lend the army the rights of the monarch than bind it to the state.'

This idea of an army without a state is the most radical and revolutionary alternative to Frederick the Great's military conduct during the Seven Years War. Here we see the underlying message in Mirabeau's assertion that Prussia was not a state with an army, but an army with a state. Clausewitz followed this to the most extreme of conclusions. To the end, Frederick did nothing else but defend his lands at the cost of terrible sacrifices and by means of desperate measures. At the peace talks, he haggled over every single piece of territory, finally over the County of Glatz. It was always about the indivisibility of the territory. The army was in the service of the state. The wars it fought only had a single political goal: to preserve and enlarge the state. This is where its and Frederick's greatness lay, and also the limits of its impact upon history.

CHAPTER 9

Philosopher-King

Of all literary forms, the recording of history is the most suited to the political sphere, since there is a close identification between the subject and his actions. Many statesmen have left memoirs but, as a rule, these are valuable only as source material for historians. Such accounts are frequently highly unreliable due to their biased and subjective nature, the author's need to justify his own conduct often obscuring the true course of events. Frederick, too, wrote '*Mémoires*', but these were closer in form and intention to '*Histoire*' (i.e. to a historical chronicle) and in fact he named his first effort, an account of the two Silesian Wars of the 1740s, the final edition of which was completed in 1775, *History of My Own Times* (*Histoire de mon temps*). Every volume in his historical output was to become a component in a comprehensive *Histoire de Brandebourg*. The appellation '*Mémoires*' continued to be applied to the *History of the House of Brandenburg* which was 'memoirs' in the sense of personal reminiscences. It covers the history of the Hohenzollern rulers, from the transfer of the Electorate of Brandenburg to Frederick I in 1415 until Frederick William's death in 1740.

Frederick's models were not diarists such as the Duc de Saint-Simon. He aimed instead to emulate Voltaire's ambitions to produce literary history. When Voltaire sent him the first section of his *Essai sur les moeurs et l'esprit des nations*, the King was extremely impressed by this unique form of historical account which he regarded as well-considered, unbiased and free from all superfluous detail and called 'Termini' – these he would return to in the introductions of his own historical works. On 13 October 1742, he instructed the poet to treat an account of the recently completed decisive war ('the war of Pharsalas') as an element in Voltaire's planned historical work. This was clearly little more than flattery on the King's part, since almost simultaneously he began working on his own '*Mémoires*', as he informed Voltaire on 15 November 1742. Frederick's first attempt at historical writing was clearly based primarily on the literary ambitions awakened by Voltaire. When well into his seventies, the King worked unremittingly on his own historical works, correcting, rearranging, recasting introductions and adding to his *Memoirs on the History of the House of Brandenburg* begun in 1746 and completed in February 1748. The second version of his history of the two Silesian Wars had been completed as long ago as 1746; after a further revision it eventually appeared in 1775 under the title *History of My Own Times* (*Histoire de mon temps*). This was followed immediately after the end of the fighting in 1763 by the *History of the Seven Years War*. It was a task which had obviously required overcoming certain personal scruples. He finalised the preface in March 1764. The King's account of the post-war decade, the *'Mémoires depuis la paix de Hubertusbourg jusqu'à la fin du partage de la Pologne'* followed in 1775, and this was continued in fragmentary form for the years until the Peace of Teschen and included an account of the War of the Bavarian Succession. Once the final parts had been published, which did not happen until 1788, two years after the King's death, these writings constituted a body of work which provided an account, in the King's own words, of Frederick the Great's entire reign with the exception of the interwar period 1745–56 and the last years. For the most part, of course, domestic matters are largely ignored except for the piecemeal information on internal reconstruction which is provided for the years 1763–73.

The work as a whole, however, is not homogeneous. Although early literary aspirations were never entirely abandoned, Frederick's own creative powers either diminished or were neglected under the pressure of events. With the *History of the Seven Years War*, his character also changed. One would be doing the politician and military leader a disservice if one did not recognise that Frederick appreciated at an early stage the importance of historical writing as a political instrument in the hands of a man whose life had been shaped by his own deeds. His assurances, therefore, that his intention was always to view events impartially and with the eyes of a philosopher, and his claim that the most important duty of the historian was to record the truth, must not be dismissed as mere literary form. He was fully conscious of using his account of the Seven Years War as a political weapon to demonstrate to posterity 'that the conflict could not have been avoided and that the honour and well-being of the state forbade my acceptance of other peace terms than those which eventually ended the fighting'. He therefore denied responsibility for the outbreak of the war and for its extended duration. This purpose was also served by an extensive documentary appendix. The editor of the German edition of Frederick's works described the King's account of the Seven Years War as a tendentious treatise. If this means that certain sections, particularly the first part, were an exercise in self-justification, then this claim is correct. It is not, however, a description which fits Frederick's treatment of military operations, which were very much to the fore in his study of the war of 1756–63. The subsequent volume dealing with events up to 1779 is truly a masterpiece of diplomatic and domestic history. The War of the Bavarian Succession is described as 'a remarkable mixture of diplomatic negotiations and military operations'. 'No one knew if it was war or peace.'

Certain characteristics of Voltaire's historical writings were absorbed by Frederick the Great's own works of history. The King, for instance, followed his mentor when he included cultural and intellectual developments in his historical account. In the *History of the House of Brandenburg*, the accounts of the policies and reigns of individual Hohenzollern rulers appear in chronological sequence, interspersed by unrelated chapters on Brandenburg's changing political condition, which included discussion of the country's internal system of government and its army, of 'superstition and religion' and finally a superb *résumé* of 'customs, practices, manufacturing, and the advance of the human spirit in the arts and sciences'. This corresponded precisely to the structure of Voltaire's *Siècle de Louis XIV*. The *History of the House of Brandenburg* is the clearest illustration of Voltaire's influence, which is much less apparent in the King's subsequent works of contemporary history. In style and tone, these are much more akin to the Political Testaments. They are instructive and intended to inform, although the King occasionally forgot that he was addressing a wider readership and not just his successor.

If Frederick agreed with Voltaire that historical writing should be philosophical in nature, that is to say, it should not be a purely chronological account of events but a reflective and thoughtful record, then one has to ask what guided these reflections. What were the most important principles in Frederick's 'philosophical' interpretation of history? This is a point the King raises frequently, often mentioning it in passing in the midst of an historical account. History, he believed, is not the result of acts governed by reason, but of the uncontrolled and uncontrollable human passions interacting with the prevailing forces of chance. To support this theory, the King cites the example of his father's relationship with his cousin, George II, King of Great Britain and Elector of Hanover. Even as youths, the two men could not stand one another (*'ne peuvent se souffrir dès leur tendre jeunesse'*). 'When both [succeeded] to the throne, their personal animosity threatened to become an additional factor complicating relations between their two countries. This enmity was soon transferred from [their] personal relationship to matters of state and clearly influenced political relations between their two countries.' Frederick drew from this a fundamental conclusion: 'It is the lot of human affairs to be guided by the passions of men, and reasons which were originally childish can ultimately lead to great upheavals.' Similar observations are taken to extremes in the age of Enlightenment, although to a King skilled in matters of state it was also clear that the politician's own room for manoeuvre was often limited while his personal intentions, in any case, served only the general good. The origins of the fall of monarchies and republics, Frederick concludes in his *History of the House of Brandenburg*, lie in the unchanging laws of nature. Human passions serve merely as a driving force continually to create new adornments on the world stage.

To Frederick the ruler and man of the world, with his remarkably acute understanding of the motives behind political events, the personal factor in history ranked highly. Frederick the philosopher, however, was more inclined to rate its influence as rather less. To him, there were higher imperatives at work than the will of a single individual. Chance always played a part, although its influence could not be determined until events had run their course. The surprising outcome of the Seven Years War gave him occasion to ponder the mysterious ways of history: 'Is it not astonishing,' he writes, 'that all of man's cunning and might is so often thwarted by unexpected events or blows of fate? Does it not seem as if some unknown power is playing a scornful game with the plans of men? Is it not clear that at the outset of [this] chaotic war, every rational person predicted a quite different outcome?' Whether or not a greater plan existed, to which the schemes of men were subordinate, is left open.

Personalities, nevertheless, held a great attraction for Frederick the historian. The King succeeded in creating character studies of considerable charm, especially when he admired his subject. One such case was the Great Elector whom Frederick metamorphosed into the ideal of his own wishes and goals in the *History of the House of Brandenburg*. Although its text is usually restrained in tone, the King's portrayal of his predecessor oozes spontaneous Prussian patriotism. Only in a postscript does he try to put the impact of the Great Elector into context by comparing him with Louis XIV. This painstakingly thorough exercise undoubtedly served to enhance the historical assessment of the Elector. It was achieved by means of an examination of similarities and contrasts:

> In their lives, there are many instances of remarkable similarity and others where circumstances make a comparison impossible. If one were to compare both rulers using the extent of their power as a yardstick, it would be like juxtaposing Jupiter's thunder and Philoctete's arrows. If, however, one leaves aside political might and concentrates on their personal attributes, it becomes clear that the soul and deeds of the Great Elector are not far removed from the spirit and achievements of the French King.

Frederick came to the conclusion that both Frederick William and Louis XIV deserved the epithet 'the Great', 'which their contemporaries had given them and posterity had unanimously endorsed'. This was rather curious since it was an epithet not generally applied to Louis XIV: for example, it was not employed by Voltaire. Personal enemies and political opponents were not spared Frederick's character analyses, which were often coloured by acerbic disdain. The King employed the weapon of irony in his historical writings in the same way he would in daily life. Of the many available examples it is best to quote only the polished lines describing Peter the Great, Augustus the Strong and Charles XII: 'Peter favoured cunning above courage, Augustus pleasure above work, Charles adored glory more than possession of the entire world.' So Voltairian is this vocabulary that one is forced to ask how far these words were influenced directly by the text's proofreader.

In the introductions to his historical works, Frederick constantly asserts that his aim is only to tell the truth and to be neutral. One could interpret this as a kind of escape clause with which the King sought to protect himself against accusations of bias – a kind of topos which many historians have used and continue to employ. But doubtless it was also an enlightened comment upon, and a critical reaction to, those historians of Prussia who had preceded him and, confusing truth with a multitude of facts, had indiscriminately assembled 'a pile of building blocks'. He makes no mention, however, of his own particular situation and simply passes over the fact that his impartiality was limited by his close personal involvement with the events he describes. The *Histoire de mon temps* was not only the history of his times, but also his own story, the justification of which was bound to flow from his pen. Doubts about the decisions he had taken – although never about his larger goals – are seldom mentioned in his historical works with one exception: mistakes in his handling of military campaigns are often admitted and then always measured against those of his opponents. The account of his unsuccessful Bohemian campaign in 1744 is one example of this. It serves to create the impression of unbiased objectivity; but is, in effect, no more than a misleading smoke screen. Fundamental strategic decisions taken by Frederick are never questioned, and the controversies which occurred within the Prussian high command, particularly with Prince Henry, are not touched upon.

The changing strategic goals and tactical methods imposed by the demands of the Seven Years War are nowhere discussed in any detail. A mere few sentences are devoted to the great plan for the 1757 campaign which had emerged only after lengthy deliberation and involved a concentrated invasion of Bohemia. Mention is made of a decisive battle (*action décisive*) which was intended to decide the fate of the whole war – but the course of the latter became dependent upon a second battle, not envisaged in the original plan of campaign. Had the King won these engagements, one reads, his superiority over the Imperial forces would have been securely established:

> Then those rulers of the Empire who were already wavering and indecisive would have begged him to grant them neutrality. French operations in Germany would have been disrupted and perhaps even halted. Sweden would have become more pacific and cautious, and even the court at St Petersburg would have considered its steps more carefully. The King could then easily have strengthened his forces in East Prussia and perhaps sent reinforcements to the Duke of Cumberland as well.

This account of the possible consequences of a Prussian victory omits one decisive factor: such military success would have forced the Empress Maria Theresa to conclude peace. Had the King dismissed this as unrealistic, or simply failed to mention such a possibility since the whole exercise was no more than one of hypothetical hindsight in any case? Clearly after a 'lost' victory, he was both unable and unwilling to secure the most complete benefits from what might have been a 'potential' victory.

What is never clearly stated is the fact that the war's entire character was changed by the defeat at Kolin. Only the battle's immediate repercussions, such as the evacuation of Bohemia and the abandonment of the siege of Prague, are discussed. Indeed, a veil is drawn over the considerations which dictated strategy during the following years: these have to be painstakingly deduced from the commentary which the King provided upon events. If one considers as examples his 1758 advance into Moravia and the projected siege and capture of Olmütz, Frederick notes only that these were undertakings with strictly limited goals, but their outcomes were surely more limited still than the results originally hoped for. With the benefit of hindsight an unfavourable turn of events was glossed over: it was, we read in the King's account of the Seven Years War, merely a diversionary tactic decided upon 'in order to occupy the Austrians during the whole campaign in an area situated as far as possible from Prussian territories'. There is no hint that this resulted in a shift towards a defensive strategy, which took place at the latest around the end of 1758 and the beginning of 1759. We do not read of a fundamental change in Prussian strategy until after the Austrian capture of the fortress at Schweidnitz in the autumn of 1761. Thereafter the King could only, Frederick recounted, 'think of retaining as many fortresses and as much land as possible in the face of the superior strength [of the enemy]. Without arousing Laudon's suspicions, he now had to limit himself strictly to defence.' In this way, either intentionally or unintentionally, the broad lines of the military struggle are lost and the account becomes submerged in the detail of developments on the various fronts.

Throughout, the King never missed an opportunity to mention both his own campaigns and those in western Germany. Yet Frederick's account of the war does shed some light on his strategic principles through its discussion of particular points. One example is that, when decisions for battle were taken, these are almost always expressly justified as unavoidable: particularly in cases when the Prussian army was defeated. This applies to Kolin (1757) and especially Kunersdorf (1759). In this second battle, writes Frederick in his own defence, the King had been forced to act swiftly: 'He had to defeat the Russians as quickly as possible in order to rush to the defence of his forces in Saxony. Since Prussian territory had been stripped of troops, with only a few contingents remaining in certain places, the way lay open for the Imperial army to advance as far as Berlin.' Explanations of this kind, employing the benefit of hindsight, do not always correspond with the King's motives in the heat of battle. Later reflections on his actions in war are occasionally at variance with his conduct at the time, above all when his decisions led to disaster. In his *History of the Seven Years War*, the King makes the observation that the death of one woman, the Empress Elizabeth, had led to Russia's resurrection when all statesmen had believed her cause to be lost. During the war itself, however, the possibility of defeat was something which he never admitted. In the conclusion, he corrects himself and deems *four* factors, rather than one, to have together allowed him to survive; after careful examination, three of these can still be considered acceptable today: lack of agreement between the members of the anti-Prussian alliance, the death of Empress Elizabeth, and mistakes by coalition military commanders 'which one would not have forgiven in a novice'.

The Prussian King's historical works – apart from additional misconceptions and mistakes, and occasional brevity – can undoubtedly be exploited as valuable source material as long as one bears in mind the psychological prerequisites of its author's attempt at historical writing. Frederick's principal motive was not to strive for self-justification since he already believed that he had been vindicated by his eventual success. The missing pieces in his account instead stem from a natural reluctance to lay all his cards on the table or, at least, not to make public the principles which guided his actions. Such secretiveness was second nature to him. His reserve – indeed, his impenetrability – was a character trait which he developed as a result of his experiences while a youth. It was something which hardly predestined him to be a historian of his own life. Wilhelm Dilthey's verdict that the King was 'the most sincere of all historians' would not be generally accepted, except perhaps with respect to the frankness with which he constantly reaffirmed his commitment to the principle of the absolute imperative of state interest. 'The interest of the state', he wrote, 'acts as a law for the ruler and that law is inviolable.' It probably necessitated the occasional deliberate falsehood in his historical writings. Reason of state was an extremely complex term as far as Frederick was concerned. In his analysis of the interests of the individual European powers, each state is subjected to a precise dissection of its various component parts: internal structure, defence capability (particular emphasis always being laid upon the latter), but also their relative economic productivity and financial strength. These are examples of the theory originally developed by Samuel von Pufendorf, who argued that sovereign states should control the course of historical development, in opposition to the contemporary propagandists for the Empire who upheld the centrality of the ideals of Imperial law.

All these factors must be taken into consideration when one examines the historical value of Frederick's writings within the corpus of eighteenth-century historiography. Are they of independent merit? The answer is categorically yes, and we must remember that their significance lies precisely in the fact that they are the testimony of a man of action who chose to compose history rather than autobiography since the former offered him greater opportunity to disguise his personal feelings. Voltaire's literary influence first impelled him to try his hand in this field, but it alone would not have been sufficient. Nor could Frederick ever attain his mentor's easy flow and often amusing vividness, however hard he tried. A greater proportion of practical observations upon the ways of the world made his account more cumbersome and, as a result, it took on a rather more documentary than aesthetic character. This set him apart both from the '*Mémoires*' produced during the *ancien régime* and from the deliberate reinterpretation of the truth as, for instance, Bismarck embarked upon in his *Thoughts and Reminiscences*. Frederick was too much of a rationalist for that. He did not possess Bismarck's eloquence because he was not writing in his native German but in the French of the educated élite. He did not address himself to the wider public as would be possible in the nineteenth century, but to his successor and to the Prussian princes and military commanders of his own time.

To ask whether Frederick's historical works would have gained recognition had they not been written by a King, who in his own century was considered a famous author, is a pointless question. They were and are notable precisely because they were penned by such an author, with all the attendant drawbacks and advantages. They cannot, of course, be considered to be of the same calibre as Caesar's *Commentaries*, for example, but nonetheless they offer some insight into a great life. Although they do not reveal the true motives of a man of action who, by avoiding the use of the first person, constantly strove to distance himself from his inner self, what resulted was a combination of detachment and involvement which is perhaps the most interesting dimension of Frederick's historical writing.

PHILOSOPHICAL REFLECTIONS

King Frederick was always a thoughtful, philosophical person who, in the midst of turbulent events and difficult decisions, reflected upon himself, other men and the human condition, the individual's influence or lack of influence over his fate. He did so in letters, writings, and conversations recorded in sources written by third parties. In this sense, according to the contemporary meaning of the word, he was a philosopher; but he was by no means an original thinker or writer. In contrast to his surviving historical works, only a few philosophical writings survive and these were either intended to inform or were the product of polemical debates with contemporary writers such as that provoked by Baron d'Holbach's *Système de la Nature (The Natural Law System)*, published in 1770. The need and, one must add, the ability to develop his own philosophical system was lacking, although the King poured out a constant stream of philosophical observations. Philosophy served him as a means of reflecting on the (available) options for practical action. If he could have succeeded in one area, it would have been in producing philosophical, anthropological aphorisms in the style of the French moralists. Unlike the latter, however, Frederick was engaged in a constant search for metaphysical problems and solutions. In his essay on 'The Philosopher of Sans Souci', Eduard Spranger points out that the kind of philosophy articulated by Frederick was an inadequate expression of his overpowering personality and his own need for dramatic action. The intellectual climate of his day did not provide the King with the philosophical tools to describe his historic mission, his daring leap into the unknown. Eighteenth-century Germany, according to Spranger, had not yet developed a philosophy of history, of politics or of the state. By this, he clearly meant the great philosophical movement of German idealism which certainly influenced Frederick's own attitudes, for example in his dedication to the ethics of duty. This argument, however, is far from entirely convincing. The portrait provided by historical hindsight, that of a

great man of action's unsatisfactory contact with the literature of French clas-
sicism, the lifestyle dictated by Rococo *mores* and the philosophy of the Enlightenment, surely says more about Frederick's own internal conflicts than
a debate about his position among world-ranking philosophers could ever do.
In many ways, Frederick's philosophy, despite its deficiencies, speaks a language suited to the King's character: its lack of internal harmony and the
unresolved tensions and contradictions in its pronouncements on morality and
duty, between the concepts of an ideal humanitarian state and practical
Machiavellianism, would not necessarily have been glaringly obvious within a
closed philosophical system.

Frederick was well acquainted with contemporary and, to an extent, ancient
philosophy. During his youth he was intensely preoccupied with Christian
Wolff, and through him, Leibniz, although a progressive rejection of metaphysical ideas led to the King gradually distancing himself from such notions.
He then became acquainted with John Locke and Pierre Bayle and sympathetic towards the ideas of the French Enlightenment, particularly its moral-
humanitarian doctrines. Here the influence of Voltaire, despite his occasionally
strained personal relationship with the King, was crucially important. Enlightened mathematicians and natural scientists such as Newton or his own
contemporary, d'Alembert, were of little interest to Frederick, although he
did seek to secure the latter for the presidency of the Berlin Academy. He
completely rejected the thinkers of the later French Enlightenment such as
Holbach, not least because of their political radicalism which anticipated the
French Revolution. The extent to which Frederick's interest lay primarily in
the area of practical moral philosophy is demonstrated by his attitude towards
the ancient world: the great Greek philosophers, Plato and Aristotle, exercised
little influence over him, whereas he praised Cicero's *De officiis* as 'the best
work on ethics' and sponsored its translation by Christian Garve. He also
admired the Stoics, above all the Emperor Marcus Aurelius who to Frederick
represented the ideal prototype of a Philosopher Prince. His growing sympathy towards Stoicism was inextricably bound up with the Seven Years War,
during the fateful course of which he clearly found it a philosophy to help him
through life; as well as discovering where the limits of its usefulness lay.

Very few of the philosophical stimuli absorbed by Frederick found their
way into his essays and other writings. He preferred to discuss philosophical
themes in his correspondence, for instance with Voltaire, with whom as Crown
Prince he exchanged letters debating the problems of free will and determinism and, later, with the more sober and restrained d'Alembert. Frederick's
letters are a treasure trove of information on his philosophical attitudes and
the changes which these underwent. Even more informative are the ideas set
out in his poetry. This largely followed the French tradition of a lyrical flow
of ideas, combining elements of playful Rococo verse with a 'consoling private philosophy' (E. Spranger). It was often poetry produced on the spur of
the moment and dedicated to those close to him. Deep emotions, such as the
King's feelings, or mind-set, can only rarely be detected, but they are certainly

noticeable in the poems composed during the critical period of the Seven Years War when Frederick wrote by way of distraction and occasionally out of sheer despair and exhaustion. After the conclusion of the war, his need to write poetry waned and was replaced by an inclination towards philosophical reflection. During the 1770s the King therefore produced a series of philosophical essays. His treatise, *Self-esteem as a Moral Principle* (*Essai sur l'amour propre envisagé comme principe de morale*) appeared in 1770, as did a *Dialogue on Morality* (*Dialogue de morale à l'usage de la Jeune Noblesse*). Both are of particular importance because of the fundamental arguments which they set out.

Having formally rejected the metaphysical doctrines of Wolff and his disciples, Frederick's subjective mind concentrated on questions of practical reason, for instance those ideas which could provide philosophical grounds for human actions. Metaphysics, he claimed, represented 'a vast sea of shipwrecks'. Yet, ultimately, the questions which occupied Frederick's inner self were of a metaphysical nature: speculation surrounding the existence of God and His relationship with the individual or society as a whole; His influence on the way of the world and on history; questions of the immortality of the soul, of free will versus determinism, of the purpose of life. Hence the brief ode to the Earl Marshal, George Keith, in December 1758: 'I do not know my destiny – where do I come from?; who am I?; where am I going?' Leopold von Ranke in his description of Prussia's position in spring 1745, characterised Frederick as a man who acted without knowing the metaphysical reasons for his conduct:

> Had Frederick been a religious man, his Protestant faith would have lent his self-abandon a certain impetus and made his actions more palatable for his subjects . . . But he was far removed from this and stood alone in his belief that he could expect no help from any quarter, not even Heaven. It was part of his stoical approach to life, summoning all his energies to confront imminent danger while always being prepared for the possibility of defeat. He feared nothing and hoped for nothing; he lived only for the need to fulfil his duty.

But is it ultimately possible to shoulder alone the enormous burden which the King took upon himself, relying only upon his own strength of will? This is a question which has never been satisfactorily answered. Almost two centuries after Frederick's first important political crisis and his initial experience of warfare during the 1740s, Eduard Spranger, writing during the far more desperate crisis of the Second World War, produced an essay on the philosopher of Sans Souci and called the King's mental attitude 'service to an unknown God'. 'It is a courageous belief which relies solely on earthly understanding (*Weltsinn*) without professing to know the ways of the Almighty.' This interpretation accords well with modern knowledge, but precisely for that reason should Frederick's inner motivation not be further investigated?

As this example makes clear, questions of underlying metaphysical factors can become very important in explaining practical actions. This is also the case with the question of free will and the associated problem of the degree of man's and, by extension, history's dependence upon the uncertain forces of fate. Throughout his life, with all its vicissitudes, the King constantly sought an answer to the question of whether man was free to decide the course of events and so influence his own destiny. Was chance not a far more powerful force? Indeed, what was exactly chance? Was it this unpredictability which changed the preordained course of human history? Another problem was posed by the concept of duty which Frederick referred to so frequently and, finally, the essence of virtue. In the philosophical essay on self-esteem (*amour propre*) and the treatise linked to it, the *Dialogue on Morality*, its royal author cites virtue as the driving force of action. Chance (*le hasard*) is the central theme of a poem dedicated to his sister, Amalia; first composed in September 1757, it was revised on several occasions during the years up to 1760. Chance, duty and morality as expressed in self-esteem are all inextricably linked to the theoretical speculation involved in daily military and political practice. The logical progression from the notion of self-esteem as a moral principle was the analogous interest of the state and therefore the use of *raison d'état* as the justification for establishing a balance of power in the political system.

The term 'Fate' – 'His Highness Fate'; 'the Holy Father, Fate' – was employed by Frederick from his early days as philosopher and throughout his years as military commander. In the *General Principles of War*, written before the bitter experiences of the Seven Years War, a whole chapter (Chapter 27) was dedicated to the concept of chance. The King's pragmatism compelled him to define it in rational terms as an ever-present problem in war, but the topic nonetheless was analysed with a certain philosophical depth. Indeed, the lessons drawn from chance act as a link between military experience and philosophical theory. Even in the midst of good fortune, wrote Frederick, one could 'never rely on anything', nor should 'success make one arrogant'. 'Rather one should remember that we, with our limited wisdom and foresight, often became the plaything of chance and the victim of unexpected events through which an unknown fate seeks to humiliate the conceited.' This statement was the product of the King's relatively limited military experience gained during the first two Silesian Wars but, nevertheless, revealed the intense theoretical consideration he had already given to the role of chance. Later, convinced of the inconstancy of luck during the Seven Years War, chance came to represent to the King a force capable of determining his fate.

On this theme, he dedicated an 'Epistle on Chance' to his sister Amalia, a poem which according to his reader, the French Huguenot *émigré* Henri de Catt, was to become his favourite during the most difficult stage of the war in December 1759. Frederick had begun working on it in September 1757 and continued to do so until January 1760. As a piece of poetry, it seems linguistically formal and laboured. It was philosophy rather than verse, but its content represents the most complete and vivid account of Frederick's attitude to nature and the workings of the forces of chance in history. Interestingly enough, it was a poem which also contained a distinction between the definition of the term 'chance' as interpreted by a philosopher and that seen from the perspective of a politician. The philosopher knows that the matrix of causation always produces the consequence. Only after the event can analytical thought establish its origin. He knows chance to be the result of *'causes secondes'*, that is to say the product of a second level of causation and, as its roots are deeply hidden, its misleading manifestation can easily dupe us. The politician on the other hand, presumptuous, ambitious and groping his way in the dark, attempts to shed light on this twilight world with a strong hand; he believes he has foreseen the future without being truly aware of what the future entails. Like a blind man, he feels his way through life, mistaking superficial appearances and the vicissitudes of human existence for certainties. Here the author performs a dual role: Frederick tries to represent the philosopher in him as superior to the politician. The philosopher would serve to impart a sense of calm which both the statesman and the military commander do not possess in his hour of need.

Using the example of unusual strokes of fate which changed the anticipated course of events, the King tries to dispel the misleading appearance represented by the presence of chance: the ascent of Madame de Pompadour, Prince Eugene's luck in battle, Marlborough's downfall caused by 'a little-known lady', the destruction of the Armada by a gust of wind and other inexplicable occurrences. All this however served merely to provide a backdrop for Frederick's inability to comprehend his own fate. There were the initial successes which he now attributed solely to luck and not at all to rational calculation. Fortune then turned away from him and towards Daun, his opponent on the battlefield. Would it not be right to say that in this accursed world there is only chance? Despite all the calculations involved in making decisions, arrogant reason is ultimately limited and one is forced to admit that man, with all his short-sightedness, will be swept along by the torrent of fate. The following verse has been omitted in the German text, but because it conveys the King's mood so aptly is quoted here in the original French:

> *En ce monde maudit il n'est que des hasards*
> *Malgré tous les calculs qui règlent sa conduite*
> *L'orgueilleuse raison se trouve enfin réduite*
> *A confesser ici que l'homme, en tout borné,*
> *Suit le torrent du sort dont il est entraîné.*

This sounds like utter resignation, even despair, in the face of the impenetrable ways of the world and its contradictory relationship with the forces of reason and rational thought. But even in this poem, reflecting the relentless assault on his ability to withstand the various setbacks of the war, the King reminded himself that it was his duty as a philosopher not to succumb to the illusion which these events seemed to represent. He interpreted these chance occurrences to have been the result of 'secondary causes' which by their very nature are hidden from the active politician or commander because they only come to light subsequently. This basic philosophy of chance was adopted by

Frederick since it corresponded with his own philosophical world view and allowed for the possibility that behind all this irrationality a greater reason prevailed. It was this philosophy which – however often he stood close to the edge – ultimately prevented Frederick from falling into the abyss of utter despair.

Chance is a term which provides an axis along which philosophical speculation and political-military practice meet. The King's military experiences undoubtedly inspired constant reflection. Similarly, the term 'duty' (*devoir*) was frequently used and clearly constituted a crucial element within the King's personal philosophy. Like chance, however, it was a concept which he never clearly defined. A connection with Kant, which at first glance seems an obvious one, cannot be established with any certainty. The Königsberg philosopher's first published work, his discourse on duty, *The Metaphysics of Morals*, did not appear until 1785, only a year before the King's death. There are also differences of interpretation: Frederick seems to have considered duty to be something which one is morally and customarily obliged to fulfil. But who ultimately imposes this obligation? It is interesting to note that duty is usually mentioned in conjunction with the state, the fatherland, the *patria*. Duty is therefore what is required in one's service to the state. Frederick could earlier have encountered such ideas in Cicero's writings in which, of all the social norms requiring a large measure of duty, the individual's responsibility towards the state was placed first. Devotion to the fatherland was to Cicero the most valuable of the ties which bound a man to his state. Almost verbatim, Frederick reproduced similar statements. The King sponsored a German translation of *De officiis* and was clearly a great admirer of Cicero. In a letter to the Marquis d'Argens dated 18 September 1760, we read: 'You must know that it is not necessary for me to survive but to do my duty and fight for my fatherland in order to save it, if that is still possible.' In the same vein there is the classic sentence which opens the Political Testament of 1768: 'It is the duty of every good citizen to serve his fatherland, to consider that he is not on this earth for his benefit alone but that he must work for the common good of the society in which nature has placed him.'

Instead of using the term 'fatherland', Frederick often replaced it with the more enlightened concept of 'general good' (*bien public*) as, for instance, in his Personal Testament of 8 January 1769. Duty to him was not an abstract idea, but a definite task with a single goal, the welfare of the state. This was precisely what divided him from Kant, who in the *Metaphysics of Morals* defined duty as 'a necessary action induced by respect for the law' where the law represented an objective principle, that is 'a practical principle which would also serve all rational beings subjectively when reason has fully conquered sentience'. Ethics as such were identical to the teaching of duty. The King did not draw the same conclusions. His view of duty was linked to the concept of a virtuous citizenry; for the sovereign himself the concept demanded a far higher degree of commitment and also of freedom. The King's duty towards the state is far more elevated than that of the private citizen. In the 'Ode to

Earl Marshal George Keith', written in December 1758, shortly after the death of Keith's brother at the battle of Hochkirch, this point is made with particular force: a King, we read, is less his own master than are his own subjects. His duty to preserve the state takes precedence over all other considerations. Only when this task has been accomplished successfully has he earned the right to relinquish his post and freely determine his own life, which should include the right of abdication or voluntary withdrawal from life. This course of action certainly would be dependent on the absolutist nature of monarchical authority, but in contrast to other conclusions which may be drawn from it, this would only affect the ruler himself and not his subjects. It would be quite a different matter if the King were to impose a separate moral code on his citizens from that to which he as statesman adhered. In the final version of the introduction to the *Histoire de mon temps* (1775) he expresses his unequivocal objection to the idea:

> Only the unhappiness of an individual may be affected by the word of a private citizen but the fortunes or misfortunes of whole countries are dependent on the word of the sovereign. The point at issue can be put as follows: is it better for the ruler to break his word or for his people to perish? Who in their right mind would hesitate when confronted by this decision?

And so we come to the question of *raison d'état* ('reason of state'), a concept which pervades the whole modern period and ultimately other epochs as well. Friedrich Meinecke dedicated his most important work to this subject. The distinction between private morality and state morality as highlighted by Meinecke is not, as Max Weber claims, identical to the difference between personal convictions and those dictated by responsibility. Private morality, after all, is not exclusively dictated by personal convictions, while state morality can easily be influenced by personal principles. Throughout his life, Frederick was concerned by the problem encapsulated in this question; here his point of reference was always Machiavelli. He failed, however, to explore the problem in sufficient depth. On the other hand, he made full use of the power of *raison d'état* without ever allowing himself to be completely subject to it.

All this was far from the ethical rigour of Kant, whose philosophy was at odds with the King's in other respects as well. There is ample evidence to support this argument. In the essay *Self-esteem as a Moral Principle* (1770), an attempt was made to base ethics on self-respect rather than the Christian principles of selflessness and altruism. Self-respect was here understood to mean love of life and, above all, self-preservation, though physical deliverance was less important than the preservation of one's good name and glorious reputation. Frederick listed as desirable attributes 'the pursuit of happiness, fear of reproach and ignominy, the desire for respect and glory and, finally, a passion for all that is useful for one's self-preservation'. More than in the King's other theoretical assertions, this unconventional set of ethical principles, where good deeds are done out of fear of reprimand or in order to preserve a glorious reputation and name, displays a respect for the code of conduct of a closed feudal society in which adherence to the prescribed forms took precedence over all other personal motivation. The pedagogical conclusions of these principles are drawn in the King's *Dialogue on Morality* which appeared in the same year and was intended to serve as a political catechism for young noblemen. As with the decision of 1740, glory is once again vaunted to be the most effective medium through which 'to perpetuate my name until the end of time'.

Self-esteem as a moral driving force is, in Frederick II's perception, a question of individual ethics. It would be easy to assume that if transferred to state institutions, the dichotomy between private and state morality mentioned earlier could be bridged. But the King failed to take this step. To him, the interest of the state remained substantially separate from the ambition of the individual, though he was never able to define where the dividing line lay. Only in one area did the old King concede, in an exchange of letters with d'Alembert, that there was a similarity: the interest of states and human will could not be encapsulated in the term 'necessity'. It was a term which in his old age, Frederick abjured as a result of the convictions gained in his youth. The word 'necessity', in the sense of Machiavelli's *necessità* as a basis for *raison d'état* was, in any case, rarely employed by the King; reason of state was something which always left room for free decision-making. As far as the will of the individual was concerned, Frederick – with the benefit of hindsight conferred by the experiences gained through the vicissitudes of his own life – polemicised against anything deemed to be 'a necessity'. In his *Examen critique du système de la nature*, a response to Baron d'Holbach, he adopted a passionate position defending freedom against the system of fatalism. Firm in the belief that necessity determined man's choice between differing decisions, he pointed out a misuse of the term 'necessity', a confusion of cause, motive and reason. 'Clearly nothing happens without a cause, but not every cause is a necessary one.' He admitted that human beings were, in some matters, at the mercy of fate but 'in others, their actions could be independent and free'.

But let us return to the basic point at issue: to what extent did the concept of duty form a fundamental element in Frederick's moral code and how far was this linked to ideas of the 'fatherland'? If duty consists primarily of dedication to the 'fatherland', then the further question has to be asked: what did this mean to Frederick II of Prussia? His thoughts on the matter are recorded in a series of fictional letters entitled *Letters on the Love of the Fatherland (Lettres sur l'amour de la patrie)* (1779). These marked the divergence of the King's thinking from the later French Encyclopaedists who condemned the concept of a fatherland as a meaningless abstraction and argued that the individual was only of value as a citizen of the world. They have made a love of the fatherland, which has been the source of the noblest of deeds since Antiquity, seem as absurd as possible, wrote Anapistcmon, the more sceptical of the two authors of the letters. Frederick, as usual, here defended himself against attacks on his 'creation', his country, but he was only able to describe what this represented in conventional terms. The 'fatherland', according to his definition, was composed of a group of citizens bound together by a social contract and subject to the same laws and customs. 'Since our interests are closely linked to its [fortunes], we owe [the fatherland] love, devotion and our service.'

The author lets the 'fatherland' speak for itself in reply to its critics, citing 'the services and safeguards one owes the state in which one lives'. The response to this appeal was in the style of ancient rhetoric and included a piece in praise of dying for one's fatherland. Philopatros, the second of the two correspondents, apologised for his *'mouvement d'enthousiasme'*, but it is clear that Frederick could not lend his characters the voice to propound a concept which cannot be understood by means of either the terminology of the law of nature or the formulaic approach of Antiquity. The artificial nature of the state of Prussia, its lack of homogeneity and relatively brief historical tradition were clearly perceptible here and the two correspondents only rarely acquired a warmer tone, as was possible in the account of their Seven Years War experiences: 'Our customs, laws and traditions are the same.' This rather conventional statement by Philopatros was followed by the more emotive line, 'Not only do we breathe the same air, but share with them our sorrow and our joy.' The war had indeed heaped more than enough sorrow on the citizens of Prussia. The rights which were consequently to be accorded to them were not mentioned, however, only a litany of duties, which every subject was expected to perform. Even Frederick the Great's Enlightened Absolutism could not transcend the limitations of his own times. A generation later, as a new Prussia was being created in the aftermath of a shattering defeat at Napoleon's hands, Baron vom Stein (the reforming Prussian official and statesman) wrote, in a letter dated 8 December 1807, to his colleague, Count von Hardenberg, in a very different spirit: the nation had to become accustomed to administering its own affairs and to progress from its adolescent state towards developing a government which was constantly alert and ready to serve the people it represented.

VOLTAIRE'S POLITICAL ROLE

Frederick II's acquaintances among his contemporaries were drawn from all social ranks and backgrounds, from those who were well known to those who were not. Among all of these, none was as dramatic or as loaded with tension, as filled with intellectual and aesthetic attraction and yet, at the same time, fraught with endless disappointments, intrigues and conflicts, as the King's friendship with François Marie Arouet, known as Voltaire, who occupied a central place in the intellectual world of eighteenth-century Europe and entered the literary pantheon through his prolific philosophical writings. Their relationship was initially conducted not in person but on paper, through an extended period of correspondence which had been initiated by Frederick while still Crown Prince in 1736. Thereafter, the two met on five separate occasions between September 1740 (their first, brief meeting at Castle Moyland near Cleves) and March 1753, when Voltaire's almost three-year sojourn at the Prussian court ended with a bitter dispute with Frederick. The final phase of their relationship saw an intermittent correspondence and intellectual exchange, punctuated by protracted silences, which continued right up to the writer's death on 30 May 1778.

The encounter between the two men was quite unique. More than any other ruler, Prussia's monarch promised to fulfil the expectations of many contemporaries and personify the ultimate phase of the Enlightenment by establishing a state created along just and humanitarian lines, while Voltaire was the intellectual and spiritual architect of that Enlightenment. Other eighteenth-century monarchs did, of course, cultivate relations with philosophers and writers in an attempt to import the spirit of the Enlightenment into the world of courtly society. Catherine II, for example, invited Diderot to Russia and carried on a prolonged correspondence with Voltaire. Yet nowhere did a relationship of such intense attraction as well as repulsion develop as that between Frederick II and Voltaire. One can safely assume that each party exerted an appeal on the other, and quite apart from all the flattery and Byzantine intrigues, it was a friendship genuinely based on a shared belief in certain ideals. It is a testament to their relationship that it survived considerable differences apparent from the very beginning. These surfaced during the early stages of the correspondence and centred on fundamental problems such as the question of free will. Frederick's admiration was initially awakened by Voltaire's universal genius, as a poet who thought and wrote about metaphysics, as a genius who had mastered all literary forms and a writer whose historical works on Charles XII and the age of Louis XIV had demonstrated the 'superiority of a mind [which sees] everything within the framework of a wider context'. In this respect, the Crown Prince's initial letter establishing contact in 1736 corresponds almost exactly to the King's epitaph for the poet in 1778. In his opening letters, Frederick described Voltaire's writings as the 'thesaurus of understanding' and praised his ability as a poet who added to his great worth 'by an unending wealth of other knowledge'. In the obituary presented to the assembled Berlin Academy, it was asserted that Voltaire merited a whole academy to himself. In seventeen centuries his only possible rival was Cicero. In these less than objective words, one must recognise the personal ideal which Voltaire represented to Frederick: a man conversant with every area of intellectual activity, the type of figure the ruler himself strove to be, especially when he first sought glory as a man of action.

Voltaire was to contribute towards the King's aim by means of an exchange of ideas by correspondence or, preferably, through personal visits. Frederick sought inspiration and enlightenment, and only instruction as far as use of the French language and acquaintance with the rules of poetry were concerned. He wanted to 'possess' the poet, as he wrote as early as 1736 as well as in his epitaph of 1778. Herein lay the root of all the twists which subsequently occurred in the relationship between the two men. Even had Voltaire not been Voltaire, in his own mind he was determined to dominate and could never be content with the role of a courtier, even one of exalted rank. He wanted to reign supreme in the realm of ideas, and not merely be the companion and entertainer of a monarch. When Voltaire's stay at the Prussian court between 1750 and 1753 ended in disagreement and even open conflict, it was undoubtedly due to his character failings and his wilfulness. He quickly became embroiled in unedifying disputes and finally in an open clash with the President of the Berlin Academy, the mathematician Pierre Louis Moreau de Maupertuis, a confrontation which had its roots in the respective positions which each occupied. In the dispute, Frederick defended Voltaire's claim to be superior in birth and intellect, even though the reality was quite otherwise. Even as Crown Prince, he wrote on 8 August 1736 that monarchs deserved little respect 'in our age', but he hoped that Voltaire would 'make an exception to the rule' in his favour. The strict hierarchy of eighteenth-century society thus appears to have been turned on its head: the King is asking to be considered as an equal. Such a relationship, however, was the stuff of an ideal, intellectual world order, embodying the doctrines of the Enlightenment, and could not actually be adhered to in reality. At court, at the centre of the monarchy, the King remained the King, and everyone had to comply with this, even the French guest, who had been appointed chamberlain, but whose position was in any case widely resented. Real parity could not be established, except perhaps at Frederick's dining table at Sans Souci. The King's wishes determined the relationship between the two men: he set the agenda as to when (or if) he wished to converse with the poet. Often enough, he refused.

It is hardly surprising that the divergence of rank between the King and the writer was far less apparent in their correspondence than when they were together. It was easier to find a common voice in their letters, something that was apparent during Frederick's time as Crown Prince and was again evident in the 1750s when their correspondence was once again resumed. It was easy for the young Frederick, who had never met Voltaire, to idolise the great master. As an ageing King who had long since lost any propensity to adore, Frederick nevertheless remained capable of reverence. Indeed, the 'philosopher of Sans Souci' requested absolution from the 'patriarch of Ferney' and admitted that, even if he would see him damned, he could not cease to love him, as he expressed it on 31 January 1773. In such letters, the fiction of a spiritual relationship was upheld, and hierarchical status and moral distance both suspended. This was true also of the eulogy of 1778 in which no disparaging words about the writer's disagreeable character could be found. A veil is even drawn over the actual reasons which led to his acrimonious departure from Berlin, which instead was linked to the outbreak of the Seven Years War, although this is chronologically inaccurate.

The constant role reversal between Frederick and Voltaire must be borne in mind when attempting to comprehend the inexplicable contradictions which underpinned their relationship. Other, additional factors came into play; it is therefore impossible to overlook the fact that the two men were divided by their different nationalities. Although Voltaire declared himself to be a citizen of the world in this Enlightened age, he remained a Frenchman and had the emotions of a Frenchman; this was more pronounced the older he became. Moreover, he had to be mindful of his own King and the court at Versailles, of public opinion in France, of friends and enemies within the ruling class; he was not as independent as he thought himself to be. Frederick, as the ruler of a state struggling for its existence, at no time forgot his position as King and never let Voltaire forget it either. These two men were drawn together by philosophy and literature, but also separated by a gulf of divergent political interests. This was a major cause of the deterioration in their friendship. The responsibility for this must be borne by Voltaire, who constantly sought to gain political capital from his relationship with the Prussian King, allowing himself to be employed on diplomatic missions without ever lowering the mask of pure intellectual friendship. When one views his relationship with Frederick in this light, the picture that emerges is quite different from the traditional one. Of course one cannot entirely absolve Frederick of the wish to use Voltaire, the most influential writer of his age, as a means of adding weight to his own voice, particularly where France and French public opinion were concerned. However, in contrast to his brother, Prince Henry, he never allowed his inclination towards the French language and culture to guide his political relationship with France. Early on he was careful to separate his political outlook from his subjective preference for Francophone culture. 'Should fate or the demon of war ever turn me into an enemy of France, then you can be assured that hatred will never dominate me and my heart will punish the lies of my actions,' he wrote to Voltaire as early as June 1738.

It must be acknowledged that the relationship between Voltaire and Frederick, however much it had initially been rooted in philosophy and aesthetics, also possessed a political dimension. It was always the relationship of a Frenchman and French writer with Prussia's King. Both gained enhanced prestige from the association: Frederick secured political capital from friendship with the most admired writer of his age and Voltaire, who considered himself ruler of the realm of ideas, but was not yet fully acknowledged as such, saw his close relationship with a King as a way of promoting himself, all the more so since the role of poet and writer at Louis XV's court eluded him. Even when the two were less formal with each other before Frederick's accession to the throne, political overtones could never be ignored. Voltaire's hopes that Frederick's future reign would see the triumph of humanitarianism and justice were no mere rhetorical dreams. But concealed within them was the hope that this would also have repercussions within France which would benefit the *philosophes* and, not least, himself. Herein lay the reason for his constant urging that Frederick should complete the *Anti-Machiavel*, which was to become the 'catechism of Kings', the 'antidote' provided by an actual ruler. When the Crown Prince sent him his first political work, *Reflections on the Present State of European Politics (Considérations sur l'état présent de l'Europe)*, he gave Voltaire the opportunity to develop his own political ideas in a lengthy letter dated 5 August 1738 and thus to bring up the idea of an alliance between the Emperor Charles VI and France as a warning to Prussia's Crown Prince. When Frederick gave him the chance to revise the *Anti-Machiavel* he exploited this for his own ends, removing those sections of the manuscript he found objectionable, and those which contained the last traces of Machiavelli's ideas, such as the concept of a just war.

The synchronisation of the first edition of the *Anti-Machiavel*, in which Voltaire's alterations were clearly visible, with Frederick's accession and the crisis triggered by Charles VI's death which ensued, created very serious problems for both Frederick and Voltaire. Voltaire could easily be seen in the wrong light if the impression were to spread that his influence on the *Anti-Machiavel* was greater than it actually was or even that he was its real author. Frederick, on the other hand, could not afford to provide his opponents with the ammunition to attack his actions, particularly since these events had prevented him from carrying out his intended revisions of the *Anti-Machiavel*. The King's treatise still dominated the exchange of letters at the end of 1740, although Frederick's own thoughts had long since moved elsewhere. In a letter dated 26 October, Frederick penned the decisive sentence: 'The Emperor is dead.' This was the moment for a complete transformation of Europe's political system, but it was also one from which far-reaching personal consequences could be drawn: he did not know, wrote the King, how he could continue working on the *Anti-Machiavel* when he was so weighed down by other matters. 'Farewell my friend . . . never forget me . . .' Voltaire was at a loss to know whether this was a permanent farewell and whether under such circumstances his invitation to the Prussian court still stood. 'My trip to Rheinsberg seems to have been cancelled,' says a letter dated 3 November, 'Who would have thought that the death of Charles VI would have such unpleasant consequences for me . . . but the collapse of a pillar can also bring down an unfortunate observer of the event.' Meanwhile, the King on 7 November adopted a surprisingly different tone: he expresses the hope 'of seeing you here'. He acted as if nothing had happened, and even returned to the matter of the first edition of the *Anti-Machiavel* with which he was not satisfied and which he determined to revise. One has to ask if this was the result of one of Frederick's frequent mood swings or if he had a quite unbelievable ability to think simultaneously on several levels. The explanation, however, seems rather simpler: should he not utilise the visit of so famous a man as the basis for a deceptive manoeuvre designed to disguise his intended actions? Could Voltaire not be employed as a kind of alibi?

When he wrote the letter of 7 November, he had long since taken the decision to invade Silesia. Four days before Voltaire's arrival in Berlin on 19 November, the decisive instructions had been issued to negotiators sent on a special mission to Vienna. But the outside world remained ignorant of the King's real plans. It was this highly charged atmosphere which greeted Voltaire on his arrival and it was in his nature not only to want to discuss philosophy with the King, but also to establish exactly what Frederick's political intentions were. It is quite clear, however, that Voltaire did not have official instructions to do so. He was merely to show Cardinal Fleury's letter praising the *Anti-Machiavel* (from which, of course, passages directly critical of France's leading minister had been removed) to the King. This was clearly an attempt to get Frederick to speak, but obviously failed. From the account provided by France's envoy to the Prussian court, the Marquis Guy de Valory, we have some indications of Voltaire's impressions which he had passed on to the highly suspicious French diplomat. A few conclusions are quite wide of the mark, such as the assumption that the King had entered into an agreement with the Grand Duke Francis Stephen of Tuscany, Maria Theresa's husband; in others, they point to vague hints about future adventures which Voltaire described as being 'to seek his fortune' (*tenter la fortune*). More concrete was the comment that the King talked about being seized by the demon of war. The goal of such plans, however, was still not made clear. In the days when troops began to mobilise, Voltaire appeared unable to form a clear picture of what was going on. In his farewell letter, he complained that the King collected hearts like a coquettish woman but never submitted entirely. Did he really know or suspect more? On his return journey, he wrote to Frederick that he was fleeing to Wesel; he hoped the King's troops had found favourable roads. 'The Prussian King has found the path to glory at a very early stage'. He, Voltaire, suspected a great enterprise was in the offing. 'My King acts in the same way that he writes', though – as his unfortunate advisers remind him – he is 'almost blind' to the consequences of his venture. This was written on 6 December; Prussian troops did not cross the border into Silesia until 16 December, ten days later.

Voltaire's first visit to Prussia's capital was unsuccessful, although at this point politics had not yet become a priority for the visitor from Paris; they merely dominated the Berlin stage, and he was unable to resist its exciting tension. When the poet encountered the King for the third time, in September 1742, at Aix-la-Chapelle, the initial battles of the Silesian War had been fought, Frederick had concluded peace with Austria and thus broken his alliance with France. This desertion was greeted with outrage in Paris. Voltaire was inadvertently sucked into the maelstrom of public opinion when a letter he had written in which he congratulated the King for a 'very good treaty' and ostensibly hailed him as 'Frederick the Great', 'the pacifier of Germany and Europe', was circulated in the French capital. Voltaire's protestations that the letter was a forgery had little impact. Nevertheless, France remained interested in re-establishing good relations with Berlin and it was believed that the writer's friendship with Prussia's King could serve this end. This strategy was only pursued during the lifetime of Cardinal Fleury, whom Voltaire kept informed of Frederick's intentions. To this end, on 10 September, Voltaire sent Fleury an account of his visit to Aix-la-Chapelle and meeting with the Prussian ruler. It contained little more than an admission that 'Scipio' in his conversations with 'Terence' *after* the conclusion of the First Silesian War, revealed little more of his future intentions than he had *before* the fighting began. He did think, however, that it would not be difficult to regain Prussia's

King as an ally, since Frederick was quite aware that Austria was determined to reconquer Silesia.

The meeting at Aix-la-Chapelle took place in an atmosphere of intimate friendship; but it was a fruitless encounter if Voltaire nurtured political ambitions in his government's service. That his actions contained the 'embryo of unfaithfulness' does not seem to have troubled Voltaire; his political ambition was such that it served merely as encouragement. Events then moved forward more quickly than could be anticipated. In January 1743, Cardinal Fleury died, and French foreign policy became more proactive. A German-British force, assembled in Hanover, intervened in the war as a 'Pragmatic Army'. The Austrians were moved to greater efforts. France suffered serious military setbacks, and was forced to retreat from Bohemia and Bavaria; the Wittelsbach Emperor Charles VII, entirely dependent upon aid from France, was forced to flee from his own Electorate and arrived in Frankfurt as a 'nomadic Emperor' on the very day the French were defeated by the Pragmatic Army at Dettingen on 27 June 1743. France was increasingly interested in Prussia's position. For his part, Frederick followed the British military intervention with growing mistrust; his neutrality threatened to relegate him to the political sidelines. But what action should he decide to take?

It was precisely this question which occupied minds in Paris, where interest in Frederick's intentions had reached fever pitch. In this atmosphere, certain groups at court turned their attention towards Voltaire. He was at this point in a difficult position, having been refused admission to the French Academy and become the target of a witch-hunt incited by clerics led by Jean François Boyer, formerly Bishop of Mirepoix, who exercised considerable influence at court, and the minister Jean-Frédéric comte de Maurepas. Although Voltaire gained revenge in his own way by composing bitingly mocking poems about his opponents, his hostility towards the Church, clearly central to his philosophy, threatened to prevent public recognition of him as France's leading writer. Frederick immediately seized the opportunity to express his disdain for a nation which failed to recognise Voltaire's achievement, and to invite him to a land where his worth was appreciated, where he was loved and where bigotry did not exist. For Louis XV on the other hand, it was difficult to decide whether or not to give this controversial figure a political assignment, as he was urged to do by some influential figures at court. Among them was the King's mistress, the Duchesse de Châteauroux, and the future commander, the Duc de Richelieu. Since Voltaire's enemy, Maurepas, was now involved in this game of intrigue, it can only be assumed that this was to be a trap for the writer, who was inexperienced in the ways of diplomacy. He was to be relegated to the sidelines and, at the same time, given the opportunity to embarrass himself.

It is unclear whether Voltaire was given detailed instructions by the secretary of state for foreign affairs, Jean Jacques Amelot. Was he only to gather information or did he also have powers to negotiate? Frederick subsequently found fault with the fact that he did not possess any formal accreditation.

France's objective was, in any case, quite clear: the King of Prussia was to be persuaded to realign himself on the French side and renew the alliance he had abandoned the year before. However, was it ever Frederick's intention to do so? This was the real problem. Voltaire therefore exposed the secret purpose of his mission to Frederick, for he not only had his own political ambition but also possessed considerable self-confidence which allowed him to look down on professional politicians. He was certainly more intelligent, astute and knowledgeable about international affairs. Nor did he eschew the devious ways which diplomacy had at times to adopt. In this mission, however, he encountered in the person of King Frederick an extraordinary man who possessed a far superior grasp of the political game.

Voltaire was obliged to play a dual role, and his first mistake was to make clear his lack of interest in Frederick's ideas on poetry and metaphysics. In this way he himself contributed to the exposure of the deception in which he was engaged. This had already begun during his sojourn at The Hague to whence he had initially travelled and where he was staying with the Prussian envoy, Count Otto von Podewils, a nephew of Prussia's foreign minister. The Dutch Republic was not only a haven of toleration but also a centre for news. Voltaire gleaned a great deal of information here which he immediately sent back to Paris. He heard that Frederick was anxious to secure a loan in Amsterdam, which he interpreted as an indication that the King was about to rejoin the anti-Austrian alliance. He saw in this an opportunity for France to offer the King of Prussia subsidies, which the secretary of state Amelot only reluctantly sanctioned.

When Voltaire was on his way with Podewils to Berlin, where he arrived on 30 August, rumours of the real purpose of his trip were already circulating. On 16 August, they had been printed in a Cologne newspaper. Frederick, too, was aware of or at least suspected Voltaire's purpose. When the latter wrote from The Hague on 23/24 July, advising the King to ascend Pegasus, the poet's horse, once again and forget the political anxieties associated with his position, and that he had much to tell him, Frederick replied ironically that he (Voltaire) had apparently found a taste for being the weathervane of Pegasus. He would reveal nothing to Voltaire since he could say to the writer only things which would necessarily appear suspicious. He was greeted by the French envoy, Valory, with obvious scepticism and received by Frederick in the ambassador's presence, perhaps to demonstrate that Prussia's King had seen through Voltaire's deception. In the days of conversations between the two men which followed, it was the Frenchman's tactic to sprinkle their exchanges on literature such as the *Aeneid* and other works by Virgil with political matters, but Frederick proved consistently evasive. Instead, he sought to mislead his guest with contradictory remarks. Accordingly, he presented an alarming picture of Prussia's limited military resources and allowed Voltaire to draw the conclusion that Berlin must maintain peace and strict neutrality. Voltaire was no match for such tactics, which in fact consisted only of mockery and irony, since they gave him no opportunity to ask or answer questions.

As a result, he finally resorted to requesting responses to written questions, which Frederick agreed to provide, although only in order to continue the game. It had been Voltaire's intention to entice the King into making definite political statements, which he could impress his political masters by reporting.

The nine questions posed by Voltaire to the King must be seen in the context of the European situation in the interval between Prussia's first two Silesian Wars. They revealed France's real interest in an alliance with Berlin, attempted to arouse Frederick's anger at Britain's military intervention, sought to exploit his interest in a dominant role within Germany and the support of the Wittelsbach Emperor, and finally to play upon the King's fear that Austria might attack him in an attempt to regain Silesia. All this was cleverly formulated in a way reminiscent of modern interview techniques. If Frederick had treated it at face value, he would have had to reveal large parts of his political strategy. He was not, however, disposed to do so. Instead, he chose to answer in a form which either adopted frank mockery or haughty lecturing as its tone, while disguising political statements in wordy passages. It must have been hard for Voltaire to produce an effective and substantial report from this. The Anglo-Dutch warning is dismissed with the sarcastic remark that he did not even understand their dialect. He expresses his disdain for Louis XV; and directed his harshest criticism against France: 'That monarchy is a very powerful body, but lacks spirit and strength.'

Nevertheless, many passages in the royal answer contained hidden remarks of political substance. In reply to Voltaire's request to give him 'some news acceptable to my court', Frederick emphasised his independence from France, from whom he neither feared nor expected anything. No political circumstances existed which would bind him to France. Moreover, it was not for him to utter the first word. 'When one wants something of me, then it is time to answer. You are sensible enough to see how ridiculous I would appear if I made political overtures to France at an inopportune moment.' This meant nothing more than that the King of Prussia saw no occasion to approach France, but did not exclude the possibility of receiving French proposals. It amounted to a diplomatic statement, although it is unclear whether Voltaire quite appreciated it or whether it was sufficient for him to bring his mission to a close. When he wrote his memoirs much later, he returned to his dispute with the King and claimed that Frederick, in an angry outburst against the King of England, had ended his sentence with the words: 'If France will declare war upon England, I will fight too.' It was by no means an unbelievable claim, although it says little about the written reply to Voltaire's questions.

In a letter dated 7 September, Frederick added something of a postscript to his answers. He reached into the past to demonstrate France's untrustworthiness as an ally, he bemoaned the lax nature of French policy and military activity, all arguments against a closer union with her. By way of consolation, he added that he believed the French nation remained the most charming in Europe and deserved to be loved not feared. He praised Louis XV beyond all measure, at which point one must remember that on Voltaire's questionnaire he had offered to compose a panegyric on France's King which would not contain a single word of truth. Here again he was bordering on irony and this devalued the whole piece. Frederick was tired of the game: 'I wouldn't dream of discussing politics with you,' he wrote, 'it would be like administering a cup of medicine to a mistress. I think it would be better to discuss poetry with you; but one cannot always do as one wishes.' The final phrase was clearly a reference to Voltaire's commission.

Although this was effectively Frederick's last word on the matter, Voltaire did not give up. He accompanied the King on his journey to visit his sister, the Margravine Wilhelmina of Bayreuth, and through her tried to realise his objective. Even in the days before his final departure on 12 October he pleaded with Frederick to give him a few lines he could show the King of France. But his wish remained unrealised. His political mission had failed. Prussia's King was unwilling to view Voltaire as anything other than the adored author, whom he never ceased trying to win for Berlin. In later editions of the *History of my own times*, first completed in 1746, Frederick wrote of the episode in somewhat milder sentences:

> This century is particularly suited to unique and extraordinary events: thus I received an envoy from France who was both a poet and an aesthete. It was Voltaire, one of the most remarkable geniuses in Europe. His imagination was perhaps the most glittering which ever existed, but he was quite unsuited for politics, possessed no diplomatic accreditation, though I can vouch for the fact that he nonetheless expected to be received as an ambassador without giving any grounds for such a claim. His negotiations were a playful joke [*plaisanterie*], and remained so.

This harsh final verdict was proof that Frederick had seen through the deception. He tried to reap revenge by allowing verses which were allegedly by Voltaire to circulate in Paris, in which Louis XV was referred to in most disrespectful terms as 'the most stupid of Kings'. Both King and writer were involved in intrigues, but Frederick, who was far more cunning, intended to discredit Voltaire in Paris and in this way win him for Berlin.

Voltaire did not, however, allow himself to become discouraged. Indeed he gave the impression that his diplomatic mission had been a success. In his memoirs, he recalled: 'I return to the French court and give an account of my trip. I prepare the ground for the hopeful developments indicated to me in Berlin. This had been in no way misleading: the following spring the King of Prussia concluded a treaty with the King of France.' Much of what had happened in the interim was passed over in silence by the poet-diplomat, notably the fall of his patron, the secretary of state, Amelot. Voltaire's mission had contributed very little to Frederick's long-meditated decision to re-enter the war on France's side. The Franco-Prussian Alliance of 5 June 1744 was negotiated principally by the Prussian representative in Paris, Count Rothenburg.

The amateur diplomat had been not only exposed by Frederick, but also humiliated. This was not to say, however, that the King, who compulsively mocked almost everyone, did not continue to shower the philosopher and writer with the most flattering praise and more than that: he wanted to bring him to Berlin and keep him there. Even before Voltaire's departure he wrote to him: 'I wish my capital to become a temple of great men. Come here, my dear Voltaire, and tell me what would make life pleasant here. I want to give you pleasure, and, when one is obliged to someone, one has to enter that person's way of thinking.' This invitation was only taken up by Voltaire some years later. His stay in Berlin from July 1750 to March 1753 was a purely personal visit, without the ambiguity or impropriety of secret political objectives. It was a test whether Frederick and Voltaire could live together and if it could in any sense be useful for both. Frederick sought intellectual conversation as a distraction from the daily burden of government. 'Political matters', he wrote on 8 September from Silesia, 'and poetry are of quite different quality; the first rein in the imagination, the second gives it wings. I stand between the two like Buridan's donkey' [who had stood between two bundles of hay, unable to decide which to eat and consequently starved]. It was, of course, inevitable that the King should give precedence to the issues of government and could only spend quiet moments with Voltaire. He saw it as unnecessary to give him an account of the things which occupied his attention, since they were matters which would be of little interest to Voltaire; 'Camp life, soldiers, fortresses, finances, legal proceedings, as they can be found in every country and the newspapers are full of them . . . .'. Seven years earlier exactly these issues would have been of great interest to Voltaire. The fact that they were now once more withheld from him could indicate a legacy of mistrust from that period. But Voltaire no longer had anything to do with such matters. What he sought in Berlin was a respected position within society, a pleasant existence, contact with like-minded people, a dominant role and freedom from the pursuit and attacks of the Church authorities. In the early, euphoric days of his sojourn he believed he had found exactly that. But above all, he sought conversation with the King. Once, however, the latter distanced himself, at first because of pressure of work rather than any deliberate rejection, life in Postdam and Berlin began to seem shallow and empty to Voltaire. In the second year, 1751, by which time he had moved to Potsdam, he complained of isolation in a letter to Frederick: 'I am entirely alone from morning to night; I only find solace in going out to take the air.' But during his walks through the royal gardens of Potsdam, his way is blocked by the 'great devils of the [giant] grenadiers'. At the same time, he claimed that he was ill, that his illness was chronic, and that he spent the whole day alone. These were in fact the consequences of his own conduct, which had been astonishingly bad. He had become involved in a whole series of dubious transactions: greed for money, shady business dealings, the worst of which led to court proceedings. Although Voltaire was victorious, Frederick wrote to his sister, Ulrike, that he thought it was a case of a joker trying to deceive a swindler. The King was beside himself that his guest had brought only disruption and disturbance to his life, and not the relaxation which Frederick had intended: 'I could keep the peace in my house until your arrival,' he wrote to Voltaire on 24 February 1751,

> and I tell you that, with your intrigues and cabals, you are at the wrong address. I love gentle and peaceful people, whose conduct does not allow them to be seduced by the intense passions of tragedy. If you see fit to live like a philosopher, I would be glad to see you. But if you continue to give yourself over to these passions and cavort with anyone, you bring me no pleasure in coming here [to Potsdam] and would do better to remain in Berlin.

This was purely an expression of Frederick's personal opinion, and had nothing to do with politics. The King, whose own conduct was increasingly arrogant, now discovered that it was impossible to live with Voltaire. The final break came when Voltaire allowed himself to be persuaded to lead a malicious campaign against Pierre Louis Moreau de Maupertuis, the mathematician and philosopher, whose position as President of the Berlin Academy he coveted. This raises a significant historical problem: why did Voltaire allow himself to be swept along by his passions in such an extreme way when despite all his character failings, he had never done so before? Did he believe that Frederick's protection gave him a certain freedom which he had lacked in Paris? Or did he feel he had been badly treated by the King: being regarded as a 'piece of furniture', a plaything, serving only for entertainment, as Wilhelmina of Bayreuth once phrased it? Or did he believe himself to have been an orange which, once all the juice had been pressed, had been discarded, as he himself wrote in his memoirs, allegedly quoting Frederick. This question has never been answered. It is beyond doubt that the King's violent reactions, his unpredictability and moodiness, his frequent display of disdain for mankind undoubtedly affected Voltaire's self-confidence and caused his venomous attacks, directed principally at Maupertuis. The writer, who was used to playing the leading role everywhere, found his dignity hurt and, as long as he lived, never forgave Frederick for these insults, though he continued to admire the King. The final insult was, of course, the treatment meted out to him and his niece on their return journey to Frankfurt when they were held and arrested by the Prussian authorities. It is unclear whether this had been a case of an over-ardent Prussian official or whether it had been carried out on the King's direct orders.

These disputes lacked any political dimension, and were simply the cause of the destruction of personal trust. Years later, however, Voltaire attributed to his clash with Maupertuis some general consequences which were not without political significance. In the whole of Europe, he wrote to Frederick on 22 April 1760, the opinion is generally held by the enemies of the *philosophes* – that is, of the Enlightenment – that philosophers cannot live in peace with each other. While their opponents are united, the *philosophes* are divided and unhappy. The criticism which Frederick levelled at him, Voltaire continued, contributed to the attacks of these fanatics and added lustre to their triumph. This was not self-criticism, but criticism of the King, whose disparaging words harmed the whole Enlightenment – a highly subjective view, and one which really turned things upside down. The dispute between the two men in reality damaged Frederick less than Voltaire, although the King cannot be said to have been blameless.

After all that had taken place, a re-establishment of relations between the King and the philosopher, who never again met in person, seemed unthinkable. Certainly it would take highly unusual circumstances to bring about such a reconciliation. After the failure of the 1757 campaign, and defeat in the battle of Kolin, Frederick felt that the continued existence of his state was threatened. Enemy armies advanced towards him on all fronts, from all directions, and for the first time the advance of a combined force of French and Imperial troops posed an immediate danger for Prussia. In this situation, with the worst scenario in mind, Frederick was gripped by the thought of taking his own life. He attempted to employ the philosophy of honour to reconcile such action with his royal duty: suicide was not to be a flight from one's obligations, which would mean dishonour, but a decision taken out of love of freedom, the decision of a King 'who, unlike a free man, cannot live or die'. He wrote in these terms on 23 September 1757 to the Marquis d'Argens who was the recipient of most of his laments during the crises of the Seven Years War. A few days later Frederick sent a copy of this letter in his own hand to his sister, Wilhelmina, with the request that she should send it to Voltaire. It is difficult to establish the King's motives. It was not in his nature to seek sympathy, nor does it seem likely that he wanted to consult his old teacher of the French language and poetry on the question of suicide. It is much more probable that, in view of the seriousness of Prussia's situation, he was seeking to establish some kind of contact with the French government which might bring about his far-reaching political goals. Wilhelmina had, in any case, offered to explore the possibility of peace through one of her many contacts in France. After many failed initiatives she turned to Voltaire. The latter had not forgotten the humiliation meted out to him by Frederick; his anger seemed inconsolable; added to this was his sense of French nationalism, now highly developed. However, the opportunity to play a prominent political role was seductive. Voltaire entered the game, the appeal of which lay in the possibility that he could appear as a peacemaker by means of 'a great act of generosity' and at the same time be transported from the isolation of his estate at Ferney into great power politics. Below this lay an irresistible undercurrent of attraction which, despite all the clashes between Voltaire and Frederick, bound the two men together. The relationship cannot be explained in purely rational terms, but can only be viewed as a meeting of minds. Frederick expressed his own sense of this a few years later on 21 June 1760:

> You are the most seductive of creatures, capable of making everyone love you when you want to. You possess such a graceful spirit, that in the same breath you can wound and achieve forgiveness in all those you know. You would be complete, were you not human.

Voltaire replied swiftly to the Margravine. He suggested that Wilhelmina should contact the Maréchal-duc de Richelieu, a key figure in French politics who would be able to use his position in order to establish a 'balance' between the warring parties which would undoubtedly be of interest to the French King and his allies. At the same time, he wrote to Richelieu himself, without offering any advice but only expressing a wish for peace, in order not to compromise anyone. And he wrote to the King of Prussia to give him a lecture in morality and persuade him to give up the desire to die, a sentiment which in October 1757 he expressed in verse. With this finely woven game, he succeeded in prodding Frederick into writing personally to Richelieu: it would be very easy, the King declared, to make peace, if one wanted to. But diplomacy did not tolerate such bluntness. The King only wished that Richelieu should seek instructions from his superiors, in order to be able to negotiate. Richelieu asked the King for possible areas of negotiation and wrote: 'I will send you a courier as soon as possible to receive your suggestions.' This marked the end of the negotiations before they had really begun. Frederick complained about the arrogance of the French to his sister. The King claimed that he was about to retrieve his position and that the French would regret their impertinence and high-handedness. This was shortly after his victory at Rossbach.

This Prussian triumph seriously dented French self-confidence. Voltaire considered it a more humiliating defeat than Agincourt, Crécy or Poitiers, and clearly the battle's impact upon morale was far greater than its strategic significance. In France, the value of the alliance with Austria concluded by the Abbé de Bernis was increasingly questioned. It was an alliance undoubtedly at odds with the traditions of French foreign policy. Voltaire exploited these sentiments to make another attempt to bring about direct contacts with Prussia. He made use of Cardinal de Tencin who, although still formally a minister of state, lived away from the centre of politics in Lyon where he was Archbishop, and who in fact possessed little influence. The Cardinal was prevailed upon to write to Louis XV and to enclose a letter from Wilhelmina. But the reaction was disappointing: the King let him know that he would be informed of the intentions of the minister for foreign affairs, in other words, that he would not take advice from anyone but Bernis. And Bernis himself then dictated the answer the Cardinal was to give: it was a clear rejection of any negotiations.

In his subsequent memoirs, Voltaire provides a curious explanation for these events, an explanation which was either invented subsequently or, if true, only proves his cunning and duplicity. He claims that he was even happier to be involved in the mediation when he was obliged to concede that it would not be successful. It was sufficient satisfaction to have been personally involved in such an important matter, but perhaps Voltaire also took additional pleasure in the Cardinal's unfortunate embarrassment. He even suggested that Tencin's death two weeks later had been caused by this grief. His intention had been to get the better of him, to embarrass him but not to bring about his death. On the other hand, he recognised a certain dignity in the conduct of the French government, refusing to negotiate a peace with the King of Prussia after the humiliating defeat at Rossbach. Even if this interpretation of events was a later concoction, it does beg the question whether he feigned diplomatic ardour in order to appear in a good light with Wilhelmina of Bayreuth and ultimately with Frederick, though recognising that success was unlikely.

Nevertheless, during the next few years, when Frederick's situation continued to be desperate, the bond between the two men was not broken, in spite of the fact that their different points of view, interests and mentalities were too far apart to be bridged. The King made mistakes in his treatment of the patriarch of Ferney. He was persuaded to send Voltaire verses containing crass insults of the French King and Madame de Pompadour. They were obviously written in a playful mood, rather than being serious poetic works, and he failed to consider their potential impact at the French court. In his memoirs, Voltaire claims to have received from Silesia at the beginning of May 1759 an ode about France, in which there was talk of a 'weak monarch', plaything of Pompadour, 'characterised mainly by the scandal of his love affair'. Frederick's reader, Henri de Catt, tells of conversations in the autumn of 1758 in which he tried to dissuade the King from sending these verses to Voltaire. Catt's fears were all too justified: Voltaire recounts that when the packet containing Frederick's verses reached him, it had already been opened. He feared that it had been in other hands before it reached him and that the suspicion of authorship would fall upon him. According to Catt, Frederick believed that this would be sufficient to ensure Voltaire's silence. The writer himself gave exactly the same reason for passing them on to France's new foreign minister, Choiseul. He claimed he was in danger of being accused of insulting the French King, although it seems probable that he wanted to gain certain advantages for his new estate at Ferney. He sought to pacify Frederick by claiming his niece had burnt the offending paper, and that it existed only in his memory, a flagrant lie. Choiseul did not make a great deal of the matter, but answered with an equally sharp ode against Frederick, to whom it was sent by Voltaire. He threatened that the publication of Frederick's poem would put an end to all communication with the King of France.

All this took place a few months before the Prussian defeat at Kunersdorf, after which Frederick found himself in the most dangerous situation of the whole war. The King urgently needed help: if not military assistance, then at least political support. Voltaire, as '*négociateur occulte*', therefore remained an important contact for him, and through him a line of communication was maintained with Choiseul, who in turn cultivated his association with the patriarch of Ferney, whom he elevated to the nobility by acknowledging his seigneurial rights over his new domain. In this way peace became the central theme in the increasingly frequent exchange of letters between Prussia's King and Voltaire. But it was soon apparent that each had different ideas of how peace might be made. Voltaire was certainly no dreamer and he knew his way in politics. He stood firmly on France's side, but his idea of peace was also marked by a vision of world happiness, as envisaged by the Enlightenment. He always viewed peace in general terms, as something which would change the world. In this spirit he wrote to Frederick on 2 May 1759:

> I pray continually to God to give you peace and that His kingdom should come to us since, in truth, the numerous massacres reveal the devil's ascendancy, while the philosophers who claim it is all for the best, hardly know the world in which they live. All will not be well until you are back at Sans Souci . . .

The continuing military struggle impeded the most important task which he found bound him to Frederick: *'écrasez l'infâme'*, that is the destruction of all that was linked to religious teaching, clericalism and superstition.

Frederick developed a quite different idea of peace; 'I love peace,' he wrote in a letter dated 2 July 1759, 'no less than you; but I want a good lasting peace. Socrates and Plato would have thought as I do if they had found themselves in the damnable position in which I find myself.' 'Philosophy,' he continued, 'teaches us to do our duty, to serve our fatherland faithfully and to sacrifice for it our lives, our comfortable lives.' This was no humanitarian ethic in the spirit of the Enlightenment, but a state ethic for a particular country. It did not allow peace to represent an absolute value, but relegated it to second place after reason of state and state interest. Frederick already wrote in the aftermath of the catastrophe of Kunersdorf: 'In order to conclude a peace, I need two prerequisites: firstly, to be able to conclude it in agreement with my trusted allies; and secondly, it must be an honourable and glorious peace.' Then on 22 September 1759, followed the significant words: 'You see, nothing is left to me but my honour; I will protect it even at the price of my own life.' Here honour is substituted for state interest.

It must be remembered that this exchange of letters took place in the full knowledge of the French foreign minister. But the opinion of the French public and of Voltaire that both Frederick and Prussia needed peace was not shared in Paris, since Choiseul was not willing to give up the support of his continental allies, Austria and Russia, against England. The stubborn insistence of the King of Prussia on the re-establishment of the territorial status quo was an obstacle to serious negotiation with France. In the long term this stance was not only an emotional position, the expression of the King's overriding commitment to maintaining the territorial integrity of his state, but also a risk worth taking given the increasing war-weariness of the powers involved. In November 1759, Voltaire offered his services to Choiseul for a diplomatic mission and referred to the alleged success of his embassy to the Prussian court in 1743. It must have been at the time when the states in the coalition against Prussia were handed an Anglo-Prussian declaration suggesting the holding of peace negotiations in Ryswijk. There is no record if it was successful. Frederick, on the other hand, continued to court Voltaire as an emissary. On 19 November 1759 he gave him an explanation of the

Anglo-Prussian peace feelers which was rooted in enlightened philosophy. 'Our *démarche*,' we read,

> stems quite firmly from the heart, the feeling of humanitarianism, which makes us wish to quell the rivers of blood which run over almost all our territory, to put an end to the massacres, barbarian behaviour, all the crimes committed by men and the unhappy habit of bathing in blood which gets worse from day to day.

Frederick often described the horrors of war, but rarely as graphically as in this letter, the purpose of which was principally political. It was quickly followed by further communications in poetic form: on 3 December 1759, the '*épître à Voltaire qui voulait négocier la paix*' and on 24 February 1760 a letter containing a poem where the brokering of peace was described as the poet's '*vrai chef d'oeuvre*'. Indeed, Voltaire did work once more in the service of the French government and conveyed to the King a new French peace offer. In it Choiseul demanded that Prussia hand over the fortress of Wesel and the Duchy of Cleves. Frederick wondered about this offer, which was of little use to France and could only bring it into conflict with the Dutch Republic. He rejected it, describing it as so outrageous that he could not decide whether to answer or not, he wrote to Voltaire on 26 March 1760. In his letter, he cited Voltaire's words: these people must either be mad, or believe that they are gods.

At around this time, contact between King and philosopher was interrupted by the unexpected republication in January 1760 of the *Oeuvres du philosophe de Sanssouci* of 1750, in which Voltaire was clearly involved and which Choiseul welcomed since it provided an opportunity for some propaganda against Frederick. In the charged atmosphere which this occasioned in Berlin, the name of the deceased Maupertuis surfaced again. The former President of the Berlin Academy was blamed for the reissue since it was claimed that an exemplar of the 1750 work left by him was used as the basis for the reprint. The King was beside himself: 'What rage continues to animate you against Maupertuis? You accuse him of having betrayed me.' Once again the atmosphere had been poisoned, and after a decade of laborious efforts to improve relations between Frederick and Voltaire, each party resumed his earlier hostility towards the other. On 22 April 1760, Voltaire wrote from Geneva, sharply accusing Prussia's ruler of having caused all the humiliations which he had suffered. Almost at the same time, he summarized his anger in one sentence to d'Alembert: 'It was a hundred times better to be the protector of philosophy in Europe than the destroyer of its peace.' The destroyer of peace in Europe – this was a clear assumption of a hostile stance against the King of Prussia which made the writer quite unable to continue as a conduit between Frederick and the French government. He had become an informer purely out of wounded pride. Personal quarrels had destroyed his involvement in the politics of the great powers.

It is significant that Frederick hardly took any notice of this. He answered on 1 May 1760 with *hauteur*: 'I will not elaborate, but in two months' time, the whole European scene will change, and even you will have to admit that I have in no way exhausted my resources . . .' At the end of the letter Frederick emphasised that the pressures upon him to conclude a peace were far less than France imagined. However little this actually accorded with the dire situation facing the King of Prussia, he gave a political answer to personal invective. 'Peace has flown away like a butterfly,' we read in a letter dated 12 May, 'all talk of it has vanished.' Indeed, the desire for peace had waned in all of the powers. For the King himself, whose position seemed increasingly hopeless, the word 'peace' had not disappeared altogether from his letters. In the following weeks he spoke of not wanting to conclude a peace without the English – who then did so themselves without him – and of not understanding why Choiseul always professed to love peace when he never concluded it, as he wrote on 31 October 1760. Only in the final letter written by the King to Voltaire during the Seven Years War in November 1761, does one look in vain for the word 'peace'. Rather he ended with sentences which urged its recipient to 'pray for a Don Quixote, who must conduct an endless war and who can no longer hope for peace of mind, he was pursued to such an extent by embittered enemies. I wish the author of *Alizire* and *Mérope* the peace which a cruel fate has denied me.'

The exchange of letters between Frederick and Voltaire ends in November 1761 and does not resume again until three years later, in 1765. The unexpected turn of events brought about by the Empress Elizabeth's death and the Peace of Hubertusburg are passed over; they are touched on by Voltaire in his *Précis du siècle de Louis XV* in connection with his discussion of a world war, which the Seven Years War had actually been. Until Voltaire's death in 1778, the two men conducted a philosophical discussion, held together by a shared hostility towards '*l'infâme*'. 'I judge the work of our philosophers,' wrote the King in December 1766,

> as exceptionally useful at present, because it is necessary to point out to people their fanaticism and intolerance so that they can work in the service of humanity and fight against the cruel and terrible stupidities which transformed our forefathers into meat-eating beasts. In order to destroy fanaticism the source of the most irreconcilable enmities has to be erased from Europe's memory; bloody traces of these can be found in all peoples.

Neither man, of course, found his way back to the carefree discussions of aesthetics which they had held in the early days of their acquaintance. In this correspondence major political events can sometimes be detected from a distance, sometimes at close quarters. This was especially true of the Polish and Eastern questions with which Voltaire had become acquainted through the links he had established in the meantime with the Empress Catherine II. In the loneliness of Ferney, Voltaire now gave his ideological sympathies and hatreds full rein. He viewed Catherine's intervention in Poland on behalf of the non-Catholic Dissidents in terms of the emergence of toleration and civil rights, as he explained to Frederick towards the end of October 1769, and was in total agreement with the King who had earlier already spoken of a march of arguments 'armed with cannon and bayonets' when Russian troops entered Poland in February 1767. The two were also in complete agreement when the Catholic national movement of the Confederation of Bar rebelled against the Russian invaders. On 6 October 1771, Voltaire spoke of it as a criminal faction and on 12 January 1772, Frederick sent him the satirical 'The War of the Confederates', a disparaging piece on the Poles. Voltaire's moral support for Catherine's intervention in Poland and her war against the Turks, however, forced him into a corner. He therefore initially reacted to the first Polish Partition with a certain amount of restraint, then with admiration for Frederick's growing power, but never with criticism or distaste. Prussia's ruler did everything to assure him that this was 'an action in which no blood would be spilt,' as he put it on 1 November 1772. A year later Frederick answered the hunch which Voltaire had articulated that the Polish partition must be the King's idea since it bore the hallmarks of genius. The King admitted that he knew Europe believed this action to have been the consequence of his political machinations. Nothing, however, could be further from the truth. After various solutions had been proposed and rejected, a partition was carried out in order to avoid a general war. Such words sent to Ferney on 9 October 1773 were also directed towards Paris; Voltaire continued to stand at the heart of a great information network, and the King wanted to involve him, as he had done previously, in his unofficial communications with the French government.

In the final years of his life, Voltaire once more engaged in a flurry of activity over one particular political question: having established a friendship with Catherine II, he strove to secure military aid for Russia in her war against the Turks (which had broken out in 1768) by organising a coalition of European powers consisting of Prussia, Austria and Venice. In a letter dated 13 November 1772, he cited only ideological, philhellenic motives with which he hoped to appeal to Frederick and persuade him to participate in the expulsion of the Turks from Europe ('to drive out these villainous Turks'), 'these enemies of the fine arts who have extinguished *la belle Grèce*'. He did not, however, forget to make his suggestion attractive to the King by pointing out that it would present an opportunity to acquire this or that province. One could not always read, philosophise, compose poetry or play music. Frederick at this point was in a difficult relationship with Russia, with whom he had been allied since 1764 (an alliance renewed in 1769), and to whom he was paying substantial annual subsidies during Catherine II's war with the Ottoman Empire. He was not in the least interested in another war, so much as in the quick ending of the Russo-Turkish conflict. His reasons were similar to Bismarck's remarks on the Eastern crisis a century later: 'We are German,' said the King, 'What business is it of ours if the English or French are fighting it out in Canada or other islands in the American hemisphere – or if the Russians and Turks should be at each other's throats?' He believed that France stood behind the Turks, and this hunch even made him suspicious of Voltaire. Not without reason, he suspected that the writer's activities were part of

Choiseul's intrigues and he told him so quite bluntly. He expressed himself in quite a 'prickly manner' on the French foreign minister whom he considered the 'architect of these unrests', reported an Austrian diplomat on 8 January 1769, recounting an interview with the King. Voltaire's support of an ideological conflict of the kind that was under way between Russia and the Ottoman Empire was already difficult to comprehend, and Frederick did not miss the chance to point out the inherent contradiction to the friend of the Encyclopaedists, who abhorred anything connected with war. But Voltaire as an accomplice in a power struggle was quite unthinkable. Frederick, who in these years was determined to maintain peace at all costs and who was unwilling to engage in warlike adventures, considered Voltaire's efforts to be no more than the vanities of an old man. Circumstances had changed completely: the King was no longer the man of 1740 and 1756, but now advocated a realistic peace, while Voltaire, the proponent of the Enlightenment, advocated war. Frederick's reactions were so ironic and replete with sarcasm that Voltaire complained that the King was mocking him. The discussion was only brought to an end by the conclusion of a Russo-Turkish peace settlement in July 1774.

In the spring of 1778, Voltaire, by this time 84 years old, travelled once more to Paris and there enjoyed his final great triumph. To the public he was the great representative of his age, France's most celebrated writer. Official Paris, that is the court, chose to ignore him, however. On 1 April 1778 he wrote his last letter to Frederick, a celebration of the ruler who had subdued prejudice in the same way that he subdued his enemies. 'You are victorious over superstition, like your enemies, the backbone of German freedom . . . Frederick the Great may become Frederick the immortal!' This was the final word in a friendship plagued by argument but based upon similar ideals and convictions which had endured for decades. It was like the end of an era: eleven years later the French Revolution broke out.

Frederick heard the news of Voltaire's death on 13 June 1778 in the camp near Schönwalde during the War of the Bavarian Succession. He immediately decided to provide him with a dignified obituary. He sketched the first draft of his necrology during the retreat from Bohemia, between 19 September and 15 October. On 26 November, it was read at an extraordinary meeting of the Berlin Academy. It contained no mention of their periodically tense personal relationship nor of the political dimension which the King's friendship with the poet had possessed. Voltaire was described as the man whose mind always ruled his body, as a scholar and writer who alone had inspired a whole academy. In death, Frederick honoured the man who had broken through the hierarchy of feudal society and who, because of his personal achievement, stood far above those who left only descendants, titles, pride and riches as their legacy.

Afterword

Every biographical portrayal encounters the question of how the individual interacted with his contemporaries, the world in which he lived, and how he responded to the structural rigidities pertaining at the time. What can an extraordinary individual, bound by the constraints and exigencies of his own age, achieve? Is he to create a new structure or does he see his historical mission as that of preserving the inherited order? Or does he belong to the great destroyers who brought about the destruction of centuries-old orders without replacing them with viable alternatives? Is it not, then, the unnamed thousands and their almost inexhaustible ability for regeneration in whom the continuity of history is manifested? How small the possibilities available to the 'individuals of global historical significance' (as Hegel called them) appear, and yet how splendid their role could be in the eyes of the philosopher as the 'guardians of the spirit of the world'.

In an examination of the life of Prussia's Frederick II, also called 'the Great', a multitude of such questions arise. His greatness provides ample scope to view him from the most diverse of angles; the more human his portrayal becomes, the closer he is moved to the modern period, of which he was, in many ways, a part. He was the representative of a transitional epoch who, to quote Jacob Burckhardt, 'straddled the divide between two eras'. It would, of course, be impossible to separate him from the context of Prussia, whose rise to great power status had been his life's most important aim. But the Prussian framework was merely paradigmatic of a general phenomenon: the emergence of the modern state, changing monarchical institutions, and the erosion of the noble élite and its convergence with a new élite composed of middle-class intellectuals. It was against the backdrop of this new section of society, whose education and wealth fired its demands for participation in government, that Frederick demonstrated how to move beyond a Europe dominated by its aristocracies and representative Estates.

The many faces of Frederick mirrored not only the contradictions inherent in his personality and kingship, but also reflected the contrasting dimensions of the times in which he lived and acted. In countless ways, he remained imprisoned within the traditional mores of *ancien régime* Europe, while at the same time contributing to their destruction. What he understood to mean the Enlightenment was always a leap into something which did not yet exist, something which had yet to materialise and of which he could say, as he did of German literature, that he saw the promised land in the distance but would never walk on its soil. His internal tensions were in many ways the product of the unusual experiences of his youth. These would have destroyed a weaker personality, but in Frederick they only served to strengthen a hard, indestructible core. His ability to maintain a second existence in the world of philosophy and the arts side by side with the tasks facing him as statesman and military commander prevented the completion of this hardening. The resultant dichotomy forms the fundamental problem which any analysis of Frederick the Great's character encounters – it is not a problem which can be fully addressed in a biography which follows strictly chronological lines. The diversity of faces the King presents to us requires a constant shift of viewpoint, like a photographer changing position in order to capture his subject. Nonetheless, the course of Frederick's life must shine through any chronological analysis of political ideas and personalities and through the development of great power politics and the structures which underpinned these. The disputes with Austria, Russia and the Empire are constant features of the Frederician era, and they had a corresponding impact upon the King's life. Likewise, the statecraft of Enlightened Absolutism, with cameralism and repopulation: their main impact falls in the second half of the reign after the conclusion of the Seven Years War. When Mirabeau becomes one of Frederick's final visitors, the King's profile is enhanced during the final years of his life as a monarch during an age of transformation. The three years following his death in 1786 were the culmination of a series of developments which ultimately led to the momentous events of 1789. I hope that these remarks go some way towards providing a key to an understanding of this book.

Further reading

There are a significant number of titles available for the English reader wishing to pursue an interest in Frederick the Great and his reign. Though some of these are rather dated, an increasing number of recent publications are available and bring the perspectives of new research into focus.

Several worthwhile biographies of the King exist: Christopher Duffy, *Frederick the Great* (London, 1985) is a sprightly military life, Gerhard Ritter, *Frederick the Great* (Engl. trans., London, 1968) is a perceptive study by a great German historian, while Ludwig Reiners, *Frederick the Great: An Informal Biography* (Engl. trans., London, 1960) offers some interesting views upon the King's personality. Carl Hinrichs, 'The conflict between Frederick and his father', in Peter Paret (ed.), *Frederick the Great: A Profile* (London, 1972), pp. 3–22, is a revealing study of the Crown Prince's relations with Frederick William I.

The important administrative reorganisation undertaken before 1740 is examined from a centralist perspective in the densely written R.A. Dorwart, *The Administrative Reforms of Frederick William I* (Cambridge, Mass., 1953), while other aspects of the Hohenzollern monarchy are the subject of the same author's *The Prussian Welfare State before 1740* (Cambridge, Mass., 1971) and Richard L. Gawthrop, *Pietism and the Making of Eighteenth-century Prussia* (Cambridge, 1993).

The best study of the workings of government is Walther Hubatsch, *Frederick the Great* (Engl. trans., London, 1975), though its dense style, defective organisation and Prussophilic tone make it less than ideal. The vintage article by Walter L. Dorn, 'The Prussian bureaucracy in the eighteenth century', *Political Science Quarterly* 46 (1931), pp. 403–23, and 47 (1932), pp. 75–94 and 259–73, provides a shrewd guide to the older German-language literature. A contrasting and less convincing perspective is provided by the detailed and informative study of Hubert C. Johnson, *Frederick the Great and his Officials* (New Haven, 1975), while there is a useful article by Peter Baumgart, 'The annexation and integration of Silesia into the Prussian state of Frederick the Great', in Mark Greengrass (ed.), *Conquest and Coalescence: the Shaping of the State in Early*

Modern Europe (London, 1991), pp. 155–81. The King's central role in the formulation of foreign policy is examined by H.M. Scott, 'Prussia's royal foreign minister: Frederick the Great and the administration of Prussian diplomacy', in Robert Oresko et al. (eds), *Royal and Republican Sovereignty in Early Modern Europe: Essays in Memory of Ragnhild Hatton* (Cambridge, 1997), pp. 500–26.

The surest guide to Prussia's impact on Europe during the first half of the King's reign is the vintage Walter L. Dorn, *Competition for Empire, 1740–1763* (New York, 1940), still the best picture of the continent at mid-century. More recent perspectives are provided by Derek McKay and H.M. Scott, *The Rise of the Great Powers 1648–1815* (London, 1983), chapter 6, and by H.M. Scott, 'Prussia's emergence as a European great power', in Philip Dwyer (ed.), *The Rise of Prussia, 1700–1830* (London, 2000). Prussia's role in the complex warfare and diplomacy of the 1740s is the subject of two recent studies: M.S. Anderson, *The War of the Austrian Succession, 1740–1748* (London, 1995) is more wide-ranging and authoritative, while Reed Browning, *The War of the Austrian Succession* (New York, 1993) contains much important detail. W. Mediger, 'Great Britain, Hanover and the rise of Prussia', in Ragnhild Hatton and M.S. Anderson (eds), *Studies in Diplomatic History* (London, 1970), pp. 199–213, examines the reaction of one neighbouring state to Prussia's rise. A lively and large-scale study of Prussia's wars between 1740 and 1763 is provided by Dennis E. Showalter, *The Wars of Frederick the Great* (London, 1995), while there is an informative anatomy by Christopher Duffy, *The Army of Frederick the Great* (2nd edn., Chicago, Ill., 1996). An up-to-date military perspective on Prussia's emergence can be found in Peter H. Wilson, *German Armies: War and German Politics 1648–1815* (London, 1998), chapter 6, while the belated translation of the influential study by Otto Büsch, *Military System and Social Life in Old Regime Prussia, 1713–1807* (Engl. trans., New Jersey, 1997) provides one view of the domestic foundations of the King's military power. In many ways the best brief introduction to Frederick as military commander is still R.R. Palmer, 'Frederick the Great, Guibert, Bülow: from dynastic to national war', reprinted in Peter Paret (ed.), *Makers of Modern Strategy: from Machiavelli to the Nuclear Age* (Princeton, NJ, 1986).

Two authoritative studies of the partnership between Britain and Prussia during the Seven Years War have appeared: P.F. Doran, *Andrew Mitchell and Anglo-Prussian Diplomatic Relations during the Seven Years War* (New York, 1986) and Karl W. Schweizer, *Frederick the Great, William Pitt, and Lord Bute: the Anglo-Prussian alliance 1756–1763* (New York, 1991). The military legacies of that conflict are examined in Dennis E. Showalter, 'Hubertusburg to Auerstädt: the Prussian army in decline' and the diplomatic in H.M. Scott, 'Aping the great powers: Frederick the Great and the defence of Prussia's international position, 1763–1786', both in *German History* 12 (1994), pp. 308–33 and 286–307, while the war's considerable impact is studied in H.M. Scott, '1763–1786: the second reign of Frederick the Great?', in Dwyer (ed.), *The Rise of Prussia*. The same author's 'Frederick II, the Ottoman Empire and the origins of the Russo-Prussian alliance of April 1764', *European Studies Review* 7 (1977), pp. 153–77, examines the making of the key Russian treaty. Frederick's role in the first Polish partition can be studied in J.T. Lukowski, *The Partitions of Poland: 1772, 1793, 1795* (London, 1999). The loss of the Russian alliance can be viewed from the perspectives of Austria and Russia in Harvey L. Dyck, 'Pondering the Russian fact: Kaunitz and the Catherinian Empire in the 1770s', *Canadian Slavonic Papers* 22 (1981), pp. 451–69, in Isabel de Madariaga, 'The secret Austro-Russian treaty of 1781', *Slavonic and East European Review* 38 (1959–60), pp. 114–45, in the same author's major political biography *Russia in the Age of Catherine the Great* (London, 1981), chapters 12–15 and 24, and in the outstanding life of another of Frederick's fellow monarchs, Derek Beales, *Joseph II*, Vol I: *In the Shadow of Maria Theresa 1741–80* (Cambridge, 1987), chapters 9 and 13. A European perspective on the King's later foreign policy is provided by the outstanding Paul W. Schroeder, *The Transformation of European Politics, 1763–1848* (Oxford, 1994), chapter 1, and by McKay and Scott, *The Rise of the Great Powers 1648–1815*, chapter 8.

Prussia's social and economic history is at last beginning to receive deserved attention in publications in English: Dwyer (ed.), *The Rise of Prussia* contains some authoritative essays on aspects of this theme. The best introduction to the world of the nobility is now Edgar Melton, 'The Prussian Junkers, 1600–1786', in H.M. Scott (ed.), *The European Nobilities in the Seventeenth and Eighteenth Centuries*, Vol. II: *Northern, Central and Eastern Europe* (London, 1995), pp. 71–109, while there is also the comprehensive F.L. Carsten, *A History of the Prussian Junkers* (Aldershot, 1989) and the notably lively Robert M. Berdahl, *The Politics of the Prussian Nobility: the Development of a Conservative Ideology, 1770–1848* (Princeton, NJ, 1988), and, on the élite's relations with the Hohenzollern state, the classic article by Otto Hintze, 'The Hohenzollern and the nobility', in Felix Gilbert (ed.), *The Historical Essays of Otto Hintze* (New York, 1975), pp. 35–63. The best introduction to the East Elbian peasantry is now William W. Hagen, 'Village life in East Elbian Germany and Poland, 1400–1800: subjection, self-defence, survival', in Tom Scott (ed.), *The Peasantries of Europe: from the Fourteenth to the Eighteenth Centuries* (London, 1998), pp. 145–90; this is one of an important series of articles by Hagen which explore aspects of agrarian society: see also 'Working for the Junker: the standard of living of manorial workers in Brandenburg, 1584–1810', *Journal of Modern History* 58 (1986), pp. 143–58, and 'The Junkers' faithless servants: peasant insubordination and the breakdown of serfdom in Brandenburg-Prussia, 1763–1811', in Richard J. Evans, and W.R. Lee (eds.), *The German Peasantry: Conflict and Community in Rural Society from the Eighteenth to the Twentieth Century* (London, 1986), pp. 71–101. A wider context, both geographically and chronologically, to the issue of serfdom is provided by Edgar Melton, '*Gutsherrschaft* in East Elbian Germany and Livonia, 1500–1800', *Central European History* 21 (1988), pp. 315–49; the same author has also written helpful articles on 'Population structure, the market economy, and the transformation of *Gutsherrschaft* in East Central Europe, 1650–1800: the cases of Brandenburg and Bohemia', *German History* 16 (1998), 297–327, and on 'The decline of Prussian *Gutsherrschaft* and the rise of the Junker as rural patron, 1750–1806', *German History* 12 (1994), pp. 334–50.

The controversy over the motivation of the King's domestic policies is decisively resolved by T.C.W. Blanning, 'Frederick the Great and Enlightened Absolutism', in H.M. Scott (ed.), *Enlightened Absolutism: Reform and Reformers in the Later Eighteenth Century* (London, 1990), pp. 265–88, while other aspects of internal developments are examined in the following studies: Herman Weill, *Frederick the Great and Samuel von Cocceji* (Madison, Wisc., 1961), on the early stages of legal reform; James Van Horn Melton, *Absolutism and the Eighteenth-Century Origins of Compulsory Schooling in Prussia and Austria* (Cambridge, 1988), chapter 7 of which offers an important guide to the educational reforms; W.O. Henderson, *Studies in the Economic Policy of Frederick the Great* (London, 1963), a shrewd guide to the abundant older German-language literature; and Christina Rathgeber, 'The reception of Brandenburg-Prussia's New Lutheran Hymnal of 1781', *Historical Journal* 36 (1993), pp. 115–36, an interesting sidelight. There is a sparkling essay by T.C.W. Blanning, 'Frederick the Great and German culture', in R. Oresko (ed.), *Royal and Republican Sovereignty*, pp. 527–50. The King's intellectual world is examined in a penetrating chapter in the classic work of Friedrich Meinecke, *Machiavellism* (Engl. trans., Manchester, 1957), pp. 275–310, which is conveniently reprinted under the title 'Ruler before philosopher', in Paret (ed.), *Frederick the Great*, pp. 129–74.

Finally, there are several collections and editions of the King's writings in English translation: parts of the 1752 Political Testament, along with other documents, in C.A. Macartney (ed.), *The Habsburg and Hohenzollern Dynasties in the Seventeenth and Eighteenth Centuries* (London, 1970); Frederick's 'Instructions for his generals' [the 1747 version] in Thomas R. Philipps (ed.), *Roots of Strategy* (Harrisburg, Penn., 1940), pp. 311–400; a modern collection of the King's military writings in Jay Luvaas (ed.), *Frederick the Great on the Art of War* (New York, 1966); and *The Anti-Machiavel* in an edition by Paul Sonnino (Athens, Oh., 1981).

Chronology of major events

1712	18 Jan.	Birth of Frederick in Berlin
1713	25 Feb.	Frederick William I becomes King
1713–40		Reign of Frederick William I
1723	19 Jan.	General Directory established at Berlin
1728	Jan.–Feb.	Crown Prince Frederick visits the Saxon Court at Dresden, accompanied by his father
1730	5 Aug.	Frederick's attempted flight
	Sept.–Nov.	Trial of conspirators; execution of Katte
	20 Nov.	Beginning of Frederick's administrative apprenticeship in the Neumark War and Domains Chamber at Küstrin
1732	29 Feb.	Frederick assumes command as colonel of the von der Goltz regiment at Neuruppin
1733		Finalising of the Canton System
	12 June	Frederick marries Elizabeth Christina of Brunswick-Wolfenbüttel
1736	Aug.	Frederick and his wife take up residence at Rheinsberg
1740	31 May	Death of Frederick William I; accession of Frederick II
1740–86		Reign of Frederick the Great
	27 June	Fifth Department of the General Directory established; responsible for commerce and manufacturing
	Oct.	Death of Charles VI; death of the Empress Anna of Russia
	16 Dec.	Invasion of Silesia
1740–48		War of the Austrian Succession
Dec. 1740–July 1742		Frederick's First Silesian War
1741	Jan.	Prussian occupation of almost all Silesia
	Apr.	Prussian victory at battle of Mollwitz
	May	Bavaria and Spain sign the treaty of Nymphenburg
	June	Prussia and France conclude a treaty of alliance
	Oct.	Convention of Klein-Schnellendorf
	Dec.	Accession of Empress Elizabeth in Russia

1742	Jan.	Bavarian Elector becomes Emperor Charles VII
	May	Battle of Chotusitz; marginal Prussian victory
	June	Preliminary Prusso-Austrian peace settlement at Breslau; Frederick secures Silesia from Austria
	28 July	Definitive Prusso-Austrian peace at Berlin
1743		Austrian recovery in middle phase of the War
1744		Prussia gains East Friesland through inheritance
	Aug.	Frederick invades Bohemia
Aug. 1744–Dec. 1745		Frederick's Second Silesian War
	Nov.–Dec.	Frederick retreats from Bohemia
1745	Jan	Death of Emperor Charles VII
	Apr.	Austro-Bavarian peace of Füssen
	June	Frederick's victory at Hohenfriedberg
	Sept.	Grand Duke Francis Stephen elected Emperor Frederick defeats the Austrians at Soor
	15 Dec.	Prussian victory at Kesselsdorf
	25 Dec.	Peace of Dresden; end of Second Silesian War
1746	Feb.	Sixth Department of the General Directory established, to deal with military affairs
1747	1 May	Completion of the palace of Sans Souci at Potsdam
1748	20 May	Frederick's Instructions for the General Directory
	Oct.–Nov.	Signature of treaties of Aix-la-Chapelle; includes an international guarantee for Prussia's possession of Silesia
1751	June	Asiatic Trading Company founded in Emden during Frederick's visit to the city
1752	Aug.	Completion of Frederick's first Political Testament
1753	summer	Beginning of work on the Oder improvement scheme
1754	Apr.	Completion of first stage of legal reform with Judicial Inspection Edict
1756	Jan.	Signature of Anglo-Prussian Convention of Westminster, a neutrality convention for Germany
	1 May	Signature of Austro-French First Treaty of Versailles, a defensive alliance
	29 Aug.	Frederick's invasion of Saxony inaugurates the continental Seven Years War
Aug. 1756–Feb. 1763		Seven Years War
1757		Frederick's invasion of Bohemia
	1 May	Second Treaty of Versailles signed; an Austro-French offensive alliance
	6 May	Prussia victorious at Prague
	18 June	Prussia defeated by the Austrians at Kolin
	30 Aug.	Russian army defeats Prussians defending East Prussia at Gross Jägersdorf

	5 Nov.	Frederick's comprehensive victory over a combined Franco-Imperialist force at Rossbach
	5 Dec.	Frederick defeats the Austrians at Leuthen
1758	Jan.	Russian occupation of East Prussia
	25 Aug.	Battle of Zorndorf
	14 Oct.	Austrians defeat Frederick at Hochkirch
1759	23 July	Battle of Kay [Paltzig], a serious Prussian defeat
	12 Aug.	Austro-Russian force inflicts a very serious defeat upon Frederick at Kunersdorf
1760	15 Aug.	Austrian defeat at Liegnitz
	3 Nov.	Prussian victory over Austrians at Torgau
1761		Reduction in the size of Austrian army
1762	Jan.	Death of Russian Empress Elizabeth; succeeded by pro-Prussian Peter III, who concludes first an armistice and then a peace treaty with Frederick; in July Peter III is swept from the Russian throne by a coup and replaced by his wife, who rules as Catherine II (1762–96), but Russia does not re-enter the Seven Years War
	July	Frederick defeats Austrians at Burkersdorf
	30 Dec.	Beginning of Prusso-Austrian peace negotiations
1763	15 Feb.	Peace of Hubertusburg ends the Seven Years War on the basis of the *status quo ante bellum*
		Beginning of the construction of the *Neues Palais* at Potsdam; completed 1769
1765	20 July	Foundation of the Prussian State Bank
1766	April	Foundation of the *Regie*
1768	May	Seventh Department of the General Directory set up, to handle mines and metallurgy
	Oct.	Ottoman declaration of war upon Russia
1768–74		Russo-Ottoman War
	Nov.	Second Political Testament completed
1769	9 Jan.	Frederick's Second Personal Testament finalised
	Aug.	Meeting between Frederick and Joseph II at Neisse in Silesia
1770		Eighth Department of the General Directory established, to deal with forestry
1772	Aug.	First Partition of Poland; Prussia annexes West Prussia, the Netze district and Ermland
		Foundation of the Overseas Trading Company
1775		Settlements begin, after land reclamation, in the Netze and Warthe districts.
1778–79		War of the Bavarian Succession
1779	May	Peace of Teschen

1780	14 Apr.	Cabinet Order for the codification of the law of the various Hohenzollern territories, which produces the *Allgemeine Landrecht* in 1794
1785	23 July	League of German Princes (*Fürstenbund*)
1786	17 Aug.	Death of Frederick the Great at Sans Souci

Map 1   Prussia in the age of Frederick the Great
Source: W. Hubatsch, *Frederick the Great* (Thames and Hudson, 1975)

Fortified place
Administrative centre
Fortified place/Administrative centre

BALTIC SEA

Memel

Tauroggen

R. *Memel*

Tilsit

Königsberg
R. Pregel

Insterburg

Gumbinnen

Kolberg

FURTHER
POMERANIA

Danzig

Elbing

EAST PRUSSIA

PRUSSIAN
LITHUANIA

WEST PRUSSIA
(annexed 1772)

Marienwerder

Mockrau

Graudenz

Kulm

Bromberg

Fordon

Thorn

NIA

:ettin

DISTRICT OF
NETZ

dt

NEUMARK

R. Netz

R. Warthe

R. Vistula

Küstrin

ankfurt

Schwiebus

Glogau

POLAND

Wohlau

Liegnitz

Breslau
R. Oder

S I L E S I A

Brieg

Schweidnitz

(annexed 1742)

Glatz

Neisse

Cosel

Jägerndorf

Troppau

AUSTRIA

0   100   200km

0   100miles

Map 2 The military campaigns of Frederick the Great
Source: Dennis E. Showalter, *The Wars of Frederick the Great* (Longman, 199

Königsberg

✕ Gross-Jägersdorf (1757)

EAST PRUSSIA

R. Vistula

f (1758)

orf (1759)

KINGDOM OF POLAND

• Breslau

✕ Liegnitz (1760)

✕ Leuthen (1757)

ochkirch (1758)

✕ Hohenfriedberg (1745)

✕ Mollwitz (1741)

✕ Soor (1745)

R. Oder

1757) ✕ Chotusitz (1742)

✕ Kolin (1757)

✕ Olmütz (1758)

HUNGARY

| 0 | | 160km |
| 0 | | 100mls |

AUSTRIA

R. March

Vienna •

Index